BOMBAY

BOMBAY

1885 TO 1890

A STUDY IN INDIAN ADMINISTRATION

SIR WILLIAM WILSON HUNTER, K.C.S.I.

GYAN

Published by

Gyan Publishing House
5, Ansari Road
Daryaganj, New Delhi-110002
Phone: 011-47034999, 9811692060
E-mail: books@gyanbooks.com

Distribution Network
gyanbooks.com
India, USA, Canada, UK, Australia, France

ISBN: 978-81-212-8923-8 (PB)
First Published, 1892

2nd Impression 2023

Printed at: Gyan Press, Delhi.

BOMBAY

AUTHOR: WILLIAM WILSON HUNTER

BOMBAY

1885 TO 1890

A STUDY IN INDIAN ADMINISTRATION

BY

SIR WILLIAM WILSON HUNTER, K.C.S.I.

M.A. (BALLIOL COLL.), LL.D. (CAMBRIDGE)

LONDON: HENRY FROWDE, AMEN CORNER, E.C.

BOMBAY: B. M. MALABARI, INDIAN SPECTATOR OFFICE

CONTENTS

CHAP.		PAGE
I.	The Scope of this Book	9
II.	Physical Aspects of the Bombay Presidency	17
III.	Political Divisions of the Country—The Four Provinces of Bombay	22
IV.	The Framework of the Presidency Government	49
V.	Dealings with the Native States	80
VI.	Education	126
VII.	Forests	189
VIII.	Land Administration	225
IX.	Public Works	275
X.	Finance	340
XI.	Excise and General Taxation	362
XII.	Protection of Person and Property: Justice, Police, Jails	402
XIII.	Local Government: Municipalities and District Boards	429
XIV.	Military and Marine	449
XV.	Sind, Aden, and the Portuguese Possessions	466
	INDEX	487–504

PREFACE

OAKEN HOLT, CUMNOR, BERKS,
1st January, 1892.

DEAR MISS FLORENCE NIGHTINGALE,

Some time ago you asked me to write a book which would show the practical working of British administration in an Indian Presidency. You pointed out that while the yearly 'Statement of the Moral and Material Progress and Condition of India' supplies Parliament with the materials for judging of the results of our rule in India, there is no work readily available to the public which exhibits the local methods by which those results are attained. The constitution of the Supreme Government of India has, indeed, been ably treated of; but similar facilities do not exist for gaining a clear view of the modern mechanism of the Provincial Governments, and of their actual impact on the people.

The Presidency of Bombay discloses in a striking light the progressive and the conservative aspects of Indian administration, and the problem of State-ownership of the land in its most direct form. The recent Governor of

Bombay was peculiarly qualified to deal with questions arising in such a Province, for while trained in an hereditary conservatism of an almost archaic type, he was by personal character and conviction essentially a man of progress. I do not think that I could better fulfil the promise made to you, than by this account of the administration of Western India during the governorship of Lord Reay, from 1885 to 1890.

In laying out the work, I have not been forgetful of the points to which you drew my attention as helpful to a correct understanding of the subject. I open, therefore, with a brief sketch of the country, and of the diverse peoples which inhabit its four speech-divisions. I then explain the framework of the Presidency government, its internal constitution, and its relations on the one hand to the Supreme Government of India, and on the other to the Provincial administrative body. Its dealings with the multitudinous Native States, which form so conspicuous a feature of South-Western India, next pass under review; illustrated, I believe for the first time, by an attempt to bring out in a clear light the various personal types presented by the Feudatory Chiefs.

Having thus exhibited the system of Provincial government, alike in regard to its internal constitution and its external relations, I proceed to exhibit it in contact with the population of the British Districts; and first of all its attitude to the progressive classes as expressed by the great Department of Education. The State ownership and State management of the land, from the initial questions connected with the conservation of scarcely inhabited forest tracts to the complex problems arising out of tenant-right in densely peopled and closely cultivated areas, occupy the central chapters of the book. The functions which the Government, as at once the chief landlord and the chief capitalist in India, is called on to undertake for the material progress of the country by means of public works, follow. I then endeavour to explain the new and extremely interesting developments which the decentralisation of Indian finance is bringing about. The Provincial taxation, apart from the land revenue, leads to a discussion of the much-vexed question of Indian excise, with its effects on public morals and on the discouragement, or the spread, of intemperance. The chapter on the protection of person and property reviews the judicial and police systems. I next pass to the question which is, perhaps, the crucial question of Indian Provincial administration in our time, and to which you asked my particular attention—the development of local self-government by means of municipal institutions and District Boards. An account is then given of the changes in the armament and defences of Bombay during the five years under review: and the volume concludes with certain questions which may materially affect the Presidency government at a not distant date.

Now that the work is done, to whom can I more fitly dedicate it than to you, dear Miss Nightingale—to you whose life has been a long devotion to the stricken ones of earth; to you whose deep sympathy with the peoples of India, no years of suffering or of sickness are able to abate?

I am,

Your Sincere Friend,

W. W. HUNTER.

BOMBAY

1885 TO 1890

A STUDY IN INDIAN ADMINISTRATION

CHAPTER I.

THE SCOPE OF THIS BOOK.

IN 1869 Lord Mayo directed me to visit the Indian Presidencies and provinces with a view to drawing up a Plan for a Statistical Survey of that empire. Among his instructions was one which dealt with the relations of the Government to the land and the landed classes. I was to gain a knowledge of the different provincial systems by which the State discharged its fundamental duty as owner of the soil, and of the local variations in administrative methods to which those differences in the land-system gave rise.

The part of India which struck me as the most interesting in this respect was Bombay; for in that Presidency the problems of State-ownership in the land are presented in their most direct and irreducible terms. In other provinces of India the Government deals with great landholders, or with coparcenary village bodies, or with joint communities claiming from a common ancestor, or with peasant proprietors or occupiers. In Bombay it deals with each field. In other provinces the State-demand is fixed by a series of complex inductions as to the average value of the crops, the average cost of tillage to be allowed, and the usages which should determine the division of the remainder between the cultivator or tenure-holder and the Government. In Bombay the State fixes its demand by laying out the whole arable area into little blocks, and then minutely ascertaining and classifying the natural qualities of the soil in each.

Further experience disclosed how profoundly the whole scheme of administration in Bombay is affected by this extremely direct form of State-ownership in the land. In the first place, the headquarters staff for working the system struck me as very large in proportion to the population, when compared with the corresponding establishments in the northern provinces. This applied not only to the honorific entourage of the Governor of Bombay, but to the actual number of working-officials in the Council, secretariats, and central departments or bureaux. In the next place, the demands made by the system on the general body of the rural administration seemed especially onerous. In Bengal, with its large proprietors intermediate between the State and the cultivator, a District Officer is seldom in tents for more than sixty days in the cold weather, and spends the remaining ten months of the year under the shelter of a good roof. In the North-Western Provinces and the Punjab, with their village communities and coparcenary bodies, the ordinary District staff, not specially told off for settlement work, may spend perhaps ninety days of their longer cold season on tour through their districts. But in Bombay the period under canvas, and in defiance of the more vertical sun, is nearer 180 or 200 days. Indeed, the good Assistant-Collector of the Bombay Presidency is the young man who is only driven into the Station from his tent life among the villagers by the deluge of the monsoon. To an officer from Bengal the Bombay Civil Service seemed a small but exceedingly active body with a very big head.

Not less interesting are the native races among whom this very precise form of State-ownership has been introduced. In Northern India the most quick-witted people with whom the British system has come into contact are the inhabitants of Lower Bengal. But the Bengalis, notwithstanding their capacity for administrative work, have never been a conquering race, nor, until the establishment of the British Power, had they been a governing class. On the other hand, the Maráthás of the Bombay Presidency were essentially both a conquering and a governing race in India. It was they who gave the *coup de grâce* to the Mughal Empire, and who pounded to pieces the States which that Empire left behind. On the ruins they very nearly succeeded in erecting a Hindu Empire of their own. The provinces which they did not seize upon and actually subjugate to their own authority, they laid under a heavy tribute. The British did not conquer India from the Mughal Emperors. Nor did they conquer

India chiefly from the revolted Muhammadan Viceroys of those Emperors. The final British conquest of India (apart from the Punjab) was mainly effected by three wars with the Maráthás, and by the subjection of the five Maráthá Houses who had parcelled out the provinces of the 'Great Mogul.' The destruction of the Maráthá power not only gave us the larger part of the Bombay Presidency, but also removed the last rival for the over-lordship of India.

The practical working out of the most direct form of British State-ownership in the soil among the most aggressive of the Hindu military races in India is full of significant problems. In no other province has the impact of the British land-system been so close, and in no province has it met with a Hindu race so capable of resisting it. It will be seen from the following pages that the Maráthá Bráhmans, instead of adopting a policy of resistance, have adopted a policy of acceptance, and that they are at this moment the chief native administrators of the system which superseded their own.

Another feature of the Bombay Presidency which struck me in 1869, was the many-sided character of the interests with which the Government has to deal. Not only does it contain four distinct British provinces, each inhabited by a well-defined population speaking a language of its own, but it controls a vast collection of Native States that have not been brought under direct English Rule. These Native States are the survivals of a condition of things which in some parts of India has almost disappeared. In no other Presidency do the Native States occupy so large a proportionate area or furnish so considerable a part of the population. Nor are they in any other Province so intricately interlaced with the British districts. Bombay presents an object-lesson of British and Feudatory Rule in the closest contact with each other, without analogy on an equal scale in any other part of India.

Bombay is, moreover, the essentially maritime province of India. In length of seaboard it may be rivalled by Madras. But the Madras coast is destitute of harbours, and its open roadsteads during many months of each year lie at the mercy of the monsoon. The great port of Bengal, Calcutta, is really a river emporium, whose communications with the sea are only kept open by a marvellous combination of human energy and skill.

The Bombay Presidency contains the ancient historical harbours of India, long since decayed and silted up. It was also the chief scene of that Indian maritime activity which, in its early phase, took the form of pirate fleets, and now finds vent in lawful commerce. The modern port of Bombay is one of the largest, safest, and most beautiful harbours in the world. The Port of Karáchi, with its railway system tapping the long valley of the Indus and the wheat-bearing plains of the Punjab, is one of the world's harbours of the future. On the southern coast, Kárwár and Marmagáo afford fair facilities for sea-borne trade during the greater part of the year.

This distinctively maritime character of the Bombay Presidency affects many questions connected with its local administration. But perhaps its most conspicuous result is the commercial activity which it has developed. That commercial activity is on one side essentially of a modern type. But on another side it is the natural evolution of the native methods of ancient trade. Commerce in Bombay thus helps to bridge over the gulf between the old and the new order of things in India, to a degree unknown in the other provinces. At this day the bankers' guild in Surat devotes a part of the fees that it levies on bills of exchange to animal-hospitals; true survivals of King Asoka's second edict, which provided a system of medical aid for beasts, 250 years before Christ.

Bombay is essentially the progressive Province of India on the modern commercial basis, yet its progress has its roots deep in a conservatism of its own. The competition of races, European and Indian, although as keen as in any other province, is tempered by common interests, mutual forbearance, and a certain reciprocal respect, which impart a moderation to Bombay public opinion and to the Bombay press in political crises.

When, therefore, it was suggested that I should write an account of Bombay and its administration, with special reference to the five years ending 1890, I gladly accepted the proposal. Ample materials, official and non-official, were made available to me for the purpose, but on the clear understanding that whatever views or conclusions I might arrive at should be my own personal conclusions and my own personal views. I entered with the greater willingness on the task, as the conditions and problems of Western India are comparatively a fresh field for independent research. The administrative system of Northern India, its local institutions, its land tenures, and its races, have been rendered familiar subjects to Englishmen by the many biographies of District Officers and Administrators whom the Mutiny brought to the front. If I were asked how a man may best learn the actual facts of rural administration in Northern India, I should answer read Bosworth Smith's Life of Lord Lawrence, Merivale's Life of Sir Henry Lawrence, Sir Herbert Edwardes' Year on the Punjab Frontier, Captain J. Forsyth's Highlands of Central Asia, Colonel Sleeman's Tour, and Sir Charles Elliott's District of Unáo.

No such literature, of equally general interest and of recent date, exists for South-western India. Its place is taken, and most effectively taken for administrative purposes, by Mr. James Campbell's Gazetteers of the Bombay Districts. I can speak with knowledge of the value of these works, for it was my duty to follow each stage of their preparation, and to read each volume as it issued from the press. They supply materials for an accurate knowledge of the Bombay Presidency, perhaps unequalled and certainly unsurpassed by the corresponding publications for any other part of India. But the very merits of Mr. Campbell's work, its minute accuracy, its patient elaboration of detail, and its completeness invaluable for administrative purposes, tend to place it beyond the range of the non-official public. To find a literature for South-western India equally copious and of equally general interest to the books mentioned in the last paragraph as illustrating the modern conditions of the northern provinces, one has to go back seventy years to the times dealt with in the Lives of Mountstuart Elphinstone, Malcolm, and Munro.

I offer the following pages merely as a short study of the Bombay Presidency in our own time. It makes no pretensions to the fulness of knowledge which a District Officer of that Presidency would bring to the subject. My official life in India was spent in other provinces. But it formed part of my duty to visit from time to time each of the different sections of the Bombay Presidency, and it was my privilege to be permitted to see some of its ablest District Administrators at their actual work. I have done my best to sift out the facts of permanent interest from the mass of reports and documents issued by the Bombay Government during the recent period with which this volume more particularly deals, and to fill in gaps by personal enquiries from those who were engaged in the administration. But I have not confined myself to that period. My aim has rather been to get at the permanent essentials of the Bombay administrative methods, and to use the special period as a practical illustration of the working of the system. Those who desire a complete record of the administration of an Indian province during any specified year, must go to the local Administration Reports. The mass of details with which they deal are not susceptible of presentment in a popular form. My humbler aim is, by the aid of historical retrospect and recent illustration, to give a general view of how a great Presidency of British India is governed in our own day.

CHAPTER II.

PHYSICAL ASPECTS OF THE BOMBAY PRESIDENCY.

THE Bombay Presidency consists of two distinct geological areas divided, roughly speaking, by the Narbadá River. The north-western area includes the maritime, deltaic, and fluvial provinces of Gujarát, Cutch, and Sind. The southern division is made up of a coast-strip and the inland tracts behind it, known as the Konkan, the Deccan, and the Maráthá country. The geological differences of these two main areas are accentuated by their climatic conditions, as the monsoon, after deluging the narrow coast-strip of the Konkan, is checked before it penetrates to the broad inland districts of the Deccan, while to the northern maritime provinces of Gujarát and Cutch it brings an abundant rainfall.

To begin with the southern area. In the Maráthá country the surface is, for the most part, composed of basalt and similar rocks. It rolls out in wide plateaux, broken by long ridges of hog-backed hills which descend by natural terraces to the lower ground, or are at places cut off from the plains by black precipitous crags. The tilth formed from the disintegrating basalt or trap-rocks yields the famous black cotton-soil of South-western

India. In the Deccan the rocks are similar to those of the adjoining parts of the peninsula. The Konkan is a coast-strip, rich in alluvial detritus, and furrowed by torrents from the adjacent hills.

In the northern geological region of Bombay, which stretches north-west from the Narbadá, a striking change takes place. 'The rocks of Gujarát, Cutch, and Sind,' wrote Mr. Blanford, when Deputy-Superintendent of the Geological Survey of India, 'are only partly represented in the Indian peninsula, and must rather be considered as belonging to continental Asia, being continuous, as has long since been shown by Dr. Carter, with the formations found in Persia and Arabia. To the northward, the Sind rocks extend to the foot of the Himálayas. To this striking change in the geology is due, to no small extent, the difference in the physical features of the countries north-west of Gujarát. Instead of plateaux covered by black soil [as in the Deccan], we find undulating sandy plains, with scattered craggy hills. The immense alluvial flats to the north of Cutch and Gujarát are for the most part deserts of blown sand, and the fertile country consists of a belt rapidly diminishing in breadth to the westward, along the borders of the sea; its verdure is due to the humidity caused by the neighbouring ocean. In Sind even this ceases, and the country, except on the banks of the Indus, or where reclaimed by irrigation, is an arid tract of gravel and sand, from which arise the steep scarps of limestone ranges.'

The geological characteristics of the two great divisions of the Bombay Presidency have profoundly affected their fortunes, and underlie their administrative problems at the present day. But, geographically, the Presidency may be divided in a different manner. There is a long coast-strip, swelling out into broad deltas and fertile valleys in the northern part of the Presidency, and contracting to a narrow line on the southern seaboard. Behind this strip rise the Arávalli Mountains in the regions of the Narbadá and Tápti Rivers. On the south of the Tápti commences a rugged and mountainous country which trends southward down the coast under the general name of the Sahyádri or Western Gháts. This great range runs almost parallel to the sea, for five hundred miles, with a general elevation of over 2000 feet, and with peaks rising to more than double that height. Generally speaking the strip between the Gháts and the sea is from forty to fifty miles, but much narrower in some districts. The Western Gháts thus form a true mountain wall, often as much as twenty miles broad, which intercepts the rain-bearing monsoon. Behind it, to the eastward, stretch the plains of the Maráthá country and the Deccan, broken by spurs or masses of rock jutting inland from the maritime mountain wall, and diversified by isolated peaks and hog-backed ridges of basalt.

The great rivers of the Bombay Presidency lie in the northern division. The Indus ends its long course, of 1800 miles from beyond the Himálayas, in the wide-spreading delta of Sind. The flood-season begins about March and continues to September. The river, which in the dry season varies from a quarter of a mile to a mile in breadth, spreads across the country in irresistible inundations at places three miles wide. The depth increases at sections from nine to twenty-four feet, the velocity of the current from three to seven miles an hour, and the discharge of water from 40,857 cubic feet per second in December, to over four million cubic feet per second in August.

The chief rivers of Gujarát are the Narbadá and the Tápti. But the Narbadá spends only a short part of its course, of 800 miles from central India, within the British Districts of Bombay. The alluvial plain of Broach which it has silted up near its mouth forms, however, one of the richest Districts of the Presidency. The Tápti, although inferior in length and size, plays a more important part in the Bombay Districts. After 150 miles among the Sátpura Ranges of the Central Provinces, the Tápti waters, during its next 180 miles, the uplands of Khándesh in the Bombay Deccan. At the narrow passage of the Deer's Leap it descends by a wild course of rapids and deep basins, crowned by high cliffs, through the Dáng forests into Gujarát. It gives fertility to the rich central plain of Surat, and falls into the sea at the ancient, but now silted up, harbour of Surat city.

Two minor streams also water the province of Gujarát. The Sabarmati and Mahi rise respectively at the northern and the southern end of the Mahi Kantha Hills, and pass through northern Gujarát to the head of the Gulf of Cambay. The silt which they bring down, together with the detritus of the Narbadá and Tápti, have blocked up with shoals and mud-banks the sea-approach to that once famous resort of Indian maritime trade.

While the northern provinces of Bombay are thus abundantly supplied with rivers, the southern tract is destitute of great streams. The Gháts stand as a wall against the monsoon. The drainage which rushes down their western escarpment and across the narrow strip to the sea are destructive torrents in the rainy season, and often dry beds of rock and sand in the hot weather. The drainage from the Gháts to the inland or eastern side supplies the head waters of the Godavari and the Kistna. But these mighty rivers do not attain their full dimensions till they pass beyond the eastern boundary of the Bombay Presidency, on their long course towards the Bay of Bengal. Together with their tributary streams such as the Bhíma, the Tunga, the Bhadra, and the united Tungabhadra, they form the somewhat scanty water-system of the Maráthá country and the Deccan.

CHAPTER III.

POLITICAL DIVISIONS OF THE COUNTRY.

HISTORICALLY, the Bombay Presidency is divided into four Provinces, or speech-divisions. Each of these divisions has a language of its own, customs of its own, and a population traditionally distinct from its neighbours although merging into them. In the north, Sind or the lower valley and delta of the Indus River had in 1881 an area of over 54,000 square miles and 2½ million inhabitants[1]. Gujarát, or the well-watered northern coast districts, had an area of about 70,000 square miles, with a population of 10 millions. The Maráthá country, including both the Maráthí-speaking coast districts of the Konkan and the inland districts of the Deccan, comprised about 56,000 square miles, with also nearly 10 million inhabitants. The Kánarese-speaking districts extended over about 25,000 square miles, with a population of under 4½ millions. I shall very briefly describe each of these speech-divisions of Western India.

[1] All figures of population are taken from the Census of 1881, unless otherwise mentioned, as those were figures on which administration was based during the five years, from 1885 to 1890, more particularly dealt with in this book.

Sind is essentially a Muhammadan province, alike in regard to its history and its population. It is divided into five British Districts[1] and the large Native State of Khairpur. Sind was the earliest province of India invaded by the Muhammadans, whose conquering fleets reached its delta from Arabia about the year 713 A.D. During the next century the Khalifas, however, lost their hold upon this distant province beyond the sea. Native kingdoms rose and fell, and after various invasions by northern Muhammadan races who poured into India *viâ* the land route through Central Asia, Sind was regularly incorporated as a province of the Mughal Empire under Akbar in the sixteenth century. On the decline of that Empire, at the close of the seventeenth century, a long and sanguinary conflict took place between the Dáúdputras, weavers and wandering warriors by profession, and the equally wild Mahars, a race of Hindu origin. In the next century, the eighteenth, the Talpur dynasty established itself firmly in Sind amid the general break-up of the Mughal Empire. They partitioned the province between their three branches, and maintained a Muhammadan rule for a further period of over fifty years, until it was subverted by Sir Charles Napier in 1843, when Sind became a British Province.

The Muhammadan conquest of Sind was thus begun from the sea nearly three hundred years before the Musalmáns entered India by the land route from the north, and during eleven centuries Sind has been

[1] Namely, Karáchi, Haidarábád, Shikárpur, Thar with Párkar, and the Upper Sind Frontier.

more or less continuously under Muhammadan rule. In 1881, 78½ per cent of the population were Muhammadans, while the Hindus only numbered 12½ per cent, the Sikhs 5⅓ per cent, and the non-Hindu aborigines 3½ per cent. The Sindís represent the ancient Hindu population converted to Islám under the Ummayide Khalifas, and by a long succession of Muhammadan dynasties. Little admixture of Arab blood seems to have taken place. But Afgháns have settled in several localities, and the Balúchís, or mountaineers from the wild barren hills to the westward, crowded into the armies of the Talpur dynasty, and can easily be distinguished from the surrounding population at the present day.

The Sindís are of dark complexion, but taller and more robust than the corresponding population in the Gangetic delta of Bengal. Their detractors represent the bad type of Sindís as idle, apathetic, intemperate, and with a name for untruthfulness among the neighbouring races. On the other hand, the Sindís as a whole are quiet and inoffensive, kindly, faithful to their friends, and honest in their dealings. In religion they are Sunnis, and are subdivided into about three hundred clans or tribes, without, however, the strong caste demarcations of the non-Islámised Hindus. Their language belongs to the pure Neo-Sanskritic group, and contains less of alien admixture than any of the cognate tongues. It stands closer to the old Prákrit than does either Maráthí, Hindí, or Bengálí, and it has preserved many ancient grammatical forms which have dropt out of the other vernaculars. Its literature consists mainly of translations from the Arabic, chiefly theological, and a few national ballads.

The Balúchí settlers are comparatively fair-skinned, taller, more muscular, and hardier than the Sindís; with genuine although peculiar ideas of honour; brave soldiers, and strongly imbued with the pride of race. On the other hand they are quite illiterate, rougher in their manners, violent, revengeful, and fond of a hard drinking-bout. About eighty clans of them settled on the plains, and like the native Sindís they are now Sunnis. The chief trade of the province is in the hands of a small residue of the population, Hindus, Jains, Parsís, Jews. The Khwájas, or the Muhammadan commercial class of the Bombay coast, have also a strong body in Sind. They profess the Shia doctrines of Islám.

The commerce of Sind is centred in its seaport and modern capital, Karáchi, situated on the bay of the same name. Notwithstanding its admirable position for sea-going commerce, Karáchi scarcely emerged into importance under the Native dynasties. The town may be regarded as almost a creation of British rule. Its extensive commerce, splendid harbour-works, and flourishing institutions, have all sprung up since the introduction of our settled administration in 1843. In 1843–44 the total sea-borne trade of Karáchi, with the neighbouring villages, only amounted to £121,150. In forty years it had increased in 1882–83 to over seven millions sterling, and to twelve millions sterling in 1890[1]. Karáchi has an importance in Sind much

[1] Taking the rupee at the old conventional standard.

greater than the number of its population (73,560) would seem to imply. For the only other large towns in the province are Shikárpur (pop. 42,496), the depôt of transit trade across the Bolán Pass into Khorasan; and Haidarábád (pop. 48,153), the capital of the old Talpur dynasty[1]. But the two railway-stations at the point where the magnificent cantilever bridge crosses the Indus at Sukkur, and whence the Sind Punjab and Delhi line branches southwards to Karáchi and eastwards to the frontier, are rapidly springing into importance, with an aggregate population of about 40,000 persons in 1881.

The problem of British rule in Sind is how to adapt its administration to an old-fashioned, unenergetic, declining Muhammadan people, once the governors of the Province. The fundamental principle of our administration is to secure the most efficient men for its work. But while the Hindus of the Western Presidency, and conspicuously the Maráthá Bráhmans, press on in the paths of Western education, and strenuously fit themselves for administrative employments, the Muhammadans in Sind have, until within the past ten years, held comparatively aloof from modern progress. Down to the time of the Indian Education Commission in 1884, they were classed among the Backward Races. The British system of *la carrière ouverte aux talents*, if inconsiderately worked, would fill all the public offices in Sind with Hindus, and might practically subject a Muhammadan province to the

[1] For the reason already stated, all populations are taken from the revised Census of 1881.

Maráthá Bráhmans. This volume will disclose the methods by which the Bombay Government endeavoured, during the five years ending 1890, to deal with this difficult problem, and to help forward the Muhammadans of Sind to their proper position in the body politic.

Proceeding southwards from Sind, the next speech-division of the Bombay Presidency is Gujarát, including the peninsula of Káthiáwár. It is bounded on the north by Rájputána, on the east by the spurs of the Vindhya and Sátpura Ranges, on the south by the Konkan, and on the west by the sea. This fertile province[1] comprises five British Districts, a large collection of Native States under the Bombay Government, and the extensive scattered territories of the Gáekwár of Baroda, the premier Hindu Feudatory Prince of India, who is in direct relations with the Supreme Government. The Native States of Gujarát contained an aggregate of seven millions of people in 1881, as against three millions in round figures in the British Districts. On the other hand the three millions of British subjects dwelt in thickly peopled Districts, covering only 10,000 square miles, while the seven million inhabitants of the Native States were spread over thinly populated tracts aggregating 60,000 square miles.

Gujarát is in several respects the antithesis of Sind.

[1] It is divided into the five British Districts of Ahmadábád, Kaira, Panch Maháls, Broach, and Surat; the State of Baroda in the centre; the Mahi and Rewá Kántha states in the east; Rájpipla, Sachín, Bánsdá, and Dharampur in the south; the peninsula of Káthiáwár with numerous native states in the west; the isolated states of Cutch in the north-west; and of Pálanpur and Rádhanpur in the north.

The most important period of its history is Hindu, and its population remains essentially Hindu to the present day. It figures from the third century B.C. to the seventh century A.D. in rock inscriptions, in the Greek geographers, and in Indian chronology, as a seat of Hindu dominion in which the struggle between the Bráhmans and the Buddhists fought itself out. Between the seventh and the fourteenth centuries Gujarát was subjected to thirteen Muhammadan invasions, the first eight of them by Arab fleets from the Persian Gulf. In the fourteenth century it passed for 170 years under the rule of the Muhammadan local Sultáns of Ahmadábád, and was afterwards incorporated in the Mughal Empire of Delhi.

But from the middle of the seventeenth century Gujarát began again to pass under Hindu sway. Sivají, the founder of the Maráthá power, pillaged Surat in 1664 and in 1669; his son plundered Broach in 1686. On the breaking up of the Mughal Empire, Surat was attacked by the Maráthás in 1702, Ahmadábád in 1707, and the Maráthá power was firmly established in Baroda about 1720. During the next century Gujarát became the seat of a military Hindu government, chiefly represented by the Maráthá House of Baroda. This is, for present political purposes, the essentially important period of Gujarát history. For it is this period which has bequeathed the characteristic land customs and that intricate commingling of Feudatory territory with the British Districts, which furnish the administrative problems in the Gujarát of our day. The final Maráthá war in 1817 left the English as the

Paramount Power in Gujarát. Their authority was formally accepted by the Gáekwár of Baroda, who entered into subordinate dependence to the British Government and agreed not to interfere with the tributary chiefs except through the medium of that Government.

The task of administration in Gujarát divides itself, as may be inferred from the foregoing paragraph, into two branches. A large collection of Native States have to be managed for their own good with a light but firm hand. A closely packed Hindu population, occupying the smaller territory under our direct rule, have to be governed in such a way as, on the one hand, not to interfere with their religious prejudices or to press unduly on their industry, but on the other hand, so as to extract an adequate revenue from the fertile districts in which they dwell. The Muhammadans of Sind are an ex-ruling race. The local Hindu population of Gujarát have during six centuries been accustomed to a more or less alien rule, whether by the Muhammadans, or by the Maráthás, or by the English. Until recently they did not disclose the keen activity of the Maráthá Bráhmans in pressing into public employments, or advancing themselves generally in the struggle for life. As in Sind, although for different reasons, the British Government has found it necessary to stimulate the Gujarátís in the path of progress, if they were not to be outstripped by the practical Maráthá intellect ever on the watch to make the most of the changing circumstances of the times.

The third speech-division of the Bombay Presidency

is the Maráthá country, consisting of two distinct tracts, the Konkan or Maráthí-speaking coast, and the Deccan or Maráthí-speaking districts inland from the Gháts. The Konkan includes the lowland maritime strip, running southwards from Thána district and Bombay Island, in all 11,400 square miles with a population of 3½ millions in 1881 [1]. The Konkan first emerges into history under the Mauryan dynasty in the Eighth Edict of Asoka, 250 B.C.—the edict found in the Thána district thirty-seven miles north of Bombay. The period of Buddhist rule left behind it the great rock temples, specimens of which may still be seen in the districts of Thána, Kolába, and Ratnágiri. The notices in Ptolemy (*circ.* 150 A.D.) and in the Periplus of the Erythraean Sea (*circ.* 247 A.D.) indicate that Greek traders from Egypt had dealings with the Konkan coast. After a succession of Hindu dynasties, the Konkan passed for a time under the loosely established authority of Muhammadan invaders from Delhi (about 1315 A.D.); and subsequently under the Muhammadan Báhmaní dynasty of Southern India. It was next partitioned between the Musalmán rulers of Bíjapur and Ahmadnagar.

From 1500, and onwards, the Portuguese appear as a conquering power in the Konkan, with Goa as their capital. Arabs and Abyssinians, both before and after that date, established themselves in the strongholds along the coast. After a short period of almost

[1] It is divided into the four British Districts of Thána, Bombay Island, Kolába, and Ratnágiri, with the Native States of Jawhár, Janjira and Sáwantwádi.

nominal rule by the Mughal Emperors, the Konkan became one of the central seats of the Maráthá power. In 1662 Sivají chose the hill-fort of Ráigarh in the Konkan as his capital, was there crowned with much pomp in 1674, and there died in 1680. From that time down to the establishment of the British power at the beginning of the present century, the Konkan remained one of the most important dominions of the Maráthá confederacy. The English had, however, rooted themselves firmly in Bombay Island, which was ceded by the Portuguese to Charles II in 1661 as part of the dowry of his Queen, Catherine of Braganza. At the end of the Maráthá war, the Konkan finally passed to British rule in 1817–18.

The great area of the Maráthá country, however, consists of the districts which run inland to the eastward from the Gháts, and comprise about 45,000 square miles with a population of nearly six millions of people in 1881. It is divided into six British Districts[1], and seven Native States or groups of States. This extensive tract, the ancient Maháráshtra, figures prominently from the earliest times as a powerful Indian kingdom. Asoka is said to have sent a missionary to convert its people to Buddhism about 240 B.C. During the first centuries of the Christian era the country formed the centre of the over-lordship or empire of the Andhrabhritya dynasty. After an obscure period of Buddhist or Rájput invasion from

[1] The British Districts are: Khándesh, Násik, Ahmadnagar, Poona, Sholápur and Sátára. The Native States are: the Dángs, Surgána, Akalkot, Bhor, Phaltán, Aundh and Jath.

the north, it again rose to power under the Chalukya rulers from about 560 to 1190 A.D. During most of this period the Maráthá country was a Buddhist, or Buddhistic Hindu, over-lordship, and its splendid rock temples at Ellora and elsewhere attest the zeal and the wealth of its sovereigns.

After the year 1190, the supremacy of the Maráthá country passed to the Yadava dynasty, under which it became conspicuous for the Sivite revival of the Brahmanical faith. The Yadavas remained more or less continuously in power until the Muhammadan invasions from Delhi early in the fourteenth century. The Musalmán power gradually established itself in the Maráthá country from 1310 onwards; and in 1340 the Emperor Muhammad Tughlak even resolved to transfer his seat of empire from Delhi to the Maháráshtra capital of Daulatábád. But Hindu potentates still remained both within and around the Maráthá country. It was not until 1565 that the great Hindu dynasty of Vijayanagar, the most powerful over-lordship in Southern India, was destroyed by a confederacy of the Muhammadan kings of the Deccan at the battle of Tálikot.

The Maráthá country forms the heart of Southern India, and is known in history by the loose general designation of the *Dakshina*, or Deccan, literally the South. For 1¾ centuries, from about 1350 onwards, it formed the backbone of the Báhmaní dominions, that is to say of the independent Muhammadan sovereigns who set up for themselves in Southern India. When that dynasty broke up (1489 to 1525), it was partitioned among the five Musalmán kingdoms which established themselves in the Deccan.

To subdue those kingdoms, and to incorporate them in the Delhi Empire, was the one fixed idea of the Mughal sovereigns of Northern India. During the sixteenth and seventeenth centuries this enterprise dominated the whole military policy of the Delhi Court. But the task was beyond its strength. The intervening tracts of mountains and forests, now pierced by railways, but which then separated Northern India from the South, presented insuperable difficulties to an effective incorporation of the Deccan into the Delhi Empire. Akbar and his successors down to Aurangzeb succeeded, indeed, in destroying the independent Muhammadan kingdoms of the Deccan, and in subjecting them more or less completely to the authority of military Viceroys, supported by standing armies from the North. But before the last of the Muhammadan kingdoms was conquered, towards the close of the seventeenth century, a third party had arisen in the Deccan, which was destined to ride roughshod over the ruins both of the independent Muhammadan kingdoms and of the Mughal Empire itself.

This third party in the Deccan was the Maráthás. As already mentioned, they developed into a powerful Hindu confederacy under their leader Sivají, in the second half of the seventeenth century. Aurangzeb, the last of the really Great Moguls, solemnly devoted himself to the conquest of Southern India, alike from the heretic Muhammadan dynasties and from the infidel Maráthás. It was his self-appointed life task, commenced in youth as the lieutenant of his imperial father, and continued with unshaken resolution throughout his own reign of half a century (1658–1707). During the first five-and-twenty years of his reign he endeavoured to accomplish this task by hurling powerful armaments against the South, while he himself from his northern capital directed the resources of the Empire to the work. Finding that the South could not be subdued by his generals, he deliberately gave up the splendours of Delhi, and consecrated the second twenty-five years of his reign to the accomplishment of his task, leading a soldier's life from one great camp to another, and heading his armies in the field.

So much persistence and self-devotion, spread over a vigorous reign of fifty years, was not without its reward. The last of the independent Muhammadan kingdoms of the South were submerged by the successive floods of invasion which Aurangzeb brought down upon them from the North. There were however by that time, as I have indicated, not two parties, but three parties in the Deccan: the imperial armies from the North, the remaining independent Muhammadan kingdoms of the South, and the Hindu military confederacy of the Maráthás. Had Aurangzeb been as far-seeing as he was zealous, he would have discerned that the real peril to his Empire lay in this new third party. He would have patched up the quarrels among Muhammadans (whether orthodox Sunni or heretic Shia), and combined the whole force of Islám in India to crush the Hindus. The task before him was not merely the old one of subduing the independent Muhammadan kingdoms of Bijápur and Golconda, but also of stamping out the more dangerous indigenous growth of the new Hindu power.

In 1683 Aurangzeb arrived at the head of his grand army in the Deccan, where he was destined to spend his old age in the field until death at last released him in 1707. After a fiercely protracted struggle, the last of the independent Muhammadan kingdoms of the South fell before his arms in 1688. But their destruction only left the arena bare for the Maráthás. Indeed, it was with the aid of the Maráthás that Aurangzeb had prepared the way for the extinction of the independent Muhammadan States. The remaining twenty years of the Emperor's life (1688–1707) was one long miserable struggle against the rising Hindu power. Their first great leader, Sivají, had (as we have seen) proclaimed himself King in his hill-fort in the adjoining Konkan in 1674, and died in 1680. Aurangzeb captured his son and successor, Sambhají, in 1689, and cruelly put him to death; seized the Maráthá capital, with many of their forts, and seemed in the first year of the new century to have almost stamped out their existence (1701). But after a guerilla warfare the Maráthás again sprang up into a vast fighting nation. In 1705 they recovered their forts; while Aurangzeb had exhausted his health, his treasures, and his troops, in the long and fruitless struggle. His soldiery murmured for arrears; and the Emperor, now old and peevish, told the malcontents that if they did not like his service they might quit it, while he disbanded some of his cavalry to ease his finances.

Meanwhile the Maráthás were drawing closer round the imperial head-quarters. The Grand Army of Aurangzeb had grown during a quarter of a century into an unwieldy camp-capital. Its movements were slow, and incapable of concealment. If Aurangzeb sent out a rapid small expedition against the Maráthás who plundered and insulted the outskirts of his camp, they cut it to pieces. If he moved out against them in force, they vanished. His own soldiery feasted with the enemy, who prayed with mock ejaculations for the health of the Emperor as their best friend.

In 1706 the Grand Army was so disorganised that Aurangzeb opened negotiations with the Maráthás. He even thought of submitting the Mughal Provinces to their tribute or *chauth*. But their insolent exultation broke off the treaty, and the despairing Aurangzeb, in 1706, sought shelter in Ahmadnagar, where he died the next year. Dark suspicion of his sons' loyalty, and just fears lest they should subject him to the fate which he had inflicted on his own deposed father, left him alone in his last days. On the approach of death, he gave utterance in broken sentences to his worldly counsels and adieus, mingled with terror and remorse, and closing in an agony of desperate resignation: 'Come what may, I have launched my vessel on the waves. Farewell! Farewell! Farewell!'

As the Maráthás were the proximate cause of the destruction of the Mughal Empire, so they were the principal gainers by its downfall. They gradually overran the whole provinces of India from the Rohilla country at the foot of the Himálayas to the southern districts of Madras. Some of the provinces they made their own. Five powerful Maráthá Houses established themselves at Poona in the Deccan, at Baroda in Gujarát, at Indore in Central India, at Nágpur in the Central Provinces, and at Gwalior on the fringe of the Gangetic Valley in the north. Quickly reviving from their defeat at Pánípat, in 1761, they sprang upon the metropolitan districts of the shattered Mughal authority, seized Delhi, and kept the blinded Emperor in their hands from about 1771 until he was delivered by the British troops in the campaign of 1803–4.

The provinces which the Maráthás did not bring under their direct rule, they subjected to crushing contributions. This system of organised pillage developed in the hands of their Bráhman financiers into a regular revenue-system of black-mail. They claimed one-fourth of the revenue of such provinces as they did not actually subjugate. The miserable Muhammadan Viceroys or generals who had more or less openly set up for themselves amid the disintegration of the Mughal Empire, had to choose between incessant invasions or the payment of *chauth*, i. e. 'quarter-revenue,' to the distant Maráthá Courts. Even the remote valleys of the Lower Ganges had to accept these degrading terms. In 1751 the Viceroy of Lower Bengal gave a formal grant of *chauth* to the Maráthás, together with the cession of Orissa.

The three critical wars, by which the British gradually broke down this new Hindu Empire of plunder, form the essential history of the establishment of our rule in Southern India. The Muhammadan usurpers of Mysore were finally crushed at Seringapatam in 1799. But during forty years, from the first Maráthá war in 1779–81, to the last Maráthá war and its resulting treaties in 1817–18, the English and the Maráthás were the two great powers in India which stood face to face. That long struggle has, however, been so fully described, that a mere reference to it must suffice here. But in order to understand the present problems of government in Southern India, and the aptitude which the Maráthás disclose for administrative employment and political combinations under British rule, it is necessary to realise the strong elements of which they consist, and which seemed for a time to point them out as the successors to the Mughal Empire.

The Maráthás of the first half of the seventeenth century formed the ideal type of a Hindu people in arms. The bulk of their troops was derived from the hardy Hindu peasantry of the Deccan or Konkan, and particularly from the highlands of the Gháts. Their military leaders were either soldiers of fortune who rose from the ranks, or petty chiefs, some of whom had more or less well-founded pretensions to Rájput descent, while others bluntly acknowledged their humble origin. Thus of the two great northern Maráthá Houses, Holkar was descended from a shepherd and Sindhia from a slipper-bearer. This military array was skilfully organised and consolidated into a political power by the Maráthá Brahmans.

The Maráthá Confederacy realised, therefore, in a striking manner the ancient theoretical constitution of a Hindu State, consisting of the peasantry, the war chiefs, and the Bráhman ministers, as sketched out in Manu, with a royal family as the cope-stone of the edifice. The royal family, or descendants of Sivají, soon became a shadowy power, and the Bráhman ministers, or Peshwás, practically superseded the Maráthá kings. The Bráhmans supplied the brain power to the whole. They directed the internal councils, controlled the external policy, and monopolised all the lucrative posts in the administration.

The Maráthá Confederacy stands as an example in modern history of both the strength and the weakness of a national organisation on strictly Hindu lines. It was firmly welded together by the spiritual authority and the secular abilities of the ablest class, the Bráhmans. On the other hand the strength of the Bráhmanical control became the weakness of the royal power. While the religious forces of cohesion were strong, the civil forces of cohesion were weak. As during the invasion of Alexander the Great, and as throughout the whole history of the Rájput races, so in the Maráthá Confederacy, there was no central force strong enough to maintain an effective and a permanent over-lordship. The Maráthás, therefore, with their tremendous energy of destruction against external States, were unable to unify their power against their own military leaders. Their internal dissensions and the conflicting interests of their five Ruling Houses, form the domestic history of their ruin. Those dissensions and internal conflicts rendered the issue of a struggle with a persistent Power like the British, animated by common aims and directed by a permanent central authority, only a question of time.

We have been so long familiar with the results of the struggle, that it requires almost an effort of the imagination to conceive that it might have had any other issue. But the contemporary records prove that in the minds of the early British rulers of India, the result was by no means a foregone conclusion. If an effective over-lordship had been maintained at Poona by a dynasty of warlike kings, worthy to be the successors of Sivají, a Maráthá Empire might have been established which would have altered the present map of India. It must be remembered that not till 1565 did the last of the great Hindu over-lordships of Southern India go down before the Muhammadans on the field of Tálikot. That within less than a century from that date, the Hindu military revival in Southern India had commenced under Sivají, and that in less than a century and a quarter the Maráthá leader had publicly crowned himself a Hindu king. That in a century and a half from the field of Tálikot the Maráthás had practically shattered the Mughal Empire. That in just a little over two centuries (1565—1771) the Maráthás had subjected almost the whole Indian provinces of that Empire to their actual rule or to their system of revenue tribute, and were holding prisoner the successor of the Mughal Emperors as a convenient puppet at Delhi.

The problem of administration in a Maráthá country is, therefore, to deal not with a quick-witted Hindu people like the Bengalis who had long been accustomed to foreign subjection, but with an equally able Hindu people who had been accustomed to consider themselves a conquering and a governing race. The problem is further complicated by the circumstance, that while war meant misery and exactions in Bengal, it meant prosperity and a most profitable business to the Maráthás. During nearly a century, I repeat, the Maráthás elaborated armed aggression into a lucrative revenue-system. Their troops returned laden with pay and plunder from their distant expeditions; their financiers swept into their central treasuries a quarter of the income of the provinces which they did not actually subject. For a time the wealth of India poured into the Maráthá kingdoms. Under such a system agriculture became a merely secondary occupation for the Maráthá peasantry during the intervals when they had not more profitable work on hand. Even a high rate of land-tax would have pressed lightly on them, but the exactions from other provinces enabled their rulers for a time to deal lightly with the peasantry of their central districts in the Maráthá country.

With the gradual establishment of the British Power a double change took place. The cessation of the *chauth* or revenue contributions from distant provinces, and the increasing difficulty of deriving an income from external invasions, compelled the Maráthá rulers to force up the taxation from their own peasantry. The Maráthá peasantry, deprived of predatory excursions as a source of profit, had to turn again to agriculture as their sole means of livelihood. They on their side could not so well afford to pay a high land-tax, as in the days when they enjoyed the plunder of other provinces, while their rulers were compelled to levy a more stringent taxation on the Maráthá lands. We shall see how this aspect of Maráthí history affected the British land-revenue system of Bombay. With the fall of the Maráthás as a predatory power, the collapse of the Maráthá system of finance ensued. When the British took possession of the Maráthá country, they found that the extortions which the Maráthá rulers formerly practised on external provinces, had been concentrated upon the peasantry of the Maráthá country itself.

The Maráthás have in them the grit of the best of the old Dravidian races, combined with the quick perception and constructive energy of the Aryan or Bráhman stratum which, in pre-historic times, superimposed its higher religious conceptions on the earlier peoples of the South. The result has been to develop in a high degree alike the active and the reflective sides of the Maráthá character. For the Maráthás are scarcely more distinguished as a military than as a literary race. Their language while of an advanced Aryan type and possessing structural complications attractive to the Indian student, bears witness to the strong original element which still forms the backbone of the Maráthá peasantry. Bishop Caldwell, while estimating the non-Aryan element in the modern Aryan languages of Northern India at one-tenth of the words in their vocabularies, placed the same non-Aryan element as high as one-fifth in Maráthí[1].

The Maráthás are a people proud, not only of their history as a conquering and governing race, but also of their national literature. One of the earliest Maráthí poets of fame was the famous Nám Deva, about the end of the thirteenth century. Like his fellow-countryman and contemporary, Dnyánoba, the author of the Dnyáneshwarí, he was deeply impressed with the spiritual aspects of life. Indeed, almost all the Maráthí writers are religious poets. About the year 1571, Srídhar compiled his Maráthí paraphrases or translations of the Sanskrit epics, the Mahábhárata, the Rámáyana, and the Bhágavata.

Maráthí poetry reached its highest flight in the Abhangas or spiritual poems of Tukarám or Tukoba (*circ.* 1609). This famous devotee started life as a petty shopkeeper; but also applied himself to religion and literature. The object of his adoration was Vithoba, whose shrine he regularly visited twice a year. Tukarám was the popular poet in Western India of a reformed Vishnuite faith, similar to that which Chaitanyá had taught in Bengal. He inveighed with peculiar unction and beauty against the riches of the world. In the eighteenth century, Mayúr Pandit

[1] It is right to mention that the more recent investigations of Beames, Hoernle, and Grierson render such *dicta*, alike of Bishop Caldwell and Lassen, doubtful.

or Moropanth poured forth his copious song in strains which some regard as even more elevated than the poems of Tukarám.

Besides its accumulation of religious verse, Maráthí possesses a prose literature, among which the chief compositions are the Bakhars or Annals of the Kings. It is also rich in love songs, and in farcical poetry of a broad style of wit.

A very brief sketch of the fourth speech-division of the Bombay Presidency, namely, the Kánarese districts, must close this chapter. For a considerable portion of the Kánarese-speaking country lies beyond the limits of the Bombay Presidency, while another considerable portion of it is really a debateable land between the true Kánarese districts and the Maráthá country in which both languages are spoken. Including Kolhápur, the Kánarese-speaking section of the Bombay Presidency has an area of about 25,000 square miles, with a population of 4¼ millions in 1881. It is divided into four British Districts[1] and eight principal Native States[2]. When it came within the cognisance of the British, it was under the rule of the Poona Peshwás, and it thus obtained its popular English name of the Southern Maráthá Country. The more accurate official phraseology of the present day prefers the designation of the Bombay Karnátik.

Like the true Maráthá country the Kánarese-speaking districts of Bombay have a history which goes as

[1] Namely, Bijápúr, Belgáum, Dhárwár, and North Kánara.

[2] Namely, Kolhápur, Miráj, Sángli, Jamkhandi, Kurundwád, Mudhol, Rámdrúg, and Savanúr.

far back as the reign of Asoka, who sent a missionary to preach Buddhism in this tract about 240 B.C. After a long succession of Buddhist and Hindu dynasties it passed for a time under the local Muhammadan kingdoms of Southern India, and for a still shorter period under the nominal control of the Mughal Empire. But for practical purposes the modern history of the Kánarese country begins with the establishment of Maráthá power under Sivají in the seventeenth century. After the breaking up of the Mughal Empire in the eighteenth century, the parts of the Bombay Karnátik not included in the home-territories of the Maráthás were ruled by the Muhammadan princes of Haidarábád (the Nizám) and of Mysore (Haidar Alí and Tipu). On the general pacification by the British, which followed our final overthrow of the Maráthás in 1817, the Bombay Karnátik was brought under the Company's rule by Colonel Munro, almost without opposition. The secret of his success consisted, to no small extent, in his recognition of the ruling families or native chiefs in the newly annexed territories. The British accepted the *status quo*; and the Native States of the Bombay Karnátik or Southern Maráthá Country form a prominent feature in this speech-division of the Bombay Presidency at the present day.

The foregoing brief account of the four historical areas which make up the Bombay Presidency, although a mere sketch with many details not filled in, suffices to bring three essential administrative facts before the reader.

In the first place it shows that the Government of that Presidency has to do with races and populations distinct alike in their history, their speech, their intellectual capacity, and their political needs. An administrative organisation which is to deal satisfactorily with these deep-lying differences, must be no hard and fast system prescribed on *à priori* principles from a central bureau, but one which is freely susceptible of local adaptations to meet local necessities and local facts.

Secondly, it places in a clear light the special feature of the Presidency Government of Bombay, as compared with most other of the Provincial Governments in India. This feature is that the Bombay Government has in every part of its territories to deal not only with a population of British subjects, but also with a population under Native Chiefs, situated in the very heart of our own districts, and often interspersed among, or interlaced with, them in a perplexing and intricate manner.

In the third place, it indicates what may be called a fundamental problem of British government, as contra-distinguished from British administration in Southern India. That problem is as old as the earliest military occupations of the South by the Delhi kings six centuries ago. It is the problem of uniting Southern India into one strong Empire ruled from the North, in spite of the physical difficulties imposed by distance and intervening tracts of mountain, forest, and desert. To the early Delhi dynasties those difficulties proved insuperable. It was the fixed idea of the Mughal Empire to overcome them, and that Empire, in the height of its power and in the plenitude of its despotic authority, shattered itself in vain efforts to accomplish this self-imposed task. The attempts of the East India Company to march troops from Bengal to Bombay proved how precarious would have been the control of Southern India by the Governor-General in Calcutta, if the British had had to depend upon the land route.

It was the maritime power of England which enabled her to weld together Northern and Southern India into one Empire. It is the maritime power of England which enables her to uphold that Empire. But her hold upon India no longer depends solely on her fleets. Since the time of Dalhousie the longest distances within India itself have, for the purpose of strategic movements, been brought under the control of the railway system. England as a basis of great military operations is now many weeks nearer to Bombay than Delhi was under the Mughal Emperors. For immediate striking purposes, our most distant cantonments of the North, Calcutta, Lucknow, Ambála, or even Pesháwar on the Punjab frontier, could concentrate their forces upon the districts of Bombay in one-tenth of the time that a Mughal army took to march from the military centres in Northern India to the nearest districts of the Maráthá country.

It was as a Sea Power that England won India. It is as a Sea Power and as a Railway Power that she has welded Northern and Southern India into one Empire under a strong central control. If, therefore, this book is to reach the heart of the matter, and to deal adequately with the problem which underlies all other problems of British Rule in Southern India, it must devote some space not only to the relations of the Bombay Government to the Supreme Government in Northern India, but also to the naval, or in official phraseology the 'marine,' resources of Bombay itself, and to the railway system by which every part of the Presidency is now brought within striking reach of the whole military power of the Empire.

CHAPTER IV.

THE FRAMEWORK OF THE PRESIDENCY GOVERNMENT.

THE Government of Bombay is the historical development of the government of the old factory of the East India Company at Surat[1]. Until towards the close of the seventeenth century, Surat was the principal seat of the Company as a trading power in India. It was ruled by a President and a Council of eight members, five of whom were to be always resident. In 1687 the seat of the Presidency was finally transferred to Bombay. It was at this same time that the Company's servants in Bengal, broken in spirit by the oppression of the Native Viceroy, resolved to abandon their factories; and embarking themselves and their goods, sailed down the Húglí, and despondently anchored off Balasor on the Orissa coast. It was not until nearly a century later that the Regulating Act in 1773 appointed the Governor of Bengal to be Governor-General of India, and

[1] This chapter is to some extent based on the 'Report on the Administration of the Bombay Presidency for 1882-83,' issued in 1884, the year previous to the five years with which the present volume deals. Printed at the Government Central Press, Bombay. I have also freely used the information collected for the Gazetteers or Statistical Accounts of the Bombay Districts, by Mr. J. M. Campbell, and my *Imperial Gazetteer of India*, and *Indian Empire*.

laid the foundation of that central control which has knit together the scattered fragments of the Mughal dominions into a new and stronger Empire.

In 1884, the year preceding the period with which this volume deals, the Government of Bombay consisted, as it still consists, of a Governor as President; and a Council of two Ordinary Members selected from the covenanted Civil Service, together with the Commander-in-Chief of the Bombay Army. The Governor and his Council, thus constituted, form the Executive Government of the Presidency. For legislative purposes the Executive Government is expanded into a Legislative Council consisting of the Governor, the Members of his Executive Council, and a certain number of Additional Members, at that time (1885–90) four to eight in number, selected from the non-official community, European and Native, or from officials of rank.

The Governor is President of both the Executive and Legislative Councils. For the sake of convenience, the business of Government is divided into Departments, of which the Political, the Judicial, the Educational, the Revenue, the Public Works, and the Military and Marine, are the chief. The supervision of each Department forms the special work of one or other of the Members of the Executive Government. The practice of regarding each of the Executive Councillors as a Minister holding the portfolio of a separate Department, which has gradually developed with such good results in the Supreme Government of India, has thus reproduced itself, although not with so strongly marked lines of demarcation, in the internal government of Bombay.

The Governor has by law the power to overrule the decisions of his Council, and to set aside their unanimous opinion in exceptional cases, recording his reasons. He has, moreover, the casting voice when his Council is equally divided—a power of considerable importance. It is, however, the object of every wise Governor, by patiently threshing out each question, to reconcile differences of opinion among his councillors, and thus to render his decisions in reality as well as in official style the united action of himself and his Council. While, therefore, Government by Parliament as in England is a government by debate and voting, Government by Council in Bombay is a government by discussion and agreement.

'The result,' says the authoritative Report[1] on the 'Form of Administration,' 'is that the chief is individually and effectively responsible for every act of the Government. The Members of Council have only an individual responsibility; but it is always known, from documents capable of being produced, and which, if called for by Parliament or public opinion, always are produced, what each has advised, and what reasons he gave for his advice: while from their dignified position, and ostensible participation in all acts of Government, they have nearly as strong motives to apply themselves to the public business. and to form and express a well-considered opinion on

[1] *Report on the Administration of the Bombay Presidency for* 1882–83, folio 20.

every part of it, as if the whole responsibility rested with themselves.

'All papers connected with public business reach Government through the Secretariat, where they are properly arranged, and submitted to the Member in charge of the department to which they belong, together with all available material for coming to a decision in the shape of former correspondence, Acts or Resolutions relating to the same or an analogous subject, and also with the recorded opinions of the Secretary or Under-Secretary in the department in question, or of both. The strength of the Secretariat is as follows. For the Revenue, Financial, and General Departments, a Secretary and Under-Secretary, who are covenanted civilians, and an Assistant-Secretary who is an uncovenanted officer; in the Political, Judicial, Educational, and Secret Departments, a covenanted Secretary and Under-Secretary, the latter of whom also officiates as Secretary to the Legislative Council, and two uncovenanted Assistant-Secretaries; in the Military, Marine, and Ecclesiastical Departments, a Secretary who is a military officer, and an uncovenanted Assistant-Secretary; and in the Public Works, Railway, and Telegraph Departments, a Secretary, a Joint Secretary, and three Under-Secretaries, who are either Royal or Civil Engineers, and two Assistant-Secretaries, one of whom is a Civil Engineer and the other an uncovenanted officer. The senior Civil Secretary to Government is entitled the Chief Secretary.' Certain changes have since been made.

The constitution of the various Departments of the

Government, Political, Revenue, Judicial, Police, and Public Works, &c., will be explained under the chapters dealing with these branches of the Administration. The present chapter treats only of the Government at head-quarters which directs the whole.

The central figures in the Government of Bombay are the Governor, his two Civilian Councillors and the Commander-in-Chief of the Bombay Army. During the five years, from 1885 to 1890, with which this book deals, the Governor was Lord Reay, and his Civil Councillors were successively Sir James Braithwaite Peile, Sir Maxwell Melvill, Sir James Richey, and Sir Raymond West. The Commanders-in-Chief of the Bombay Army during the same period were successively Sir Arthur Hardinge, Sir Charles Arbuthnot, and His Royal Highness the Duke of Connaught. This book is not written in the praise or dispraise of any living man, and with one exception, Lord Reay and his colleagues are still in the world of the living. That exception is the late Sir Maxwell Melvill, and in a later part of this chapter I shall endeavour to show what manner of man he was.

The Governor, however, stands in a different category from his colleagues in Council. He is not only the central motive power but the conspicuous figurehead of the Government for the time being. It largely depends upon his personal character whether his Government is strong or feeble, courageous or timid, skimming over the surface of things or going to the root of each matter. It is, therefore, necessary in order to understand the attitude of the Bombay

Government towards the successive grave questions which came before it in the five years from 1885 to 1890, to have some idea of the personality of the Governor during that period. I hope that in attempting the most delicate of tasks, a biographical notice of a living man, I shall be found to confine myself strictly to a narrative of the influences (hereditary and personal) which shaped his mind and gave direction to his views on public affairs.

Donald James, Chief of the ancient Scottish clan Mackay and eleventh Baron Reay in the peerage of Scotland, took his seat as Governor of Bombay on the 30th March, 1885. He represents one of the famous Scottish families who sought service about three centuries ago in the armies of Europe, and gained for themselves high positions in their adopted countries. 'When King James Sixth of Scotland became also King of England,' says the historian of Mackay's regiment, 'there followed a lengthened period of peace and quietness throughout the two kingdoms,' during which 'numbers of brave and adventurous men,' who 'could not remain idle,' 'left Scotland in search of fame and fortune, and took service under the banners of the various princes who were then warring for supremacy on the continent of Europe[1].'

One of these gentlemen, Sir Donald Mackay[2], raised a regiment among his clansmen, and headed the Scots

[1] 'An Old Scots Brigade, being the History of Mackay's Regiment, now incorporated with the Royal Scots.' By John Mackay (late) of Herriesdale. Blackwood & Sons. 1885. Dedicated to the present Lord Reay.

[2] Born 1590; knighted by King James, 1616; created a baronet, 1627, and Baron Reay, Peerage of Scotland, 1628; died 1649.

Brigade which did splendid service for Holland and Sweden in the Protestant cause during the Thirty Years' War. A scarce monograph of the last century gives a stirring account of the battles and sufferings of this gallant body of Scotchmen[1]. Its Chief, the first Lord Reay, on hearing of the distress of his sovereign Charles I, hastened over to England from the Continent to join the losing cause, was taken prisoner on His Majesty's surrender, and thrown into gaol. Being liberated by the intervention of the King of Denmark, Lord Reay returned to that country. He 'continued in the s^{d} King's service during the remainder of his days; and upon hearing of the murder of his G[racious] Sov. K[ing] Ch. I, he took it so to heart that he took his bed and dyed in 3 days y^{r} after' (February, 1649)[2]. The King of Denmark sent over a frigate with the body of the loyal old soldier, to be interred in the ancient burying-place of his House in the Scottish highlands.

The tyranny of James II led to as hard a struggle between loyalty to the Crown and fidelity to the Protestant religion among the Scottish regiments serving in Holland, as among his subjects at home. The Dutch regiments of the Scots Brigade, under General Mackay, made up a large part of the armament which brought over the Prince of Orange to England in

[1] 'An Historical Account of the British Regiments employed since the reigns of Queen Elizabeth and King James I in the formation and defence of the Dutch Republic, particularly of the Scotch Brigade.' T. Kay. London. 1795.

[2] John Mackay's *An Old Scots Brigade*. Appendix H, p. 252. From a family manuscript written between the years 1678 and 1700, in the possession of the present Lord Reay.

October, 1688. It fought for him at Killiecrankie, where indeed the commanders on both sides, Viscount Dundee for King James, and General Mackay for King William, had been bred to arms in the Scots Brigade. On the fall of Lord Dundee in the battle, another ex-officer of the Brigade, General Cannon, who had commanded one of the Scots regiments brought over from Holland on the occasion of Monmouth's rebellion, took command of the Royalist Highlanders. In 1691 at the siege of Athlone, the storming of the fortress was allotted to the Scots Brigade under General Mackay.

From this period the careers of the regiments of the Brigade which had been brought over to England and those which remained in Holland diverge. Until the close of the eighteenth century the Mackays and their followers in Holland considered themselves Scotchmen, and indeed were almost ready to mutiny rather than to give up their national colours or uniform. They had the keen *animus redeundi* which still characterises the Scot in foreign countries. But from the end of the eighteenth century the Dutch section of the Scots Brigade began to consider Holland as their fatherland. Colonel Aeneas Mackay, of the Scots Brigade (born 1734, died 1807), the great-grandfather of the present Lord Reay, fairly settled in Holland, and through his marriage with the Baroness de Haeften in 1763 brought the Dutch estate into the family. His son Barthold, the present Lord Reay's grandfather, wore the uniform of the Dutch navy. His son, the 10th Baron, the present Lord Reay's father, was the first of the race to enter a

Dutch University, and to take an important part in the government of their adopted country. He became Minister of State and Vice-President of the Privy Council of the Netherlands. The present Lord Reay's mother was the daughter of Baron Fagel, a distinguished Dutch statesman [1]. One of his mother's uncles was the Dutch Ambassador in London, another held the same post in Paris.

The present Lord Reay (born 1839) was educated at the gymnasium at the Hague and at the Leiden University. His tutor at the latter seat of learning was the eminent jurist in Roman law, Professor Goudsmit. The Dutch Mackays were high Conservatives of the old type, philosophical Tories and Divine Right men. Lord Reay's father combined these principles with the doctrines of free trade, and was a Liberal in colonial policy. Lord Reay himself chose for his dissertation when he took his Degree at Leiden, a purely colonial subject, namely, the administration of Netherlands India under Field Marshal Daendels, the road-making Governor-General in Java. On leaving the University, Lord Reay entered the Dutch Foreign Office, and was attached to the Dutch Legation at the Court of St. James's to study English institutions. From the Foreign Office he was transferred to the Dutch Colonial Office to get a thorough knowledge of its Colonial system. In 1866 he made a tour in America to examine the institutions of that country, and there laid the foundation of life-long friendships with some of

[1] The Fageliana of the Dublin library belonged to the Fagel family.

its most distinguished citizens, including Lowell and Longfellow.

Being appointed President of the Society for the Promotion of Dutch Industries, Lord Reay gave special attention to questions connected with capital and labour; and in 1869 organised an industrial exhibition at Amsterdam, for the benefit of the working classes—the first attempt to illustrate in this way the relations of capital and labour in Holland. The exhibition proved a great success, and although the more extreme Conservatives looked on it as a Socialist innovation in disguise, the late Queen of Holland gave it her cordial support, and continued to the young politician the intimate friendship with which she had honoured his parents and grandparents.

In 1871 Lord Reay entered the Chamber of Dutch Representatives as a Liberal Member for Tiel, the district in which his family estates lie, and was again returned in 1875. In the Chamber his special subjects were foreign and colonial politics, secondary and agricultural education, and industrial questions, especially those connected with co-operative labour. His father succeeded to the Scotch title in 1875, but died in the following year. The present Lord Reay succeeded to the family honours in 1876, and was naturalised by Act of Parliament as a British subject in 1877. This step gave considerable umbrage to many of his Dutch friends, the more so as the family then held a very conspicuous position in the political life of the Netherlands. Lord Reay's cousin and heir-presumptive was President of the Second Chamber, and was till

August, 1891, Prime Minister of Holland. In 1881, Lord Reay was raised to the peerage of the United Kingdom under the title of Baron Reay.

Throughout his career, both in Holland and England, Lord Reay's attention had been strongly directed to foreign politics and to colonial administration; and in 1885 he was appointed Governor of Bombay. A Liberal, of what is now known as the federal but decentralising type, Lord Reay brought to his task a life-long conviction of the necessity of binding together the Colonies and India with the mother-country; by strengthening the interests which the various parts of the Empire have in common; and by non-interference with local institutions and susceptibilities. In home politics, which however interested him less than Indian, colonial, and foreign affairs, Lord Reay was a decided Liberal and free-trader of the Cobden and Bright school. That is to say, of the school which resisted with equal firmness any steps in the socialistic direction on the one side, or any tampering with free-trade principles on the other. In foreign and colonial politics, Lord Reay was, alike by hereditary training and by personal conviction, opposed to the *laissez faire* policy, and in favour of great vigilance in the maintenance of British interests. He was one of the original members of the Federation League, and heartily went with Lord Rosebery and his friends in their programme of making India and the colonies living factors in the national organisation of Greater Britain. It follows that he believed in the necessity of a strong army and navy for the mother-country, and of a cautious but vigilant frontier policy in India.

There was one question of domestic politics to which he had given much attention. He had always been a steady and powerful advocate of popular Education, and especially of Technical Education. He regarded the instruction and true enlightenment of the people as the best, perhaps the only permanent, weapon of civilisation against the socialistic tendencies which threaten to divert the democracy in Europe from the sure although slow paths of economic progress.

On Lord Reay's arrival in India he found himself associated with a military colleague of great ability. The Commander-in-Chief of Bombay, General Sir Arthur Hardinge, K.C.B., knew India and the Indians well and was a thorough man of the world, with literary tastes and varied social accomplishments. As the head of the Bombay Army his strong point was believed to be infantry tactics. He rendered a lasting service by enforcing the principle of selection for regimental commands on the ground of personal qualifications, rather than on hard and fast seniority claims. In the discussions which then occupied the attention of the Government with regard to the reform of the 'Silladar' system of Irregular Cavalry, he also took a decisive part. His successor, Sir Charles Arbuthnot, K.C.B., R.A., was in many respects Sir Arthur's complement—a hard-working soldier, of retiring manners, whose elaborate and carefully considered Minutes on the Bombay, Aden, and Karáchi defences form State

Papers of high historical importance. His successor in turn was the Duke of Connaught. The popularity of His Royal Highness with the army both European and Native, the plans which he set on foot or supported for its welfare, the mark which he left on the military organisation of Bombay, and the universal regret testified at his departure alike by the Native Chiefs and by the various races and communities in the British districts, will long be remembered. During his tenure of office there was no detachment of the Bombay Army which he did not personally inspect. His colleagues in Council had special reasons for appreciating the tact with which His Royal Highness reconciled his rank as the son of the Sovereign with his official position as second in the governing body of an Indian Presidency. The Duke and Duchess of Connaught made every one feel that they really enjoyed India and Indian service, and that they frankly identified themselves with the life of those around them.

The Civil Members of Lord Reay's Council, men of my own service and some of them personal friends, I must touch off with a light hand. Sir James Peile, K.C.S.I., was the Revenue Member until 1886, when he was advanced to the Council of the Governor-General of India. He was regarded as the representative civilian of the 'head-quarters' type' in the Bombay Council; reserved in manner, very methodical in work and preferring to do it in writing rather than by oral discussion, fond of old lines, but in educational matters progressive. In forest and excise affairs he was opposed to change, and a steady supporter of the permanent officials of those departments; strongly putting forward the revenue aspect of each question. He had acquired valuable experience in dealing with Native States as a Political Officer, and had mastered the working of the central mechanism of Government, both in the Secretariat and in various special employments. He knew Káthiáwár thoroughly, with its multitudinous petty States, and rendered important service to education in our own districts as Director of Public Instruction. In 1885 he acted as Governor and President in Council in Bombay, during the brief interval between the date on which the out-going Governor laid down his Office and Lord Reay's arrival. The Feudatory Chiefs held him in reverence, and the new Governor heartily acknowledged his obligations to him in questions connected with their management. Although best known as what is called in India 'a strong departmental man,' Sir James Peile recognised the necessity of according a more effective voice to Native opinion, and proved a firm supporter of Lord Dufferin's policy in regard to an extended Native representation in the Legislative Councils.

He was succeeded by a civilian of a different but equally well-marked type. Sir James Bellot Richey, K.C.I.E., was essentially a 'District officer,' with the minute and painstaking knowledge of the local administration and of the people which that term connotes. An agreeable colleague in Council, very open-minded, not afraid of innovations, conciliatory, and popular, he inclined to the more liberal view in the forest and excise measures which were destined to form so important a feature of Lord Reay's administration. Sir James Richey unfortunately suffered from bad health, and when compelled to go home on leave, Mr. Pritchard, C.S.I.[1], acted for him. Mr. Pritchard was a strong representative of the revenue interests in all measures. He had himself increased the revenue from the excise, and this subject was with him one of keen personal conviction. In forest questions he inclined to what was regarded as the Liberal party in the Government. Both Sir James Peile and Sir James Richey were Oxford men, the former of Oriel, the latter of Exeter College. Together with their colleagues, Sir Raymond West and Mr. Naylor, to be presently mentioned, they were among the early fruits of the competitive system for recruiting the India Civil Service.

Sir Raymond West, K.C.I.E., M.A., became a Member of the Bombay Council in 1887. His service had been chiefly in the Judicial Department, and it was as Judicial Member that he proved of great value to Lord Reay's Government. In addition to the ordinary acquirements of a barrister-at-law and a High Court Judge, Sir Raymond West had the enthusiasm and special learning of a jurist, and as such was apt to be regarded as tending towards the doctrinaire type of administrator. A writer of erudite Minutes, exceedingly loyal to Bombay interests, and opposed to any undue interference of the Government of India, he fought effectively with pen and tongue for the views

[1] Now Sir Charles Pritchard, K.C.I.E., C.S.I.

of himself and his colleagues. Generally speaking he belonged to the Liberal party in the Government, was a scientific political economist, a strong advocate of education, and very popular with the Natives. Sir Raymond West was probably the best debater in the Legislative Council of Bombay during the five years under review.

Mr. Naylor, C.S.I., who acted as a temporary member of Council on two occasions, belonged to the less strongly pronounced type of judicial officer; conscientious, avoiding friction, fond of a tough piece of work, he will be remembered as the practical author of the new municipal constitution for the city of Bombay.

The most brilliant member of the Bombay Council during the five years under review was, by common consent, Sir Maxwell Melvill. This genial and accomplished man is now no more, and I may therefore with propriety give a somewhat fuller sketch of his character and career than would be suitable in the case of his colleagues still living. Arriving in India in 1855, he early disclosed a bent towards the judicial branch of the administration, and marked himself as a man certain to obtain the highest positions which it offered. Having served as an Assistant Magistrate and Collector, and as an Assistant Judge in the Bombay Presidency proper, he won distinction as Judicial Assistant Commissioner in Sind. After not more than about eight years' service he was offered the coveted and lucrative appointment of Judicial and Political Secretary to the Bombay Government by

Sir Bartle Frere, one of the finest judges of men who ever ruled Western India. This extraordinary piece of promotion the young civilian declined, out of friendship for Mr. Mansfield, under whom he had served in Sind, and who, he knew, desired the post. He acted for a short time as Registrar-General of Assurances, and in 1866 was appointed Judicial Commissioner and Judge of the Sadr or Chief Court in Sind. In 1868 he was selected as one of the Commissioners to enquire into the failure of the Bank of Bombay, and in the following year, 1869, he took his seat as a judge of the High Court. This office he held for fifteen years, until advanced to the Bombay Council in 1884. He declined the offer of a membership of the Viceroy's Council—the highest appointment open to a Bombay civilian—on the ground of weak health.

But Sir Maxwell Melvill, or Max Melvill as he was affectionately called throughout his career, was an important personality and a living influence quite apart from his official work. In economics he did not shrink from declaring himself a protectionist of the American type—that is to say an advocate for protection not for a single isolated country, but for a great continent like America or India made up of a number of States, possessing within them the resources for almost every kind of production, indeed for almost every form of human industry, and capable of a self-sufficing economic development. One of those who knew him best believes that it was this consciousness of holding views not in accordance with the prevailing doctrines of the Government of India, which influenced him in declining the seat in the Viceroy's Council. The same friend writes to me:—'What used to strike me most in the character of his mind was that he combined a strong turn for the poetical and picturesque, with the most accurate matter-of-factness. In dealing with a question he would puff away all the froth of exaggeration and false sentiment with a few witty remarks, and present what remained in a manner that always interested. There was nothing didactic about him, and his cleverness was of an infectious sort that made the person he talked with feel on equal terms. He always liked to hear what others had to say, and mended or adjusted his own views as the conversation proceeded. A dispute with him was a real pleasure.

'I used also to be struck with his many-sidedness: for he was a keen sportsman, and a man of society as well as a worker. He was always a centre of refinement and cheerfulness, and had a happy knack of finding something humorous in all the minor troubles of life. And the wonder was that he could do all this with a fragile constitution that would have excused a life of apathy and inertia. He was scarcely ever really well, and on two or three occasions at death's door from weakness. His work would of course not compare with that of some others in India from the elaborative point of view; and one may say that its characteristic was ease, not effort. But his work was sound, and true all the same—and probably few men have made so few mistakes.' His hospitality was proverbial even in hospitable Bombay. He moved through life with a grace and tolerance that made him a favourite among a wide circle, and with a capacity for sincere and self-abnegating friendship that will long dwell in the memory of the few who knew the inner nature of the man.

I have dwelt on the different types of Lord Reay's civilian colleagues in Council, because those types are truly representative of the Bombay Civil Service at large—the Service whose varied experience and often conflicting opinions have to be amalgamated and harmonised in the corporate measures of the Presidency Government; the Service, moreover, by which those measures have to be practically carried out. For although made up of widely diversified component parts, the Government of Bombay, as of other Indian Provinces, presents the outward form of an entity firmly compacted together, and wielding the strength of the Greek ideal of 'the one in many.' In its external relations it ordinarily deals with the Supreme Government practically represented by the Governor-General-in-Council at Simla or Calcutta, but on certain occasions with the Secretary of State direct. Its internal business with the Bombay Presidency Administration it discharges through the medium of the Secretariat, assisted and humanised by the personal intercourse of the Governor with the District Officers and the Heads of Departments.

It is necessary here to say a few words in regard to the external relations of Lord Reay's Government towards the Supreme Government of India.

The decentralisation policy which Lord Mayo

inaugurated, in 1871, in Indian finance has, in its later developments, given a new importance to the relations between the Central and the Provincial Governments. The remarkable feature of those relations at present is that on mere matters of detail constant reference to the Central Government may be necessary, while on many large questions involving important principles, such references may almost be avoided. Thus to take an example in the Department of Public Instruction. I am informed that the foundation of the Fergusson College in Poona, which amounted to a new departure in the self-education of the Maráthá country, did not necessitate a single communication between the Simla and Bombay Secretariats; while the endowment of a new Professorship at the Grant Medical College, affecting no question of general principle, required a lengthy correspondence between the two Secretariats. Even in legislative matters the lines of local initiative and of Central control are not clearly demarcated. Theoretically the Local Legislature deals with local legislation. But, speaking practically of the period under review, the Bombay Government passed several important acts without interference by the Central Government, whilst other bills not of a strictly local character, yet not more important in their consequences, were considered to require amendment in detail by the Governor-General-in-Council.

It is not possible, therefore, in the present transition state of India, to define exactly the limits of local legislation and administration in regard to the Central control. But the growing burdens imposed on the Supreme Government by the extension of the Empire, steadily make for decentralisation, and the centrifugal force is always gathering strength: Lord Reay, like other self-reliant Provincial Governors, believed that this tendency is in the right direction. He regarded the spectacle of the ablest and most experienced administrators in India, one set of them at Simla and another at a provincial capital, spending their best days in keen dialectic controversy over administrative details, as a spectacle altogether unsuited to the India of the present day. As a matter of fact, although the demarcating lines as to which questions are imperial and which provincial are nowhere clearly defined, a tacit understanding has gradually grown up. It is right to add that the influence of both the Viceroys, Lord Dufferin and Lord Lansdowne, during the period under review, was opposed to needless interference by the Simla Secretariat with the Provincial Governments.

Personally, Lord Reay was in full accord with Sir Stafford Northcote (Lord Iddesleigh) in favour of further decentralisation. Routine is the bane of bureaucracy. It is a natural parasite of the Anglo-Indian form of government, and to it a peculiarly dangerous parasite. Lord Reay regarded a cautious extension of the powers of the Provincial Governments as a practical antidote to the paralysing influences of routine, and in his relations with the Supreme Government of India he acted frankly on this conviction.

As regards the internal division of labour within the Government of Bombay itself, the Governor's relations are primarily with his Members of Council, and in a secondary although an almost equal degree with his Secretariat. Lord Reay retained in his own hands the more special charge of the Political, Military, Ecclesiastical, and Public Works Departments, throughout his whole tenure of office. During the last year of his Government he had also charge of the Department of Public Instruction. The Judicial Department, including the judicial side of our political relations with the Native States, formed the particular charge of one of the two Civilian Members of the Council, commonly known as the Judicial Member. In like manner the other Civilian, or Revenue, Member of Council was responsible for the initiation and conduct of the Government in the Revenue Department, including under that comprehensive term the relations of the Government to the land and the cultivators, besides the various branches of administration which it ordinarily embraces in European countries. The questions in the Revenue Department are, however, so vitally important to the welfare of the people, and their economic side is so deeply interesting to any one accustomed to deal with landed property in Europe, that no conscientious Governor can divest himself of an enormous amount of work connected with them. As a matter of fact, very few Minutes written by Lord Reay's colleague in Council in the Revenue Department were returned to the Secretariat without some exchange of thought between the Governor and the Revenue Member.

The branch of the administration which came least

within Lord Reay's direct and personal management was the Judicial Department. Lord Reay's studies under one of the most accomplished of continental jurists made him realise the extremely intricate and technical character of the mixture of English with Hindu and Muhammadan law administered in the Indian Courts. Indeed, it would have been unwise for any Governor appointed from England to attempt to override the long and comprehensive experience of such colleagues as Sir Maxwell Melvill and Sir Raymond West in the practical conduct of Indian judicial questions. Such questions are even more essentially matters for Indian experts, and of even a more technical character, than those which arise in the Public Works Department itself.

Lord Reay took the view that the constitutional advisers of the Governor are his Members of Council in a much more direct sense than his Secretaries. He held that to govern chiefly on Secretariat Notes is a dangerous although a not uncommon error in India. The Secretaries to an Indian Government are very important functionaries, younger and often personally more vigorous than the Members of Council, with their further careers still before them, and chosen for their powers of quickly grasping questions and smoothly performing many kinds of work. Lord Reay carefully chose the strongest men he could find in the Service for his Secretaries, quite independently of whether their personal views coincided with his own. But he realised with great distinctness the tendency of the Secretariat to run in bureaucratic grooves, and he endeavoured to correct this tendency by freely and constantly consulting with the District Officers direct, and with the heads of the European and native communities. He believed that as an English Chancellor of the Exchequer maintains personal communication in regard to the larger matters of finance with the leaders of the City, so an Indian Governor should maintain a personal communication with the non-official leaders of the Provinces which he administers. The Secretaries had always the right of stating their views to him with absolute frankness in their Secretariat Notes, and of giving personal explanations if they desired to do so. But having a Council appointed under Act of Parliament, it seemed to Lord Reay that personal discussion should ordinarily take place between himself and his Members of Council, rather than with the Members of the Secretariat.

As this is a question which arises under every new Governor in India, and as Lord Reay held strong opinions in regard to it, it may be proper to state at a little further length his own views. He held that a Governor must not allow himself to become the mouthpiece of his Secretariat. That it is as President of his Council, and with the Members of his Council, that all important business should be transacted. That it is even necessary to guard against the Secretariat invading the province of the Council. That when a Secretary and a Member of Council take divergent views with respect to any question, the difficulty is aggravated if the Governor backs his Secretary, unless his Council are well aware that he is not under Secretariat influences. Acting on this conviction Lord Reay departed from the system of receiving regular weekly visits from the Chief Secretaries, and of transacting work with them in person. He thought that that system, while certainly saving trouble, and while necessary in the more complicated mechanism of the Supreme Government of India, exposed a Provincial Governor to the temptation of not looking himself so closely into each question as he would otherwise be forced to do. Lord Reay preferred reading what the Secretaries had to say, and then talking over their opinions with the Members of Council in cases where a difference of opinion arose.

On matters of trade and finance Lord Reay was always anxious to consult the Members of the Bombay Chamber of Commerce, and especially Sir Forbes Adam, the distinguished head of that body. In railway matters he advised freely and personally with the managers of the chief lines; in the Public Works Department with the leading engineers; on Military matters with experienced officers; on Educational questions with the leading professors and inspectors of schools, in addition to the Director of Public Instruction; on Revenue questions with the District officials, both European and Indian, and with the Native Inámdárs or landholders who were qualified by their special knowledge to give an opinion. This system of consultation outside the Council and Secretariat, added both to the labour and to the interest of Lord Reay's work. It is a system which all energetic Governors make use of, to a larger or smaller extent.

But with Lord Reay it formed a cardinal principle, as he believed that it helped to counteract the tendency to bureaucratic onesidedness which he regarded as a constant danger to Indian government. On the one hand it increased the knowledge of the Governor, and the confidence of the public which soon became aware that the Governor did not act on *ex parte* statements and that his was not a government by 'file.' On the other hand it was sometimes not altogether agreeable to the immediate entourage of the Governor, and perhaps tended to temper the enthusiasm with which some Governors have been regarded by their Secretariat.

In the difficult matter of patronage, Lord Reay endeavoured to make all other considerations subordinate to individual fitness. Where two candidates were of equal fitness, seniority prevailed. But Lord Reay made it clearly understood that for the higher or more special appointments, fitness, not seniority, guided his selection; and that, for example, a Commissionership of a Division was not necessarily given to the senior Collector on the list. This principle was not always popular with the Service, but it was fully endorsed by the Government of India.

The presence of an officer at head-quarters, constituted, in Lord Reay's opinion, no special title to promotion. Good district work, knowledge of the people and of the living forces among them, were regarded by Lord Reay as superior claims to an indoor acquaintance with rules and regulations. Appointments based on such considerations did not always give complete satisfaction in a Service in which seniority has, and rightly has, strong rights. But similar principles were adopted by Sir Arthur Hardinge as Commander-in-Chief, in filling up vacancies, conspicuously in the case of colonels of regiments; and Lord Reay believed that the Bombay Army was indebted to Sir Arthur Hardinge for an increase of efficiency on this as on other grounds.

In regard also to the difficult question as to the employment of military officers in civil or political appointments, Lord Reay entertained distinct views of his own. On various occasions he expressed his opinion as to the high character of the Civil Service in general and of the younger members of it in particular. Very few services in the world, he thought, could show such an amount of honest hard work, or so high a standard of personal honour in positions of isolation, where a man's work and a man's conduct have to be regulated so decisively by what is right in his own eyes. Lord Reay was not in favour of employing military officers in civil departments. He heartily acknowledged that a good soldier makes a good official. But he thought that the system of drawing away the most promising among the young regimental officers for civil employ meant a serious loss to the army, especially at a time when the military authorities were complaining of the insufficiency of officers for regimental duty. He believed that the reasons which in former times rendered it expedient to employ military officers in the political department, that is to say in the relations of the British Government towards the Native Chiefs, had lost much of their old force, and that other imperative considerations had arisen on the other side. In the majority of cases he thought we are now bound to place at the Native Courts civil officers who have had experience in the working of the rural administration in British Districts, and who carry with them into political employment the knowledge and standards which they have thus acquired. Such men seemed to him best qualified to aid the rulers of Native States in the improvement of their territories.

The Governor of a Presidency like Bombay, divided by the history, language and character of the people into four distinct Provinces, is essentially a peripatetic ruler. Lord Reay attached great importance to his tours, as they brought him into personal contact alike with Native Chiefs and their Ministers, with the District Officers, and with the heads of the local communities. As he carried on the business of government with the same personal care while on tour, as when residing in one of his three administrative headquarters (Bombay, Poona, and Mahábaleshwar), a very large amount of his work had to be done on paper. He preferred to personally discuss questions with his Members of Council individually, to the more formal meetings of the Council itself. It so happened that his principal colleagues during his five years of government took the same view, and two at least of them were famous as Minute writers. The result was that Councils were only held when the collective decision of the Government was required, while on the other hand the State Papers and Records referring to the five years under review are particularly full and able. The shortest Minutes are those by the Governor, and few heads of Indian Provinces have been more studious of brevity in this respect. Lord Reay's own view was that by steady individual discussion with his colleagues a question was more likely to be thoroughly threshed out, than at a formal meeting of Council at which it might be more difficult for a member to give way after once delivering his opinion.

Lord Reay regarded the Secretariat as an instrument of administration, not of Government. This is an important distinction, and one which, with the growth of municipal and other organisations of local self-government in India, becomes every year more significant. It is one thing to deal with administrative principles and to practically work them out; another to deal with the principles of government which underlie alike the principles and details of administration. With regard to the first class of business Lord Reay, with a special knowledge of the bureaucratic régime in European countries, has recorded his opinion that it would be impossible to assign too high a place in all the essentials of efficiency to the Anglo-Indian bureaucracy. He became more and more impressed with the administrative merits of that bureaucracy, the more intimately he became acquainted with its inner working. He believed that the Indian Service presents a combination of theoretical and practical ability, together with a high standard of personal character not to be found in either of the two European Countries in which the bureaucratic system has been carried to its highest perfection, Germany and France. But he held, not the less firmly, that a bureaucratic administration must understand that its horizon is limited by the nature of its duties, and that there are other and higher functions which must be reserved to the Government.

There is something to be said in favour of a clearly defined view of this kind; something, too, against it. Sooner or later an Indian Governor has to recognise that in India, with its vast territories and diversified local peculiarities, the district administration is, in a much more than European sense, the actual Government of the country. By 'government' Lord Reay understood the grasp of the political and social situation, and the reaction of the one on the other. For example, the Indian administration is apt to look upon what has been called the temperance movement, or the opposition to excise facilities for the liquor traffic, as a spurious movement. Lord Reay, on the other hand, believed it to be a movement which represented a certain amount of conviction on the part of many concerned in it, and an engine of agitation by which others sought to win the sympathies of a powerful party in England. Or to take another and more important example. Many Indian officers hold that local self-government spoils good administration. Lord Reay was willing to acknowledge that a thoroughly good civilian works an Indian District more efficiently than municipalities or local boards can at present be expected to do. But he also held that municipal self-government is the necessary school for the extension of local institutions, and of that expansion of the Legislative Councils which he regarded as inevitable in the near future of India.

He believed that an unchecked bureaucracy in India would, with the progress of Indian education and enlightenment, produce sooner or later the same unfortunate results which it has produced in Ireland. But, on the other hand, that no man can be a good Indian Governor who does not appreciate and make full use of the wonderful administrative instrument which he possesses in the bureaucratic organisation of the Indian Civil Service. He thought it possible to reconcile these two views, and he never lost sight of them in the practical work of Government. Whether it is really possible to reconcile them without a considerable amount of friction, is one of the chief problems in governing India during its present transition stage.

CHAPTER V.

DEALINGS WITH THE NATIVE STATES.

LORD REAY retained in his own hands, throughout the five years under review, the charge of the 'Political Department' which conducts the relations of the British Government towards the Native States. For the duties of this Department his early diplomatic training had given him both a personal taste and a special aptitude. The territories under Native Princes or Chiefs formed more than a third of the whole area of the Bombay Presidency and aggregate 82,324 square miles [1]. This is inclusive of the great Hindu State of Baroda (8570 square miles); of which the political control was transferred, in 1875, from the Bombay Government to the Governor-General in Council. The Native States which remain under the supervision of the Government of Bombay have an area of 73,753 square miles [2], and a population in 1881 of seven million inhabitants.

The relations of these Native States to the British

[1] *Imperial Gazetteer of India*, vol. iii. p. 48. Ed. 1885.

[2] *Parliamentary Statistical Abstract relating to British India.* Statement I, 1889. The areas and population are always given according to the Census of 1881—the Census which regulated administrative statistics during the five years under review.

Government are regulated by a long series of Treaties and Engagements many of which date from the third quarter of the last century. But broadly speaking, and for present purposes, they rest upon the general settlement effected for Western India at the close of the third Maráthá War in 1818–20[1]. Some of the States are of great extent and are thickly peopled; others are under petty chiefs, thinly inhabited and in a backward state; others again are mountainous or jungly tracts. For administrative purposes, and exclusive of Baroda, they are divided into eighteen States or groups of States, presenting many varieties of internal government, and wide differences alike as to the powers exercised by their Chiefs and as to the social condition of their people. Thus the great Káthiáwár group had in 1881 an area exceeding 20,000 square miles, and a population of close on 2½ millions. The little State of Savanúr had barely 70 square miles, while Nárukot had only 6,440 inhabitants. With regard to the pressure of the population on the soil, which forms a dominant factor in the problems of Indian administration, they present equally striking contrasts. Starting from the Khándesh States (the Dángs) with 15 persons to the square mile, or Khairpur with 21 persons to the square mile, they proceed in an ascending scale through a general average of 110 persons to the square mile, to the densely peopled districts of Kolhápur with a population of 284 to the square mile.

[1] Sir Charles Aitchison's '*Treaties, Engagements and Sunnuds*,' vol. iv. Foreign Office Press, Calcutta. Ed. 1876.

The political relations between the British Government and the Native States are maintained by the presence of a British Agent or representative at the principal Courts. The position and duties of this Agent vary in the different States, and are regulated either by the terms of the original Treaties or by more recent *sanads* or patents granted by the British Government. In some instances, as in Cutch, the function of the Agent is confined to giving advice, and to a general surveillance of the policy pursued by the Native Chief. In other cases the Agent is invested with an effective share in the administration; while States whose rulers are minors—and the number of these is always large—are directly managed by European or Native officers, or by mixed Regencies, appointed by the Government of Bombay. In all cases the Political Agent is in close and confidential communication with the Political Department of the Bombay Government—the Department which Lord Reay retained as his special charge.

Perhaps the most characteristic feature of the eighteen groups of the Bombay Native States is the extraordinary number of petty principalities into which they are sub-divided. The Káthiáwár group alone contains no fewer than 187 separate States. The recognition of these multitudinous jurisdictions is due in part to the circumstance that the early Bombay administrators regarded the *de facto* exercise of civil and criminal jurisdiction by a landholder in Feudatory territory as carrying with it a *quasi*-sovereign status. In most of the States the British Agent exercises not only a political but a judicial control. A large amount of judicial work accordingly devolves on the Governor-in-Council, who in criminal cases acts as a Court of Reference and Appeal, and in civil matters as a Court of Appeal, from decisions in the Native States.

But greatly as the Bombay Native States differ in respect to their size, to the condition of their people, and to the degree of political control exercised by the British Government, they present still more striking diversities in regard to the characters of their ruling chiefs. We are apt to speak and to think of the Native Chiefs of India as if they were a homogeneous class, differentiated indeed by religion into Muhammadans and Hindus, but governing on the same old-world patterns, and regulated as to their motives and conduct by a common love of *laissez faire*. In the following pages we shall see how wide apart is this popular conception from the actual facts. The comparative isolation of the Indian Princes tends to develop in each of them a strong individuality, whether for good or for evil. Indeed, so important is the personality of the Chief of a Native State, that any attempt at a comprehensive survey of the separate types which they exhibit would involve an elaboration of treatment quite beyond the scope of the present book. Instead, therefore, of losing the thread of this chapter in multitudinous details, I propose first to exhibit the general principles which guided Lord Reay in his dealings with the Native Chiefs; then to give a sketch of certain of them with whose characters he became personally intimate; concluding with a summary of the principal transactions in the various groups of States during the five years of his government of Bombay.

Lord Reay believed that in the political control of the Native Chiefs, there should be a minimum of interference, a maximum of encouragement to those who had at heart the good administration of their States, and in confirmed cases of misrule such a form of intervention as should protect the interests of their people without trenching on the hereditary right of succession vested in the family of the Chief. He did not expect the Chiefs to introduce all our methods of administration. On the contrary he held that while we are trying to develop local self-government in our own municipalities and Districts, even at a possible sacrifice of efficiency for the moment, it would be unreasonable to deny a free hand in local self-government to the Native Chiefs on their own lines, even if those lines are not exactly those which we should prefer.

Thus the regular payment of a fixed Land-Revenue in cash is a fundamental principle in the British Districts. But if a Native Chief thought it better to preserve the more elastic method of paying in kind, or of paying a large sum in favourable seasons and a smaller sum in bad ones, Lord Reay did not deem it needful to press for uniformity. Again, if Native Chiefs applied for officials trained in our service, the Bombay Government made a point of complying, but equally made a point of not urging the Chiefs to make such applications. On the other hand it steadily kept before them the advantages of improved roads, and in certain States of railways, of irrigation, of education, and of the abolition of those grievous internal tariffs or customs duties which strangle trade in a conglomeration of petty separate Chiefdoms such as Káthiáwár and other of the Bombay groups. The surrender of revenue derived from this latter source was in some instances considerable during the five years under review, and reflected the highest credit on the Chiefs.

The question of jurisdiction over railways in the Native States demanded the serious attention of the Bombay Political Department. It is natural that the Chiefs should wish to keep that jurisdiction in their own hands, when the railways are constructed out of their own revenues. In States where there are fair magistrates and an efficient police, and which are willing to introduce our Railway Act, Lord Reay thought that not much harm would probably arise from such independent jurisdictions, as long as the line of railway did not form part of a trunk system. On the whole, however, he held that, in a gigantic railway system like that of the Indian Empire, the safety of the travelling public and of goods in transit requires a continuous police and magisterial supervision which can only be secured by a central control, and an unbroken chain of responsibility. The post and the telegraph are Imperial departments for this reason, and the railway system will in time probably become so, alike in the British Provinces and the Native States.

During the period under review, the Bombay Government acted on the principle that, where the public interest did not clearly demand interference, no interference should be exercised. In States like Bhaunagar and Morvi, in which an intelligent initiative introduced important railways, the Bombay Political Department held it impolitic to disquiet the Rulers by any curtailment of their railway jurisdiction, unless the public safety absolutely and imperatively compelled it. Lord Reay believed that the spread of railways through Native Territories is of much greater importance than the immediate exercise of British jurisdiction along the lines; and that our efforts should rather be directed to persuade the Chiefs to adopt our Railway Act, and thus secure to travellers and goods the safeguards which it provides.

Non-interference was thus the key-note of Lord Reay's policy towards the Native States, but where the Governor felt that intervention was necessary to protect a people from callous and obdurate misrule, he did not hesitate. In the State of ——, for example, extreme measures were found needful. The Chief represented a peculiar type. A religious devotee and a miser, with little concern for his people, obstinate as Pharaoh but a man of pleasant manners and a good deal of humour, he filled his garners with hoards of grain which he allowed to rot rather than serve it out to his subjects during famine. After many fruitless remonstrances, Lord Reay's government found it needful to depose this Chief, and to bring his State for a time under a British officer. An English Administrator was accordingly appointed, with instructions to put an end to the abuses of which the people had justly complained, but to refrain from any sudden or violent reforms which might shock native prejudices.

This temporary measure completely altered the condition of the State. The treasure which the Chief had accumulated at the cost of the misery of his people, was brought forth from his palace and employed in giving wages to a multitude of labourers, employed on railway and other useful public works. The people soon forgot their old discontent, and it was found possible to introduce cautious yet beneficial reforms not only in the judicial and revenue administration, but also with reference to education, forests, public works, and the coinage and miscellaneous cesses current in the State.

Perhaps in no position has a civilian a better opportunity for the exercise of his powers, than in a Native State which has been suffering from misrule. Assisted by good native officials, and not hampered by too minute instructions from his own Government, he can bring order out of chaos in an incredibly short time. Indeed, the moment that British rule is established in such a State, the people take for granted that extortion will cease and justice will prevail. But the reforms, although easily introduced, do not always take deep root under such a system of temporary administration. Lord Reay realised this, but he felt it his duty to make it clear that our administration could only be of a temporary character; that the rights of the ruling house were only in abeyance; and that its restoration was only a question of time.

In the State of ——, the Bombay Government

had to deal with a Chief of a more hopeless class. The personal habits of this petty potentate at length rendered him unfit to discharge the duties of his position, and a British officer was appointed to reform the abuses into which he had allowed his Administration to sink. The other Native Chiefs felt no alarm, being well aware of the temporary character of the remedy applied, and of the causes which rendered that remedy imperative. In a very short time the State recovered under its British superintendent, and the hereditary rights of the ruling family were clearly maintained throughout.

In regard to the vital question of Adoption, the Bombay Political Department while under Lord Reay's charge maintained its liberal policy. The more important Chiefs hold *sanads* or patents conveying the right to adopt a son not only to succeed to their private property, but also to their public *status* as Ruler of the people. The principle was laid down in the Queen's Proclamation on the transfer of India from the Company to the Crown in 1858, and received immediate effect by a multitude of *sanads* granted shortly afterwards. Acting on this principle, Lord Reay favoured a policy of further extending the grant of *sanads* to Chiefs not previously in possession of them. In his speech on the Jubilee of the Queen-Empress, Lord Reay could truly state: '"We shall respect the rights, dignity, and honour of Native Princes as our own" are the words of Her Majesty's Proclamation. This pledge also has been carefully redeemed.'

In connection with the right of adoption, Lord Reay felt very deeply the responsibility which devolved on him personally, when the minor sons, whether natural or adoptive of Native Chiefs were left to the care of the British Government by the death of their father. His provision for the education of the young Rájá of Kolhápur will serve to illustrate this side of his political work.

The Rájás of Kolhápur, a Maráthá Principality of the first class with a population of nearly a million, have long held a conspicuous position among the Native States of Bombay. The great Maráthá houses of the Gáekwár, Sindhia, and Holkar, esteem an alliance with the Kolhápur dynasty as an honour. The tragic fate of the last two Rulers of Kolhápur appealed in a special manner to the sympathies of the British Government on behalf of the present minor. In 1866, the Rájá of Kolhápur died without a natural heir. His adopted successor, a young Prince of great promise, died at Florence, while returning to India from a European tour; in his turn leaving no natural heir. His adopted successor became insane, and dying in 1883 without issue, was again succeeded by adoption, by the present minor, who was the son of the Regent of the State.

Lord Reay endeavoured to discharge his duty to this representative of an ancient and powerful, although recently unfortunate family, by a close personal care over his education. The young Rájá was at first sent to the College for Native Princes at Rájkot in Káthiáwár, accompanied by his younger brother the

Chief of Kágal, a youthful uncle, and another boy. After a time Lord Reay thought it right to bring the young Chief nearer to his own dominions, and devised a special scheme for his education. He selected as his place of residence the healthy town of Dhárwár, a British Station of the first class in the southern Maráthá country, where the young Chief would be surrounded by manly English influences. At the same time he took care not to segregate him from his own countrymen, and to this end formed a group of five other youths of princely or noble birth, to be educated along with him. The group of six consisted of the young Rájá of Kolhápur, his brother the Chief of Kágal, his juvenile uncle, and another young Maráthá nobleman, together with the son of His Highness the Mahárájá of Bhaunagar and a young companion from Káthiáwár. An able junior civilian, Mr. Fraser, was appointed tutór to the six youths, aided by picked instructors. Lord Reay kept up a friendly personal intercourse with the lads, and was rewarded by their confidence and esteem. His ward, the young Rájá of Kolhápur, came frequently to visit him, and still continues to write to him in England.

The main object of our education of young chiefs, Lord Reay maintained, should be to give them a high sense of honour, of truthfulness, and of responsibility towards their people. The branches of knowledge which he considered most important for them, are English and Indian history and literature, Political Economy, and the principles of Jurisprudence. He urged the employment of men of talent for the instruction of Native Princes, men who had the gift of interesting their pupils, and rousing their faculties, so that the Chiefs should not abandon their books when raised to the State-cushion. He held that as much of their education as they can receive in India, should be given to them there; and that they should as a rule only be permitted to go to England after they have obtained a complete command of English. He insisted that we ought never to lose sight of the fact that the Chiefs are to spend their lives among their own people, and that we cannot with impunity sever in early life the ties which bind a Chief to his native country. The benefits of an English education or of a visit to England would be too dearly bought, if the Chief were to reach manhood devoid of sympathy for his people or bereft of their affection and confidence.

Several of the Chiefs are now on their own initiative sending their boys to obtain a complete liberal education in England. Lord Reay did not deem it his duty to throw impediments in their way, but still less did he think it his duty to urge such an experiment upon them. He believed that the true policy of educating the Native Chiefs was to adhere firmly, although temperately, to the lines laid down by Lord Mayo, and to encourage Colleges for Chiefs, like those at Rájkot and Ajmere which will ever be identified with Lord Mayo's name. But he realised the very great difficulties with which such Indian Etons have to contend. The boys are of all ages, with every conceivable deficiency in their previous education, so that it becomes almost impossible to work a well-regulated class-system. The usual incentives to steady work are absent in the case of the eldest sons; and for the younger sons of the Indian Princes there is unhappily, at present, no career which they can make for themselves by proficiency in any branch of knowledge.

This latter consideration weighed heavily both with the Governor and with His Royal Highness the Duke of Connaught during their residence in India, and a partial remedy suggested itself to both their minds. They believed that, not only would it be an excellent opening for the younger sons of Chiefs, but also an additional source of stability to our rule, if a Military education and commissions in the Army could be granted to the élite of the young Indian aristocracy.

The Supreme Government did not however find it possible to give immediate effect to this proposal. For the present organisation of our Native Army is based upon regimental promotion from the ranks, on the ground of tried courage and proved fitness. This system has great merits. It not only secures a steady upward flow through the non-commissioned to the commissioned grades in the Native Regiments of a most valuable class of officers, but it also maintains the *status* of military service in the ranks as an honourable profession alike for gentle and simple in Native society. The problem of the future is how to combine the two systems, so as to allow of direct commissions to specially qualified sons of Chiefs, without rendering the ranks less attractive to the upper rural classes and the sons of small landholders. The Governor and

His Royal Highness the Duke of Connaught favoured the establishment of an Indian Sandhurst, as a step in this direction; with due provision also for promotion by merit from the ranks.

The possibility of employing the younger sons of Chiefs in our civil or political administration also formed a subject of anxious thought with Lord Reay. At present a Native Chief and his younger brothers are practically debarred from taking any part in the British administration. Lord Reay had hopes that the College for Chiefs at Rájkot might receive such a development as would render it an avenue to civil employment under our Government. He did not advocate its affiliation to the Bombay University, because a University education does not proceed upon the lines best suited to the requirements of the native aristocracy. But he thought that a certificate of good conduct, merit and capacity by the Rájkot College might be recognised as a ground for granting to the younger sons of Chiefs an admission to certain offices under the Bombay Government. In order that such certificates should carry real weight, however, he perceived that it would be necessary to raise the standards of the College, and to require a more satisfactory previous education than that which the younger sons of Chiefs usually bring to it.

It would be unwise to hide the difficulties underlying these proposals, and the further difficulties arising from the fact that the young gentlemen are not in the strict sense of the word British subjects. But the importance of the results to be obtained seemed to the

Governor to justify some elasticity in the methods employed. The Bombay Presidency has so large a number of States and especially of petty States under its Political Supervision, that if their co-operation could be secured by the conviction that the Rájkot College afforded a practical outlet for their sons, the College might be equipped on a perfect footing by the aid of contributions from the States themselves.

The intimate personal relations which the Governor had with many of the Native Chiefs, convinced him of the excellent material which, with vigilant care and more elastic methods, may in the future be developed out of their order. The most important of the Bombay States, Baroda, is, as I have mentioned, in direct relationship with the Supreme Government. But the Governor of Bombay has necessarily much intercourse with His Highness the Gáekwár of Baroda as the Premier Hindu Prince of India. His Highness talked freely and earnestly with Lord Reay as to his views and hopes in life. It was the great ambition of His Highness that Baroda should become a pattern Native State, and that the standards of rural administration should be assimilated as nearly as possible to a British District. His careful education by Mr. Elliot and His Highness's residence in England, have taught him a contempt for a merely superficial appearance of good government, or for administrative shams of any sort. His aim is not to have a show capital with fine palaces, hospitals, colleges, a public library, and public gardens (although his large revenues and careful finance permit him also to enjoy these luxuries), but to have his districts well administered and to spread education among his people.

To assist him in his task the Gáekwár recruits from the best of the Native officials in the Bombay Presidency. Every year the number of rural schools in his territories is increased. The Gáekwár won Lord Reay's sincere admiration by the great pains he took to master both sides of each question as it arose. His Highness is a discreet and cautious ruler who, while appreciating the high results attained by British administrative methods, thoroughly realises the necessity of carrying his subjects with him, and of suiting the pace of progress so as not to break away from what is good in Native tradition, or to sacrifice the confidence and affection of his people.

The Gáekwár has strong sympathies with his own race the Maráthás, and is in an especial manner bent on promoting their interests and raising their status. He never forgets that, although the Premier Hindu Prince of India, he is first of all and above all the foremost man of the ancient Maráthá race. He clearly sees that the progress of that race must now be made on industrial lines. He devotes both time and money to the spread of education in all parts of his territories, to the construction of railways, the introduction of a plentiful supply of good water to his capital, and to numerous public works. As an illustration of the pains which His Highness takes to master administrative details may be mentioned a lengthy conversation which he had with the Governor on the vexed question of the subsoil water assessment—a question which, as we shall see, has exercised the ingenuity of the ablest of our own administrators in Gujarát.

The value of the Gáekwár's moral influence, alike upon his Court and upon the upper classes of his subjects, can hardly be exaggerated. His home life is pure. He does not spend money on costly trifles, and his palaces are furnished like English country-houses. Hospitable to strangers, and fond of a quiet talk with an English visitor, he appreciates chief of all straightforwardness and candour among those by whom he is surrounded. His subjects are proud of him, and the more His Highness resides among his people, the more they grow to understand and to like him. Being a strong ruler, he is naturally sensitive to interference with his own affairs, and in the matter of railway jurisdiction he objects to it stiffly. As the Baroda territory overlaps and intercepts the British districts of Gujarát in every direction, the public works carried out by the Gáekwár are of great benefit to our own subjects, and involve close personal relations between the British and Baroda administrators—relations which the Governor, as the Member of Council in charge of the Bombay Political Department, maintained on an amicable footing of reciprocal confidence.

Perhaps the most important group of Native States under the Political Department of the Bombay Government are the 187 Chiefdoms of Káthiáwár. Of these, 13 pay no tribute, 105 pay tribute to the British Government, 79 to the Gáekwár of Baroda; while 134 also pay a tribute to the Nawáb of Junágarh. They exhibit a perplexing congeries of jurisdictions, with a mixed tributary responsibility to the British Government and to the two Native Princes just named, the result of a long history of disquiet and warfare brought to a close by numerous treaties.

The delicate and complicated control required for the management of so large a group of Chiefs, some of them ancient and powerful, others of them poor, and all of them proud, must ever be a subject of personal and peculiar interest to a Governor of Bombay. As many of them are connected by marriage with the Princes of Rájputána, Lord Reay thought it his duty to cultivate cordial relations with the great Rájput houses. He visited Udaipur, Jodhpur, and Jaipur, and brought away with him very pleasant remembrances of their hospitality, and a high impression of the loyalty of these Chiefs to our rule. The Mahárána of Udaipur, the most ancient of the Rájput princely families, struck Lord Reay by the simplicity and strength of his character. His private life is regulated by the same pure standards as those of the Gáekwár, although he did not have the same educational advantages as those which the Gáekwár has enjoyed. The Mahárájá of Jodhpur seemed to Lord Reay a real native king—living in affectionate friendship with his family and dependents, supporting his distinguished brother Sir Pratab Singh in his plans for improving the condition of his army and his subjects, wisely generous in his expenditure on railways and irrigation, and sparing no effort to rear up the heir to the State in liberal and manly instincts, so that he too may be a true Rájput ruler. At Jaipur Lord Reay was especially impressed by the vitality of Hindu art under an enlightened Native Prince aided by able European advisers.

Even careful writers are apt to speak and think of the Káthiáwár group of States as an entity. As a matter of fact their 187 Chiefs present as widely different types as are to be found among the nobles of Europe, from the semi-Tartar Russian prince to the haughty and languid Spanish grandee. If we are to understand the problems involved in our political control over Káthiáwár, we must first realise the striking diversity in the character and the aims of its Rulers. Let me endeavour, therefore, to place a few of their strongly marked personalities before the eyes of the reader.

In Bhaunagar for example, the Chief, although he has never visited England, forms his system of administration upon British models. Educated at the College for Chiefs at Rájkot under careful European supervision, he determined after consulting Lord Reay to re-cast the framework of his government upon the basis of a Council, each member of which should have a special Department. Among these, his most trusted adviser is the English head of his Public Works Department. His Judicial Councillor is an experienced Parsi, formerly a Presidency Magistrate in Bombay. His Revenue Councillor is a Bráhman. By means of this Council, the Mahárájá of Bhaunagar has quietly but effectively freed the State from the monopoly of offices formerly exercised by the too-powerful caste of Nágar Bráhmans. He spends the revenue of his State wisely and liberally on State purposes, promotes railways, and is thoroughly loyal to the British power. The Grand Cross of the Star of India was conferred on His Highness, in recognition of his merits as the Ruler of a pattern State.

In the Káthiáwár principality of Gondal[1], on the other hand, the Chief has been much in England, and is again, studying medicine in the University of Edinburgh. Extremely reserved, but hospitable in a princely manner to visitors, well aware of his own treaty rights, and determined to allow no infringement either on his political status or his personal dignity, his single grievance against the ruling power was the permission accorded during his minority to his Muhammadan subjects at Dhoráji to slaughter kine for food. He is an example of the new type of Chief developed by frequent visits to England. Such a Chief sees for himself how Englishmen treat each other, and he returns to India, disposed neither to fear nor to flatter the English political officers with whom he has to deal. He accordingly bears himself with a more manly personal attitude towards the Government than the older school of Chiefs; but at the same time with a more complete conception of the strength of the Paramount Power, and of the unity of interest which has grown up between that Power and the Native Princes. His Highness is perhaps the only Rájput Chief in India whose princess accompanies him to England, and drives out with her husband and visits English ladies in Bombay.

[1] Area, 1024 square miles. Population, 159,741 persons in 1891. Revenue, Rs. 1,200,000. Tribute, Rs. 110,721.

The Thákur of Gondal has a Parsi as his Prime Minister, and his State is admirably managed. The State took an active part in the construction of the Gondal-Bhaunagar Railway, and during Lord Reay's tenure of office the Chief carried out his share of the important line which connects the town of Dhoráji with the harbour of Porbandar. Having studied medicine in the University of Edinburgh, he maintains six hospitals which, in the year 1890–91, gave relief to 49,914 patients, and performed 1,466 operations. His system of State medical relief includes a travelling hospital, and it has succeeded to a remarkable degree in winning the confidence of his female subjects; 28,784, or over 57 per cent of the whole patients, being women and children. A vaccination department looks after the rising generation, while an asylum and orphanage provide for 792 of the aged and infirm, and for those who are left without natural protectors to the care of the State.

Seventy-five schools, aided and inspected by the State, give instruction to 4,619 pupils, with all the latest improvements for female education, and night schools for the poorer cultivating classes whose sons cannot be spared from the fields during the day. The administration of justice is conducted by seven courts, the Chief presiding in person in the Supreme Court of Appeal, and his place being taken by the Prime Minister during the absence of His Highness in England. Examinations are held of the police officers in the criminal law and rules of evidence current in the Gondal territory, and a conference with the Police

Superintendents of the neighbouring States was held to concert measures for the suppression of crime on their frontiers. An Administration Report of his State is regularly published, drawn up on the system of chapters prescribed for the similar reports in the British Provinces, and dealing quite frankly with the successes and failures of the administrative year. The result of good government in a Native State is illustrated in a very practical form by the census of Gondal taken during the year 1891. While the increase of population from 1881 to 1891 throughout the British Provinces, after adjustments for changes of area, is returned at 11 per cent,[1] the people in the State of Gondal increased by nearly 18 per cent. The progress of municipal life, a new element of hopefulness in India, has been still more rapid. Gondal has five municipal towns, each with a local government of its own. The average increase of population in these five municipalities was 19½ per cent during the decade from 1881 to 1891; and in two important towns it reached the extraordinary rates of 23¼ and 25 per cent.

The Chief of Morvi is a ruler of a different type. He has all the traditional features of the noble Rájput, is fond of every manly exercise, and a first-rate rider. Following the most vigorous examples of the old Native School, he allows no body of ministers to grow up between his own personality and the people, but governs for himself with a keen eye to the revenue,

[1] I have to take this rate from the preliminary Census tables furnished to the Secretary of State—the only returns which have yet reached England, September, 1891.

and a disdain of anything like philanthropic ostentation, although he has model schools to show when needful. In his dealings with strangers he displays the old-world courtesy of the Rájput prince, and, like other princes of that type, he has a good many troubles with his numerous brotherhood and blood relations. This type he has firmly adhered to notwithstanding a residence in England and in our North American Dominion. In his intercourse with British officers he demeans himself as a comrade and fellow-sportsman—as one who thoroughly understands and likes their ways, and who has driven his dog-cart down Piccadilly and purchased a tract of land in Canada. He thoroughly appreciates the necessity of a liberal expenditure on railways, if a Native State is to hold its own in these days, and has not only brought his own territories into the railway system, but has invested money in lines outside them. One of his most intimate friends is the English gentleman at the head of his Public Works Department. He has sent his son to be educated in England.

The Chief of Jasdán was a ruler of a still older school. A strict upholder of ancient etiquette, and a recognised referee on Káthiáwár local customs, and as to what could and could not be done by the numerous classes of Chiefs, he enjoyed in a marked manner the respect alike of his brother-rulers and of the Paramount Power. His manners were perfect, extremely courteous, dignified and full of self-respect. A fine rider, and a good chess-player, very sagacious in the management of a State upon conservative lines, he frankly declared himself a man of the old school. Nevertheless, he recognised the new condition of things which was growing up around him, and sent his son to Cambridge to fit him for the altered future of the Indian feudatory order.

The Thákur of Lakhtar clung even more closely to ancient traditions. He urged the necessity of a more religious (or orthodox Hindu) teaching at the College for young Chiefs at Rájkot, and was wont to vigorously press this view, together with a grievance which he had about the Salt Revenue, in his personal conversations with Lord Reay. The Governor deemed it a part of his duty to encourage the Native Chiefs to lay open their minds to him, and to make them feel that his intercourse with them was not merely an exchange of courtesies, but an interchange of views on the subjects which they had at heart. In thus trying to give reality to his personal relations with the Native Chiefs, Lord Reay frankly faced the fact that he could not always expect to obtain their support for his own measures.

Thus the Ráo of Cutch [1], a thoroughly well-educated man and always most courteous and friendly in his intercourse with the Governor, proved little accessible to arguments for the abolition of Customs duties, and on other subjects in regard to which His Highness thought that his State held a peculiar position. His Highness has the advantage of having a long coast-line for his main frontier, and he believed it to be his best

[1] Area of Cutch, 6,500 square miles. Population (1881), 512,084. Revenue, Rs. 1,603,050.

policy to maintain his isolated position as a maritime Chief rather than to open up his country by railways. In spite of these differences the Ráo of Cutch came frequently to see the Governor, and went to England for the Jubilee of Her Majesty the Queen-Empress. His Highness's domestic life is exemplary. He is a keen sportsman, very fond of his brother, but not seeking intimate relations with any beyond his own family circle.

Lord Reay endeavoured to become really acquainted with the personal characters of the Chiefs, and with the views, traditions and ideals which they might be chary of expressing on paper, but which regulated their action both in public and private affairs. It would be wrong, however, to let it be supposed that all the Chiefs of the Káthiáwár belonged to the pleasing types which I have indicated. Thus the Thákur of —— disappointed every effort which the Governor could make for his welfare. Addicted to drink, he lacked courtesy and dignity in his private intercourse, and wasted a keen intelligence through infirmity of moral character. He died despised by his subjects, and his death was a relief rather than a regret to those responsible for the political supervision of his State. I ought to add that this was by no means the only case of the kind with which Lord Reay had, to his sorrow, to deal.

Having thus summarised the widely different types presented by the Káthiáwár group of Chiefs, it may be well to take a single State, and to exhibit at length the system which the Bombay Government has pursued in relation to it during the present generation. As a single example is all that space allows me to select by way of illustration, I shall take the first-class Káthiáwár State of Bhaunagar, in regard to which I have some personal knowledge, and I have also to thank its former joint administrator, Mr. Percival, for much valuable information[1]. In regard to the States already mentioned, I have confined my view to the period of Lord Reay's administration. I select Bhaunagar as an illustration of the general principles of policy, steadily and continuously applied by the Bombay Government to the Native States under its care.

On the death of the late Thákur of Bhaunagar, in 1870, there was no member of the family with sufficient ability and authority to be entrusted with the control of the State. The present Thákur (since advanced to the rank of Mahárájá) was then 12 years old. Bhaunagar State enjoyed the reputation of being well governed by certain families of Nágar Bráhmans, who exercised the chief authority, and at the head of whom was Gaurishankar Udeshankar, the Diwán or Prime Minister, a man of great talent.

The Governor of Bombay at that time, Sir Philip Wodehouse, determined to place the authority exercised by the late Thákur, as the chief of a first-class State, in the hands jointly of a member of the Bombay Civil Service, Mr. Percival, and the Bráhman Prime Minister, Gaurishankar. The object was to obtain a

[1] The following account of Bhaunagar is condensed from a manuscript narrative from Mr. Percival's hand.

continuity of Native rule, improved by English influence, without introducing any new system which the young Chief might be unable or unwilling to maintain when he came to power.

The officials of the Bhaunagar State had been brought into unusually close contact with the authorities of the adjoining British district of Ahmadábád, owing partly to the position of the State on the coast near to several British ports, and also because a large portion of the State had been for half a century placed under the British Courts of Law, in consequence of an act of cruelty done by one of the previous Thákurs. Gaurishankar's conduct of the delicate relations with the Bombay Government, which finally resulted in the withdrawal of the British Courts, showed the highest ability and tact. He was also successful in the management of the turbulent Káthi landowners, who had until recent times constantly disturbed the peace of Káthiáwár by open resistance to the Chiefs, or by going into outlawry (báhirwatia) and committing atrocities upon innocent villagers, in order to force the States to comply with their demands. These Káthis are numerous and powerful in Bhaunagar, but Gaurishankar arranged terms with most of them, and kept the rest from serious outbreaks such as from time to time occurred in other parts of the province. The high price of cotton during the American Civil War largely increased the revenue of the State, and a considerable balance had been accumulated in the treasury. In 1870, therefore, the joint administration of Mr. Percival and Gaurishankar commenced under favourable circumstances.

The chief offices in Bhaunagar were held by families of Nágar Bráhmans, all more or less related to each other and to the Prime Minister Gaurishankar. It was by means of this strong organisation that he and his predecessors had been enabled to control the State. The moderation of the ruling Bráhmans, in a position of great temptation, had been praiseworthy, and they were not slow to accept new ideas.

The first matter for consideration by the joint administrators was the education of the young Thákur Takhtsingji, and fortunately it had shortly before been decided, under Lord Mayo's auspices, to build a College for the Káthiáwár Chiefs and their relatives at Rájkot. In January 1871 the College was opened, and Takhtsingji, with three of his dependents, was the first to enter it. The sons of Chiefs, who up to that time had always been suspicious and jealous of each other, now met for the first time under one roof, and, thanks to the admirable system and temper of the Principal, Mr. Macnaghten, learned to grow up together on friendly terms. Takhtsingji was just 13 years of age, and he contributed to the success of the new College by frankly submitting to its rules, by taking with him only a small retinue of servants, and by encouraging other young Chiefs to come. On his return to the College after his first vacation, his brother, aged 11, was to have gone with him, but his mother absolutely refused to part with him, and threatened to dash her head against the wall if he went. The young Thákur went without him, and it was only after considerable delay that the mother's scruples could be overcome.

After three years at the Rájkot College, Captain H. L. Nutt was appointed tutor to the young Thákur in 1874, and the Chief continued his education at home, or in travelling with his tutor.

In accordance with the custom of the family he was early married—in 1874. The joint administrators had only to arrange for the wedding ceremonies; as the young Chief had been betrothed by his father to five girls, one of whom had died, and the marriages of the remaining four were all carried out at the same time in April 1874. A new wing to the palace was built, in which each lady was provided with a separate suite of rooms, something like a modern flat. Each lady received a similar present of jewellery; the store of jewels in the treasury sufficing for most of what was wanted. It is usual to build a large temporary hall for receptions on such occasions, but a permanent iron structure supplied its place. When covered with tinsel and richly furnished, it made a magnificent hall for the ceremonials, and now serves as a market.

The accounts of the State for several years previous to the Thákur's death had been placed under seal, and, an independent examination of them being required, a special Hindu auditor, now the Diwán of Junágarh, was invited to undertake it. A mixed body of State dependents, consisting of horse and foot, household and outdoor servants, relatives, slaves, men, women, and boys, to the number of about 2000, appeared before Mr. Percival to receive a year's pay at the Diwali or New Year of 1870. A great many of these had little or no duty to perform, and their allowances had been given as pensions or as charity. A more regular system was gradually introduced, but it was probably not so economical to the public purse, for a good native master puts up with an old servant as long as possible, rather than dismiss or pension him. The same kindly careless feeling had existed with regard to the animals owned by the State. There were thirty elephants; a great and useless expense, especially since the price of their food had risen. They had grown out of date as roads and the use of carriages increased. Native Chiefs found that a four-in-hand of horses could be kept for about the same cost as one elephant, and on public occasions smart four-in-hand carriages were beginning to be the fashion.

There were 800 buffaloes, of a very fine breed, which took prizes at all the shows; besides 2000 other animals, camels, horses, cows, bullocks and goats, which had never been weeded out as they became old and useless. There was a strong feeling against selling the superfluous buffaloes and cows, and at first even against the sale of horses. No objection, however, was made to giving away the old animals, and a crowd of pious mendicants were set upon horseback and rode away whither they would. Twenty elephants and 150 camels were sold at once, and in the course of two years the other domestic animals were reduced to about half the original number.

The State requires a large supply of horses, and has facilities for breeding them. An establishment for this purpose was started with excellent results in improving the breed. The pure Káthiáwár strain is hardy and enduring, but too small for purposes of draught.

The most pressing want in 1870 was a supply of water for the town of Bhaunagar, which had become a harbour with a considerable import and export trade. Many hundreds of bullock-carts, laden with unpressed cotton, daily entered the town at the beginning of the hot season, when there was scarcely enough water for the inhabitants to drink. The animals could not stay in the town a single day, and besides the inconvenience and harm to the townspeople from a limited supply of bad water, the business of the port was carried on with increasing difficulty. A young English engineer, Mr. Monckton, had been employed by the State in the time of the late Thákur to carry out public works, and his hands were now full. The services of Mr. East, an engineer who had been on the Madras Irrigation Company's works, were engaged, and finally he took a contract to carry out a scheme of water supply to the town. The 'Gaurishankar Lake,' a body of water about two miles long, was constructed, and its waters were admitted to the town on the 22nd August, 1872. The present development of the town, with its gardens and largely increased population, could not have been possible without this assured supply of good water.

The appointment of Mr. Proctor Sims by the Bombay Government in 1875 to superintend the public works of the State, marked a new departure. He had control of an expenditure of from seven to eight lacs of rupees a year. Under his administration the High School and

Courts of Justice at Bhaunagar have been built from designs by Major Mant, lighthouses have been erected, and dispensaries, district courts, and other necessary buildings have been completed. Even more important work has been done in the construction of a good system of roads, of which 160 miles bridged and 50 miles unbridged have been brought into use. An instance of the interference which may be caused by the opposition of an unprogressive neighbouring Chief to the efforts of an enlightened administration may be here noted. The —— State prevented the erection of an important bridge over the Bhaunagar Creek, notwithstanding the serious inconvenience caused to the steam ferry by the strength of the tide. Not satisfied with roads, the joint administrators strongly advocated the construction of railways, but it was not until 1877–78 that Bhaunagar, Gondal, and other States commenced the survey for the present line at their own cost, and without insisting on a guarantee from the Supreme Government.

The armed police force which maintains order in the Bhaunagar State, consists of 200 men, and the only other disciplined body is the Thákur's escort of 50 cavalry commanded by the son of an English chaplain, who has been converted to Islám. The jail is very well managed, although on January 15, 1872, it was the scene of a serious outbreak, in which three of the armed police and fourteen prisoners were killed.

Notwithstanding the importance of its customs-duties levied on the sea-borne commerce, three-fourths of the revenue of the State of Bhaunagar is derived from the land, and the introduction of the British-Indian system of settlement has had a marked effect upon the prosperity of the country. When the joint administrators began their work in 1870, the land-revenue was levied in kind or as a share of the gross produce. This method had the usual good and bad results. It benefited the landlord in good years and relieved the tenant in times of scarcity; but it discouraged the energy and skill of the cultivator and checked the growth of capital in his hands. All produce had to be carried to the village grain-yard, where it was measured and divided between the State and the cultivator; much was begged or pilfered in transit, much was eaten by peacocks and other birds, and much was spoilt by exposure. So great was the damage caused to cotton, the staple crop, that Gaurishankar attempted to have it measured while still standing; an attempt which had to be abandoned owing to the complaints of cultivators, who were unable to pick their cotton when it was ready, because the valuer had not come in time or the 'permit' had not been given. When Mr. Percival joined Gaurishankar in the administration of the State, this wasteful system was replaced by cash payments. At the end of two years, that is by 1872, cash settlements were made of every holding in the State on the basis of the former nett receipts, and the payments were fixed for four years. The new scheme was received with unexpected enthusiasm, and though it was declared optional and not enforced by law, only 10 or 12 per cent of the cultivators preferred to continue on the old system, and these were chiefly inhabitants of poor villages.

As the necessary sequel of the introduction of the land-system in use in British territory, a careful survey of the State of Bhaunagar was undertaken. In October, 1872, Mr. T. R. Fernandez, of the Gujarát Survey, was placed at the disposal of the joint administrators by the Bombay Government, and in about seven years the country was carefully measured and mapped, and boundary marks were erected. In 1876 the first rough settlement, which had given such satisfaction, was revised, and continued for another four years. In 1878, after the Thákur had himself assumed the administration, the results were thus recorded in the annual report: 'This settlement has worked extremely well. Its advantages to the State are very great, and that the bulk of the cultivators prefer it to the old system is shown by the fact of their almost universal acceptance of it. Its financial result has been to keep the revenue of the State at much the same total as before its introduction, though large quantities of waste land have been brought into cultivation.'

The successful introduction of the land-settlement into Bhaunagar is an instance of the influence for good exerted by the Bombay Government upon the Native States politically connected with it. Not only did it render the land-revenue less onerous to the cultivators, without diminishing the income of the State, but it facilitated economic reforms in other departments. The joint administrators reduced the special tax on sugar-cane fields; they suspended the tax on fruit-trees until the trees were bearing well, with the result that in 1876 no fewer than 1660 mango and 430 cocoa-nut trees were planted by ráyats on waste land; they replaced the tax on the sale of houses by a moderate stamp duty on registered sales; and they kept the customs-duties so low that traders were encouraged to use the port, and soon raised it to an unprecedented condition of commercial prosperity. Where the country was bare of trees from its open and exposed position, the joint administrators started extensive protected plantations, one of which at Mhowa contained nearly 100,000 cocoa-nut trees. They also opened dispensaries in all the chief towns and founded numerous schools.

Bhaunagar was the first State in Káthiáwár to welcome inspection by the Bombay Department of Education, and to maintain girls' schools, the chief officials and the Thákur himself setting an example by sending their daughters to the school in the capital. Care was taken to secure the impartial administration of justice in both civil and criminal cases. A judge was appointed in each district, with a Court of Appeal of three judges at Bhaunagar, from which lay a final appeal to the Thákur. The State has a short code of law of its own; but practically the Indian Civil and Criminal Codes are in force, and supersede the old local regulations. The chief difficulty in a small Native State is to secure the independence of the judges. The revenue officer in each district is an autocrat, and expects to be consulted in every case of any importance. No change of system can alter this, but higher salaries, improved courts, and the selection of suitable men have tended to strengthen the judges and give the people more confidence in them.

The young Thákur, when he took the reins of government into his own hands, found his State in good order. He has received a greater reward than even his Grand Cross of the Star of India, or the friendship of successive Governors of Bombay, in the love of his people. 'It was interesting to observe,' writes Mr. Percival to me, 'the devoted loyalty of the people to the young Thákur. The old minister who had controlled the state for many years, passed almost unnoticed, whilst crowds followed the boy about, wherever he went. When a native State is absorbed in British territory, we destroy a source of happiness to the common people, for which we can provide no equivalent.' The Mahárájá of Bhaunagar, now a man in middle life, continued to successfully govern his State during the five years under review. By establishing a Council of heads of departments responsible to His Highness only, he started a valuable administrative and financial check on abuses and extravagance.

I have now given several examples of Hindu Native Rulers. But before concluding my account of the Native States under the Bombay Government, I must also refer to two which are governed by Muhammadan dynasties, Khairpur and Junágarh.

Khairpur is the one Native State situated within the limits of Sind. It is governed by the descendant of the only Talpur Mir whose independence was spared at the time of the conquest of Sind in 1843, and comprises an area of 6109 square miles, with a population of 129,153 according to the census of 1881. The Amir of Khairpur, Mir Ali Murad Khán, was in 1889–90 an old man of 77, but he still administered his State with the help of his sons. His administration is of the ancient oriental type. Justice is done by the Amir in person in patriarchal fashion, assisted by his sons, and is swift, summary, and cheap. The revenue is collected in the same primitive style. There has never been a survey or a land-settlement. The land-revenue is paid in kind, and not content with import and export duties at his frontier, the Amir collects them at the boundaries of each táluká or subdivision. The chief industries of the State also, metal work, loom work, lacquer wood work, and múnj grass work are managed on behalf of members of the Amir's family.

The Amir of Khairpur maintains a considerable army and military police. The men are armed with native-made guns and swords, for which purpose the Amir supports some clever families of cutlers and gunsmiths. A considerable expenditure is also devoted to the Amir's medical establishment of five hakims or native doctors, attached to his own person. These five physicians follow his camp everywhere; while another is maintained at Khairpur.

The purely oriental and patriarchal administration of Khairpur contrasts with the civilised methods of the Káthiáwár chiefs. It is interesting as one of the last survivals of the past, and is not likely to be disturbed during the lifetime of the present autocratic Amir.

He refuses to move an inch from the paths of his ancestors. But he manages to keep on good terms with the Bombay Government, and made a loyal concession to the Government of India by suppressing the manufacture of salt in his dominions. In spite of his great age the Amir is still a keen sportsman, and strictly preserves the game in his jungles. This manly old chief suffered two severe domestic afflictions during the period under review, by the death of a son in 1887 and of another in 1888. He more than once visited Lord Reay, when the Governor was on tour in Sind, and was present at the opening of the Lansdowne Bridge at Sukkur on March 27, 1889; on which occasion his salute was increased by two guns.

Another Muhammadan State which merits special notice is Junágarh. This sea-board principality has an area of 3283 square miles, with a population of about 400,000 souls, and ranks as a first-class State under the Political Agency of Káthiáwár. It presents the twofold set of problems arising from a considerable maritime trade and from a wild hilly interior, for ages the haunt of banditti, and now one of the few recesses of India in which the lion still lingers. Its chief town, Junágarh, situated under the Girnár and Dátár hills, is among the most picturesque cities in the world, and has a history dating from the ancient Buddhist period—a period to which its stronghold of Upárkot still bears witness by its rock-hewn monastic caves. The densely wooded tract of the Gír, in some places hilly, at others sinking into dark malarious hollows matted with jungle and flooded during the rainy season, formed the scene of the lion-hunt given to H.R.H. the late Duke of Clarence and Avondale by the Nawáb of Junágarh.

At the commencement of the five years under review, 1885–1890, Junágarh was much disturbed by robber-gangs, who took advantage of the breaking out of agrarian disputes to renew their old life of plunder. The peasantry, discontented with the land arrangements, and doubtful of effective protection, in some localities sided with the dacoits, and preferred to come to terms with them rather than to trust to the State police. This condition of things, and certain maritime differences arising between the Junágarh and the Portuguese authorities, attracted the serious attention of the Bombay Government, and Lord Reay twice visited the State in person during his tenure of office. On his first visit the road had to be strongly guarded: the watchmen being at places perched upon trees so as to command a view of the intervening woods.

The internal disturbances were put an end to by the deputation of a carefully selected British officer, Major Humfrey, who reorganised the State police in such a way as to render gang-robbery at once a perilous and an unprofitable trade. I shall refer more fully to the change which he effected at a later page. The Muhammadan Wazír of the State and the Hindu Diwán cordially worked together, under the encouragement of H. H. the Nawáb, to place the land-settlement on a better footing. The jurisdiction dispute with the neighbouring Portuguese harbour of Diu was adjusted with a moderation and mutual forbearance creditable to both parties. His Highness the Nawáb found his finances improve, and came forward as a large contributor to the railway system of Káthiáwár by constructing a line to the Junágarh port of Veráwal. It was Lord Reay's good fortune both to cut the first sod of this line and to open the railway on its completion. The Nawáb of Junágarh was created a Grand Commander of the Indian Empire in recognition of the progress made by his State, and of the reforms which had been quietly but firmly carried out by the efforts of His Highness and his ministers.

In the foregoing pages I have endeavoured to place before the reader the personality of several typical Chiefs of Bombay Native States, together with some characteristic features of the populations over which they rule. I shall conclude the chapter with a summary of the principal events in the history of the Native States superintended by the Bombay Government, from 1885 to 1890. The summary must be very brief. It does not pretend to completeness; but merely notes a few salient points.

As regards the supervision of the Native States, the most important innovation was the breaking up of the historic political group, known as the 'Sátára Jághírs,' by a notification of the Government of India, suggested for administrative purposes by the Bombay Government. By this alteration, which came into effect from November, 1887, the jághírs of Jath and Daphlápur were placed under the political charge of the Collector of Bijápur, that of Bhor was transferred to the Collector of Poona, and only Phaltán and Aundh remained, as the whole group had formerly been, under the supervision of the Collector of Sátára. In the internal administration of the Native States many changes occurred. The most important of them arose out of the death of princes, or their supersession by the Bombay Government; and the appointment of new ministers or Diwáns. Special attention may be drawn to an interesting experiment tried in the State of Rádhanpur, where in November, 1888, the Nawáb appointed a Hindu and a Muhammadan gentleman joint ministers of State, in order that the Hindu and Muhammadan communities might be equally represented in the government. As is inevitable in a Presidency where so many States march with each other, there were numerous boundary disputes during the five years. The most serious took place in the Mahi Kántha Agency, between the Bhils of Mewár and the Bhils of Pol. It led to armed raids, the loss of several lives, and the destruction of property to the estimated value of Rs. 70,000. Peace was finally restored in 1888 by an authoritative demarcation of the boundary.

Turning next to the maintenance of order within the several States; special police forces, including the Pálanpur Agency Police, the Mahi Kántha Agency Police, and the Káthiáwár Police, were formed. They took the place of His Highness the Gáekwár's *sowars*, or irregular horse, who had not proved efficient in the suppression of dacoity. This crime had never been stamped out in Káthiáwár. In 1886–87 it was reported[1] that 'the country is infested with bands of robbers and dacoits, who commit outrages with almost

[1] *Bombay Administration Report for* 1886–87, p. xli.

perfect immunity, and who, even when arrested, are in the great majority of cases subsequently released, owing to the difficulty of identification. In the course of the year 117 robberies and 78 dacoities took place. In these affrays, property worth nearly one lakh of rupees was destroyed or stolen, 11 persons killed, 61 wounded, and 24 carried away as hostages.' In 1887–88 the area of disorder spread from Junágarh to Gondal, Nawánagar, and other States. Property worth Rs. 1,14,365 was plundered or destroyed, 17 persons were killed, 45 wounded, and 29 carried off as hostages. The Imperial Mail was robbed on one occasion, and stopped on three others. Of the 875 persons concerned in these outrages, only 217 were captured and 63 convicted. In consideration of this serious state of affairs, the Bombay Government lent to the Chiefs of the three States above named the services of Major Humfrey. He carried on a vigorous campaign against the dacoits, and it is satisfactory to read that in 1889–90 there was 'a complete cessation of organised crime[1].' The Káthiáwár Agency Police, which helped to bring about this result, consists of 816 men, of whom 251 were mounted and 60 camel police.

These dacoities were largely attributed to the Mekránis, then in rebellion against the Junágarh State. Their most daring chief, Movar Sadháni, was captured in Jodhpur territory, after an arduous pursuit, by Captain Salmon in 1885. Movar Sadháni was a sort of Káthiáwár Rob Roy, with a good deal

[1] *Bombay Administration Report for* 1889–90, p. iv.

of popular sympathy on his side. Several persons, including one of the minor chiefs in the Pálanpur Agency, had to be prosecuted for harbouring the outlaw. An equally notorious robber-chief was 'Kadarbux,' another Mekráni, captured and executed in 1886. In 1885, an instance of sympathy with robbers was given by the armed opposition of the Bhils of the village of Jhaila in the Mahi Kántha Agency to a party of police, who came to arrest dacoits. In the affray two policemen were killed, and the Bhils of Jhaila and of the neighbouring village of Kaliánpur then decamped across the border and escaped. Two cases of bad jail management also took place in Native States during the period under review. In 1885–86 the prisoners in the Edar jail had to be fired on by the native guard, who killed eight and wounded fourteen of them. In 1886–87 eleven desperadoes broke out of Gondal jail.

The reasons which induced the Bombay Government to lease the abkári or liquor tax and salt duties in Native States will be explained in the chapter dealing with the Excise administration as a whole. The question of transit duties is more complicated. It is difficult to persuade native rulers that such duties are disastrous to commerce, and the Bombay Government endeavours to obtain their abolition by persuasion, not by purchase or by peremptory orders. Good progress was made in this direction during the five years under review, and at the end transit duties had virtually disappeared in the Bombay Native States. In 1885–86 all import duties and export duties were abolished in the State of Kolhápur; and the taxes of that nature known as deshdan in the Káthiáwár States of Nawánagar and Junágarh. In 1886–87 all transit duties were abolished in the Pálanpur and Mahi Kántha Agencies, in all the States in the Rewá Kántha Agency, except Bária, and in all the Sátára Jághír States, except Bhor. In 1887–88 they were abolished in Mudhol, one of the South Maráthá States, and in 1889–90 considerably reduced in Dhrángadrá, one of the States of Káthiáwár. Lord Reay on various occasions recognised the sacrifices made by chiefs in order to meet his free-trade views.

The influence of the Bombay Government appeared in every branch of the administration of the Native States, but especially with regard to education and public works. To enumerate even the principal schools and educational institutions for boys and girls maintained by the chiefs is far beyond the scope of this summary. Mention must, however, be made of two institutions. The School of Art at Bhúj, the capital of Cutch, was carefully fostered by His Highness the Ráo of Cutch, and its beautiful work obtained diplomas both at the International Exhibition at Antwerp in 1885, and at the Colonial and Indian Exhibition in London in 1887. In March, 1887, the Jayasing Ráo Ghatge Technical School at Kolhápur, founded in memory of that able administrator of the Kolhápur State, was opened. The most important public works in Native States during the period under review were the extension of the Káthiáwár Railways and the construction of the Kolhápur State Railway. These I shall speak of in a later chapter, as they formed part of the general extension of the railway system in the Bombay Presidency. But numerous local works, such as roads, bridges, harbour works, and administrative buildings, were also undertaken and completed. Hospitals were built by the rulers of many States. In Cutch, a private citizen, Shekh Datubhai Ibrahim, presented Rs. 35,000 for the establishment of a hospital at Mándvi in 1885. Large donations were given by many native princes to the Bombay Branch of Lady Dufferin's Fund for providing lady-doctors for the women of India. The Ráo of Cutch gave Rs. 10,000 to be expended in charitable relief of his subjects in Bombay City.

An interesting movement is going on in the Mahi Kántha Agency. A Bhagat or Bhil saint, who says he possesses a divine mission, has set up a new religion. The principles he advocates are abstinence from those vices to which the Bhils are particularly prone, namely, crimes of violence, theft, and intemperance. He encourages habits of cleanliness, and has induced the authorities to open two schools for Bhils, promising to fill them with pupils.

This chapter may fitly conclude by recording the enthusiasm and loyalty displayed by the Native Chiefs of Bombay on the Jubilee of the Queen-Empress in 1887. In addition to the public almsgivings at the time, numerous institutions were founded as permanent memorials. Most of these memorials took a useful form. Among many others may be mentioned the Jubilee Waterworks for Bhúj, the capital of Cutch, and for Bhaunagar; the Jubilee Institutes at Pálanpur and Rádhanpur; a Jubilee Clock Tower at Sádra, in the Mahi Kántha Agency; a Jubilee Municipal Hall at Bálásinor; a Jubilee Dispensary at Dharampur; a Jubilee Dharmsála, or rest-house for travellers, at Bánsdá; and a Jubilee Bridge over the Hiranyakeshi River at Ajrá, in Kolhápur. But the number was so great that I almost fear I may be accused of partiality in referring to some without enumerating others, equally important for the loyalty and liberality displayed, and for the usefulness of the purposes to which they are devoted.

CHAPTER VI.

EDUCATION.

IN the last chapter I tried to enable the reader to realise the living personalities with whom the Political Department of the Bombay Government has to deal. I now pass from the feudatory relations of that Government towards the Native Chiefs, and come to its direct administration of the British Districts. The most conspicuous branches of internal administration are the collection of the revenue and its expenditure on the protection of person and property. But in India there is a smaller special department which yields, perhaps, a clearer insight into the people as they are and as they aspire to be. This is the Department of Public Instruction. I have always considered it a fortunate circumstance in my own life, that, at an early period of my service, I was diverted for a time from the regular work of the administration, and placed in educational charge of Orissa and South-Western Bengal as Inspector of Schools. I believe that I was thus enabled to obtain fairer and kindlier views of the people than I should have gained until a much more mature stage of my Indian experience.

I propose to adopt a similar course in the present

attempt to exhibit the government and the people of Bombay. Instead of plunging at once into the chapters exclusively devoted to administration, I should like to show the administrative problems which incidentally arise in the education of the Indian races. I think we shall thus be enabled, at the outset, to get nearer to the facts of native life in the Bombay Provinces than we should, if we were to start with the more conspicuous branches of government, such as the revenues, justice, or police.

The five years under review had, moreover, a special importance from an educational point of view. A Commission had been appointed by the Supreme Government in 1882, to reconstitute the Indian system of Public Instruction on a broader basis. Its report, after consideration by the Governor-General in Council and the Secretary of State, formed the subject of an authoritative declaration of the educational policy of the Government of India in October, 1884. It fell to Lord Reay, on his accession to the Bombay Government in March, 1885, to give practical effect to that policy; and to adjust the new departures indicated and the general principles of expansion laid down by the Education Commission, to the local conditions and needs of Western India. But in order to clearly understand the educational measures then taken by the Bombay Government, it is necessary to start with some idea of the history of education in India since the British became the paramount power, and, in particular, of its progress in the Bombay Presidency.

In India education has always been highly valued,

as is testified by the wealth and the variety of the ancient Sanskrit literature. Megasthenes, the Greek Ambassador at the court of Chandra Gupta about 300 B.C., found science and philosophy honoured, and from early days the first of the four stages of a Bráhman's life, embracing his youth and early manhood, was that of a Bramachári or learner. The Muhammadan conquest introduced a new feature, and the mosques became in India, as in other countries of Islám, centres of instruction and of literary activity. When the power of the East India Company was finally established, it had, therefore, to rule over a people who were accustomed to instruction and respected learning. It found four ancient methods of education at work: (1) the teaching given by Bráhmans to their disciples; (2) the *tols* or seats of Sanskrit learning; (3) the *maktabs* and *madrasas*, or schools and colleges of the Muhammadans; and (4) the village schools.

The East India Company was not altogether unmindful of its duties in this respect, and the history of education in British India under the Company and the Crown is marked by steady, although tardy, progress. That history divides itself in Bombay into six periods. The first period lasted until about the year 1825, when the provision of the Charter Act of 1815, appropriating a lakh of rupees annually for educational purposes, was carried into effect. The characteristics of this period throughout India, and particularly in the Bombay Presidency, were the growing activity of the Christian missionary bodies and the quiescence of the State. The Roman Catholics continued to labour upon the Western coast of India as they had done ever since the establishment of the Portuguese power, when friars and Jesuits invariably accompanied the famous 'conquistadors.' The American Missionary Society opened a school for boys in 1814, and ten years later the first school for Native girls, in Bombay. The Scottish Church worked in Bombay city and the Konkan. The London Missionary Society established itself in Surat and other towns in Gujarát. The Church Missionary Society extended its operations over the Deccan, the Konkan, and even as far as Sind, while the Irish Presbyterian Missionary Society exerted itself in Káthiáwár. Stimulated by this exhibition of energy, the Bombay Education Society, supported by voluntary contributions, was established in 1815, and the Native School-book and School Society in 1822.

Mountstuart Elphinstone, that far-seeing ruler whose name is connected with many measures of progress in the Bombay Presidency, was the first chairman of the School Society. Under his superintendence it obtained help from the State [1], and endeavoured to organise and extend the work of education. It was Elphinstone, also, who applied towards its original destination a portion of the *dakshina*, or grant made by the Peshwás for the encouragement of learning at Poona, and who in his Minute on Education in 1824 defended and justified the creation of the Poona Sanskrit College, which had just been founded in the capital of the Maráthás. The services of Mountstuart Elphinstone to the cause of education in the Presidency were

[1] *Report of the Indian Education Commission*, p. 12.

recognised by the establishment of the Elphinstone College at Bombay, at the cost of nearly four and a half lakhs of rupees subscribed on his retirement from the Governorship, in 1827, to perpetuate his memory.

The second period ended in 1839, when Lord Auckland published the Minute which decided the long controversy between the 'Orientalists' and the 'Anglicists.' The 'Orientalists,' who advocated education on the old lines through the medium of the Oriental classics, were defeated. The 'Anglicists'' victory was mainly due to the eloquent support of Macaulay, at that time Legal Member of Council. They urged the use of English and the Vernaculars.

This second period (1825–1839) was, on the whole, a period of unsystematic official effort, marked, however, by the consolidation and extension of various educational societies and committees which had struggled into existence. In Bombay, the inadequacy of a system of educational institutions partially under Government management, but not directed by a special agency, became manifest. The Elphinstone College, in spite of its ample funds, did not prosper. The District Schools in Gujarát, which were removed from the superintendence of the Native School Society and placed under that of the local revenue officers, distinctly deteriorated. As the result of much experience, the Bombay Government resolved to create a special agency, and in 1840 established a Board of Education of six members, three nominated by Government, and three, as its last act, by the School Society.

The history of Bombay education during the third

period from 1840 to 1855 is the history of this Board, and of the continued efforts of the various missionary societies. The strong man of the Board was Sir Erskine Perry, Chief Justice of Bombay, who acted as its president from 1843 to 1852. He was a strenuous advocate of higher education. He believed in concentrating upon the higher education of the few the available Government grant, which he considered quite inadequate to make an impression upon the masses. He held what was called the 'downward filtration' theory, and argued that the thorough education of the upper class would react upon the ignorance of the rest of the population. Under his vigorous influence the number of English schools in the Bombay Presidency and the attendance at them doubled. In 1855, when the Board of Education resigned, there existed a High School, in which English was taught, at (I believe) every head-quarter station in the province except Kaira. The encouragement given to higher or collegiate education was a marked characteristic of this period throughout India. In the Bombay Presidency it was signalised by the foundation of the Grant Medical College, and the addition of the English branch to the Poona Sanskrit College now known by the name of the Deccan College.

The great Educational Despatch of the Court of Directors of the East India Company in 1854 closed the first epoch of the history of education in India, which, as has been seen, is divisible into three distinct periods. This despatch is believed to have been drafted by John Stuart Mill, and the principles laid down by it were accepted and confirmed by the Secretary of State for India in 1859, after the East India Company had been succeeded by the Crown. The education of the people of India was definitely declared to be a duty of the State, and means were suggested for its extension and improvement. It was recommended that Universities should be founded in the Presidency towns, that separate departments of education should be established for each Province, and that regular and consistent inspection of schools by the Government should take the place of vague encouragement.

On the publication of this Despatch, the Education Department of Bombay was formed in 1855. Its first Director, Mr. C. Erskine, C.S., mapped out its future policy, which differed in one important respect from that pursued in other provinces of India. In the words of the Report of the Education Commission: 'The work, which the Department [in Bombay] set before itself, after a careful census, was one of creation rather than of incorporation[1].' It deliberately endeavoured to supply the educational wants of the population by originating institutions under departmental management, instead of aiding the existing primary schools or stimulating the development of private enterprise.

The distinctive characteristic of this fourth period (1855–1870) of education in India, inaugurated by the Educational Despatch of the Court of Directors in 1854, was the extension of secondary education and the

[1] *Report of the Indian Education Commission*, p. 33.

encouragement of High Schools, in which English was recognised as the medium of instruction. In that respect the Department of Public Instruction in Bombay had the labours of its predecessor, the Board of Education, as a good foundation on which to build. Like the Board, it endeavoured as far as possible to keep the management in its own hands. It was not until 1863 that it offered grants-in-aid to missionary and private institutions, and not until 1865 that it offered them on a sufficiently liberal scale to elicit private effort[1]. Not less important than even this development of secondary education was the foundation of the University of Bombay in 1857, which by means of its examinations has exercised a regulating and controlling influence over the whole course of studies in the Bombay Presidency.

In 1871 the fifth period (1871–1883) was opened by the transfer of the control of education, under Lord Mayo's decentralisation scheme, to the Local Governments. This measure did not very directly concern Bombay, which has always been independent, but simultaneously with it came a great increase in the attention paid to primary education, the necessary foundation for all true educational progress. In 1882, the Indian Education Commission, after collecting evidence in the various provinces, endeavoured to consolidate what experience had proved to be the best schemes and systems, so far as consolidation was consistent with local requirements. It made provision for all classes and races of the Indian

[1] *Report of the Indian Education Commission*, p. 364.

population, and laid down the lines on which the various local Departments of Public Instruction might expand into a truly national system of education for India. The publication of the Education Commission's Report, and its adoption by the Supreme Government, in 1884, inaugurated the sixth period in the history of Indian education—the period which is still current, and with which this chapter more particularly deals.

When Lord Reay arrived in India in 1885, he found that the Bombay Government had the Report of the Commission under consideration, and he at once set himself to adapt its conclusions to the local system. Every branch of the educational administration of the Presidency was examined, and wide-reaching reforms were introduced.

Of the various classes of education perhaps the most important for the welfare of the people is primary or elementary instruction. The 'downward filtration' theory had been generally acknowledged to be untenable; the extension of primary education invariably leads to the development of an upward tendency; the converse has not yet been proved. The Missionaries and the Native School-book Societies in Bombay always recognised the paramount importance of establishing elementary schools, but it was not until 1853 that the Board of Education practically accepted it as the duty of the State to provide for primary instruction. It did so in that year by undertaking to open a school in any town or village in the Presidency, on condition that the inhabitants would pay half the master's salary and would build a school-room and supply school-books. This policy was continued by the Bombay Education Department. The first Director of Public Instruction, Mr. C. Erskine, gave every encouragement to the foundation of new primary schools, to be inspected by the Department and supervised by district school committees of the Local Boards. Efforts were made to secure efficiency by providing school-houses and training masters, and a high standard was maintained by careful and systematic Government inspection. This sustained effort to create a departmental system of primary instruction bore good fruits, but it was accompanied by a neglect of the existing popular institutions, the indigenous village schools.

It is not needful to blame the Bombay Education Department in its early years for this neglect. It may now seem that it would have been alike more economical and more consistent with sound administration to develop the village schools, and to endeavour to improve the ancient methods of instruction preserved in them, than to found new schools and introduce Western ideas. But it may well have appeared hopeless to the educational administrators of the time that any change for the better could be made in the existing village schools. To their minds the arguments for superseding them by Government institutions proved irresistible. The following account of an indigenous Bombay village school, which had preserved its character intact, to some extent justifies their attitude. The description reminds one of the old-fashioned hedge-school of Carleton's *Tales of the Irish Peasantry*.

'The ordinary daily routine of a Hindu indigenous school is nearly the same in all parts of the Presidency. Each morning at about 6 o'clock the Pantoji, who is in some cases a Bráhman and the priest of many of the families whose children attend the school, goes round the village and collects his pupils. This process usually occupies some time. At one house, the pupil has to be persuaded to come to school; at another, the parents have some special instructions to give the master regarding the refractoriness of their son; at a third, he is asked to administer chastisement on the spot. As soon as he has collected a sufficient number of his pupils, he takes them to the school. For the first half-hour a Bhupali, or invocation to the Sun, Saraswati, Gaupati, or some other deity, is chanted by the whole school. After this the boys who can write trace the letters of their *kittas*, or copy-slips, with a dry pen, the object of this exercise being to give free play to the fingers and wrist, and to accustom them to the sweep of the letters. When the tracing-lesson is over, the boys begin to write copies, and the youngest children, who have been hitherto merely looking on, are taken in hand either by the master's son or by one of the elder pupils. The master himself generally confines his attention to one or two of the oldest pupils, and to those whose instruction he has stipulated to finish in a given time. All the pupils are seated in one small room or verandah, and the confusion of sounds, which arises from three or four sets of boys reading and shouting out their tables all at the same moment, almost baffles description[1].'

In spite of the defective methods pursued in the old Bombay village schools, the Education Commission, acting on the experience gained in other provinces of India, had no hesitation in recommending (1883) the careful development of indigenous schools in preference to the creation of new departmental primary schools. Lord Reay at once adopted this recommendation, and took measures to carry it into effect. His aim was to improve existing institutions, to stimulate private enterprise and to guide it into proper channels. He did all in his power to induce the local authorities to establish and supervise primary schools, and encouraged them by greatly increasing the amount of financial support given to elementary education by means of grants-in-aid under the management of local Boards. The enhanced proportion of Government assistance given to primary instruction is best shown by the fact that during the period under review it was increased from Rs.2,90,893 to Rs.5,48,035.

The Governor was not only ready to spend money on elementary education, he also endeavoured to guide it in the right direction. Hitherto, the instruction given in the primary schools had been mainly regarded as the first step of the educational ladder, up which an apt pupil might climb through a secondary school and a college, by means of scholarships and studentships, to a University degree. This is a laud-

[1] *Report of the Indian Education Commission*, p. 65.

able idea in itself, and Lord Reay recognised its importance. But in practice it tends unduly to increase the number of University graduates, for all of whom it becomes impossible to find fitting employment in the public service; while it provides those lads who are unable to climb the whole ladder, not with a complete education suited to their needs, but with a training preliminary to a classical education, which is comparatively useless to them. Lord Reay had been familiarised with the aspects of this problem by his study of the corresponding controversies in Europe, and in a Minute, dated 12 August, 1885, he laid weight on the necessity for giving a practical turn to education, with a view 'of suggesting to the younger generation what they ought to do, to become good artisans, good cultivators, &c.' At this early date in his government, therefore, he disclosed that policy towards the encouragement of technical education which afterwards occupied so large a share of his attention. He indicated that such education should have its proper place in the elementary schools. He held that these schools ought to give a sound training to the majority of their pupils who have to labour for their bread, and should try to rear them into intelligent working men, and not concentrate their efforts on the small minority of embryo University graduates.

While neglecting no means to improve and develop the system of primary instruction, Lord Reay did not fail to perceive the importance of a simultaneous reform in secondary education. Secondary or middle education in India is the stage which leads from the primary to the collegiate course. Its goal was the matriculation standard of the Universities. It implies, therefore, in its higher grades a thorough knowledge of the English language, which is the medium of instruction in the colleges. I have mentioned that Sir Erskine Perry and the Bombay Board of Education did much to encourage English education in the Bombay Presidency, and that, before 1855, schools teaching English had been established in every district except Kaira. Notwithstanding this excellent basis, the Bombay Education Department failed for a time to make much progress in secondary education, and the lack of Government assistance led to little being done by private enterprise.

The Indian Education Commission found itself constrained to report, in speaking of the progress of education between 1854 and 1871: 'Compared with some other provinces, therefore, the development of secondary education in Bombay during this period must be pronounced to have been weak[1].' The system of grants-in-aid, however, introduced in 1863 and on a more liberal scale in 1865, although hampered by a too rigid enforcement of payment by results, led to improvement and indicated the direction to be pursued in the future. A bright side, also, was discernible in the eagerness of the people to avail themselves of the higher grades of instruction, for the Education Commissioners go on to say: 'A marked feature of the Bombay secondary system is that the schools, though few in number, have a much larger average attendance

[1] *Report of the Indian Education Commission*, p. 185.

than in any other Province in India, being between two and three times as large as in Madras or Bengal [1].'

The action of Lord Reay's Government upon secondary education was as important, though it did not involve so large an increase of expenditure, as his development of elementary education. Of his great reform, effected by a wise extension of grants-in-aid, and the abolition of payments solely by result—a reform which had a beneficial influence on every class of education, mention will be made later, when the whole subject can be discussed at length.

The special reforms with regard to the secondary schools followed the same lines as those adopted for the primary schools. An attempt was made to transfer the Government schools to the local authorities,—an attempt immediately successful only with the Ahmadnagar High School. Greater success crowned the Governor's efforts to widen the direction and the aim of the studies pursued. If it is true that the elementary schools were mainly regarded as the first step of a ladder leading up to a full University education, it is still more true of the old curriculum in the secondary schools. The Matriculation Examination of the University of Bombay became the goal, towards which all secondary education was directed. The number of passes obtained at that examination formed the official test of efficiency.

The one-sided effect of this system, which forced all the brighter minds along one path and destined all the best scholars for the crowded ranks of the Govern-

[1] *Report of the Indian Education Commission*, p. 186.

ment service or the learned professions, had attracted the notice of the Education Commission. One of the standing questions put to the witnesses whom it examined ran thus: 'Is the attention of teachers and pupils unduly directed to the Entrance Examination of the University?' The replies of the witnesses were unanimously in the affirmative, and the Commissioners go on to say in their Report: 'The University looks upon the Entrance Examination, not as a test of fitness for the duties of daily life, but rather as a means of ascertaining whether the candidate has acquired that amount of general information and that degree of mental discipline which will enable him to profit by a course of liberal or professional instruction. In these circumstances, it appears to be the unquestionable duty of that Department of the State which has undertaken the control of education, to recognise the present demand for educated labour in all branches of commercial and industrial activity, and to meet it so far as may be possible with the means at its disposal[1].'

The evidence of Sir Raymond West, Vice-Chancellor of the University of Bombay during the earlier part of Lord Reay's administration, clearly set forth the need for reform in the curriculum of the secondary schools. 'The preparation for ordinary business,' he says, 'may with advantage proceed up to a certain point along the same course as that for literature and science. It is a defect of our system, as I understand it, that it does not provide for a natural transition to the further studies which may be the most proper for a man

[1] *Report of the Indian Education Commission*, p. 220.

of business, nor even propose to encourage and conduct such studies. When a boy reaches the age of about fourteen he may have plainly shown that he has not the gifts that would make him a good subject for literary culture. His tastes or his circumstances may disincline him to be an engineer or a chemist. He ought not then to be forced on in a line in which failure is almost certain. He should be put to work upon matters that he really can master, unless quite exceptionally dull, such as arithmetic, rudimentary economics, mercantile geography, the use of manures, or others determined by the locality of the school and its needs. . . . . The extension of this knowledge should be along those lines where it will be grasped and incorporated by the interests and teachings of active life. Still it should be education, aiming at making the mind robust and flexible, rather than at shabbily decking it with some rays of "business information" or low technic skill. For these different aims the present system makes no sufficient or distinct provision [1].'

Supported by the authority of the Report of the Education Commission, and the testimony of Sir Raymond West, Lord Reay, himself well-acquainted with European theories and systems of State education, did all in his power to forward what is known as the 'bifurcation of studies.' His conviction of the necessity for technical education was not to be satisfied with any idea of 'downward filtration.' He did not think it enough to establish Technical Institutes. He endeavoured, in addition to fostering higher and special

[1] *Report of the Indian Education Commission, p.* 220.

technical education, to stimulate what is known as the modern side in the ordinary secondary schools, in which the pupils who were not fitted for a University education or not desirous of it, might be trained for the practical work of life.

Nor was this the only measure to free the secondary schools from being swayed solely by the standard of the University Matriculation Examination. To secure greater elasticity in their curriculum, he arranged that the University should undertake a School Final Examination, with a wide range of optional subjects, which was to qualify for admission to the lower grades of the public service[1]. The rules regulating this new examination were published on April 4, 1888, and were received with general approbation. Not only did they encourage the private and aid secondary schools by emancipating them from strict subservience to a single and detailed examination, but they gave room for a greater variety in teaching, and relieved the excessive pressure on the University by providing another door of entrance into the public service. The Bombay Government, under Lord Reay, thus showed in its treatment of secondary, as well as of primary schools, that it understood the real meaning of the word education, as embracing every branch of sound mental training, and not merely special literary and scientific instruction.

As the 'ladder theory' has formed the subject of much discussion in India, and as Lord Reay held a decided personal opinion regarding it, I may perhaps

[1] In 1890–91 the number of candidates who presented themselves for the University School Final Examination was 820; of whom 331 passed.

be permitted to quote a letter which he addressed to me on the question. 'I think,' he says, 'the main point with reference to the "ladder" theory is that primary education should be preparatory to secondary education as well as to the more humble walks of life; while secondary education should be preparatory to higher education but also complete in itself for those who have to enter upon a profession at eighteen. Bifurcation in the higher classes of secondary education is needed to secure this object, and also to divide the classical scholars from those who enter upon a scientific career, either as doctors, engineers, or scientific agriculturists. There are three main divisions: pure classics, pure science or modern literature, and the third division for those who do not get to the University, but stop short either after primary or after secondary education, and who therefore do not want to be prepared. The B.A. degree for the first division, the B.Sc. for the second, that is what I wished to secure, but the University did not adopt the B.Sc. as imperative for the medical students or engineers.

'A very important question was a training school for *secondary* teachers. We decided that secondary teachers should as a rule be University graduates, and then get their pedagogic training in certain specified secondary schools with good head-masters—a less expensive and more efficient method than a training school. For *primary* education, both male and female, we paid great attention to the improvement of our Training Colleges.' The pension scheme for teachers in primary schools, an extremely intricate matter most important to the teachers, also received close and successful attention from Lord Reay.

Higher, or as it may more properly be termed in India collegiate, education rests entirely in the hands of the Arts Colleges affiliated to the Universities, and of the special colleges and classes which give instruction in the different faculties recognised by the Universities. The fact of having passed the Matriculation Examination guarantees that the student has some command of English. The subsequent collegiate teaching is imparted in English by lectures, and follows Western methods. The Arts Colleges in the Bombay Presidency are nine in number. Two of them, the Deccan College at Poona and the Elphinstone College at Bombay, have a long and honourable history, and are still under Government management. Two, the Rájarám and Sámaldás Colleges, are maintained by Native States. Four are aided by the Government, the College of the Free General Assembly of the Kirk of Scotland, called the Wilson College after the famous missionary Dr. John Wilson, and St. Xavier's Roman Catholic College, both at Bombay; the Gujarát College at Ahmadábád, and the Sind College at Karáchi. One is unaided, the Fergusson College at Poona. For instruction in professional studies, there are also the Law School at Bombay and the Law Class at the Deccan College, the Grant Medical College at Bombay, and the College of Science at Poona which has developed out of the Poona Civil Engineering College.

The chief events of Lord Reay's administration in connection with collegiate education were his efforts to amalgamate the two Arts Colleges at Poona (the Deccan and the Fergusson); the transference of the Elphinstone College to a more suitable situation and the addition of another professor to its staff; the conversion of the Gujarát College from a Government into an aided institution; the foundation of the Sind College; the improvements effected at the Grant Medical College; and the development of the agricultural branch of the College of Science at Poona.

The oldest of these colleges, the Deccan College at Poona, has had a chequered history. When the East India Company annexed the territory of the Peshwás in 1819, Mountstuart Elphinstone found that it was the custom to distribute a large sum of money, called the *dakshina*, to the Bráhmans of the capital every year. This grant, originally intended to encourage education and learning by the donation of valuable prizes, had so degenerated that when the English took possession of Poona, it had become a mere dole of alms to all Bráhmans who applied. Mountstuart Elphinstone recommended that part of the *dakshina* should revert to something like its original purpose. He suggested that it should not be expended in gifts to proficients in Hindu theology, as had latterly been the case, but should be allotted to those skilled in the more useful branches of learning, such as law and mathematics, and to a certain number of professors maintained to teach those sciences.

On this subject Mr. Elphinstone wrote a memorable paper, which explains his fame as an educational reformer on pre-existing lines. 'There exist in the

Hindu languages,' he said, 'many tales and fables that would be generally read, and that would inculcate sound morals. There must be religious books tending more directly to the same end. If many of these were printed, and distributed cheaply or gratuitously, the effect would, without doubt, be great and beneficial. It would, however, be indispensable that they should be purely Hindu. We might silently omit all precepts of questionable morality, but the slightest infusion of religious controversy would secure the failure of the design. It would be better to call the prejudices of the Hindus to our aid in reforming them, and to control their vices by the ties of religion which are stronger than those of law. By maintaining and purifying their present tenets at the same time that we enlighten their understandings, we shall bring them nearer to that standard of perfection at which all concur in desiring that they should arrive; while any attack on their faith, if successful, might be expected in theory, as is found in practice, to shake their reverence for all religion, and to set them free from those useful restraints which even a superstitious doctrine imposes on the passions[1].'

These were the principles which actuated the Hon. Mountstuart Elphinstone in directing the foundation of a college for the encouragement of the study of Sanskrit and of ancient Hindu literature and science at Poona in 1821. The Court of Directors, however, did not share the Governor's enthusiasm for Sanskrit

[1] *Memorandum on the Origin and Development of the Poona and Deccan Colleges*, p. 1.

or altogether sympathise with his ideas about the education of the Hindus, and they suggested that the newly established institution should be closed. Mr. Elphinstone answered his critics in his elaborate Minute on Education of March 1824, which contains this powerful argument: 'It would surely be a preposterous way of adding to the intellectual treasures of a nation to begin by the destruction of its indigenous literature; and I cannot but think that the future attainments of the natives will be increased in extent, as well as in variety, by being, as it were, engrafted on their own previous knowledge, and imbued with their own original and peculiar character[1].' The college was, after this eloquent defence, allowed to exist under the name of the Poona Sanskrit College, and did good work on native lines until the establishment of an English Department, consisting at first of only a single class, in 1842. This department rapidly developed in importance. In 1852, instruction in English was recognised as of equal value to the teaching of Sanskrit philosophy and science, and the institution received the name of the Poona College.

The next stage in the history of the College was marked by the appointment in 1859 of Dr. Martin Haug, the celebrated Oriental scholar, to superintend the Sanskrit studies, on the ground that Sanskrit ought no longer to be taught as a vehicle of superstition, but treated as an ancient language and literature by the modern methods of scientific philology and

[1] *Memorandum on the Origin and Development of the Poona and Deccan Colleges*, p. 2.

criticism. The usefulness of the College was, however, diminished and its growing prosperity checked by its situation in the heart of the city of Poona, and by the lack of suitable lecture-rooms. This was brought to the notice of the eminent Bombay philanthropist, Sir Jamsetjee Jejeebhoy, who in 1863 offered a lakh of rupees towards the erection of a new building, on condition that Government should contribute an equal sum, and grant an appropriate site. The generous offer was accepted, and in 1864 Sir Bartle Frere, Governor of Bombay, laid the foundation-stone of the present edifice. He announced, on completing the ceremony, that its name would be altered from the Poona to the Deccan College, in order to signify that it was intended for the higher education of the whole Deccan and not merely for the city of Poona. In 1865 the Principal was able to restrict the College to its proper function, as a home for higher education, by refusing to admit students who had not passed the Matriculation Examination of the University of Bombay, and in 1868 the new building was opened.

Such had been the history of the Deccan College, typical in many ways of the growth of higher education in India during the present century, and indissolubly connected with the great name of its founder, Mountstuart Elphinstone. In its more recent developments the Deccan College has had the advantage of the able and sympathetic management of Dr. Wordsworth, one of the most distinguished public teachers who ever laboured in India. But it had no longer sole possession of the field of higher education in Poona. A young and vigorous rival existed, founded to do honour to the memory of Lord Reay's immediate predecessor, and called after him the Fergusson College.

The history of the Fergusson College is almost as interesting as that of the Deccan College. During the last days of Sir James Fergusson's government, the Poona Bráhmans, under the name of the Deccan Education Society, conceived the idea of founding an institution to perpetuate the memory of the departing Governor. The Kolhápur and Southern Maráthá chiefs subscribed liberally, and the college was started with an able principal, Mr. Apte, and a staff of young Bráhman professors. These men were enthusiastic teachers. They received hardly any pay and formed a patriotic fraternity, stimulated by an ideal view of the dignity and importance of education. The students were all poor but anxious to be taught, and the institution soon attained a high degree of success in the first stage of collegiate education, that is, in the preparation of candidates for the Previous Examination of the University of Bombay—the first examination after Matriculation towards the degree of Bachelor of Arts.

Lord Reay saw the anomaly of the existence of two Arts Colleges at Poona, when many other important cities had no provision for higher education. He foresaw the undesirable effect likely to be produced by the competition of two institutions, the one maintained by Government and the other independent. He found that the Fergusson College, although singularly successful in preparing candidates for the Previous Examination, was not able to give the necessary instruction for the whole B.A. course, and this supplied a ground for urging the amalgamation of the two institutions. The Education Commission had strongly enjoined the policy of replacing Government by State-aided education, wherever possible, and Lord Reay thought he saw an opportunity in this way for economising the resources of the Presidency. Actuated by these motives, His Excellency entered into personal negotiations with representatives of the Fergusson College at Mahábaleshwar in 1887. He proposed to merge the two colleges into one, which should be under the superintendence of the Deccan Education Society, and which should receive a liberal grant-in-aid from the Government, like the Gujarát College at Ahmadábád and the Sind College at Karáchi.

Notwithstanding the Governor's earnest intervention, the negotiations led to no result. Many of the leading native scholars distrusted the ability of the professors of the Fergusson College to prepare for all the University Arts Examinations, even with the assistance of some of the English professors from the Deccan College. It was feared that the fusion would lead to a diminution of the Government grant towards higher education in Poona. The Fergusson College fraternity were jealous of the introduction of a European element: the professors at the Deccan College naturally preferred their status as Government officials. This opposition to the scheme of amalgamation could not be overcome, and Lord Reay's failure to carry out his scheme illustrates his principle of respecting the views of local responsible bodies, even when those views were a disappointment to himself.

His other efforts to improve the condition of higher education in Arts Colleges were entirely successful. By the liberality of Sir Dinshaw Manekji Petit, who presented a suitable building for the Central Press, the Elphinstone College at Bombay was removed to a more appropriate situation, close to the University, and Lord Reay used the money saved by the reduction of the staff of European inspectors of schools to add another English professor to its staff. Of even greater importance to the cause of higher education in the Presidency were the conversion of the Gujarát College at Ahmadábád into an aided institution and the foundation of the Sind College at Karáchi.

The conversion of the Gujarát College is a good example of Lord Reay's policy of withdrawing the Government from the direct management of educational institutions, wherever practicable, and of substituting grants-in-aid. The college at Ahmadábád is not so old an institution as the Deccan and Elphinstone Colleges, but it had exercised a considerable influence upon the higher education of the Gujaráti-speaking population as a Government institution. It was, at the end of March, 1887, separated from the Government High School, to which it had been attached, and made over to the management of a Board of Control, consisting of the Trustees of the College Endowment Fund and of three representatives of Government. An English principal was also appointed in the person of Mr. Waddington, a distinguished Oxford graduate.

The establishment of the Sind Arts College at Karáchi, in January, 1887, marked an interesting stage in the history of higher education in the Presidency. When the progress of education is considered province by province, it will be seen that Sind, which had hitherto been the most backward province of all, made a remarkable advance during the five years under review. Not the least remarkable step in this advance was the establishment of the Sind College, which owed its origin to local endeavour, aided by the advice and active assistance of the Government. It is under the management of a Council, consisting of three nominees of the Government, six representatives of the Sind College Association, and one representative of each Municipal or Local Board which contributes not less than 500 rupees annually towards its expenses. A lakh of rupees was quickly raised as the nucleus of an Endowment Fund; the Municipality of Karáchi granted a site, and the Viceroy of India laid the foundation-stone of the building on November 14, 1887. This building is estimated to cost two lakhs, of which Government give half under the grant-in-aid rules. It bears the name of the late Honourable Dayárám Jethmal, Member of the Governor's Council.

The various Arts Colleges, however, fill only a portion of the wide field of higher education. The attainment of the degree of Bachelor of Arts, or even of that of Master of Arts, which is only granted by the University of Bombay after a severe examination in Languages, History and Philosophy, Mathematics or Natural Science, merely gives evidence of prolonged and systematic study. It does not qualify a young man for a learned profession. General education must be supplemented by professional education, and in the development of the professional colleges in the Presidency Lord Reay took an active part.

The most important institution for professional training in Western India is the Grant Medical College at Bombay, which bears the name of Sir Robert Grant, Governor of the Presidency from 1835 to 1838. Sir Robert Grant throughout his tenure of the governorship showed the deepest interest in medical education. He introduced the modern ideas of medicine and surgery into the medical department of the Sanskrit College at Poona. He suggested the creation of a Medical School at Bombay, and no more fitting memorial could have been devised to do honour to his memory and to perpetuate it than the establishment of the College. In 1843, the foundation-stones of the Grant Medical College and of the Jamsetjee Jejeebhoy Hospital (the gift of the famous Bombay philanthropist) were laid, and from the first the two institutions worked in harmony. The most important points in the history of the Grant College down to 1885 were its affiliation to the University of Bombay in 1860, and the consequent supersession of its diploma by the University degree of Licentiate in Medicine and Surgery; the improvements effected in its system of teaching by the appointment of a Professor of Physiology and of several other professors in 1867; the establishment of provincial medical schools at Poona, Ahmadábád, and Haidarábád in 1878 for the instruction of hospital assistants, which relieved the College of the vernacular classes; and the opening of its course of instruction to women in 1884[1]. The Jamsetjee Jejeebhoy Hospital also developed, and its usefulness was trebled by the addition of the Motlibai Lying-in Hospital and the Petit Hospital for Women and Children, due to generous donations received by Lord Reay from Motlibai, a wealthy Parsi lady, and from Sir Dinshaw Petit, Bart.

One serious deficiency of the Grant College was the absence of a proper laboratory, fitted with the modern appliances for scientific teaching and research. This deficiency was supplied under the influence of Lord Reay by the liberality of Mr. Framji Dinshaw Petit, son of the above-named baronet, who presented the College with Rs. 60,000 for the construction and Rs. 15,000 for the equipment of a first-class modern laboratory, suited for physiological, pharmacological, pathological, and chemical research. 'For his assistance in removing this obstacle to the practical work of the College,' writes the Principal, Brigade-Surgeon W. Gray, 'our Governor, Lord Reay, is entitled to the lasting gratitude of both the present and future professors and students.'

[1] *Medical Education in Bombay: an Introductory Address delivered at the Grant Medical College*, by Brigade-Surgeon W. Gray, Principal and Professor of Surgery. 1889.

The Petit Laboratory is not the only result of the Governor's interest in medical education. He induced the Gáekwár of Baroda to guarantee the salary of an additional professor at the Grant College, and filled the new Chair by the appointment of Dr. Bahadurji, a Parsi graduate of the University of London, who had paid special attention to pharmacology. The importance of trained nursing also occupied Lord Reay's attention; and his friend, the Mahárájá of Bhaunagar, gave a lakh of rupees as the endowment of a Lady Reay Nurse Fund, while a Native gentleman, Mr. Bhownaggree, gave part of the money for the establishment of a Nurses' Home in connection with the Jamsetjee Jejeebhoy Hospital. As a memorial of the services rendered by the Governor to medical education, a late very distinguished Principal of the Medical College, Dr. Vandyke Carter, Honorary Surgeon to the Queen, has founded a lectureship in the Grant College to bear the name of the Reay Lectureship.

In Bombay, as in other provinces of India, the keenest intellects are attracted in preference to the study and practice of the law. The graduates in law are scattered all over the Presidency; they represent the educated class in the municipalities and local boards; they exercise great influence on the formation of native opinion; they closely watch the administration of justice, and it is of the utmost importance that they should be properly trained and educated. The Law School at Bombay originated in the establishment of the Perry Professorship of Jurisprudence, which was founded to commemorate Sir Erskine Perry, Chief Justice of Bombay. Other professors were added from time to time, but none of them were obliged to devote the whole of their attention to teaching law. As a rule, attendance at their lectures was given merely to fulfil the obligation imposed by the University, and the students prepared for their examinations at home. The result did not prove altogether satisfactory, and the best remedy appeared to be the appointment of a principal or professor, who should give his whole time to the work of teaching. Lord Reay strongly advocated this course. Before he left India it had been resolved to have a 'full-time' Professor of Jurisprudence, and the resolution was awaiting the sanction of the Supreme Government. In filling the legal Chairs which fell vacant during his tenure of office, the Governor sought for able jurists, whether Indian or European. He nominated Mr. Kashinath Trimbak Telang, now a Judge of the High Court, and Mr. Sethna, a Parsi who had carried off many prizes at Lincoln's Inn, to professorships. It should be noted that, in addition to the Law School at Bombay, a Law Class is maintained at the Deccan College at Poona, which, however, only prepares for the first University Examination in law.

Next to medicine and law in the University of Bombay ranks engineering. Most of the candidates in this department are prepared in the Poona College of Science, formerly known as the Poona Civil Engineering College. This institution grew out of a school established by the Government at Poona in 1854 for the purpose of training subordinates for the Public Works Department. Agriculture and Forestry have been added to the old curriculum, and under the management of its able and energetic principal, Dr. T. Cooke, the Poona College of Science has become celebrated for efficiency. In extending its range, its original purpose was not forgotten. A thorough preparation is given for the Bombay University degree of Licentiate of Civil Engineering, which requires from two to four years' practical training in workshops as well as sound theoretical knowledge. So high is the reputation of the College of Science, that the Mysore State finds it both advantageous and economical to send students to be trained at Poona, and the Nizam is said to be thinking of closing the Haidarábád Engineering College and following the example of Mysore.

The development of the Agricultural and Forestry branches, and the attempt to meet the demand for technical education in its workshops, were the points in regard to the Poona College of Science which occupied most of Lord Reay's attention. The whole question of technical education will be discussed later, but something must be said here of Dr. Cooke's endeavour to secure the recognition of agriculture as a distinct subject for higher or collegiate education. The main difficulty with which he met was the refusal of the University of Bombay to grant a degree for Agriculture, or even to admit it as a subject for examination for the degree of Bachelor of Science.

The opponents of this scheme argued that the

theory and practice of Agriculture could not be taught in such a way as to give a training comparable to that demanded in the examinations for the existing degrees. Dr. Cooke contested this notion in an able memorandum, in which he pointed to the course prescribed by the University of Edinburgh for a certificate, namely the General Principles and Economics of Agriculture, Geology, Botany, Physics, Mechanics. He also added to these subjects Agricultural Chemistry and Veterinary Science. Lord Reay heartily concurred in Dr. Cooke's views, but the authorities of the University only consented to grant a diploma, not a degree, to students of Agriculture.

The Governor succeeded, however, in arranging with Sir Edward Buck, the Secretary to the Supreme Government of India in the Department of Revenue and Agriculture, for the appointment of an expert agricultural chemist, whose salary was to be defrayed by contributions from all the provincial treasuries, and who was to visit each province in turn. The Governor also arranged with Sir E. Buck for the establishment of the first Pasteur Laboratory in India in connection with the Poona College of Science, and laid the first stone of the building for this important institution in the winter of 1889. The instruction in Forestry had the practical advantage of training men for the Forest Department, but some difficulty was experienced in getting the Forest Department to take these men to fill vacant appointments.

At the summit of the educational edifice in the Presidency stands the University of Bombay, founded in 1857 in accordance with the Education Despatch of the Court of Directors in 1854. As has already been indicated, the University of Bombay is an examining body, like the University of London, not a teaching University, like Oxford and Cambridge. The control which it exercises over higher education is all-powerful, for its Matriculation Examination forms the standard of the secondary schools with regard to pupils who propose to attend one of the colleges, and its degrees form the goal of the colleges. Lord Reay, while desirous of expanding the scope of its examinations, as in the matter of an agricultural diploma, strictly respected the self-governing character of the University, and left the consideration of all proposed changes in the curricula to the various Faculties.

An important controversy arose over a measure for University reorganisation brought forward by Sir Raymond West. This measure did not meet with the approval of the Senate of the University. Sir Raymond West had proposed that the University should exercise a direct supervision over the colleges. This would not have been acceptable to aided institutions, and the Senate rejected that part of his scheme. In other clauses, the Senate inserted amendments which altered the scope of the measure. The Bombay Government decided not to accept the bill thus modified, and forwarded it to be dealt with by the Supreme Government. On the administrative side, Lord Reay bestowed much care in filling vacancies in the governing body of the University, and inaugurated a new departure by appointing, as Vice-Chancellor of the University, Dr.

Mackichan, Principal of the Wilson Free Kirk College, as a representative of the voluntary and professorial elements. In this sketch of the various classes of education in the Bombay Presidency and of their progress during the administration of Lord Reay, two principles appear to have guided his policy; namely, the desire to withdraw the Government from the direct conduct of the work of education, except in a few institutions which were to be of the highest type; and the desire to promote technical education in its widest sense. These two principles deserve a more detailed examination.

It has been already stated that the traditional policy in Bombay kept education as much as possible in the hands of the Government. In spite of the recommendations contained in the Despatches of 1854 and 1859, the first Directors of Public Instruction, Mr. C. Erskine and Mr. Howard, upheld the soundness of this policy, and consistently pursued it. When grants-in-aid were at length offered to the schools maintained by the Missionary Societies in 1863, the managers found the terms to be 'so illiberal as to make it not worth while to offer their schools for inspection under the rules in question[1].' It was not until Sir Alexander Grant came into office as Director of Public Instruction, in 1865, that a more generous scheme of aid was adopted and substantial encouragement promised to private effort. The Education Commission of 1882 reported that 'aided education [in Bombay since 1865] has made considerable progress relatively, though its total

[1] *Report of the Indian Education Commission*, p. 364.

amount is still but small[1],' and strongly recommended that it should be further developed. This was the situation when Lord Reay arrived in Bombay.

The new Governor found, as has been said, the Report of the Commission still under consideration, and he endeavoured to carry its recommendations into effect. He held with the best authorities that the proper function of the Government in State education consisted in inspection, not management. He firmly believed that institutions started by private effort, and administered or superintended by persons of local influence, were likely to have more vitality and elasticity, and to attain a greater measure of success than purely Government institutions, of which the managers were necessarily less bound by local ties. He realised that private schools afforded more variety and scope for individual ability than Government schools under the direction of a public department, and under the restrictions imposed by a uniform curriculum. His Excellency, therefore, did his best to transfer the existing Government institutions to local authorities, and to encourage private efforts, such as those of the missionary societies and native bodies.

In respect to the primary schools legal enactments secured success; but as regards secondary schools and colleges Lord Reay's efforts did not so immediately bear fruit. He managed, however, to transfer the Ahmadnagar High School and the Gujarát College at Ahmadábád to Local Committees, and to found the Sind College at Karáchi and the Victoria Jubilee

[1] *Report of the Indian Education Commission*, p. 365.

Technical Institute in Bombay, on the basis of local subscriptions and representative management.

The gradual withdrawal of the Government from the actual management of schools and colleges was not the only reform, suggested by the Education Commission, which received support from Lord Reay. The grants-in-aid given to private colleges, schools, and educational institutions had been regulated, since the introduction of the system into the Bombay Presidency in 1865 by Sir Alexander Grant, on the basis of results attained, as attested by the reports of the Government inspectors. This uniform system of payment by results, which has caused much acrimonious controversy in England, was implicitly condemned by the Indian Education Commission of 1882. In 1885 the system of fixed grants was applied to colleges. In 1887 it was extended to other higher institutions. These grants were 'in no case to exceed one-half of the local assets or one-third of the total expenditure of the institution during the previous official year,' supplemented by liberal building grants towards new institutions.

The advantages secured by the change soon became apparent. The Government inspector became a kindly visitor and critic, whose hints were valued and whose supervision was welcomed. The managers and masters were also freed from the incubus of having to satisfy one particular set of tests of efficiency. Lord Reay hoped that the reform would bring about the following results: (1) to give elasticity to educational methods and to encourage individuality; (2) to give the managers of the best schools greater freedom and security in their finances; (3) to stimulate originality in teachers; (4) to relieve inspectors from the burden of a great amount of routine work and to give them more freedom of action in adapting local educational efforts to local needs; and (5) to give to the best schools a greater amount of aid.

It is too soon to judge how far these expectations have been justified, but it is stated that not a single complaint against the changed system of grants-in-aid was received by the Government while Lord Reay remained in India. Not merely was the reform based on sound principles, it also proved economical; and it was owing to the financial saving effected by the abolition of an English inspectorship of schools, rendered possible by it, that Lord Reay found the means to found the new English professorship at the Elphinstone College.

The greater encouragement of aided institutions and the substitution of fixed grants for payments by results, which modified the whole structure of the educational system in the Bombay Presidency, were administrative reforms suggested by the Indian Education Commission. With regard to technical education, however, Lord Reay was an originator, and his fame as an 'educational' governor of Bombay rests chiefly on his clear perception of the importance of this question and on his measures for establishing a sound basis on which to build hereafter. He believed that the concentration of all energy upon the development of a purely literary education, which overcrowded the professions, could best be remedied by the co-ordination of a system of practical training. He strove to impress upon the minds of the people the necessity of education not only for the training of doctors and lawyers and engineers, but also for mechanics, artisans, weavers, and cultivators. In a Resolution of Government, published in November, 1886, Lord Reay defined what he understood by the term 'technical education,' and the lines on which he wished to work.

'It is universally felt,' he says in the concluding paragraph, 'that new channels should be opened, not to repress the intelligence of the country, so largely developed by means of the education imparted during the last thirty years, but to dissuade it from overstocking one field by providing other appropriate ground. Various gradations of technical education, forming ends in themselves for various classes of the community, must all tend to develop the material resources of the country, and to improve the general condition of the people. The public no doubt realises that financial pressure obliges the Government to be most careful in what they do, and that otherwise they would have been glad to extend the basis of operations as regards technical education. Being thus restricted financially, His Excellency in Council would earnestly appeal to all local authorities and associations, as well as to the wealthy classes, to come forward and co-operate heartily with Government in their efforts to enter the arena which several European countries have entered not so long ago, achieving signal success in a very short time; countries, which cannot be called rich, but which realised the conditions imposed upon them by the keen competition which threatened their prosperity.

'His Excellency in Council wishes to make a cautious and small beginning; to establish a basis out of which gradually a more complete fabric may be developed by the process of natural evolution; to utilise existing resources; to labour in a few and selected fields; to work out the scheme almost entirely through native agency; to improve such native agency by giving them opportunities of completing their education in Europe and of witnessing the industrial, agricultural, mechanical, artistic, and mercantile development of the western world. The scheme is not academic, does not include legal and medical education, because it is not intended for the academic, but for the producing, classes. Its success cannot be tested by examinations, but rather by exhibitions and by statistics of imports and exports, prices and wages. Its main object is to enhance the well-being of the people at large by giving increased employment in the Presidency to labour and capital, and by cementing the harmonious relations which should exist between both.' I shall briefly relate the manner in which Lord Reay endeavoured to carry out his programme.

Technical education may be roughly divided, for the purpose of the Resolution, into practical training in agriculture, the artistic industries, and the mechanical industries. Something has already been said of Lord Reay's encouragement of higher agricultural education from the scientific point of view, and of his desire that it should be recognised by the University of

Bombay. But agriculture has its practical as well as its scientific side. It would be well indeed if the servants of the Government and of the native princes thoroughly understood the science of agriculture, and the applications of chemistry, botany, and geology to it. But this cannot be hoped for from the ordinary cultivator. What he needs is a knowledge of the simple and practical facts which would aid him in his daily labour, such as the uses of different manures, and the rules for breeding cattle—a subject of vital importance to prevent the stock from degenerating. From this point of view, lessons in the practice of agriculture form a branch of technical education, and in an agricultural country like India perhaps the most important branch. Lord Reay found the Poona College of Science (under Dr. Cooke) ambitious not only to teach the science of agriculture, but also to become a normal school for instructing teachers in its practice. The Governor did what lay in his power to encourage Dr. Cooke in his efforts. The experimental farm attached to the College of Science for practical work was enlarged, and a veterinary hospital and an observatory were added to the establishment.

Agricultural classes were also developed in connection with several of the secondary schools which give practical instruction, and they are annually inspected by the Principal of the Poona College of Science. With regard to these classes, notice should be taken of the efforts made by the Education Department to transfer them to the superintendence of the local authorities. 'The farm at Sholápur,' it is stated in the Report of the Director of Public Instruction in the Bombay Presidency for the year 1887–88 [1], 'has been transferred to the District Board, and arrangements are being made to bring in Kunbi boys [2] from the *tálukás* and to give them a practical course of instruction. The farms at Ahmadnagar and Násik have been refused by the Boards, and are shortly to be abolished. The farms at Dhúliá and Belgáum are to be offered to the District Boards. At Nadiád the farm belongs to an agricultural society which is liberally disposed, as it admits the High School students to its land, and pays scholarships to two of the best boys in the class. This year five senior boys and the teacher went to the Songarh Cattle Show, the Society paying their expenses.' Lord Reay not only encouraged agricultural education in connection with the College of Science at Poona, but also induced the Gáekwár to establish a chair of Agriculture in the College at Baroda, with promising effects in the future for Gujarát.

Closely connected with the study of scientific agriculture, if indeed it may not be termed a branch of it, is veterinary science. On July 1, 1886, the Bombay Veterinary College was opened under the superintendence of Veterinary-Surgeon Steel, A.V.D. It was established in a bungalow on the Parell estate of the Bombay Society for the Prevention of Cruelty to Animals, and gives clinical instruction in the hospital belonging to that Society. It started with 69 students in the first year, of whom 28 were Parsis and 27

[1] Page 40.

[2] That is to say, boys of the hereditary agricultural class.

Hindus, and it is worthy of notice that all the first graduates and licentiates of the College at once obtained work at regular salaries [1]. It began humbly with only a forge, a dissecting-room, a lecture-room, a small museum, and a library, but its remarkable success attracted general notice, and in 1890 Sir Dinshaw Manekji Petit presented a Patho-Bacteriological Laboratory to the institution.

Practical instruction in agriculture and in veterinary medicine and surgery may seem, however, hardly to come within the popular English idea of technical education, which mainly applies to systematic training in the artistic and mechanical industries. The central institution for the teaching and encouragement of art in all its forms in the Presidency is the Jamsetjee Jejeebhoy School of Art at Bombay. Painting, sculpture, architecture, and the decorative arts were being efficiently taught in it under the management of Mr. Griffiths, when Lord Reay took up office. It has full scope for important work. The Indian eye for colour and form is famous throughout the world, but, as in Japan, the competition of the cheap machine-made productions of modern Europe is forcing the Indian craftsman to turn out more hurried and therefore less highly finished work. It even seemed as if his powers of invention and artistic imitation were diminishing, and it was feared that some of the most renowned arts of ancient and mediaeval India, such as carving and decorative metal work, were in danger of extinction.

[1] *Report of the Director of Public Instruction in the Bombay Presidency for the year* 1886–87, p. 47.

To counteract this decline the Jamsetjee Jejeebhoy School of Art was founded at Bombay. But it is not sufficient to teach the principles of art; what is wanted is to secure the application of those principles to the artistic industries. During Lord Reay's Government the Reay workshops were established under the supervision of the School of Art. He did not try to introduce new artistic industries by means of such workshops, but to revive those which were languishing or deteriorating for want of care and encouragement. His plan was to have promising craftsmen, belonging to local industries of the Presidency, sent to Bombay, and practically trained in the workshops of the Jamsetjee Jejeebhoy School of Art by the best masters of their craft, so that they might become efficient teachers in their own localities.

Lord Reay did not initiate the teaching of drawing in the primary and secondary schools of the Presidency, but he fostered it as the first step towards artistic training. New drawing-classes were being constantly opened during his administration, and were annually inspected. The advance made in this direction may best be shown by the statistics. In 1886–87, only 784 candidates from 52 institutions offered themselves for the first-grade examination in drawing, and 22 for the second-grade examination. By 1889-90, the numbers had increased to 1515 candidates for the first-grade, and to 177 for the second-grade examinations. Still more striking is the rapid growth in the number of children reported to be learning drawing in the schools for ordinary education, who in 1889–90 numbered 8413 as against 1600 in 1886–87.

Under Lord Reay's government an institution was founded for practical instruction in the mechanical industries, which should become the normal school for teachers of technical education throughout the Presidency—the Victoria Jubilee Technical Institute at Bombay. The scheme had many difficulties to surmount, among which may be noted the poverty of the Government and the suspicion of certain native gentlemen, deeply interested in educational work, that the money spent on technical education would be taken from other, and in their opinion more important branches. A grant from the Ripon Memorial Fund was obtained for the Textile Department. The Municipality of Bombay gave Rs. 80,000 and promised Rs. 5,000 annually. The Bombay Government felt justified in promising Rs. 25,000 a year, and subscriptions flowed in from wealthy merchants when the project was associated with the celebration of Her Majesty's Jubilee. It was wisely resolved not to be too ambitious at the start. The school was to be a technical, not a technological, institute. Only so much science as was required to make an intelligent and efficient workman, was to be taught; the training of millowners and managers in the higher branches of technology was not at first to be attempted.

Sir Dinshaw Manekji Petit, with his accustomed liberality, met the initial difficulty of finding an appropriate place, in which to house the infant institution. He presented a suitable building for the Government

Central Press, and the newly-erected buildings for that Press thus became available for the Elphinstone College, near the University. This left the old college in the heart of the manufacturing district vacant for the Technical Institute.

An English technologist, Mr. Phythian, C.E., was appointed the first principal, and so many students offered themselves that advertisements had to be inserted in the newspapers, stating that no more could be admitted. Work began in September, 1888, but the Institute was not formally opened until April, 1889. Lord Reay, in his inaugural speech, defined the scope of the teaching to be given. 'What we are doing here,' he said, 'is to supply to the artificer and the artisan of this Presidency that education which he wants, that education which will train his hand and eye, and through his hand and eye, also his mind, by the combination of mental and of manual training.'

The Victoria Jubilee Technical Institute consists of three separate departments. The main building, formerly the Elphinstone College, contains lecture-rooms, and the drawing-room, in which 120 students can study the drawing of machinery. The Sir Jamsetjee Jejeebhoy Technical Mechanical Engineering School contains the pattern-room, the foundry, the smithy supplied with eight anvils, the lathes, the machine-tool room, and the fitting-room. The Ripon Textile School is fitted up with a complete cotton-mill, containing the latest improvements in machinery, by means of which all the various processes connected with cotton, from the separation of the fibre from the pods to the weaving of ornamental fabrics of mixed cotton and silk, can be thoroughly learned. These are the two practical schools; but as the essence of sound technical education is to impart a knowledge of the principles involved in the use of machinery, the student has to spend two hours every day, throughout his three-years' course of the Textile or Engineering Schools, in the Physical Laboratory.

The Laboratory is divided into two sections, in one of which the laws of sound, light, and heat are taught; in the other electricity and magnetism. Students must be over fourteen years old at the date of admission, and must have passed the Fifth Standard. The latter regulation is necessary because the instruction is given in English and not in the Vernacular. As a matter of fact these regulations have caused no inconvenience, for of the 233 students who attended the first year's instruction in the new building, no fewer than 139 had passed the Seventh Standard, while their average age was twenty years. With the name of Lord Reay, in the foundation of this most useful institution, should also be recorded those of Sir Frank Forbes Adam, the Chairman of the first Board of Management, and of Mr. Nauroji N. Wadia, the first Honorary Secretary.

While the establishment of the Victoria Jubilee Institute at Bombay was the most important step taken towards a scheme of thorough technical education, other parts of the Presidency were not neglected. The workshops at the Poona College of Science afforded further scope for the boundless energy of Dr. Cooke. These workshops not only serve for the practical training of matriculated students reading for the Bombay University degree of L.C.E., but also as a junior department for technical training.

'The school there,' says Mr. Lee-Warner[1], 'is on the half-time system, the morning being devoted to mental education, the afternoon to practical training in the workshop, and the course extends from the age of thirteen to sixteen. The pupils learn drawing, mathematics, physics, chemistry, and the elements of various trades, the best practical workmen being engaged to teach these trades. It appears to me that any enterprising municipality, which is the centre of various trades, would do well to institute a school of this sort in place of the uniform Lower Anglo-Vernacular School, which is copied everywhere. But, in the first place, teachers are wanted, and I would gladly see the workshops of the Poona College largely increased, and the institution recognised as in part a sort of Technical Training College for teachers of a new class of Technical Secondary Schools, of which every District should have one.'

The people of Poona are quite aware, indeed, of the value of technical training. A large and interesting Industrial Exhibition was held there in 1888, which resulted in the formation of the Reay Industrial Museum. A group of native gentlemen have formed the Industrial Association of Western India to take over the management of the Museum, and generally to forward the cause of technical education. Technical

[1] Quoted in the *Note on Technical Education in India*, p. 23.

classes were also established in one of the Poona primary schools.

The Industrial School at Ratnágiri, under the management of a Local Committee, works on a smaller scale, as do various lesser industrial schools chiefly belonging to the Missionary Societies. It must, however, suffice to describe the schools founded by Khán Bahádur Kádirdád Khán in the backward province of Sind, in which the Governor took an especial interest. 'Mr. Kádirdád Khán's plan,' says Mr. H. P. Jacob, the Inspector of Schools in Sind [1], 'is an eminently sound one. Taking the staple industries of the district, for which there is a constant demand for young apprentices, he provides in each of his schools a thoroughly good training in the practice of these crafts. The workshops proceed on strictly business principles, every boy's work being assessed and paid for, and touch kept with the local market by the sale of the work turned out. At Moro the craft taught is turnery; at Naushahro the embroidery and needle-work for which Sind is famous; at Kàndiáro, where more elaborate arrangements have been made, joinery and cabinet-work, smithery in iron, silver-work and electro-plate, pottery, embroidery and needle-work.

'The local Zamindárs have everywhere volunteered their support, and have associated themselves with the Deputy-Collector on the committees of these schools; while the people at large have responded, simply because they have been shrewd enough to see

[1] *Report of the Director of Public Instruction in the Bombay Presidency for* 1887–88, p. 41.

that it is to the worldly advantage of themselves and their offspring that their boys should become intelligent and skilful craftsmen, able to earn better wages than the average workman now gets. Every boy spends three hours daily in the workshop, one hour in the drawing class, and three hours in the primary or Anglo-Vernacular school.'

As regards the geographical distribution of institutions, and putting on one side Bombay town as the capital, Poona is the best-endowed city in the Presidency from an educational point of view. It possesses not only the Government Deccan College and the independent Fergusson College, but also the industrial and scientific teaching given in the Poona College of Science. With such educational advantages, it is not to be wondered at that the Maráthá Bráhmans are the best-educated class in the Presidency, along with the Parsis, and that they fill a large proportion of the government offices. The Gujarátis felt this to be a grievance, and Lord Reay did what he could to remedy the supposed neglect of Gujarát by frequent personal visits, and by appointing a Gujaráti member to the Legislative Council of Bombay. The only Government College in British Gujarát, the Arts College at Ahmadábád, became an aided institution during his administration. It must be remembered, however, that Gujarát has the advantage of the College at Baroda, which is supported by the Gáekwár, and is in a very prosperous condition. An excellent division of labour would be for the Baroda College to take the scientific and the Ahmadábád College the classical side, but the difficulty is that science is not yet sufficiently recognised in India as a regular academic faculty.

Education in Sind made a vast stride forward during the five years. At the commencement of the period Sind had no college for higher education, notwithstanding its distance from Bombay, and both in primary and secondary education it was far behind the rest of the Presidency. Lord Reay endeavoured to remedy this. He gave the largest grants in his power to the Sind Arts College and to the Muhammadan Madrasa at Karáchi, and showed his sympathy towards both institutions by personal visits and words of encouragement. Both of these institutions are increasing in usefulness, and will open a new era in the educational history of Sind.

Not less noteworthy than the beginning of higher education in Sind, was the rapid development of primary and secondary education in the province. This was largely due to the sympathetic energy of the first English 'full-time' inspector of schools for Sind, Mr. H. P. Jacob, selected by Lord Reay. This gentleman was a valued member of the Indian Education Commission of 1882, and drew up the tables attached to its Report. He may be said to have breathed new life into education throughout the province of Sind. His principal coadjutor in arousing an interest in the cause was the Muhammadan Deputy-Collector, Khán Bahádur Kádirdád Khán, whose technical schools have already been noticed.

Closely connected with the state of education in

Sind is the more general question of the educational backwardness of the Muhammadans. From the days of Warren Hastings, who founded the Calcutta Madrasa in 1782, it has frequently been placed on record that the Muhammadan population of India do not take that share in the administration of the country, to which they are entitled by their numbers and previous history. This has been mainly caused by their unwillingness or inability to avail themselves of the advantages of the British-Indian system of education, which has made the Hindus able and useful servants of the Government. Muhammadan boys have to spend so much of their time in learning the Arabic Kuran and the precepts of their religion that they are not able to keep pace with the Hindu youth in the secular schools. The Education Commission of 1882 paid special attention to this problem, and a statement made by the Director of Public Instruction in the Bombay Presidency is printed in its Report. 'The Muhammadans,' he says, 'avail themselves of our lower schools, but do not rise to the higher schools and colleges. In the list of University graduates there are one Musalman M.A. and two B.A.'s. I think that the reason is to be found, not in the poverty of the Muhammadan community (for beggar Bráhmans abound in the high schools), but in their poverty and depressed social status combined. In this matter the Bráhman and Musalman are at opposite poles. Thus we have in Gujarát ten Bráhmans in the colleges and twenty in the high schools for every Musalman, but only three Bráhmans for every Musalman in the middle-class, and not two for every Musalman in the lower-class schools[1].'

In the Bombay Presidency, Mr., now Sir, J. B. Peile took measures to deal with this state of things. He obtained the appointment of a Professor of Persian and Arabic in the Elphinstone College; he drew up a course of instruction in Persian for the upper standards in vernacular schools, and for English and high schools; and he appointed Musalman Deputy Inspectors to inspect special Musalman primary schools. Yet the difficulty of getting Muhammadans to continue their education beyond the elementary stage still to some extent continues. That difficulty does not arise from any innate dislike for higher education. As far back as 1809 the Muhammadans of the Borah (merchant) class founded the Arabic College at Surat, which was for some years very successful, but 'secular studies never forming more than a nominal part of the college curriculum, the institution was never considered to be entitled to any aid from Government, and recently, for various reasons, it has fallen into complete decay[2].' In 1876, a Society, called the Anjuman-i-Islam, was started in Bombay with the object of developing Musalman education. It has done a good work in calling the attention of the Muhammadan community in the capital to the importance of the question, and has established a successful school. Similar societies are in existence at Poona and Ahmadábád, and the Honourable Kázi Sháhbudin,

[1] *Report of the Indian Education Commission*, p. 487.
[2] *Report of the Indian Education Commission*, p. 262.

the late Premier of Baroda, has founded scholarships for the reward and encouragement of his co-religionists.

The question of Muhammadan education in the Bombay Presidency is mainly concerned with Sind, for more than one-half of the believers in Islám throughout the Presidency are inhabitants of that province. When, therefore, I said that Mr. H. P. Jacob did a great work in Sind during Lord Reay's administration, it was tantamount to saying that he exercised a powerful influence on the education of the Muhammadans. This he did by his careful inspection of their primary schools throughout the province, and by the encouragement he gave to the Madrasa or Muhammadan College at Karáchi. The Madrasa, which I had the pleasure of visiting in November, 1885, when I examined the boys and recorded a favourable opinion on the management, was hampered by the want of a suitable building. Mr. Jacob urged its cause upon the Government, and he met with cordial support from Lord Reay. A Resolution of 30 September, 1889, sanctioning the building grant, stated that 'the Director of Public Instruction should be informed that Government wish to give to the Sind Arts College and the Sind Madrasa precedence *pari passu* over grants to other institutions.'

The only other religious body which deserve special notice besides the Muhammadans, are the Lingáyats, who chiefly dwell in the Kánarese-speaking districts. They, too, have formed a special educational association at Dhárwár, which raises funds to advance the education of their own sect. The association gives scholarships to Lingáyat boys to enable them to complete their education at the colleges at Poona and Bombay; and in 1888 it collected over Rs. 15,000 for the purpose of sending a Lingáyat student to England to compete for the Covenanted Civil Service or to read for the bar. As an instance alike of the loyalty and of the educational zeal of this sect, it may be noted that in 1887 fourteen Lingáyat gentlemen of Belgáum raised a sum of money in commemoration of the Queen's Jubilee, which is to be paid to the first Lingáyat M.A. and to the two first Lingáyat LL.B.'s, who may obtain those degrees from the University of Bombay. The Lingáyats, like the Muhammadans, feel aggrieved at the monopoly of administrative posts by the Maráthá Bráhmans, and presented a petition to the Governor on the subject. Lord Reay, in his reply, denied the existence of any monopoly, and advised the petitioners to study self-reliance, and to attain the same high standard of education which the Bráhmans had achieved.

The question of the education of what are known as the 'depressed castes,' arises from different causes. The unfortunate people belonging to this class in the Bombay Presidency were reckoned at about 1,100,000 in number by the Education Commission. They are probably descendants of aboriginal races, and have for ages been kept in a state of servitude and degradation. The villagers resent the idea of their former serfs receiving any education, and it was given in evidence before the Education Commission[1] that when some

[1] *Report of the Indian Education Commission*, p. 514.

promising low-caste boys were sent to the Government High School at Dhárwár a number of Bráhmans at once took their children away. In the face of this deep-rooted popular feeling the time has perhaps not come when it is possible to force the companionship of the despised Mhars and Dhers upon the boys of the higher castes. Accordingly, the Report of the Education Commission recommended the establishment of special schools for the low-castes. It expressly condemned, however, the notion that they had no right to go to the public schools, and only made its recommendation on the ground of expediency. In 1882, when the Commission commenced its labours, there were but 16 special schools in the Bombay Presidency, attended by 564 low-caste pupils. The annual Reports of the Director of Public Instruction do not contain quite complete information on this subject. In that for 1887–88 it is stated that there were 21 special schools or classes in the Southern Division attended by 554 children; besides eight special schools in the Northern Division (the number of pupils not being specified); and that there were 4,546 low-caste children under instruction in the Central Division 'distributed among the common and special schools.' A favourable distribution of Government scholarships was granted on behalf of these castes during the period under review.

The so-called aboriginal tribes are too shy to come to school at all. The two most numerous of these races in the Bombay Presidency are the Kolis and the Bhils. A Resolution of the Bombay Government in November, 1887, directed the establishment of special schools for them, six being in the Poona District near the Bhimáshankar Hills. The Bhils chiefly inhabit the Native States in the Rewá Kántha and Mahi Kántha Agencies, and it is gratifying to observe that something has been done for their education by the State of Rájpipla, where two schools for Bhils have recently been opened. Mr. Thompson of the Khedwára Mission has also opened a school for Bhils at Luseria in the Mahi Kántha Agency, and is trying the experiment of sending two Bhil boys to study at the Vernacular School at Sádra with a view to their becoming schoolmasters among their own race. The Government takes no fee from any member of an aboriginal race attending a public school.

From the education of depressed castes and aboriginal tribes to that of princes and nobles may seem a long step, but the problem with regard to the latter is equally difficult to solve. The well-known Rájkumar College at Rájkot for the education of the native princes of Káthiáwár was established to meet this demand. It has been instrumental in training many princes who have done good service to their States, and have been wise and able rulers. But it does not appear to retain its hold on the feudatory chiefs. The number of pupils sank from 44 in 1886–87 to 28 in 1889–90, and Lord Reay found chiefs like Morvi and Gondal, who were themselves *alumni* of the Rájkumar College, refusing to send their sons, and preferring England for their place of education. This decline is certainly not the fault of the Principal of the Rájkumar College, and Lord Reay attributed it to the desire of the most progressive Native Chiefs to give their sons a thoroughly English education, with English boys as their associates, if possible in England.

Another difficulty was how to dispose of the younger sons of these princes, when they were educated. As already stated, the Duke of Connaught is said to have been in favour of an Indian Sandhurst, and the admission of its cadets into the commissioned ranks of the native army. Sir Frederick Roberts, the Commander-in-Chief in India, and Sir George Greaves, the Duke of Connaught's successor as Commander-in-Chief in Bombay, were opposed to this idea. They felt the difficulty of having English officers under the orders of natives, however excellent in themselves, and feared the demoralisation which a wealthy prince might produce in a small regimental mess. In the social grade below the Chiefs, Lord Reay encouraged the Girasia School at Wadhwán for the education of the sons of the tálukdárs of Gujarát, and took special interest in the Mirs' School established for the descendants of the former rulers of Sind.

Public opinion in India is not yet unanimously in favour of female education. A good education is becoming generally recognised as a provision for a boy. But a daughter's education does not present itself to an Indian parent in the same light. Early marriages, moreover, cut short the course of female education, and what school-teaching a Hindu or Muhammadan girl is to obtain in India, she must practically get before she is eleven or twelve years old. Another difficulty is to provide female teachers to give even this amount of elementary instruction. The prejudice against widows (as persons stricken by the chastisement of the gods) makes them unacceptable. The ordinary Indian wife has no inducement to continue her education; and the most promising source of female teachers consists of the wives or future wives of schoolmasters. Miss Hurford, the Principal of the Poona High School for Girls and of the Poona Female Training College, and Mrs. McAfee, the Principal of two similar institutions at Ahmadábád, both give their particular attention to this class, and with excellent results. Indian youths who are training themselves as schoolmasters, quite understand the advantages of having an educated wife and a partner in the labours and the emoluments of teaching.

These institutions are directed by able ladies, but very great caution is required in ascertaining the characters of the girls who are admitted. Lord Reay met the difficulty at Poona by placing the responsibility for admission on a committee of native gentlemen, who would be more likely to know about the personal characters of the girls than any European. Mention should also be made of the Roman Catholic Convent School at Bándra, which Lord Reay visited with Archbishop Porter. His Excellency considered it a model institution. He also held a high opinion of the Alexandra Native Girls English Institution at Bombay, which is mainly under the management of Parsis and used for the education of their daughters.

Even more important for the true prosperity of a country than the scholastic results of its system of education is the tone of morality which it inspires. If its highly educated men lead good lives and are actuated by lofty aims, the influence of their careers reflects back on their education. If on the other hand, education is perceived to make men more cunning but not better, an equally evil effect is produced. This was felt to be the touchstone of the educational system in India, and on 31 December, 1887, the Supreme Government addressed a letter to the Local Governments and Administrations drawing their attention 'to the growth of tendencies unfavourable to discipline, and favourable to irreverence, in the rising generation in India,' and formulating certain suggestions, including the 'preparation of a moral text-book based on the fundamental principles of natural religion.'

On 2 October, 1888, the reply of the Bombay Government to this circular letter, founded on an elaborate minute by Lord Reay, was forwarded to the Supreme Government. It was observed that the problem was more complex and serious than a mere question of school discipline in Indian schools, and involved the influence of Western thought on Oriental minds. The moral defects attributed to the Indian schoolboy were not unknown among the rising generation in other countries. Irreverence, superficial scepticism and even immorality are not wholly absent from the public schools and Universities of Europe. The Government institutions of Bombay never aimed at more than the production of good conduct and intellectual discipline. Never having attempted a moral regeneration they could not be charged with failure because they had not effected it. Such a regeneration would be of very slow growth, and must lie in the hands of the people of India rather than in the hands of the Government. Internal reforms could alone cure the evil, and the first step was to raise the moral standard of those whom the people regarded as their natural leaders. Nevertheless, what Government could do would be done.

The importance of training-schools and colleges increased as Government retired from the direct management of schools, and measures were indicated by which the supply of better qualified teachers, especially in secondary schools, could be assured. It was proposed to introduce practical training-classes into specified high schools for graduates; to direct teachers to call the attention of their pupils to a consideration of their duties in life by illustrations of a patriotic, moral, and parental character derived from history. The extension of the boarding-house system involved serious financial difficulties, but much might be done by increased and more sympathetic intercourse between the professors or masters and their students—such as had been maintained successively by Sir Alexander Grant and Dr. Wordsworth. The monitorial system suggested by Mr. Jacob should be extended, increased attention given to the provision of playgrounds and manly games, and the experiment of conduct registers and rewards for good behaviour attempted.

I cannot more fitly conclude this chapter than in the words of a gentleman who took an active part on the Education Commission of 1882, and who has closely watched the efforts to give effect to its recommendations throughout the Bombay Presidency. 'The history of education in Bombay since 1885,' writes Mr. Lee-Warner, 'will hereafter be mainly known by the systematic efforts made to encourage private enterprise, and to give education a practical turn. Higher institutions of general education have been relieved of an undue strain and enabled to become real institutions for higher education. The University arts-examinations are no longer sought as mere passports to the public service, and the idea that education may assist the rising generation to become good mechanics, good agriculturists, and good men of business has been fostered. The establishment of the Victoria Jubilee Institute was regarded as an educational revolution, but its extraordinary initial success has disarmed opposition. The Government standards of education no longer dominate the whole course of aided schools. Variety and freedom have been generally introduced. Self-help has been evoked by the transfer of the management of schools to local bodies, and the Department has learned to look upon itself as responsible rather for the direction and encouragement of educational activity, than as a State Department for giving education and managing schools.'

CHAPTER VII.

FORESTS.

ANOTHER branch of the administration which brings the Government to very close quarters with the people is the Forest Department. As education exhibits the Government chiefly in contact with the progressive and well-to-do classes, so the Forest system discloses its dealings with the poorer cultivators and the hill and woodland communities. Circumstances gave special prominence to the Forest Department in the Bombay Presidency during the five years under review, and it is convenient that its measures should be explained at an early stage of this volume.

India was in ancient days a land of forests. The Mahábhárata contains direct and indirect evidence that forests covered the country, including many tracts now bare of woodland, such as the banks of the lower Jumna. The Ramáyána, which treats of a time when an Aryan Empire had been established in Oudh, speaks of forests dark as a cloud in the wilderness of Taraka. In the north of the Punjab, the Salt Range in the Pabbi was clothed with forest sufficiently dense to conceal the movements of the army of Alexander the Great. In the forests dwelt wild primitive races, who lived by hunting and on the produce of the woods. The Aryan settlers, as they slowly made their advance and introduced agriculture and civilisation, destroyed the forests before them; and the burning of the Khandava forest, probably situated between the Ganges and the Jumna, is a very early example of such a clearing on a great scale. The necessity of the nomadic tribes for wide stretches of grazing ground was perhaps even more destructive than the advance of an agricultural population, and hills and plains covered wth forest were fired to make new pastures for their flocks and herds.

The long-continued destruction of the forests is believed to have diminished the rainfall, and certainly to have rendered it less effective, in many parts of India. The numerous deserted villages which attest the former existence of a dense population, sites in now barren deserts, are pointed to as evidence of the change—a change also supported by the analogy of other countries, which have been deforested within historical times. The once well-wooded Dalmatia is in modern times a stony desert. Persia, formerly one of the granaries of the East, is barren and desolate over a large extent of the country. North Africa, the richest corn-producing colony of the Roman Empire and the chief granary of ancient Rome, is subject to the severest droughts. Parts of Spain, Italy, Sicily, Greece, and Asia Minor are also cited as examples of agricultural deterioration due to the denudation of the forests.

It is through their influence in absorbing, storing, and re-evaporating moisture, and so husbanding the rainfall, that forests affect the climate and productiveness of countries. Where rain falls upon a well-wooded forest area, it percolates slowly into the soil, whence a large quantity is gradually pumped up again through the roots of the trees, exhaled by their leaves, and again assists in forming rain-clouds. On the other hand, where it falls upon barren hills or open plains, it either rushes away in torrents or sinks into the sand with diminished facilities for re-evaporation. As long as the freshets, the streams, and rivers, carry fertile soil, the plains are benefited by the inundations caused by the rapid rush of water from mountains and high grounds. But when the good surface-soil has been scoured away, the cultivated fields are covered by the floods with unproductive sand and stones, and are ruined instead of benefited. The influence which forests exercise in controlling and regulating the water-supply is, however, now generally recognised. Specialists have analysed the causes of that influence, and have laid the bases for the study and practice of scientific forestry.

Scientific forestry is a creation of the present century, and first developed in France and Germany. Great results were hoped from it; the waste places of the world were to be made rejoice. Its natural limitations were forgotten. The fact that forests would as a rule only grow again where forests once had flourished, was not realised, and attempts were made to plant trees in unsuitable localities; attempts which, as in the case of the steppes of Russia, were foredoomed to failure. India was not behindhand in welcoming the new science. It was known that extensive areas had been denuded of their forests within historical times, and it was expected that careful conservation would do much to insure the country against periodical famines by regulating the rainfall. Efforts were made in different provinces, and in 1864 Mr., now Sir Dietrich Brandis, was appointed Inspector-General of Forests to the Government of India, and a Forest Department was regularly organised. In 1865 the first Indian Forest Act was passed, and in 1878 the second. These measures strengthened the idea that it was the duty of Government to preserve forests and to subject them to a separate jurisdiction. The working of a Forest Department demanded a special Forest service. It was at first recruited from members of the other services, possessing a special aptitude for forest work. But the need of a thorough scientific and professional training soon made itself felt. Young Englishmen educated at the Forest School at Nancy were then sent to India, and in 1884 a regular Forest School was established at Cooper's Hill.

In the Bombay Presidency the importance of preserving timber-trees had impressed itself on the Government before the idea of systematic and scientific forest conservation was introduced into the country. The right of the British Government, as the successor of the Maráthá power, to the possession of teak trees was already recognised in 1839 and acted upon. In 1847 Dr. Gibson was appointed the first Conservator of Forests in Bombay, and the scope of his authority steadily enlarged. The lopping of teak trees was prohibited in 1852; the prohibition was authoritatively extended to blackwood trees in 1859; and when the first general Forest Act for India was passed in 1865 considerable advance had already been made towards a system of conservation in Bombay. During the period between the two Acts of 1865 and 1878 the Bombay Forest Department increased in efficiency and energy. Its staff contained many able men full of énthusiasm for their work, convinced of the importance of forest conservancy as a factor in the prosperity of the Presidency, and ardent advocates for the extension of their powers. They were supported in their views by successive Governors, and especially by Sir Richard Temple (1877–80).

The Bombay Forest Department is divided into three divisions, the controlling, the executive, and the protective staff. The controlling staff consists of three Conservators of Forests, and of a certain number of Deputy and Assistant Conservators, each entrusted with the superintendence of a division. The executive staff includes Sub-Assistant Conservators, Forest Rangers, and Foresters. The protective staff consists of forest guards. The territorial unit of management is the 'range,' which is sub-divided into beats or protective charges; while a collection of ranges forms a division, or controlling charge. The upper places in the forest service are reserved for the trained Europeans from Nancy and Cooper's Hill; the rangerships and foresterships are destined for natives, specially educated for the service in the Forest Branch of the Poona College of Science. It is hoped that, as time goes on, selected men from among these trained rangers may be fitted by their experience and education for the superior charges.

The most important forests which the Bombay Department has under its charge, are those that clothe the Western Ghâts and spread down their slopes into the Konkan, between the mountains and the sea. These forests abound in teak and in all the most valuable timber trees which grow in India. Of only less importance are the forests in the thinly populated parts of the districts of Khándesh and Násik and the Panch Mahâls, and upon the eastern or inland side of the Ghâts. In Sind, what forest exists is of a totally different character. The nature of the soil there prevents the growth of the fine timber of the Ghâts; but the babúl (*acacia arabica*) flourishes within the range of the inundation of the Indus, and babúl reserves have been formed for the protection of these useful trees. Their extent, however, is comparatively small, and on March 31, 1889, there were only 624,026 acres of reserved or protected forest declared to exist in Sind out of the 9,407,549 acres of forest in the whole Presidency. In speaking of the administration of the forests in Bombay, therefore, it will be understood that Sind is practically excepted, by reason of its limited forest area, and the difference of the local conditions which prevail.

The first step towards the introduction of a sound forest administration, which should not only preserve existing forests, but also regulate their growth so as to make them yield the maximum of advantage with the minimum of expense, is to ascertain and record the situation and extent of the existing forests before placing them under special jurisdiction. This work of demarcation was provided for in both the Indian Forest Acts, and was carried out with special vigour in the Bombay Presidency during the government of Sir Richard Temple, when as many as six or seven Civil Servants were employed as special Forest Settlement Officers at the same time, besides those engaged in the work in addition to their ordinary duties.

During the vigorous period of forest development which followed, it was complained that a tendency appeared to make popular or customary rights subservient to the improvement of forest conservancy. The result was ascribed in part to the absence of sufficiently exact rules as to the manner in which the demarcation of forests ought to be carried out. The attention of Lord Reay's Government was drawn to the deficiency, and by a Government Circular dated September 22, 1885, precise instructions were laid down for the guidance of officers employed in this important preliminary work. Detailed orders were issued as to what facts and proposals each scheme of demarcation should comprise. Directions were given as to what share the Forest Settlement Officer, the Divisional Forest Officer, the Conservator of Forests and the Revenue Officers, should respectively take in furnishing them. Distinct information was to be given under three separate heads: (1) the disposition and (2) the capacity of the proposed forest area; with (3) the popular requirements for its use. The principle was at the same time enunciated that the only satisfactory forest settlement scheme is one which, after full consideration of all interests concerned, is unanimously recommended by both the Revenue and the Forest Departments with clear evidence that it adequately provides for the wants of agriculture as well as for beneficial forest conservancy.

Two classes of the population are affected by the demarcation of forests in India, those living in the forests, whose means of subsistence would be taken from them under a strict system of conservancy; and those who need the products of the woods and have been accustomed to use them, but are not so dependent upon them for existence. Both these classes have to be considered in any scheme for the demarcation of forests, and any forest policy which ignores their customary usages, even although short of legal rights, runs the risk of strenuous and well-founded opposition.

The first class of forest denizens consists of the aboriginal and semi-aboriginal tribes, who have from an almost prehistoric period dwelt in the woods, and who still lead the same life of savage freedom as their fathers before them. The Government of India has always wished to be considerate to these wild children of the forests. While trying to induce them to settle down and become civilised, it has recognised the impossibility of making a sudden change in their habits and mode of life. The Forest Department is, therefore, obliged to make allowance for the primitive tribes, and is not allowed to deprive them of their customary means of subsistence.

The use which they make of the forests is twofold. They earn what money they need by collecting forest produce, such as the nuts of the hirda-trees, the 'myrobalams' of commerce, gum, honey and beeswax, resins, and firewood. They also grow a small quantity of grain by a peculiarly destructive process of nomadic cultivation, known in different parts of India as dahya or dalhi, júm, or kumri, and in Burma as taungya. The system consists in setting fire to a tract of forest, and raising a crop from the ground thus cleared, with the ashes as manure. When they have exhausted the clearing by a rapid succession of crops, they move on to another tract and renew the wasteful process. Such a system, if unrestricted, is incompatible with any system of conservancy. At the same time the complete and sudden stoppage of all nomadic cultivation would inflict grave hardship on the wild tribes, who live by it; and it has to be allowed for in any scheme of forest demarcation. On the other hand, the collection of forest produce only needs careful regulation. There is no reason why the Bhils and Kátkaris, the Thákurs and Kolis, should not continue to collect and sell the articles which they best know how to find; and the Forest Department may perhaps make use of their knowledge of their native woods by employing them in subordinate positions.

The second class which has to be considered in the demarcation of forests consists of the inhabitants of villages in the neighbourhood of forests, who have been accustomed to graze their cattle beneath the trees, to take the timber they require for house-building or implement-making, to gather firewood, and to lop branches for burning into ash-manure. The unrestricted exercise of these customs for generations gives them the effect of popular rights, so that a sudden or total closure of the forest areas must cause great suffering and discontent. The Forest department in Bombay Presidency failed, at one period, to adequately realise this. In their zeal for forest conservancy, some of the Forest Settlement Officers closed woodland districts to the neighbouring hamlets, and curtailed the free use of the materials which the villagers had been accustomed to enjoy. The Revenue Officers urged the consideration of such customary rights, and came to open issue with the Forest Department. Indeed, it was the opinion of some of the most experienced of the District Officers that the continuance of a policy of wholesale demarcation of forests without sufficiently providing for existing customs would lead to outbreaks. The grievances of this class of forest borderers in the two districts of the Konkan nearest Bombay, Thána and Kolába, were brought to Lord Reay's notice immediately after he assumed office, and the measures taken to satisfy them form an important feature of the five years under review.

The district of Thána and the northern part of the district of Kolába, comprising the Northern Konkan, is a region particularly well suited to the growth of timber trees. Mountstuart Elphinstone speaks of it as formerly 'a thinly inhabited forest, from which character it has even now but partially emerged. . . . The descriptions of Captain Dickenson in his reports on the inland parts of this Collectorate show that at the end of the Peshwá's rule the whole country was lying waste and unpopulated. That up to about 1850 waste land was everywhere so abundant as to create a feeling of despair as to the future of the district; that the increase of cultivation was so much desired that the poorest people were allowed to cut down as many trees as they liked merely for the purpose of clearing the land, and that wood itself was so abundant that every one cut where and as he liked[1].'

The rapid growth of the city of Bombay made inroads upon these forests, for firewood and building timber. A lucrative trade sprang up, which absolutely denuded the hills nearest to the city and threatened to denude the whole district of Thána. The first Conservator of Forests in the Bombay Presidency, Dr. Gibson, confined his measures of conservation to the preservation of teak trees during several years after his appointment. But in 1850 he found it necessary to take further action, and replaced the transit duties on timber which had been abolished in 1836, by a system of fees on all jungle wood. This met with violent opposition, and in view of the agitation which Lord Reay found existing in Thána, it is curious to notice the existence of a similar popular ferment more than thirty years before. 'Of such clamour we had an example in 1851,' writes Dr. Gibson[2], 'when the Gujarát merchants and others in

[1] *Report of the Bombay Forest Commission*, vol. i. p. 21.
[2] *Ibid.*, p. 26.

the Sanján *táluká* shipped about 300 of the Várli tribe for Bombay, and marshalled them on the steps of the Council-room in order to concuss (coerce ?) the Government into a repeal of the jungle fee scheme, which had just then come into operation; and when I proceeded to Sanján in 1852, in order to make a final settlement, I was surrounded by some thousands of persons, all of them with the same object, and little disposed to stop short even of personal violence.'

If this was the attitude of the people of Thána in 1851, on the imposition of a slight restriction on the timber trade, it can be easily imagined that the procedure of the Forest Settlement Officers after the passing of the Indian Forest Act of 1878 led to a much more serious agitation. It was no longer a question of merely checking the export of timber to Bombay. Large areas were demarcated into forests, in which the inhabitants of the neighbouring villages were prohibited from getting wood for their own use, and were no longer allowed to graze their cattle. The agitation was, however, conducted in a lawful manner. So far as I have discovered, no acts of violence against forest officials were reported. They do not even seem to have been mobbed like their predecessor, Dr. Gibson. But a 'Thána Forest and Abkári Association' was formed; the native vernacular press was incited to take up the case against the Forest Department; and the powerful assistance of the Sarvajanik Sabha of Poona was granted to the agitators. Even more vigorous than the diatribes of the vernacular press was the language used in a pamphlet entitled 'A Few Words about Forest Conservancy in the Thána District of the Bombay Presidency,' published at the beginning of 1885.

'The citizens of Bombay, "who sit at home at ease,"' begins this vigorous philippic, 'will possibly be surprised to learn that within from twenty to seventy miles of their palatial residences lies a vast tract of country, in which nearly a million of inhabitants have been goaded, by the best-intentioned mismanagement, into a state of aggravation which might, at any time, culminate in a serious outbreak. It is fortunate for us, here, that the natives are, as a rule, patient and law-abiding; had any European population been subjected to the treatment that has fallen to the lot of the people of Thána, they would, despite the purely philanthropic motives of their rulers, have long since broken out into open rebellion, and, as it is, the local civil officers have more than once expressed the apprehension that the restrictions imposed upon the people would lead to "scenes of violence and possibly widespread disturbance."'

The gist of the writer's argument is contained in the following paragraph. 'Far worse than such illegalities,' he says (p. 10), '*to me* is the crying injustice on which the entire scheme of forestry in this unhappy district appears to have been based, rendering it to my view indefensible from first to last, and thoroughly rotten to the core. It is one thing for Government to appropriate almost virgin forests, in which at most a few hundreds of people, often mere savages, have enjoyed the privilege of taking such produce as they needed, and enclose these, leaving still to the excluded persons an ample open area, from which to supply unquestioned all their possible wants. Another for them to appropriate a vast wood-bearing area, over which the entire population of a densely populated district has from time immemorial exercised unchallenged all forest rights; to close this arbitrarily without any pretence of compensating any one for the losses thus entailed, and to commence charging a price for all those articles that the people have hitherto supplied themselves with without any payment to any one.'

The publication of this pamphlet, which attracted great attention in India and some in England, co-operated with other considerations to render it expedient for the Government of Bombay to vindicate, or to amend, its forest policy. Lord Reay had not been many days in office, before—on April 9, 1885—an influential deputation of native gentlemen from the disturbed districts waited upon him. They laid their views before the Governor in a somewhat lengthy, but on the whole temperately worded memorial, and concluded their petition by saying: 'Our prayer is that, being satisfied of the substantial accuracy of our statements, your Excellency will (1) direct a temporary suspension of the present Forest Rules, which are harsh and illegal, and (2) appoint a Commission of Enquiry, composed partly of experienced European officials and partly of independent Native gentlemen.'

Lord Reay decided to accede to the second request of the petitioners, and on July 24, 1885, a strong Commission was appointed, whose Report is of the utmost value and marks an epoch in the history of Forest Conservation in Bombay. The words of the Government Resolution appointing the Commission defined its aim with brevity and precision. 'The Governor in Council—wishing to secure an efficient management of forests, and believing that the conservancy of forests and the maintenance of the rights of the Crown is beneficial to the interests of the people in providing for a continuous supply of timber; wishing to secure the agricultural wants of the people and the privileges they have hitherto enjoyed for the legitimate fulfilment of these wants; convinced that where friction has arisen in the management of forests, especially in Thána, such friction is due to a misunderstanding which can be removed; desirous to give to all parties concerned the means of bringing their views before Government—institutes a Commission, &c.'

The Commission consisted of four English and three Native members, and represented every type of opinion. The English members were Mr. G. W. Vidal, the Chairman, Acting Collector of the District of Thána, and one of the ablest members of the Bombay Civil Service; Lieutenant-Colonel Peyton, Conservator of Forests, Southern Circle, a forest officer of the old school, famous as a sportsman, who had killed more tigers than almost any other man in the Presidency; Mr. R. C. Wroughton, Deputy-Conservator of Forests, a representative of the scientific school of forest officers; and Mr. E. C. Ozanne, C. S., Director of Land Records and Agriculture, Bombay. The native members were Ráo Sáheb Rámchandra Trimbak Achárya, District

Government Pleader, Thána, and member of the Thána Local Board and Municipality, representing local discontent, who succeeded Ráo Bahádur Dáji Govind Gupte (originally nominated) before any evidence was taken; Ráo Bahádur Krishnáji Lakshman Nulkar, formerly president of the Poona Sarvajanik Sabha, and now a member of the Viceroy's Legislative Council; and Ráo Bahádur Yeshvant Moreshvar Kelkar, Assistant to the Commissioner S.D. who acted as Secretary to the Commission, now Oriental Translator to the Government of Bombay.

The Bombay Forest Commission was formally opened in the Council Hall at Poona on August 27, 1885, on which occasion Lord Reay delivered a speech, which attracted great attention at the time, and which it is necessary, for the proper appreciation of the subsequent measures, to quote at some length. 'Mr. Chairman and gentlemen,' said the Governor, 'I have asked permission to attend here to-day to thank you in the first place for the way in which you have placed your services at the disposal of the Government. You have a very delicate and difficult task to perform. You will, I am sure, acquit yourselves of the trust reposed in you with complete independence. The value of your labours will be enhanced, if you lay down in your report the conclusions to which you may have been led by the inquiry, however varied they may be. It is perhaps not superfluous for me to add that the members of the Commission who represent the Civil Service, are not acting in any way on the Commission as delegates or representatives of Government, but have been appointed to give their own views, the results of their own experience. You will, on the other hand, have to deal not with individual actions or the opinions of individual Government officers, but with the effect of Resolutions for which Government is alone responsible. As long as the actions of a Government officer are sanctioned by the open or tacit approval of Government, Government is responsible.

'I need not here enter elaborately on the various causes which have led to the appointment of this Commission, but it is a remarkable fact that both the late and present Secretary of State have approved of the institution of this inquiry, and the sanction of His Excellency the Viceroy has also been obtained. The importance of the subject has been recognised, therefore, on all sides. Since I have had the honour of being charged with my present duties, the matter has been a constant source of anxiety to me. Agricultural problems have always struck me as peculiarly interesting, and the more one looks into the various agricultural systems of various countries, the more one becomes convinced that over-legislation in agricultural matters is a mistake, and that in the present condition of agricultural science, which is not by any means as far advanced as it ought to be, we must be careful to interfere as little as possible. Agricultural centralisation would certainly lead to disastrous consequences.

'In his speech on the Indian Budget, the Secretary of State asked the question, how are you on the one hand to obtain the most desirable objects of preserving and renewing the forests, without on the other hand entailing hardships on the people by depriving them of valuable and long-established rights? That is the question which has constantly presented itself to me. I believe, however, that if Forest Conservancy tends to increase the supply of fodder and fuel for the people of this country, the enterprise will meet with their support, and has a right to their sympathy. I also believe that the hardships can be mitigated, and that we have recently done a great deal to reduce them to a minimum. My chief object is to substitute co-operation for antagonism, confidence for mistrust, contentment for disturbance. The worst result of centralisation is that measures, which must inevitably benefit the people ultimately, take a longer time for their acceptance than if they had been settled locally.

'In every forest settlement which I have dealt with, I have always carefully considered the peculiar circumstances of the locality, the existing resources for the feeding of cattle and for the extension of cultivation, and the advantages which would accrue to the inhabitants from Forest Conservancy. And here, gentlemen, let me say that I believe that if your district boards had to deal with these questions, they would not in their decisions come to conclusions differing very materially from those to which we have come. We are at great disadvantage, because we have very often to decide at a distance intricate questions, and I for one have very keenly felt the responsibility of deciding between the conflicting opinions of local officers, who perform their difficult duties with great care.

'One thing, however, is quite clear. If you wish to

have improved fodder and more fuel, you must allow your plantations to grow; you must protect the young growth by closing such areas; you must close those areas in such a way that you cause a minimum of inconvenience to those who used to find on such areas pasture for their cattle. On the grazing question your report will no doubt throw light, but meanwhile you may take for granted that it is the determination of Government that, wherever free grazing has been lawfully enjoyed, it will be continued by giving a full equivalent in all those cases where the area hitherto used has been absorbed. I do not think that the people will have anything to complain of, as the equivalent will be an improvement on what formerly provided them with an insufficient supply. How, when, and where areas are to be closed; how, when, and in what numbers cattle are to be admitted to open areas, and on what conditions, seem to me to be essentially questions which must be settled on the spot by the combined action of the revenue officers and the forest officers, and on which Government can only lay down general principles.

'Your Commission will fulfil the mandate contained in the Government Resolution of July 24, unhampered by any extraneous influence. A speedy, full, and local investigation of the Forest Conservancy of the district of Thána will, however, be most welcome to the Government, as it wishes to obtain your advice in detail on the situation of that district, which affords scope for the examination of nearly all the questions with which Government have to deal. You will, I doubt not, assist the Government in its endeavours to remove legitimate grievances. You will also assist Government in preventing wanton destruction of timber—a proceeding utterly unwarrantable, and most demoralizing and injurious to the local and national interests.

'A strong Government does not stand in need of exceptional measures to put a stop to such vandalism. This Commission will strengthen, not weaken, the ultimate action of Government. It will uphold law and order; promote one of the chief elements of agriculture, namely, good pasture; promote harmony between the administration on the one side and the people on the other, whose interests will be ably represented on this Commission, not only by those whom they will perhaps more especially consider as their representatives, but also by officials, whose desire I know, from personal experience, it is to preserve to the people privileges, to which naturally they attach great value.'

The Bombay Forest Commission held 123 meetings for the examination of witnesses and the preparation of its Report between August 27, 1885, and December 18, 1886. The completed Report was submitted to Government in April, 1887. The printed record of the labours of the Commission fills four volumes, and it is not too much to say that a careful study of these volumes is indispensable for every one who wishes to form a correct estimate of the difficulties which beset the demarcation of forest areas in the Bombay Presidency. Fortunately for the members of the Commission, they were saved the waste of time and trouble that would have ensued if they had had to deal with the complaints against the Forest Department individually. The local population entrusted its case in Thána District to the Thána Forest Association, which had by its vigorous agitation secured the appointment of the Commission; and in Kolába District to the Kolába Forest Sabha, a similar body. This procedure simplified matters. An experienced pleader, Mr. S. H. Chiplonkar, arranged the grievances complained of in an intelligible order, and brought the evidence to bear with some regularity upon each point.

From the Report issued by the Forest Commission it appears that the customs or rights of the inhabitants of villages bordering on forests or included in demarcated forest areas, which must be recognised and either allowed or compensated in future forest settlements, may be divided into two general heads, namely, grazing and wood-cutting. These are common to the whole Presidency of Bombay, but special consideration must be given in the Thána and Kolába Districts to their peculiar system of cultivation.

The question of grazing is almost certain to arise wherever a line of forest demarcation runs near a village boundary. The inhabitants of such villages generally pasture their cattle in the nearest suitable locality, whether it is covered with trees or not. The gáirán or communal grazing ground, in the case of a village on the plains usually a plot of waste or uncultivable land, might in a wooded district form portion of a valuable forest. But the grazing of cattle, and still more of sheep and goats, does incalculable damage to the growth of young trees. There is therefore a natural inclination on the part of energetic forest officers to wish to exclude cattle from the forests under their charge; it is equally natural for the villagers to resent being deprived of a valuable prescriptive privilege; and the land-revenue officers, whose interest it is to promote cultivation, are the natural allies of the villagers against encroachments by the Forest Department.

The Government of Lord Reay had therefore to mediate between the Forest Department and the villagers. In this matter it did not wait for the Report of the Commission, but on September 15, 1885, issued a code of rules for the regulation of grazing rights in forest areas. It directed that, wherever gáirán or village pasture-lands had been taken into forest, free grazing must be granted, either in those parts of the forest lands not actually occupied by the forest officers for the purpose of forest conservancy, or in those parts which had been closed for the preservation of young trees, as soon as they can safely be opened. This privilege is reserved for cattle kept for agricultural purposes, and is not permitted for cattle kept for profit or trade. The code was followed by a Resolution, on October 9, 1885, which, in passing orders for the Forest Settlement of Sholápur táluká, instructed the land-revenue, *not the forest*, officers to prepare an estimate of the amount of grazing available outside the forest area, especially in waste lands; and of the legitimate grazing requirements of each village. It provided that where the outside grazing was insufficient, the deficiency must be supplied by permitting grazing over part of the forest land. On February 25, 1886, the term 'cattle kept for agricultural purposes' was ruled to mean the cattle required for the proper cultivation of the agriculturist's holding, and a cow or she-buffalo kept to supply the agriculturist's family with milk for their home consumption.

While discouraging professional graziers in the border forest villages by the imposition of grazing fees, the Government was not unmindful of the necessity of encouraging cattle-breeding where the local conditions were more favourable for that industry than for agriculture. The Panch Maháls District, for instance, is specially adapted for the rearing of cattle, and by a Resolution dated April 29, 1887, the Governor in Council directed that this natural advantage should be carefully fostered, and every reasonable encouragement given to the industry in that particular locality.

On August 27, 1889, the Bombay Government reviewed the recommendations of the Forest Commission with regard to grazing in the Thána and Kolába Districts. These recommendations, arranged in thirteen articles, had laid down elaborate rules and precautions on the subject. They were approved and sanctioned by the Government for the two districts, but the approval was accompanied by various observations and modifications, of which the most important concerned free grazing. Thus, that the exercise of this privilege be limited by the closure which the Forest Department, after approval by the land-revenue officers, might impose in areas for necessary purposes of forestry; and that the number of cattle admitted to graze free of charge should not be in excess of the number for which the area open could be expected to furnish a sufficient supply of grazing. Further, that the cattle should not be allowed access at the season when it is deemed requisite to close the forest to permit the growth of the young grass.

The Government issued definite orders on September 14, 1889, that where land originally gáirán had been included in forest, free grazing must either be allowed over it, or, if its closure for afforestment is deemed absolutely necessary, over an equivalent area of other forest or waste land, possessing equal grazing capabilities. It is important to clearly apprehend the scope of these provisions with regard to grazing. They illustrate the even balance maintained by Lord Reay's Government between justice to the villagers and the needs of forest conservancy. They also explain the standpoint from which that Government dealt with the pre-existing forest agitation, and quieted it.

The other general question which almost necessarily arises during the demarcation of forests bordered by or including villages, has reference to the right of wood-cutting or timber-felling. If forest officers dislike cattle-grazing on their domains, they more strenuously oppose unlicensed cutting and felling. There are two distinct sides to this latter question. Just as villagers in forest villages had been always accustomed to pasture their cattle in the wooded districts, so they had been wont to fetch what wood they wanted, whether for fuel, or for making implements or mending their ploughs, &c. This unlimited liberty had to be checked. For the first requisite of forest conservancy is the power to preserve the trees. But the Forest Commission, and in accordance with its recommendations the Government, resolved to deal liberally with fair prescriptive rights. The people were, indeed, forbidden to cut at their pleasure, but the wild tribes and the poor were permitted to pick up dead wood for fuel, and to take away, free of charge, the small branches and twigs lopped off at the periodical Government fellings. Free grants of timber for building purposes and for agricultural implements were also allowed as some compensation for former privileges.

The trade in timber or firewood, a brisk one in the neighbourhood of a capital, further complicates matters in the Thána District, which is the nearest timber-producing region to the city of Bombay. It was the Gujarátí timber merchants who fomented the agitation against Dr. Gibson's jungle-fee in 1851—the agitation which led to the first Conservator of Forests in Bombay being mobbed at Sanján in the following year. Ever since the Department was established, the difficulties caused by the extensive timber trade from Thána, and by the temptation given by its large profits to evade the regulations issued for its control, had been the source of numerous schemes and expedients. The Bombay Forest Commission made a bold effort to grapple with the situation. The difficulty of identifying timber had always afforded the chief opening for fraud. It was quite impossible to assert that any particular log of wood came from a Government Forest when once it was on the road. The invariable allegation was that it came from a private owner. Government trees were therefore frequently felled and passed off as the products of occupied holdings.

The practical method of dealing with this difficulty seemed to the Forest Commission to obtain legislation for the control in transit of all tree produce, whether obtained from forests or private holdings. In return for this interference with a private owner's rights in the timber growing on his own soil, it was proposed that all Government trees, such as teak and blackwood, in occupied lands, should be guaranteed to the occupants for domestic and agricultural purposes: subject to the restrictions that (1) the tree produce of occupied lands should be utilised exclusively to meet local as distinguished from trade demands, and that (2) if the land on which the trees grew had been uncultivated for ten years or more, it should not be cleared for cultivation. The Bombay Government laid the request for special legislation before the Government of India. The Supreme Government complied, and on February 28, 1890, the Forest Act Amendment Bill became law. The legislation required by the Forest Commission for the success of the experiment being thus fulfilled, the Bombay Government issued a Resolution, dated April 8, 1890, dealing with the scheme proposed by the Commission on somewhat modified lines.

The right of grazing and the right of cutting wood have to be reckoned with in every scheme of forest demarcation, where the boundary approaches or encloses parts of inhabited villages. But in Thána and Kolába

Districts there was another prescriptive right peculiar to the local method of rice cultivation, which also brought the inhabitants into collision with the Forest Officers. According to this method, known as *ráb* cultivation, the beds for the rice seed are prepared by burning layers of cow-dung, tree-loppings, leaves and grass. The Forest Conservators naturally object to the collection of the tree-loppings, which form an important part of the ráb or ash manure. It was argued that this system was wasteful and barbarous, and little, if any, superior to the nomadic cultivation by burning down temporary clearings and then deserting them for new ones. Rice was grown in other parts of India without destroying the branches of the trees, and it was asserted that the innate obstinacy and backwardness of the local cultivators alone maintained the ráb system.

Whether this system was to be permitted or prohibited was one of the points to be investigated by the Forest Commission; and Mr. E. C. Ozanne, the Director of Agriculture in the Bombay Presidency, and a member of the Commission, made a series of experiments with regard to it. They proved that at least twice as good a harvest of rice could be raised from seedlings transplanted from a nursery or seed bed prepared with *ráb*, as from one treated with ordinary manure[1]. The words in the opening address of the Governor to the Commission thus received an unexpected confirmation. 'In many instances,' he had said, 'a scientific justification for local agricultural

[1] Mr. Ozanne's experiments are detailed in an Appendix to vol. i. of the *Report of the Bombay Forest Commission*, pp. 221–241.

practices unconsciously observed by the population will be forthcoming.'

In consequence of these experiments, the Forest Commission recommended that the cultivators in villages of the Thána and Kolába Districts which had contributed lands to the Forest Department, might, as a temporary privilege and until further orders, make up the deficiency of their ráb supply by taking loppings from certain specified kinds of trees from the unclosed portions of forests, in addition to removing grass, leaves, reeds, and brushwood from these areas, and that they might also remove grass from the closed portions of the forests. In reviewing this recommendation the Bombay Government observed on August 27, 1889, that to prohibit absolutely the lopping of all trees and the cutting of all shrubs and brushwood in the State forests would doubtless facilitate Forest Conservancy, and increase the timber-producing capacity of the forests. But the prohibition would, in some tracts, be disastrous to agriculture, and check superior cultivation. The Forest Department would have to superintend, not to check, the ráb supply in order to avoid waste, as it was undesirable and impossible to withdraw all the privileges in respect of ráb supply hitherto enjoyed. At the same time it was to be remembered that the available supply, whether from the forests or from trees in occupied lands, is limited, and it is necessary in the interests not only of the present but also of future generations, that the cultivators should practise economy in the consumption of their own ráb resources, as well as of those of the State.

The chief points to be considered in the demarcation of forests from cultivated land in the Bombay Presidency have now been noticed, together with the principles laid down by Lord Reay's Government for the guidance of forest settlement officers. It remains to examine the treatment of the wild aboriginal tribes, who are absolutely dependent on the woods for their living. Their nomadic system of dalhi or kumri cultivation, which is much more primitive and wasteful than ráb cultivation, notwithstanding the analogy drawn between the two by enthusiastic forest officers, has been over and over again condemned by the Bombay Government, as it has been by the other Provincial Governments in India. The ordinary custom of these tribes to wander from place to place in the forest tracts, and to burn down patches for temporary clearings, has done more to check the progress of Forest Conservation than ráb cutting in its extreme and most abused forms. Lord Reay's Government recognised the evil, and made several attempts to check it. A Government Resolution, dated August 3, 1885, ordered that all possible inducements should be offered to the dalhi cultivators in the Peint Táluká of the Násik District to abandon the practice and to resort to less destructive methods of agriculture, and it was distinctly laid down that no expansion of the custom would be permitted in the future. A more stringent Resolution was published on April 13, 1888, with regard to the same District, declaring that the custom must be extinct after the next generation.

But it is one thing to proscribe their wasteful method

of cultivation, another to deprive the wild tribes of the means of earning their livelihood in the woods. In this regard the Bombay Government cordially endorsed the views of the Bombay Forest Commission. 'There is every reason to hope,' say the Commissioners in the Report[1], 'that much additional work will be found for the wild tribes, when the completion of working plans will enable the Forest Department to carry out felling operations up to the maximum legitimate yield of the forests. All the labour in connection with the annual fellings should, in future, be entrusted to the wild tribes as far as possible.' With reference to the subsistence to be derived from the collection of forest produce, such as gums and resins, myrobalams, and the flowers of the mahuá tree, the Commissioners also speak hopefully. 'The wild tribes,' they say[2], 'owing to their local knowledge of the jungles and the localities where the different products are to be obtained, now have, and probably always will have, a practical monopoly of the right of collection. Without their co-operation, collection of forest produce on a large scale would be difficult, if not impossible. This fact will, we believe, always ensure fair rates being paid to them, whether they sell to private customers or to the Forest Department.'

In spite of the favour shown to the wild tribes, it was believed that certain criminal proceedings on the part of the Kolis, an aboriginal tribe, in the Junnar Táluká of the Poona District, which were brought to

[1] *Report of the Bombay Forest Commission*, vol. i. p. 122.
[2] *Ibid.*, vol. i. p. 106.

the attention of the Bombay Government in 1887, were caused by the strictness of Forest Conservancy. A special inquiry was ordered into the condition of the Kolis, not only in the Junnar Táluká, but also in the Khed and Máwal Tálukás of the Poona District and in the Akola Táluká of the Ahmadnagar District. The officer who conducted the inquiry reported that the Kolis were moderately well off, deriving a considerable income from the sale of myrobalams, and that they were in no way hampered or aggrieved by Forest Conservancy. He attributed their tendency to form dacoit bands to their hereditary customs and instincts. Among the remedies he suggested was the provision of more land for the extension of cultivation; and accordingly in July, 1888, one hundred and thirty-three acres of reserved forest were disforested, and nearly twenty thousand acres, which had been included in the demarcation scheme for the Junnar Táluká, were abandoned.

The difficulties and popular agitation which Lord Reay found on his arrival in Bombay were largely due to the circumstance that the forests were not properly defined and demarcated. It took some further time for the rural population to become generally acquainted with the privileges which were restored to them. Before Lord Reay left India the important work of settlement had greatly advanced. It is work which can be done once for all, and the real aims of Forest Conservancy cannot be pursued until it is done. When the Forest Department knows the exact limits of the forests under its charge, and what local or tribal rights exist over them, it can turn undisturbed to its proper functions, the preparation and carrying out of regular working plans.

Lord Reay's activity was mainly concerned with the principles of demarcation, but he also took a keen interest in the development of the working plans. The object of these plans is to ensure the working of the forests in such a way as to carefully husband their resources. They take account of the forest capital and growing stock; they arrange for regular fellings at periodical dates; they re-stock the cleared areas and preserve the young trees until they are strong enough to be left to themselves. As the work of forest settlement approaches completion this becomes the essential duty of the Department.

Another measure undertaken by Lord Reay's Government was the reorganisation of the subordinate Forest Establishment. For this purpose the Bombay Government appointed a Special Committee in July, 1889, to settle the details of reforms. It consisted of the chief officers of the Forest Department, the Commissioners of Divisions, Dr. Cooke (Principal of the Poona College of Science), and Mr. G. W. Vidal, who had been the Chairman of the Forest Commission. The Committee presented its report on February 14, 1890. It deals chiefly with the reorganisation of the executive and protective staffs, and proposes that the number of Sub-Assistant Conservators of Forests and Rangers, who form the executive staff, should be increased from thirteen and forty respectively to twenty-four and one hundred and sixty-three, and that the protective staff and the office establishments shall also be strengthened. It recognises the importance of employing trained natives, who have passed through the course of instruction in the Forest Branch of the Poona College of Science, and proposes a liberal scale of pay and travelling allowances for them. The requisite additional expenditure to carry out this scheme of reorganisation is estimated at slightly over two lakhs of rupees.

The necessity for defining the relative position of the forest officers to the general administration of the Presidency was not less needful than the reorganisation of the Forest Establishment. A Bombay Government Resolution, dated April 8, 1890, on the eve of Lord Reay's departure from India, pointed out that responsibility for a wise and efficient management of forest matters rests upon Collectors and their assistants as well as on officers of the Forest Department. Forest administration was stated to be as much a branch of the general administration requiring the direct supervision of the Collector and Magistrate as any other branch of Revenue or Police Administration.

It was clearly inexpedient that the forest officers should exercise independent authority when the Collector is made responsible for the welfare of the people of the district. The Forest Department, like all other special departments, supplies the general administration with technical knowledge. But in providing a special establishment for forest purposes, Government did not intend, and it could not allow, the ordinary executive to be relieved of any responsibility which before attached to it. It remained a part of the duty of village and revenue and police officers to protect Government property in trees, as it was a part of their duty before trees were transferred to the Forest Department. This being the case, it is obvious that the members of the lower grades of the Forest Service, such as the forest guards, who form the protective staff, and must depend largely for the efficient discharge of their duties on the co-operation of the village officers and the police, ought to be placed to some extent under the supervision of the Revenue and Police officers.

This question was referred to the Forest Establishment Reorganisation Committee, who in an Appendix to their Report have drawn up seven simple rules on the subject. The most important of them provide that, 'when a Mahálkari or Chief Constable, or any Revenue or Police Officer of higher rank, camps in the limits of a forest village, or in the limits of a beat or round, the forest guard shall report himself to such officer, and bring his diary with him for inspection'; yet that 'No Revenue or Pòlice Officer shall punish or censure a forest guard, but, if he deems it necessary, shall report the result of his enquiries and observations to the Divisional Forest Officer.'

From one point of view, the forest administration of the Bombay Presidency may be dealt with as a system instituted for the good of the country, for the preservation of an important source of its natural wealth, and for the advantages believed to be obtained from it in regulating the rainfall and preventing erosion. This was the point of view from which Lord Reay himself mainly regarded it. But it has another side, as a source of revenue, and this was not neglected during the period under review.

The result of the vigorous forest policy inaugurated in 1879, after the passing of the Indian Forest Act of 1878, and consistently carried out under successive Governors of Bombay, may thus be briefly stated.

Excluding Sind, where forest revenue and expenditure have hardly altered, the gross revenue from forests in the Bombay Presidency proper has risen from Rs. 11,14,254 in 1879–80 to Rs. 24,34,322 in 1888–89, or rather more than doubled. The nett revenue has grown from Rs. 3,40,888 in 1878–79 to Rs. 10,31,309 in 1888–89, or more than trebled during the ten years. The totals for the whole Presidency, including Sind, were in 1878-79, gross forest revenue Rs. 15,24,712, nett forest revenue Rs. 4,64,095; and in 1888–89, gross forest revenue Rs. 28,50,189, nett revenue Rs. 11,61,065.

The forest administration of Lord Reay will repay careful study. He found the Forest Department at issue with the Revenue officials and disliked by the people, and he set himself to remove the causes of the official dissension and of the popular dislike. He found discontent and agitation in Thána and Kolába Districts; he put an end to the disturbances by the issue of special orders, by the appointment of an impartial Commission, and by promptly giving effect to the equitable changes which it proposed. He found that the vigorous impulse given to forest policy in previous years had gone so far as to exceed the limits of justice to the people; he gently but firmly restrained the ardour of the Forest Department without diminishing its efficiency. In his speech at the opening of the Forest Commission, during the first year of his government, Lord Reay used these words: 'My chief object is to substitute co-operation for antagonism, confidence for distrust, contentment for disturbance.' He succeeded in attaining his object.

CHAPTER VIII.

Land Administration.

ONE distinction between the administration of India and the administration of a modern European State is, that in India the British Power not only governs the country but owns the land. It is, theoretically, the universal landlord as well as the administrative authority, and its servants in the executive department are not only rulers but estate agents. This conception, that the *dominium* of the soil vests in the ruling power, formed the basis of the mediaeval theory of sovereignty in the West, but has now little more than an historical interest in Europe. It is still, as it has always been, practically recognised in the East.

As the East India Company conquered and annexed province after province in India, it placed itself in the position of the former rulers, and assumed their rights and duties. It also continued their administrative and financial policy, modified by the introduction of modern ideas. This was a main cause of its success. It attempted no violent revolution or subversive change, but was content to adopt the attitude of its predecessors to the people and to the land.

The East India Company found that all former

governments, whether of Hindu rájás, or Muhammadan kings and emperors, or Maráthá conquerors, had derived nearly the whole of their revenue from their position as the supreme landlords. Their subjects paid them a large aggregate rental, besides less productive although sometimes vexatious and numerous taxes. This rental was collected by different methods and under various systems, but it formed and still forms the most important portion of the revenue of India. Sometimes the sovereign took one-half, sometimes two-thirds of the produce of the soil. Sometimes an estimated money equivalent was received in place of a share of the produce; sometimes the rent was remitted as an allowance for certain services. Sometimes it was exacted by officers of the government, sometimes let out to farmers, who paid a lump sum for the privilege and made what profits they could.

Local circumstances had much to do with these differences. It might be more convenient to take the State rental in money, where there was a recognised revenue unit, such as an organised village system; but in backward districts and among primitive communities, it was only possible to take it in kind. It might be more economical to collect the State rental directly from the cultivator; but in distant provinces with imperfect means of communication, or in times when the government was weak and unable to enforce its demands, it was necessary to have recourse to revenue farmers, with all their attendant evils. When the government was at once strong and enlightened, as under the Emperor Akbar, it recognised its duties as chief landlord. It understood that if the cultivators were to pay a high rent, and the State to collect a large land-revenue, something must be done to encourage agriculture, by irrigation and other public works. The British Government, on becoming the supreme landlord, acknowledged these obligations to the land, and has spent large sums on irrigation, on means of communication, and on measures to improve the knowledge of agriculture among the people.

The wide differences in the systems of collecting the land-revenue adopted by the East India Company for its various territories were mainly due to historical reasons and local conditions. The point common to them all was the recognition of the Company as the supreme landlord. In Bengal the employment of farmers of the revenues was found at work. The first English administrators, therefore, adopted this agency; and eventually in 1793 the amount of rent was fixed in perpetuity.

This converted the mixed body of Bengal Zamindárs and revenue-farmers into proprietors, subject to their regular payment of the stipulated rent. The Company believed that it thus secured the advantages of a body of responsible landlords, of rendering the revenue-collection more secure, and of encouraging agriculture by granting fixity of tenure. In the North-Western Provinces it found, *inter alia*, a system of co-parcenary village communities, and arranged to levy the rent from them as units, but on a settlement for a term of years, and not fixed for ever as in Bengal. In Madras an attempt to create a homogeneous body of proprietory

Zamindárs failed; the village communities were also found to have there lost much of their cohesion (if they had ever possessed it in a high degree), and it was arranged to collect the rent directly from the cultivators or ráyats.

There is no need to censure any of these systems. Each has its advantages and disadvantages. The Bombay system, which I am about to describe, differs from all three, and if its advocates claim for it the maximum of the advantages of the other methods with the minimum of their disadvantages, it must be remembered that it was initiated at a later date and after much experience gained in older Provinces. There were, moreover, historical causes which led the Bombay land-settlement to assume its present form, and it is by an examination of these causes that it can best be explained and understood.

It may be premised that the same ideas lay at the root of the Bombay, as of the Bengal, North-Western Provinces and Madras systems. The importance of fixity of tenure for a long term of years, in order that the cultivator might not be disheartened by fears of a sudden and arbitrary re-assessment of his rent; the duty of equitably demanding only such a share of the produce in the shape of rent, as would allow the tenant a fair margin of profit; and the necessity for providing a machinery which could collect the revenue economically and without its being fraudulently diverted; all these points were in the minds of the Bombay administrators, as well as in those of their colleagues in Bengal and Madras. The large proportion which the revenue derived from the land bore to the total revenue made its fair incidence and collection a task of vital importance. More than one-third of the gross revenue of the Bombay Presidency is still derived from the land-revenue or rent, and the proportion was much greater in the early days of the British power in India.

For practical purposes the land-settlements of the Bombay Presidency proper (for in the following sketch I omit at present the consideration of Sind) start from that of Málik Ambar, the Abyssinian finance minister of the Nizám Sháhi dynasty of Ahmadnagar, at the end of the sixteenth century. This great administrator, who resembles in his bold policy Rájá Todar Mall and Abul Fazl, the famous ministers of Akbar in the north, took the villages as his revenue units, and exacted from each of them a lump sum or quit-rent. His assessment, known as the 'Tankha' land-settlement, was not very heavy, and the inefficient administration of the Muhammadan kings of Ahmadnagar, and afterwards of their distant Mughal conquerors, caused it to be collected intermittently during frequent periods of war, and with laxity at all times.

On the decline of the Mughal power in the Deccan, the Maráthás, who took the administration into their hands, made a fresh and more severe assessment, popularly known as the 'Kamal' land-settlement. The Bráhman ministers of the central Maráthá authority at Poona were keener men of business than their Muhammadan predecessors, and their tax-gatherers were more skilled in extracting the largest possible amount of money. Theoretically, each individual cultivator in the home districts of the Maráthás was rigidly assessed; in more distant provinces 'chauth' or tribute was exacted wholesale. But in spite of their heavy individual assessment, the Maráthá cultivators of the Deccan managed to pay and to thrive. For these peasants were also the soldiers of the Maráthá armies, and not only cultivated their fields, but also plundered the rest of India from Tanjore to Delhi. They could afford to pay a heavy rent, as they supplemented the income derived from their own land by the booty which they brought home from their forays in distant provinces.

The gradual establishment of the British dominion in India put an end to this state of things. A limit was placed on freebooting expeditions and exactions of 'chauth,' and the Maráthás were forced to rely on their own districts. This acted in a double way to the detriment of the Maráthá peasant. On the one hand, as I have mentioned in a previous chapter, the Maráthá Court, deprived of its income from foreign tribute, became more severe in exacting the assessments in the Maráthá districts; on the other hand, the Maráthá cultivator, deprived of his former plunder, was less able to pay. Under the strain the financial system of the Maráthá Government broke down; land went out of cultivation; the people took to the hills and became robbers.

This was the state of things when the domains of the Peshwá were annexed to the British Presidency of Bombay, at the close of the third Maráthá war in

1818. Mountstuart Elphinstone, who became Governor of Bombay in the following year, made it his first aim to restore prosperity by giving a sense of security and fixity of tenure to the cultivators. This could only be done by limiting the demand of the State for rent for a period of years, in other words, by a new land-settlement. Elphinstone had before him the systems adopted in other parts of British India. The Maráthá administrators had been too keen to allow any powerful body of intermediaries to grow up between them and the cultivators, like the revenue-farmers and Zamindárs of Bengal. The Madras 'ráyatwárí' settlement, by which the Government dealt directly with each cultivator, seemed to involve an amount of detail too great to be thoroughly superintended by the English civil servants, while it could not be safely entrusted to natives. There remained the system of treating the villages as revenue units, which had been adopted *inter alia* in the North-Western Provinces, and leaving the villagers to apportion the general village assessment among themselves.

This was the system of land-settlement which Elphinstone would have liked to adopt. But he found that co-parcenary village communities were the exception, not the rule, in the Bombay Presidency. They had either not been so generally developed and so completely organised as in North-Western India, or they had been broken up by the Maráthá system of exacting the uttermost from each individual cultivator. Elphinstone therefore resolved to take the hereditary village head-man as the representative of the village community and to arrange with him for the village land-tax. He felt that this would not be quite the same as the North-Western system, for the husbandmen would not be co-parceners, accustomed to joint responsibility and to the joint management of the village affairs. He therefore determined to protect the actual cultivators by recording their individual tenures and holdings. 'The settlement,' he said, 'would still be with the head-man, but the right of every cultivator would be known and fixed.'

A first settlement was accordingly made on these principles under the direction of Mr. Pringle, and by Native agency. The assessment was based on a measurement of fields, and on estimates of the yield of various soils, as well as of the cost of cultivation, and the revenue or rent was fixed at 55 per cent of the estimated nett produce [1]. In theory this sounded well; but, as a matter of fact, Mr. Pringle's settlement effected little improvement. The Native agents (the relics of the late anarchy) proved incapable or dishonest. The measurements were faulty, and the estimates on which the assessment was fixed often proved erroneous. The former assessments of the Muhammadan and Maráthá rulers were somewhat reduced, but the rate was still too high, and the cultivators, in spite of Elphinstone's precautions, often remained at the mercy of the village head-men. The native officials levied contributions for themselves and intercepted remissions allowed by the Government to

[1] *Bombay Administration Report*, 1882–83; Bombay, 1884, p. 28.

the husbandmen. For a time, however, it was believed that the peasants would not, rather than that they could not, pay. Every effort, including torture and other cruel measures of the old Maráthá revenue gatherers, was resorted to by the native officers in spite of the benevolent intentions of the Government. Numbers of the cultivators deserted their homes for the hills, or fled into the neighbouring Native States. Large tracts of land were thrown out of cultivation, and in some districts no more than one-third of the cultivable land remained in occupation [1].

Such severities were felt to be disgraceful to a British administration. The necessity for a better system brought forth the right man, and in 1832 Mr. Thomas Williamson, of the Bombay Civil Service, was appointed Revenue Commissioner for the Presidency. He brought two fixed convictions to his new duties. First, that if the land-settlement was to be effected without oppression to the people, it must be conducted by a better-paid and honester class of native officers. Second, if it was to be effected without frauds on the Government, it must be carried out by a more minute and searching process. Local inquiry and European supervision—these were the two ideas which dominated Mr. Williamson's policy. He pressed their adoption upon the Bombay Government; his views were accepted; and in 1835 Mr. H. E. Goldsmid and Mr. Bartle Frere, two young Assistant Collectors, were despatched at his request to 'settle' the sub-division or 'táluká' of Indápur in the Poona

[1] *Bombay Administration Report*, Bombay, 1884, p. 23.

District, 84 miles from the old Maráthá capital of the Deccan.

The revenue history of the Indápur sub-division, which was the first tract completely settled under the improved method during the years 1835–37, illustrates the revenue history of the Bombay Presidency at large. It was one of the home-districts of the Maráthás, and there is no reason to believe that it was more harshly treated than others. Under the 'Tankha' assessment of Málik Ambar, Indápur had been directed to pay Rs. 1,02,000 to the treasury of the Muhammadan kings of Ahmadnagar; a sum roughly estimated to be a third share of the produce. Under the later 'Kamal' assessment of the Maráthás, the revenue or rent was raised to Rs. 2,22,800 by 1785, levied from the individual cultivators. When it was no longer possible for them to add the old profits of pillage to those of tillage, the peasants fled to the hills, and in 1807 special measures had to be taken to repeople the depopulated districts.

The first assessment after the British occupation in 1818 was far more moderate, and under Mr. Pringle's settlement the revenue to be paid by Indápur was fixed at Rs. 64,000. But even this reduction, sweeping though it may appear, was insufficient, and in 1830 only Rs. 12,880 were collected. To try to make up the deficiency, unauthorised pressure amounting to torture was resorted to, with the result of still further ruining the people. 'It was at this crisis, with the district half-depopulated,' wrote the Commissioner thirty-three years afterwards, 'that the late Mr.

Goldsmid proceeded to inaugurate that system of survey-settlement, which has since formed the groundwork of the revenue administration of the entire Presidency.'

Mr. H. E. Goldsmid, assisted during 1835 by Mr. [Sir] Bartle Frere, and afterwards by Lieutenant [Sir] George Wingate and Lieutenant Nash, carried out the settlement on a new basis. He measured out the country into fields, classified the soils, and fixed the revenue to be paid according to the ascertained quality of the soil, allowing for contingent circumstances, such as facilities of communication. He adopted the field as the revenue-unit and not the cultivator. But an equitable settlement would have afforded little encouragement to the peasant, if his rent could be raised as his land improved. Mr. Goldsmid clearly realised this, and persuaded the Government to sanction the rent for ten years, a period eventually extended to thirty. Boundary marks were authoritatively set up and permanently protected by law.

Moderate assessments and fixity of tenure for a term of years began to work wonders in Indápur. In the second year of its settlement, the Revenue Commissioner reported 'that the sum actually collected has never been so great except during the first four years of our occupation, when it is generally acknowledged our demands were much too high'; and 'the outstanding balances have never yet been so low at the end of the official year as they were last year.' Cultivation rapidly extended, and by the end of the second year nearly 68,000 acres of waste land had been brought under the plough. The average annual collections during the thirty years' settlement, at reduced but fixed rates, exceeded by 86 per cent the average annual collections under excessive assessments and yearly rents during the ten years before Goldsmid and Bartle Frere were sent to the district.

These excellent results opened the eyes of the Government. It resolved to extend the system to other parts of the Presidency, and within ten years of the completion of the Indápur Settlement, the important districts of Násik, Ahmadnagar, the rest of Poona, Sholápur, Dhárwár, and Kaládgi (now Bijápur) were settled in a similar manner. As experience was gained, various modifications were introduced and improvements made, but much was still left to the discretion of the officers employed. It was therefore decided to lay down uniform rules for the future, and the three Superintendents of Survey in the Bombay Presidency were summoned to Poona in 1847 for that purpose. The three Superintendents were Mr. Goldsmid, Captain Wingate, and Captain Davison.

They embodied their conclusions in the famous Joint Report of August 2, 1847, which forms the charter or title-deed of the Bombay Land Revenue system, and a manual for all who desire to study it or who have to put it in force. The three Superintendents, after explaining the objects of a revenue survey and the general principles on which the assessment of land should be conducted, laid down rules for the definition and demarcation of fields, the settlement of boundary disputes, the classification of soils, the interior regulation of surveys, and the administration of settlements. The Bombay Survey and Settlement Department has followed the recommendations made by them with certain improvements and modifications until the present time[1].

For purposes of survey and settlement Bombay is divided into territorial areas each under a separate Superintendent of Survey. Four Revenue Surveys were at work from 1885 to 1887, the Gujarát, the Poona and Násik, the Southern Maráthá, and the Ratnágiri; and three, the Gujarát, the Deccan, and the Konkan from 1887 to 1890—on the revision of expiring settlements. Each Survey consists of a number of Survey Parties, under the management of Assistant Superintendents. There were thirty-one such parties employed in 1886–87 and thirty-four in 1889–90. Some of these parties are employed in measuring, or actual surveying, others in classing the soil. Their maps and reports are forwarded to the Superintendent, who examines and controls the whole and fixes the assessment. The Superintendent submits his proposed assessment of a táluká, or group of villages in a táluká or sub-division, to the Collector of the district, who in turn forwards it with any remarks he may desire to make through the Survey and Settlement Commissioner to the Commissioner of the division. The scheme is then laid before the Government,

[1] This account is mainly based on *A Manual of the Land Revenue Systems and Land Tenures of British India*, by B. H. Baden-Powell: Calcutta, 1882, pp. 551–572, and on the *Bombay Administration Report for* 1882–83: Bombay, 1884, pp. 29–31.

which reserves to itself the power of sanctioning it or sending it back for further revision. When sanctioned, the assessment is introduced into the táluká or group of villages by the Superintendent of Survey, and fixed from that date for a term of thirty years.

The process consists of three distinct series of operations, the survey of the land, the classification of the soil, and the assessment of the revenue, each of which requires separate notice.

The first stage is to obtain an accurate survey of of each village about to be assessed. This work was originally done very roughly. The early settlement officers, such as Goldsmid and Bartle Frere, were not trained surveyors. They desired to do their work quickly, and remembered that they were making a revenue settlement, not a geographical survey. At the present time conditions have altered. Expert native surveyors are employed, and the village maps which they draw up now exhibit not only boundaries, but roads, village sites, tanks, and local or physical features with considerable fidelity. So accurate indeed is their work that the Great Trigonometrical Survey of India finds the revenue village maps an aid in its more scientific field of labour. But, as in former days, absolute precision calculated on large geographical areas is of comparatively little practical importance to the revenue survey.

The crucial work of a measuring party in a Bombay Revenue Survey is the delimitation of 'fields.' The revenue unit of the Bombay Settlement System is, as has been said, the field, and the determination of the areas and boundaries of fields is the first requisite for adjusting the assessment. These fields are technically termed 'numbers,' and one of the most important conclusions of the Joint Report of 1847 was its definition of a field or 'number.' It took as the standard, the area which a ráyat could cultivate with a pair of bullocks. This naturally varied according as the soil was light or heavy, or as the cultivation practised was wet or dry, and generally with the climate and circumstances of the locality.

It was assumed in the Joint Report that twenty acres would be the extent of such an area for light, dry soil; fifteen acres for a medium soil; twelve acres for heavy soil; and four acres for irrigated rice land. It was then laid down that those areas should be the minimum, and double them the maximum of a field or 'number[1].' But of course these were arbitrary standards, and existing plots of cultivated land would not always fit them. It was therefore determined that where a man's holding approached the standard it was reckoned as a separate number; where it much exceeded the standard, it was divided into two or more numbers; and where it greatly fell short, different holdings were counted together as forming one number. This last class gave rise to little difficulty, for in the case of several holdings being included in one 'number,' each share was separately recorded and distinguished into 'pot numbers,' if the sharers so desired. The measuring party sets up

[1] Mr. Baden-Powell's *Land Revenue and Land Tenures of India*, p. 553, ed. 1882.

permanent boundary marks for the 'numbers,' a precaution necessary in tracts devoid of hedges; commonly by placing stones or making earthen ridges at each corner.

Usually in the next season after the measuring party has done its work, the 'classing' party enters the field. Its duty is to classify the soil in each 'number' and to record the 'accidents' affecting its value. This double work was reduced to a definite system by Lieutenant Wingate, afterwards Major Sir George Wingate, a successor of Bartle Frere as assistant to Mr. Goldsmid in settling the Indápur táluká. The 'classer' first takes into consideration the nature of the different species of holdings, which are, whenever practicable, kept in separate numbers. The main divisions under this head are unirrigated land, rice land, and garden land watered by wells or small watercourses[1]. Then he classifies the soils. The varieties in the unirrigated land, taking the Deccan as an example, are found to be uniform black soil, which is very productive; coarser red soil; and light soil.

But, further, the actual fertility of these soils depends upon their depth. Three feet is considered the maximum depth of practical importance to the agriculturist. The classer divides the 'number' into ten classes, according not only to the nature, but the positive or relative depth of the soil.

He next considers the 'accidents' which affect the

[1] Artificial irrigation from canals or reservoirs formed by the Public Works Department is, I believe, dealt with separately.

soil of the 'number' and depreciate its productiveness. These 'accidents' are seven in number, and they may be worth enumerating to show the thoroughness with which the classification is carried out. They are (1) admixture of nodules of limestone, (2) admixture of sand, (3) sloping surface, (4) want of cohesion, (5) impermeability to water, (6) exposure to scouring from flow of water in the rains, and (7) excessive moisture from surface springs. Each of these 'accidents' is held to lower any soil by one class, and if it occurs in excess by two or more classes.

Having done this work, the classer makes a sketch of the number and divides it into compartments, each of which he marks separately on a regular system according to the nature and depth of the soil and its 'accidents.' He then takes the average of the value of the compartments, and shows the proportion of the rate of assessment it should pay.

Finally, the classer has to note the value of irrigation on the 'number.' He has hitherto considered all land, whether irrigable or not, and classified it. He now calculates the advantage of irrigation, where it exists, according to the supply, depth and quality of the water, and even the distance of a garden-ground from the village as affecting the cost of manuring. He next fixes an extra irrigation value to be applied either to the whole or part of the acreage of the field[1]. This work is (together with a percentage of the measurements) tested by the Assistant-Superintendent, as is

[1] Baden-Powell's *Land Revenue and Land Tenures of India*, pp. 557–562, ed. 1882.

also that of the measuring parties, and the maps and sketches are sent in to the Superintendent.

The Superintendent of Survey has now to fix the assessment. He considers the circumstances of each village and examines various points with which the measuring and classing-parties had nothing to do, such as climate, facilities for market, communications, average prices, and the effect of previous settlements, British or Native. He then fixes the maximum dry-crop rate for the village, or group of villages, the conditions of which are homogeneous. His proposals are forwarded through the Collector of the District, the Survey and Settlement Commissioner, and the Commissioner of the Division, to the Secretary to Government. The maximum dry-crop rate and the accompanying rates for irrigated land and rice land are carefully considered by Government, and if accepted the Superintendent proceeds to work out the revenue demand for each Survey 'number.' The classer has, as already mentioned, fixed the proportion of the standard rate which each 'number' ought to be able to pay; and, the maximum rate once declared, it is a mere mechanical and arithmetical process to assign the equitable amount of rent to each number for the ensuing thirty years.

I have described in some detail the history and procedure of the Bombay Land Revenue System. For while the Permanent Settlement of Bengal, the co-parcenary village system in the North-Western Provinces, and the Madras *ráyatwárí* system, are all more or less understood in England, the Bombay system has seldom been presented in a popular form. It may be asserted with truth that in no country in the world has greater care been taken than in Bombay that the cultivator of the soil should pay no more rent than he is fairly able to pay. In its simplicity of principle and in its minute conscientiousness of detail, the Bombay Settlement system ranks among the triumphs of British administration in India.

It not only secured to the rấyat a full measure of justice from his landlord, the Government; it also gave him a property. As long as the occupant paid his rent or revenue, he owned his holding. He could sell it, bequeath it, or mortgage it, and the limits of his land were clearly laid down in the village revenue map, and preserved by boundary marks. A 'survey' tenure was in fact created, a firm right of occupancy subject only to the payment of the fixed assessment and to the liability of its being revised after thirty years.

This right was definitively established by the Bombay Survey and Settlement Act of 1865, a measure now absorbed into the Land Revenue Code Act of 1879. By these Acts the occupant was still further secured, for it was enacted that all revised settlements 'shall be fixed, not with reference to any special improvements made by owners or occupants from private capital or resources, but with reference to general considerations of the value of land, whether as to soil or situation, prices of produce or facilities of communication [1].' The right of occupancy was declared to be conditional solely on the payment of the Government

[1] *Bombay Administration Report for* 1882–83, p. 31.

demand, and to be 'a transferable and heritable property, continuable without question at the expiration of a settlement lease, on the occupant's consenting to the revised rate [1].'

Unfortunately the Deccan cultivator did not make the wisest use of his newly acquired property. He freely mortgaged it to astute money lenders, who held him in thrall and who made use of the British laws to reduce him to the condition of a tenant at will, or at a rack-rent. This led to agrarian disturbances. In 1879 the Government found it necessary to step in, and to protect the cultivators against the results of their own unwisdom by the Deccan Agriculturists' Relief Act, which was a sort of Encumbered Estates Act and Peasants' Insolvency Act at the same time. The Act has now (1891) been referred afresh for inquiry by the Government of India to a Commission.

Notwithstanding this need for relief the legal status of the peasant has greatly improved under British rule. The old Muhammadan kings had levied a lump sum from every village, and left the villagers to distribute its burden among themselves. The Maráthás had come to closer quarters, and levied a heavy assessment from each cultivator, sometimes with very little regard to the actual yield of his holding. The English Government in Bombay took the final step, and based its more moderate demands upon the carefully ascertained capacity of each field.

In Bengal, the British authorities had, in 1793, rid themselves of the toil and perplexities of a detailed

[1] *Bombay Administration Report for* 1882–83, p. 31.

land-settlement by leasing out the country in wide tracts to so-called landholders, thus practically leaving the cultivators at their mercy until the tardy legislation of 1859 came to the relief of the tillers of the soil. In Madras, the British Government had not shrunk from the difficulty of dealing with the individual husbandmen. But its arrangements involved what amounted to almost a yearly resettlement with each cultivator, according to the land which he took up for the individual season, and the amount of crop which he secured for the year. The Madras system of annual revision, with its former 'opportunities of extortion, peculation, chicanery, and intrigue of all kinds [1],' has been slowly organised into an orderly procedure by seventy years of hard English work. All this is now clear enough to Indian administrators. The merit of Williamson, Frere, Goldsmid, Wingate, and their brother-officers in Bombay, is that they, in their various separate departments, clearly perceived it fifty years ago, and devised a new and better alternative for the Western Presidency.

By taking the field as their unit of revenue, and laying on it an assessment so moderate as to leave a liberal profit to the cultivator, they secured a regular revenue from the lands then under tillage, and they supplied inducements for bringing large areas of waste under cultivation. The margin between their assessment and the actual produce of the soil gave a saleable value to each field. But, unhappily, the rights which

[1] These are the perhaps too unfavourable terms in which Sir George Campbell speaks of the Madras system. (*Modern India*, p. 362, ed. 1853.)

they conferred on the cultivators to sell, or sublet, or mortgage, enabled improvident husbandmen to turn their little holdings into cash or to raise loans upon them. It is now clear that the peasantry of the Deccan, with their extravagant marriage expenditure and other occasions for throwing away money upon domestic display, had not at that time been sufficiently prepared for the wise use of those rights. The evils of agrarian indebtedness, with forced sales of their holdings, resulted. These evils were intensified by the usurers' frauds on the ignorant ráyats, and to some extent by the rigid regularity with which the English Government enforced its assessments in a country peculiarly at the mercy of the rainfall.

But, while acknowledging that the Bombay system has indirectly led to evils, it has been productive of far outweighing benefits. It is now recognised, even by Bengal officers like myself, as the best solution of the complicated land problem of India, in a province where the co-parcenary system of joint village responsibility did not exist or had become inoperative.

I have mentioned that while the Bombay system still rests on the basis of the Joint Report of 1847, modifications have been introduced. The surveys and classifications made before that year were necessarily imperfect. A staff of surveyors and classers cannot be trained in a day, and even after that date the importance of getting the work done quickly somewhat impaired its thoroughness. As the thirty-years' leases fell in, it was found necessary, therefore, to re-survey and re-class as well as to re-settle. But the work of revision, whether total or partial, is now being done once for all as far as the Survey Department is concerned, and the survey and classification record can in future be kept in order by the local officers of each district.

Before noticing the points which were brought before the Bombay Government between 1885 and 1890, in connection with the revised settlements, it is necessary to draw attention to a change in the law, emphasising the doctrine that the Government, as chief landlord, should not make any increase in the revised settlement for improvements effected by a tenant. This had been affirmed in the Bombay Survey and Settlement Act of 1865, as has been already said, when the 'survey tenure' was legally defined. It was re-affirmed in the Bombay Land Revenue Code of 1879, but a clause was added reserving to Government the power to consider, in fixing a revised assessment, the increased value arising from certain classes of improvement. This clause had never been put into effect, but complaints were made that its mere existence affected the tenant's property in his holding. Act IV of 1886 was therefore passed, which amended the clause objected to, and enacted that 'when a general classification of the soil of any area has been made a second time, or when any original classification of any area has been approved by the Governor in Council as final, no such classification shall be again made with a view to the revision of the assessment of such area.' Further, 'if any improvement has been effected in any land during the currency of any previous settlement made under Act V of 1879, or under Act I of 1865, by or at the cost of the holder thereof, the increase in the value of such land or in the profit of cultivating the same, due to the said improvement, shall not be taken into account in fixing the revised assessment thereof.'

Nothing can be more clear or precise than this declaration of the principle, all important for the encouragement of good tenants, that the value of the tenant's improvement shall not accrue to the landlord. The discussion which took place in the Bombay Legislative Council on the second reading of the Bill which became Act IV of 1886 was of a very important character, not only as containing a complete vindication of the practice of the Survey and Settlement Department in the matter of re-classification, but as establishing the moderation of its assessments. In Lord Reay's speech on this occasion proofs are adduced that the doubts stated by certain non-official members to be entertained by the general public regarding the action of the Department, were opposed to facts and figures derived from the records.

The discussion led to an important result bearing on the practice of settlements. It had been the custom for the Superintendent, after the proposed maximum rates were sanctioned by the Government, to work out the individual assessments which resulted, and then to assemble the cultivators and announce the revenue demand on each field. It was objected that by this course no opportunity was given to the ráyat to be heard as to enhancements before the enhancement became an accomplished fact.

After minute inquiry into the numerous administrative objections to any alteration of practice, it was decided by a Government Resolution dated October 16, 1886, that not only should increased facilities be given to cultivators to make known their objections to the Survey officers while the survey was in progress, but that the Superintendent of Survey should announce to the villagers by public notification the maximum rates he proposed to use, as soon as such rates were determined on, and that the cultivators should be allowed a period of two months within which to forward their objections to the Collector. It was decided, moreover, that the Collector should submit all such petitions, with his criticism, to Government, through the ordinary channels, and that in this way Government should have the objections of the ráyats before them when the proposals came under their consideration. This decision, the fairness and justice of which cannot be doubted, is in full force, and although many difficulties tend to impair its usefulness, the large number of petitions and objections advanced show that the cultivators appreciate the opportunity, and are not slow to avail themselves of it.

Turning to administrative questions which arose in the work of re-settlement during the five years now under review, the most important was as to the rate to be imposed on dry-crop land which had been converted into rice land during the past thirty years. It will be remembered that rice lands and dry-crop lands are differently assessed, and it was pointed out that it would be a hardship if a cultivator spent much labour in turning his dry-crop land into rice land, and was then assessed at the higher rate. It would be, in fact, a tax on improvements, and a violation of the great principle just affirmed. The question came before the Bombay Government in May, 1885, soon after Lord Reay's assumption of office, with respect to the Igatpuri táluká in the Deccan. After careful consideration it was decided that such converted rice land should be assessed not as rice land, but at the maximum rate for dry-crop land. The question was again raised in 1889 with regard to the re-settlement of the Khalapur Peta táluká in the Konkan, and after a long discussion was settled on the same basis.

This controversy led to an innovation in the rules for classification. It was argued that some 'warkas' or dry-crop lands in the Konkan could be very easily converted into rice land owing to their natural position, and that the Government should take this circumstance into consideration. It was therefore resolved that the classer should include in his classification a new gradation or 'position class.' This was not to affect the immediate assessment, but was to be entered on the record, so that at the next settlement it might be known what tracts had been converted into rice lands, not so much by the labour of the tenant as because of their natural advantages.

A change was also made in the instructions to survey parties, arising out of the excessive subdivision which had been taking place in the unit of survey. It will be remembered that subdivisions of numbers, called 'pot numbers,' might be marked off in the numbers. Since the settlement, many numbers had been divided by partition among relatives or otherwise. The practice developed until it had been laid down by the Land Revenue Code that 'every separate occupancy recognised in the village accounts is required to be made into a Survey number, or subordinate Survey number, and to be measured, demarcated, classified, and assessed on its own individual merits.' This record of minute subdivisions was laborious and expensive. It was therefore ordered in 1889 that, in future, subdivisions of numbers should only be made at the request and at the cost of the occupant.

Among other reforms during the five years under review the following may be particularised. When any large addition was made to the original assessment at the revised settlement, it was only to be introduced gradually. A system of sub-soil classification of water advantages was substituted for the former well assessment in Gujarát, and various other new regulations were made, which need not be detailed here.

Of all common agricultural improvements in the Bombay Presidency the most important is the sinking of wells not only for securing the ordinary crops in seasons of drought, but also for the raising of the finer descriptions of produce. The treatment of wells with reference to assessment gave rise to frequent discussion, and the question attracted much attention during the five years (1885–1890). After the passing of Act I of 1865, by sec. 30 whereof improvements made by the occupant with his labour and capital were exempted from consideration in fixing the assessment, the principle acted upon by the settlement officers was to treat all lands irrigated from wells sunk after the preceding settlement as purely dry-crop only, while lands watered from wells existing at the time of the former settlement were not to be rated in excess of the highest dry-crop rate prevailing in the village. A slight difference therefore existed in the treatment of wells recorded at the former settlement and wells found to have been newly built, but even lands watered by the older class of wells were considerately dealt with according to a fixed scale, and such lands were not placed uniformly on the highest existing dry-crop rate.

The difference, however, attracted notice in the press and elsewhere, and it was pointed out that the pioneers of the well-sinking industry, who had taken early steps to irrigate their fields, were burdened by heavier taxation than those who had delayed. About 1885–86 the question was much discussed, with special regard to the circumstances of the province of Gujarát, which was just coming under revision, and where well assessment formed a considerable portion of the land revenue and the opportunities for digging wells were abundant. In this province, the soil is chiefly alluvial, and the water-bearing strata are generally found at an easily ascertainable level, and can be utilised under circumstances calculable with accuracy. For many years previously, suggestions had been made by experienced officers that the true solution of the question of assessment of wells lay in doing away entirely with taxation of water when brought to the surface and utilised, and in imposing a slight additional rate on lands which were known or believed to possess the advantage of sub-soil water within easy reach and free from difficulty of utilisation. Government now affirmed this principle, and decided that it should be the basis of settlement 'whenever the Superintendent can safely and conveniently apply it.'

The system was introduced into the first tálukú of Gujarát, which fell in for revision in 1886[1], under rules carefully framed by the Survey Commissioner, by which the advantages of sub-soil water were graduated according to depth and character of soil to be pierced, distant or questionable advantages being left out of consideration altogether. The result is that in Gujarát there is no well assessment in revision, the facility for obtaining sub-soil water and not the use of it being the point to be decided.

In 1889 the attention of the Government was drawn to the method by which this small additional revenue on account of sub-soil water was worked out and imposed. Under the rules applied to the Ahmadábád Collectorate in the first instance, the addition was made to the soil classification and the result ascertained in the ordinary way, but Lord Reay, who gave this subject very close attention, disapproved of the maximum addition for sub-soil water being fixed with a view to recouping the amount of well assessment which had been hitherto collected in the tálukú—a limit which had been observed from the first. Differences were created in the several tálukás for which no real reason could be adduced, except that they had by their former well

[1] The Dholka Tálukú in Ahmadábád.

assessments subscribed more or less to the revenue. Lord Reay considered that the method should be changed and a moderate cash addition should be made to the rate per acre which resulted from the soil classification, in this way avoiding unnecessary and unreasonable anomalies. The alteration was duly made in calculating the assessments for the Daskroi and succeeding tálukás of Ahmadábád, and its working is being carefully watched.

The following paragraph shows the actual work done by the Survey and Settlement Department during the period from 1885-6 to 1889–90 inclusive; the addition which it yielded to the revenue; and its cost.

During the five years in question from 31 to 34 surveying parties were employed, who measured 8,460,669 acres, or nearly 13,220 square miles, and classed 8,079,956 acres, or nearly 12,625 square miles. Revised, and in a few parts of the Konkan original, settlements were introduced into 3,891½ villages, or excluding Native States and *inám* villages belonging to individuals, into 3,621½ villages. The revenue from these villages was assessed at Rs. 42,99,320 instead of Rs. 34,40,703 as it had formerly been, a gain of Rs. 8,58,617 to the revenue; or, excluding again Native States and *inám* villages, at Rs. 39,58,604 instead of Rs. 31,40,177, a gain of Rs. 8,18,427 a year. To obtain this increase of yearly revenue there was expended on the Survey and Settlement during the five years Rs. 28,04,526, being an average of Rs. 5,60,905; or excluding payments by Native States Rs. 27,26,130, being an average of Rs. 5,45,226 a year.

The expense is undoubtedly great but the gain is great also.

The foregoing description of the Bombay Land-Revenue System, and the statistics of work done, deal only with the Bombay Presidency proper. The land-revenue system of Sind stands apart, with a separate Survey Department of its own. Sind cultivators depend entirely for their harvest upon irrigation; without it the province would be a desert. Attempts from time to time made to introduce the elaborate Bombay land-settlement have proved futile. The Sind peasant does not stick to one place; he moves about and is difficult to assess. When measurers and classers were imported, the former did useful work; the latter were quite out of their element. It is almost useless to classify soil, or to estimate 'accidents' in a country which depends entirely upon one resource, irrigation, and where 90 per cent of the assessment is derived from it.

Temporary settlements and other expedients had been tried in Sind, but without success. In 1887 it was decided to introduce irrigation settlements—a laborious and delicate task which was carried out with great ability by the Commissioner in Sind, and his officers. By this plan, the one distinctive feature of Sind is fully recognised, and tracts and groups of villages are assessed solely by their irrigation facilities. There are no village communities in Sind to arrange with; the cultivators move so rapidly that in extensive tracts there are not even 'fields,' i.e. continuously inhabited and cultivated 'numbers,' to assess. The estimate of irrigation-facilities takes the place of the classification of soils in the Presidency, and on this basis irrigation settlements for a period of ten years have been rapidly introduced into Sind, with the best results both to the Government and the cultivator. A difficulty constantly arose in the Sind assessment from the fluctuations in occupation and the frequency of fallows. The irrigational settlements, based on the irrigational facilities of the land, form a most important series of measures in the land-administration of the Province.

To return to the Presidency proper, it is interesting to notice some of the land-tenures which survive in spite of the advantages offered by the simple survey tenure. Only two have any political importance, the tálukdári tenure in Gujarát and the khoti tenure in the southern Konkan, but one or two of the others, such as the bhágdári and narvádári tenures in Gujarát, and the shilotri tenure in the Konkan, have an historical interest of their own. There are many curious local varieties [1], such as the máleki and sarákati, but they only exist in a few villages, and all tend to be absorbed in the universal survey tenure.

The tálukdári tenure in the Bombay Presidency is only to be found in Gujarát, principally in the western part of Ahmadábád District, bordering on Káthiáwár, where it used to cover, until recently, 1931 square miles; and in Broach District and the Panch Mahals, where it is the prevailing system over 266 square miles. The tálukdárs are usually of pure Rájput descent: gentlemen who consider manual labour de-

[1] *Bombay Administration Report for* 1882–83: Bombay, 1884, pp. 32–40.

grading and who live on the hereditary share of the produce of their lands, which are cultivated by tenants at will. The tálukdári estates are of all sizes, but seldom exceed one, two, or three villages, owing to the custom of subdivision among the kinsmen. With regard to the Government the tálukdárs are absolute owners of their estates, but are bound to pay a certain *jama*, which is a tribute rather than a rent. On the other hand the tálukdárs are answerable for the pay of the village police and for the village expenses sanctioned by custom.

The relations between the tálukdár and his tenants are regulated in the following manner. The village crops are stored in the village grain-yard. A fixed proportion is deducted for seed and certain perquisites, and the remainder is divided between the tálukdár and the ráyats according to the village custom. The average demand has been assumed to be 50 per cent of the common grains, 40 per cent of wheat, and 48 per cent of cotton. The tálukdárs are interesting as a survival, but as a rule they are heavily in debt. A special Act was passed for their relief in 1862, and a special officer has been appointed to look after them.

During the period under review the decline in the status of the tálukdárs and their privileges formed the subject of a further Bill[1], which was discussed in the Legislative Council in 1886. The Bill provided for the better revenue administration of the estates of the tálukdárs, and more clearly fixed their position with regard to the British Government. As one of the

[1] 'Act No. VI of 1886.'

results of this Act, a survey is now in progress with a view to revise the data upon which the *jama* of the several tálukdárs is fixed. Special attention is paid to the cultivation of waste lands which has taken place, and the former classification is tested and, where necessary, corrected.

The khoti tenure differs in its nature in the northern and southern Konkan. In the north the khots are practically leaseholders of a certain number of villages and exercise no proprietary rights. In most of these villages the survey tenure has been introduced, and the cultivator is little affected by the fact that his village is held from a leaseholder, instead of directly from the Government. But in the southern Konkan, in the whole of the district of Ratnágiri and in the greater part of Kolába, the khots are recognised as proprietors of their villages. It is believed that they were originally farmers holding on leases for the improvement of the country, and they have been compared to the Bengal zamindárs. The chief features of the khoti tenure in the southern Konkan country are that they hold their villages on payment of a lump sum to Government; that they may rack-rent all lands in which there are not rights of permanent occupancy; that they may resume all lands which may lapse by the absence or failure of the permanent occupant; and that they have to collect the assessment from permanent occupants without remuneration. The rights of the permanent occupants as against the holders of khoti tenures are very various, and the tendency of the Government is to maintain these rights.

Shilotri lands, which are also found in the Konkan, are lands which have been reclaimed from the sea and embanked. These reclamations are known as khárs. The tenure is of two sorts. Shilotri proper, under which the khár belongs to the reclaimer or his representatives. These shilotridárs have a proprietary right; they let their khárs, and they are entitled by old custom to levy a maund of rice per bigha in addition to the assessment for the repair of the embankments. Where however the Government has made the reclamation or become possessed of the khár, the cultivators hold the shilotri lands like any other survey tenants, but they pay an additional assessment, which represents the shilotri maund of rice for the repair of the embankment.

Finally, mention must be made of the bhágdári and narvádári tenures. It was said in the historical sketch of the Bombay Revenue system that Mountstuart Elphinstone found hardly any traces of the coparcenary village in the Bombay Presidency. These two tenures represent the few that did and do still exist. The bhágdári tenure is only found in the Broach District, while the narvádári chiefly centres in the District of Kaira, but is also represented in a few villages in Ahmadábád. The main point of interest in them is that they are genuine survivals of an old system, for the whole village inhabited under their arrangements is jointly responsible for the Government revenue. The distinction between the two tenures is that under bhágdári there was a fixed assessment on each field, while under narvádári the revenue was paid in a lump. While interesting as remains of the ancient village community, these tenures are not found by their holders to work satisfactorily at the present day, and the survey tenure is felt by them to be superior. In 1887 the narvádárs or shareholders of the village of Kanjári in Nadiád táluká applied to have their special tenure abolished and replaced by the ordinary system [1].

The superiority of the survey-tenure is a noteworthy fact. It might naturally have been expected that the Survey and Settlement Department, which was engaged in enhancing assessments, would have been hated, and in recent times it was unpopular. But in the early years of the Department the Survey was designed to remedy the effects of long periods of faulty revenue administration, and was applied to districts which were reduced to poverty and wretchedness. The system, therefore, was liberal from the outset, large reductions being made in the Government demand to encourage fixed cultivation and the re-occupation and fresh cultivation of waste lands. The introduction of the Survey came to be regarded as the signal for moderation and reduction of rents. In the opinion of some the sacrifices made were almost too great. Sir George Campbell relates that when the Madras officials were twitted with the success of the Bombay system, they used to say that it would be very easy to give as much satisfaction if the revenue were as completely sacrificed as in Bombay [2].

[1] *Bombay Administration Report for* 1887–88, p. 53.
[2] *Systems of Land Tenure in various Countries*: Cobden Club, p. 172.

The renewal of revision operations, 1860–1866, marked a new era in settlement procedure. When the Department came to deal with the subdivisions settled at an early date, it found that the exceedingly moderate assessment of the first leaders of the Survey had borne their full fruit, and that owing to the development of the country by roads and railways, and the establishment of convenient markets, the cultivators were enjoying large increments of profit which ought justly to be considered in fixing the Government demand. Consequently a considerable enhancement of assessments resulted from the first batch of revisions. The cultivators were unprepared for this new phase of the Survey operations, and in parts of the Poona District there was much dissatisfaction. The revised rates were freely attacked in the public press, and, notwithstanding that considerable reductions were made in the case of some revised settlements, agitation continued with more or less force until the year of the famine (1876–77).

In 1881, in consideration of the great losses the cultivators had sustained from famine and destruction of crops, temporary remissions of revenue were granted in all cases which had come under revision, and it was ordered that before the full revised rates were again levied there should be a further enquiry, and the sanction of Government should be obtained. Notwithstanding these precautions, doubt and suspicion continued to be entertained against the Survey up to 1886; and in the discussion which preceded Act IV of that year to amend certain sections of the Land

Revenue Code, the Survey Department was attacked by several non-official members of the Council speaking on behalf of the cultivators. Since 1886, however, there has been a marked difference of attitude towards the Survey on the part of the leaders of the people and the press.

This is due, in part, to the explanation of the system and refutation of the complaints against the Survey during the debate on the Bill, and to Lord Reay's resolve that the cultivators should be allowed as many opportunities as were possible to bring forward objections to the treatment of their holdings at the Survey and the resulting assessments. Those who were agitating against the Survey found themselves compelled to acknowledge the tenacity with which the Bombay Government kept to its pledges of moderation of rates, notwithstanding conflicting opinions, and could not fail to see that adequate precautions were being taken to prevent the operations of the Survey Department from becoming arbitrary or oppressive. While the number of revenue-paying occupancies only varied from 1,300,643 in 1885–86 for the Presidency, excluding Sind, to 1,292,927 in 1889-90, the number of distraints for rent fell from 3186 in 1885–86 to 1111 in 1889–90.

The vigorous and sagacious administration of the Survey and Settlement Department has made it possible to bring it to an end ere long, and its successor has already been appointed. When the thorough survey and classification, now in progress, are completed, this branch of the work will, it is hoped, be finished once for all, subject to such rectifications as are inevitable; and it will then only be necessary to preserve the records and keep them up to date. The work of future settlement officers, when the settlements again come up for revision, will be comparatively simple. In the words of the Government of Bombay: 'When these operations are finished, the record will remain as an authoritative and sufficient standard of relative values by which assessment may be adjusted to each field through calculations made in the Collector's office[1].' The work has been expensive while it lasted, because it has been thorough; and because it had to be done by a special agency instead of by the ordinary executive officers as in most other provinces of India.

The succession to the Survey and Settlement Department is destined to be inherited by the officers of the Land Revenue Department with the aid and advice of the Director of Land Records and Agriculture. The latter Department was founded in accordance with the recommendations of the Famine Commission, and it was at one time under consideration to make it sole heir of the Survey and Settlement Department and the custodian of the traditions thereof. Subsequently, however, it was decided that the Circle Inspectors, who were to keep the Survey maps and records up to date, and the officers appointed to superintend their work, should form part of the district revenue establishment of the Collector, acting with the advice and assistance of the Director of Agriculture. It was not

[1] *Bombay Government Letter*, No. 6340, dated Aug. 27, 1883.

thought expedient that, in direct control, the Director should be substituted for the Collector, although in passing rules and selecting subordinates the utmost advantage should be taken of the Director's knowledge and experience.

The Circle Inspectors will be chosen principally from the Survey Department when its operations are ended, and the supervising officers will be Survey men. It is hoped that in this way the traditions and practice of the Survey Department will be efficiently maintained. The additional words 'and land records' were added to the title of Director of Agriculture, when the records of the Dhárwár and Bijápur revised settlements were completed and made over to the charge of the Collectors. The regular treatment of the land records at the various Head-quarter Stations, and the compiling of comprehensive land revenue statements for the Presidency, will form important duties of the Director.

It is appropriate that the Department of Agriculture should thus be interested in maintaining the records of the Revenue Survey. For there can be no question that the Survey has done much for agriculture by securing fixity of tenure and a fair rent. During the five years under review, the cultivated land in the Presidency proper, exclusive of Sind, rose from 24,035,256 acres in 1884–85 to 24,481,639 acres in 1889–90, an increase of 446,383 acres. What is now urgently needed, is to improve the quality as well as to extend the area of Indian agriculture, and one of the most hopeful methods of effecting this is a system of agricultural education. The subject received the earnest attention of Mr. Ozanne, the Director of Land Records and Agriculture, during the five years under review. Besides promoting a graduated scheme of agricultural education, and an 'agricultural diploma' in the University of Bombay, he rendered important services to the actual administration. His valuable ráb experiments largely influenced the report of the Bombay Forest Commission. He also carried on a series of investigations for the improvement of Bombay agriculture at the Government experimental farms and in other likely localities. Lord Reay took a special interest in these efforts.

Alienation Settlements are somewhat similar in character to the regular settlements made by the Survey and Settlement Department, in that they regulate and define the rights of certain holders of land. But they differ in that they are, as a rule, permanent, and not for a term of years only. They fix, as their designation signifies, the grants of land alienated from the Government, and the tenures on which they were granted and by which they are held.

The tenures of alienated holdings may be divided for general purposes into four classes, political, service, religious, and personal[1]. Lands held under the first of these heads include political pensions and the grants known as 'jághírs' and 'saranjáms,' the former being of Muhammadan, the latter of Maráthá origin. These grants were made by the State for the perform-

[1] *Bombay Administration Report for* 1882–83: Bombay, 1884, p. 41.

ance of civil or military duties, or for the maintenance of the personal dignity of nobles and high officials. Under the British Government the duties attached have either been abolished or commuted for a money payment, but many grants are continued on political considerations. Far more numerous are the assignments held on 'service tenure.' Such grants were originally made to ensure the performance of certain specified services in each village or district. But owing to the introduction of the revenue survey and the organisation of a regular police, the duties attached to many service assignments have come to an end, and the holders of them now pay a portion of their estimated value and are freed from liability to serve. Holdings granted by native governments for the support of religious or charitable institutions, and continued by the British Government, are classified as held on 'religious' tenure. Lastly are included under the head of 'personal' tenure a vast number of estates and holdings, alienated by former rulers under various denominations and for different services, and continued to the present day as personal inâms.

A more systematic enquiry into the titles to alienated holdings in the Bombay Presidency was suggested in 1851 by the large number of unauthorized and fraudulent alienations, gradually brought to light by the Revenue Survey in the Southern Maráthá country and elsewhere. The enquiry then commenced in that portion of the Presidency developed into an organised investigation, which, under the title of the Inám Commission or the Alienation Department, was extended to the whole of the Presidency. The work was, however, done with inconvenient slowness, owing to the minute detail with which the scrutiny was conducted. It was accordingly resolved in 1863 to give such persons as claimed an exemption from the payment of Government land-revenue the option of avoiding a scrutiny of their title by the payment of a quit-rent, and in that year Acts II and VII of 1863, known as the Summary Settlement Acts, were passed.

The results of the operations of the Alienation Department and of the summary settlements which followed were most advantageous to the revenue[1]. The annual revenue alienated at the commencement of the enquiry was Rs. 132,51,008. The amount was reduced to Rs. 80,38,361 by 1876–77, causing an addition to the revenue of Rs. 51,86,398. This great additional revenue was secured at a comparatively small expense, the cost of the Alienation Department up to 1876–77 having only amounted to Rs. 26,10,179. It is curious to observe how these alienations are distributed under the four classes already mentioned. Rs. 33,67,892 are included under 'personal' tenure and Rs. 33,65,482 under 'service' tenure, while only Rs. 6,72,604 appear under 'political' tenure, and Rs. 6,32,383 under 'religious' tenure. The enquiries respecting alienated lands have now been completed in the majority of the districts of the Bombay Presidency, and in 1889–90 the only districts in which any considerable amount of work

[1] I derive these figures from the Standing Information prefixed to the *Bombay Administration Report for* 1882–83.

remained to be done were Sátára, Ratnágiri, and Kolába[1]. The settlement of alienations formed an essential complement to the labour of the regular Survey and Settlement Department, and it has this advantage, that it will not have to be revised, as the titles are granted in perpetuity and not for a term of years only.

The collection of the land-revenue is one of the main duties of the district officer, and the nature of the Bombay system demands a most exact supervision. The Assistant or Deputy Collector in the Bombay Presidency travels about the tálukás or subdivisions placed under his charge for about seven months in the year, and the Collector of a district for four months[2]. Under them are the Mámlatdárs, each of whom is responsible for the general business of one táluká. It is the Mámlatdár's business to get in the revenue for the villages from the Revenue Pátel or head-man, and to see that the village accounts are properly kept by the village accountant, who is called a Taláti in Gujarát and a Kulkarni in the Deccan. The Survey register is the record of title. Every occupant is given a separate receipt-book, in which the head-men and accountants of the village are obliged, under heavy penalties, to record each instalment of rent as soon as it is paid. A general scrutiny and record, termed the jamábandi, of the village is annually made, at which time the amount of revenue due from the village is worked out, the village

[1] *Bombay Administration Report for* 1889–90, p. 37.
[2] *Ibid.*, 1882–83, p. 25.

accounts are examined, and transfers of numbers are verified and recorded. During this scrutiny the Assistant or Deputy Collector is brought into direct contact with the villages under his charge, and is enabled to judge of their wants and requirements.

For the district officers are not merely rent-collectors. The British Government endeavours according to its lights to play the part of a wise and tolerant landlord, and is ready not only to remit rent or revenue when such remissions are rendered necessary, but to advance sums of money to its tenants for agricultural improvements. This work is conducted by the district officers on their tours. Floods, droughts, and plagues of locusts are taken into consideration, and remissions of revenue made on account of them. Equally important are the advances made by Government to the cultivators. By Act XIX of 1883 such advances were allowed to be granted for permanent improvements, and by Act XII of 1884 for the purchase of cattle and seed. An aggregate sum of Rs. 4,36,619 was advanced for these purposes during the years 1885–86 to 1889–90. Such loans bear interest of one ana in the rupee, or 6¼ per cent per annum. But this is not always exacted, and during the five years under review Rs. 37,039 were advanced to the Bhils in Khándesh free of interest. Government advances are largely taken advantage of by the cultivators in Sind and in the district of Belgáum. The latter district, indeed, received the large proportion of Rs. 1,80,000 out of the total Rs. 4,36,619. Among the purposes for which such advances were granted may be noted the construction and repair of wells, the clearing of waste land, the conversion of dry-crop land into wet-crop land, and the removal of prickly pear and rank grass. A sum of Rs. 5,250 was granted in the Panch Mahāls in 1888–89 for the rebuilding of houses destroyed by fire.

Another duty of the revenue administration is to take care of the estates of holders who are unable to take care of themselves. These may be ranked in two classes: (1) wards or minors, (2) improvident landholders. The absence of large estates in the Bombay Presidency, arising from the nature of the settlement field by field, renders the management of wards' estates a smaller and less interesting branch of the work of the local officers in Bombay than in Bengal. In the districts of Ahmadábád, Broach, and Kaira, wards' estates are placed under the care of the Tálukdári officer; in the other districts they are directly managed by the ordinary district officials for the advantage of the wards. The number and extent of these estates vary from year to year. In 1885–86, at the commencement of the five years under review, they were 91 in number, amounting to 110,051 acres, including one in the Haidarábád district of Sind of 64,765 acres. In 1889–90 they were 79 in number, extending over 111,523 acres, including three in the Panch Mahàls, aggregating over 60,000 acres.

In addition to the care of wards' estates, the Government had in 1884–85 two officers specially engaged in administering the estates of improvident landlords. These were the Manager of Encumbered Estates in

Sind, and the Tálukdári Settlement Officer in Gujarát. The former official had 143 estates under his superintendence in 1885–86, but the number steadily diminished. In 1887 the special establishment in Sind was abolished, and the encumbered estates were placed under the charge of the district officers. It was not found possible, however, to dispense with the services of the Tálukdári officer in Gujarát. I have already described the Tálukdári tenure on pp. 256–258.

The Tálukdárs personally are distinguished for loyalty. They celebrated the Jubilee of the Queen-Empress with the utmost enthusiasm at Ahmadábád in 1887. Her portrait was hung with garlands of flowers, a congratulatory address in a silver casket was forwarded to Her Majesty, and Rs. 20,000 were subscribed by them for a memorial of her jubilee year. Yet with all their good qualities, it is difficult to save them from the consequences of their hereditary habits of improvidence, and it is stated that many of them are hopelessly involved. In spite of the efforts made for their rescue, they are reported to have 'succumbed anew to the wiles of the money-lenders, with a readiness and ignorance which showed that they had not benefited by past experience[1].'

In the year after this statement was made, an interesting account was given of the causes of their embarrassments. 'The result of legislation in regard to the Tálukdárs of Gujarát has not been altogether successful. It is a matter of notoriety that already very many of the estates freed from debt in the manner

[1] *Bombay Administration Report for* 1886–87, p. xv.

provided by the legislature are again seriously encumbered. In some cases, the second state of the Tálukdárs is even worse than the first. The causes ordinarily assigned for this state of things are the reckless improvidence of the Tálukdárs, the exaggerated view they entertain of their own position, their wasteful expenditure on marriages and other domestic ceremonies, their open-handed extravagance at all times, and the enlargement of credit which followed the recognition of absolute proprietorship in the soil accorded by section 20 of Act VI of 1862. But experience has shown that there are other causes, perhaps not so well known.

'Amongst those causes may be mentioned the following: (1) Litigation—most of which is wholly unnecessary—with co-sharers. (2) Intrigues of kárbháris (managers). (3) Malpractices of creditors of the sáukár (money-lending) class. And (4) Extravagance of sons. In most cases the kárbhári is a creditor of the Tálukdár: he encourages quarrels and litigation among the bháyáts (co-sharers), lends pecuniary assistance, and thus obtains a control over his master. Still more helpless are the Tálukdárs in their relations with their Wánia creditors. Debts equivalent to from four to twelve years' revenue have already been contracted by Tálukdárs, whose estates have been recently released[1].'

The disturbances caused by the indebtedness of the Deccan peasantry, who had used the credit given them and created for them by their possession of the 'survey tenure' to borrow freely, and thus to make themselves practically the tenants of money-lenders instead

[1] *Bombay Administration Report for* 1887–88, pp. 59, 60.

of the Government, occurred before the period under review. The passing of the Deccan Agriculturists' Relief Act in 1879 therefore lies beyond the scope of this work. The indebtedness of the peasantry still continues a source of anxiety in the Deccan; and the working of the Deccan Relief Act is, as already stated, again under enquiry (1891).

It remains to see the effect upon the land, as apart from the cultivators, of the establishment of the 'survey tenure' and of the land-rights which it has conferred on the peasantry of Bombay. In 1885-86 it was estimated that in the Bombay Presidency excluding Sind there were 27,111,272 acres of cultivable land; of which 24,035,256 acres were cultivated, and 3,076,016 were cultivable waste. During the five years from 1885-86 to 1889-90, no less than 1,004,104 acres of the waste were reported to have been taken into cultivation. The nett actual increase of cultivated land after all deductions was, as already stated, 446,383 acres.

The proportion of the cultivated to the cultivable area is very large in all the inland districts except the Panch Mahâls and Khândesh, and it is a noteworthy feature that immigrants are beginning to move freely into the latter districts. Of the coast districts, only Ratnâgiri, perhaps the most closely cultivated district in the Presidency, is as yet completely occupied. There is much cultivable waste both in Thâna and Kolâba; and in each of these districts it is found more profitable to reclaim the salt marshes than to break up new land towards the interior. North Kânara is still capable of a considerable extension of cultivation, and there is a large demand for labour in the spice gardens of this wealthy district. It is difficult, owing to the want of data, to speak with precision regarding Sind, but it may be asserted that the improvement, which is there due to increased facilities for irrigation and to the Irrigation Settlements, is as great as, if not greater than, in the rest of the Presidency.

CHAPTER IX.

Public Works.

THE Department of Public Works in India conducts many undertakings which in England are left to private enterprise. The position of the British Government as chief landlord, and the absence of an adequate organisation of capital in India, render this inevitable. If the Government did not construct large and necessary works of public utility, they would not be undertaken at all. The English administrators have tried to efficiently discharge the duties thus laid upon them, and have organised a special department in each Province to deal with the multifarious subjects which come under the head of Public Works. The labours of the Public Works Departments, central and provincial, have transformed the face of the country, and have done much to consolidate India from a collection of territories into an empire.

The Public Works administration of any province, like Bombay, is complicated by the circumstance that the Supreme Government keeps the financial direction, though not the executive management, of certain important divisions of the Public Works Department, such as the main lines of railway and irrigation, in its own hands. In regard to many important questions a provincial Governor may suggest improvements or reforms, yet he cannot carry them into execution without the previous assent of the Government of India. This dual control is inevitable; but it makes the connected study of the progress of public works in a particular province a task of no small difficulty.

The work performed by the Public Works Department in the Bombay Presidency arranges itself into five main branches. (1) The development of means of communication, such as railways, roads, bridges and ferries. (2) The superintendence of irrigation, one of the most important duties of the Indian Government, as the great State-owner of the land. (3) The facilitation of commercial enterprise by the construction of harbours, docks, &c. (4) The maintenance of the material fabric of government, such as court houses, police lines, schools, and public or quasi-public buildings of many sorts. (5) The construction of sanitary works and appliances, such as schemes for drainage and water-supply. The really important functions of the Public Works Department, from the civil point of view, may be brought under one or other of these heads. The branch of military works, including the construction or maintenance of barracks, fortifications and schemes for general defence, stands on a different footing, and is therefore treated in another chapter.

Dealing first with Means of Communication, a brief notice must suffice for the railways and the growth of the different railway systems in Bombay. For there are, strictly speaking, no provincial railways in the

Presidency, that is to say, no lines constructed out of provincial revenues. The great arterial systems are all under the Government of India, and the Provincial Governments have no pecuniary interest in them. But they are decentralised to a certain extent for the sake of convenience in administration, and the Bombay Government exercises immediate control over the three great lines running out of Bombay City, with a total mileage of 5001 miles, of which, however, only 1988 miles are within the actual limits of the Presidency. It also supervises the railways in the Native States of Káthiáwár and those constructed by the Gáekwár of Baroda.

The three trunk lines referred to are the 'G. I. P.' or Great Indian Peninsula Railway Company, the 'B. B. and C. I.' or Bombay, Baroda and Central India Company, and the Southern Maráthá Railway Company. The two first are guaranteed lines, which the Imperial Government has, at certain dates and under certain conditions, the option of purchasing. The North-Western State Railway, originally constructed mainly for military purposes, runs along the right bank of the Indus from Sukkur to Karáchi, and is throughout that section in the province of Sind, but it is not managed by the Bombay Government.

The most conspicuous engineering work accomplished by the Great Indian Peninsula Railway, during the five years under review, was the doubling of the line from Bhusáwal in the Bombay Presidency to Khandwá in the Central Provinces, where it joins the Málwá line. This was completed in January, 1889.

Perhaps even more important for the future prosperity of Bombay City was the development of the Indian Midland Railway Company's system by the opening of the lines to Jhánsi, and from Jhánsi to Gwalior, on February 1, 1888, and March 1, 1889, respectively. A shorter route has thus been provided from Bombay to Cawnpur, *viâ* Bhusáwal, Khandwá and Itársi on the Great Indian Peninsula Railway, and thence *viâ* Bhopal and Jhánsi on the Indian Midland Railway; and also from Bombay to Agra *viâ* Jhánsi and Gwalior, where a junction is formed with the old Sindhia Railway. These lines have not been in use long enough to determine how far the trade from Cawnpur and the North-Western Provinces will be diverted from Calcutta, and adopt Bombay for purposes of export. The recent completion of the Nágpur-Bengal Railway will also exercise an important influence on the fortunes of the Great Indian Peninsula line, as a continuation of its Nágpur branch, and the most direct route from Bombay to Calcutta.

In regard to the working of the Great Indian Peninsula Railway, an improvement was effected by permitting mail and passenger trains to traverse the Bhor Ghát at night all through the year. This had been forbidden during the monsoon months, but time has shown that the Bhor Ghát is now safe from serious slips, and the prohibition was provisionally removed by the Agent during the five years under review. His action was confirmed by the Board of Directors on June 5, 1891, to the great convenience of the public and the Post Office. In the construction of permanent buildings, considerable energy was shown by the Great Indian Peninsula Railway during the period from 1885 to 1890. A new and handsome station was completed at the terminus in Bombay; large additions were made at Nágpur to meet the requirements of the increased traffic expected on the opening of the Nágpur-Bengal line; and extensive alterations were taken in hand at Poona, where the Southern Maráthá line forms its junction with the Great Indian Peninsula Railway.

In the Southern Maráthá Railway system, important extensions were completed during Lord Reay's administration. Originally projected and undertaken as a famine relief work, it has developed into one of the most useful railways in India. The section from Dhárwár to Bellary in the Madras Presidency was opened in September, 1885; the extension from Hubli to Harihar in October, 1886; the section of the West Deccan line from Poona to Koregaon in November, 1886; the whole of the West Deccan line in December, 1887; and the connection with the West of India Portuguese Railway in February, 1888. Further works are in progress to connect the system with the Madras Presidency. The Mysore Railways were transferred to the Southern Maráthá Railway Company in July, 1886.

The Southern Maráthá Railway thus developed during Lord Reay's tenure of office from a local line of 457 miles into a railway system of 1339 miles. It is premature to forecast the prospects of the Southern Maráthá system. Originally started as a famine line and extended for the same reason, it traverses a somewhat poor and sparsely populated country. But along its route lie several highly productive tracts and valuable forests, and the traffic has exceeded the amount anticipated. If it further develops, it may fairly be expected to earn 4 per cent on the capital expended on its construction. If this amount be reached, the Bombay Government will have spread a net-work of railways over a great area, at times terribly stricken with famine, without imposing a further burden on the general revenue.

The most interesting addition to the Southern Maráthá system was the connecting line with the West of India Portuguese Railway. This line runs through the Portuguese territory eastward from the port of Marmagáo, and was projected under the treaty made with Portugal in 1878. It has been constructed by a British Company, the interest being met by the hypothecation of the four lakhs of rupees, which the Portuguese Government yearly receives under that treaty from the Government of India, in return *inter alia* for the concession of the excise and salt monopoly. It proved a costly line to build, and the completion of its junction with the Southern Maráthá line near the frontier at Castle Rock was celebrated in January, 1888, by an imposing official ceremony, at which Lord Reay and the Governor-General of Portuguese India were present. It seems likely to command a large traffic, as Marmagáo will now be the most accessible seaport for the cotton grown in Bellary and the adjacent districts, which formerly had to seek an outlet by Madras. The railway is maintained by the company which constructed it, but the locomotive arrangements remain entirely under the management of the Southern Maráthá Railway Company.

These developments of the Great Indian Peninsula and the Southern Maráthá Railways, although completed during the administration of Lord Reay, were projected and commenced before his arrival. Lord Reay himself obtained sanction from the Supreme Government for the construction of a line from Godhrá to Ratlám in connection with the Bombay, Baroda and Central India Railway system. The main line of this system runs from Bombay to Ahmadábád, but it also works the Rájputána-Málwá and Cawnpur-Achnera railways, by which it controls the direct communication from Bombay to Delhi and the Punjab. The growth of the Bombay, Baroda and Central India traffic, and of the Rájputána Railway system, in bringing down produce (especially wheat) to Bombay, made it imperative that some relief should be given.

'This recurring pressure has again brought before the Company,' wrote Major Bisset, the Agent of the Bombay, Baroda and Central India Railway on June 4, 1889, 'the question of what is to be done to enable it to fulfil its duty to Government and to the public, for we see, and I think Government will see, that we cannot go on much longer without breaking down. . . . We can no longer dally with the question of increasing the carrying power of the line between Ajmere and Ahmadábád. At the present moment, a week's bad weather in England, or an unfavourable telegram of the prospects of the American crop, may pour upon us an overwhelming traffic. Even now, although our officers and staff are doing very well, and are running every train that can be run, I believe we do not get all traffic that would be offered, if we could clear our export grain platforms more rapidly, and I am in daily expectation of a block.'

Lord Reay took measures to meet the views of the Bombay, Baroda and Central India Company. Two schemes were proposed, the one to double the line from Ahmaḍábád to Ajmere, the other to continue the existing branch from Anand to Godhrá to the eastward and form a junction with the Málwá line at Ratlám. The latter plan presented great advantages. It would provide two distinct routes from Bombay and Baroda to Ajmere, the one *viâ* Anand, Ahmadábád and Abú Road, and the other *viâ* Anand, Godhrá, Ratlám and Nímach, and would open up direct railway communication between the rich province of Gujarát and Central India. Throughout the period of his administration, Lord Reay persistently pressed the importance of this scheme on the Supreme Government, and just before he left India, he obtained its sanction to the construction of the Godhrá-Ratlám link railway. The line will be about 115 miles in length and is estimated to cost 100 lakhs of rupees.

The question of railway development in Sind also occupied Lord Reay's attention. At present the only railway communication possessed by Karáchi, one of the most important and most promising ports in India, is by means of the North-Western State Railway. This line was primarily constructed for military purposes. It runs along the right or west bank of the Indus to a point opposite Sukkur, where it crosses the river. It proceeds thence *viâ* Baháwalpur to Múltán, where it branches out on the right to Lahore, and on the left to Miánwáli, whence an extension is in progress to Ráwal Pindi. This circuitous route to Delhi is unsatisfactory to the merchants of Karáchi, who have for many years been pressing for the construction of a more direct line to Delhi and Agra, and for direct railway communication with Bombay. They urge the excellence of their harbour, and point out that it lies some hours nearer England than Bombay. If, therefore, they had a more direct inland line than the circuitous route by Lahore, they argue that much of the produce of North-Western India would come to Karáchi for shipment. In the second place, they complain that their only postal communication with Bombay, with which most of their correspondence is carried on, is by a bi-weekly steamer service, and that there exists an imperative necessity for a daily post by rail.

On the other hand a railway across the arid deserts of Bikaner and Jaisalmer, through which any line from Karáchi *viâ* Haidarábád to Delhi would have to run, holds out but little prospect of becoming a profitable undertaking. It would pass through a country with few resources in itself and apparently not susceptible of much improvement. However, the Government of India, in response to the representations of the Karáchi merchants, consented to make a reconnaissance of the proposed route in the cold season of

1888–89, and on a more detailed scale in 1889–90. Whatever direction the line[1] may ultimately take, it must first run to Umarkot,—an historic town and important mart, the birthplace of the Emperor Akbar, about ninety miles east of Haidarábád. From Umarkot the line could be continued either across the desert for 550 miles to Delhi or for about 150 miles to Pachpadra on the Jodhpur Railway.

Direct railway communication between Haidarábád in Sind and Bombay might be secured by the prolongation of this Umarkot line *viâ* Dísa to Pálanpur on the Rájputána State Railway. But it would be more convenient for Karáchi if a direct line were made along the southern coast of Sind and then through the Native State of Cutch to a junction with the Káthiáwár system. Such a railway would do much to open up the State of Cutch, through which it would run for more than 100 miles. But that State is not a rich one, and does not seem able to bear the expenses of constructing its section unaided. There are no serious engineering difficulties in regard to the Rann of Cutch. Karáchi has good ground to complain of its isolation alike from Bombay and from direct communication with Central and North-Western India, and an effort will doubtless be made to improve its railway facilities.

Apart from the general question of uniting Karáchi with the main railway systems of India, stands the project of opening up the province of Sind by a local railway from Gidhu Bandar (which is connected by a ferry across the Indus with Kotri on the North-Western

[1] Since sanctioned as far as the Nára valley, and commenced.

State Railway), through Haidarábád to Umarkot. The importance of such a line as the first link in a scheme for directly connecting Sind with the rest of India has been already noticed. But local reasons are also urged for the line being undertaken at once and as a provincial project. The district of Thar and Párkar has been provided with a splendid system of irrigation works by the Eastern Nara Canals, and is now extremely prosperous, but it has no means of obtaining a market for its produce. It would be most costly to make metalled roads for want of proper material on the spot, and every year the difficulty increases in obtaining camels, which alone can provide efficient transport.

'It appears,' wrote Mr. A. F. Baillie, Secretary of the East India Tramways Company, on November 23, 1885, 'that formerly the trade between Haidarábád and Aláhyár-jo-Tando [the first stage on the way to Umarkot] was chiefly conducted by means of camels, and that up to some seven or eight years ago, the returns arising from the octrois amounted to say Rs. 9000 per annum, but that they have now fallen to Rs. 5000. This arises from the fact that of late years the demand for camels for military transport and other purposes has greatly increased, and that the supply for trading purposes has in consequence decreased. Camel transport on an adequate scale having failed, it has to some extent been replaced by the ordinary country bullock carts, but as the roads are totally unadapted for this description of traffic, the cart owners dislike the route, and charge high rates; and in consequence trade has languished, and, as already stated, the returns for octrois have been reduced by nearly 50 per cent. Some allowance must be made for the feelings of the cart owners, for, without exception, the road connecting this city [Haidarábád] with Aláhyár-jo-Tando is the worst that I have ever had the misfortune to travel. Throughout the march of twenty-two miles I have never found one hundred consecutive yards of sound way; and although mounted on an extremely capable *Mahri* I was never able to proceed except at the slowest walking pace. In other countries that I have visited, where the soil is equally loose, and where a similar description of cart is in use, huge ruts are created, but ultimately a solid foundation is reached, and the ruts themselves serve to form the permanent way: but in the district of Sind that I have just visited, there would appear to be no bottom, for the carts sink deeper and deeper, until the loose soil between the wheels reaches to the axle, and further progress is impeded. I am far from imputing mismanagement to any one, and can bear witness that attempts have been made to improve the way; but with the class of material on which to work, it seems to me impossible, except at an enormous expense, to form a permanent road for the carts, and a recurrence to the old system of camel transport, for the reasons already stated, is equally impossible.'

Under these circumstances two successive Commissioners in Sind, Mr. Erskine and Mr. Pritchard, urged the construction of this railway upon the Bombay Government. They showed that owing to the nature of the country it would cost but little more to build a light railway than to make a road, and it was suggested that second-hand rails and rolling-stock could be obtained from the North-Western State Railway. It was estimated that such a railway from Gidhu Bandar to the banks of the Eastern Nára, a distance of 75 miles, could be constructed with babúl sleepers from the local forests, for 16 lakhs of rupees. According to this project, the line would stop 15 miles short of Umarkot, because of the expense involved in bridging the Eastern Nára. Towards the 16 lakhs, the Local Boards of Haidarábád and Thar and Párkar offered to contribute a lakh and three-quarters, and the Bombay Government expressed its willingness to finance the remainder.

The Secretary of State for India sanctioned the construction of this railway, and the Government of India sent an officer to enquire into the matter. Regarding it from the imperial point of view, he estimated the construction of a line, up to the standard of the great trunk railways, with steel sleepers and an expensive ferry across the Indus from Gidhu Bandar to Kotri, which should transport the loaded railway waggons, at 31½ lakhs of rupees. The Government of India forwarded this estimate to the Bombay Government with expressions of approval, and evidently hoped that the construction of the line would be the first step towards a through railway to Pachpadra or Delhi.

This point of view did not commend itself to the Bombay Government. On December 5, 1889, it replied: 'The scheme, as now foreshadowed, is designed more for the future than for the present, and requires a very much larger outlay from provincial resources than is considered necessary by this Government for probably many years to come. In fact, this Government is asked to construct the line up to a standard which would only be required should it become an imperial highway, and thus to incur expenditure the interest on which may never be recouped so long as the section remains as a local provincial railway.' In the last letter upon this subject during Lord Reay's administration, written upon February 6, 1890, the position is still more clearly defined: 'However desirable it may be to make the line more substantial in character from the outset, the Governor in Council regrets that the finances of this Presidency cannot bear the extra expense that is sought to be entailed. Under ordinary circumstances that part of the country would have been opened out by roads, but as the first cost of a road and its maintenance would not be much less than a cheap railway, the Governor in Council is prepared to make the railway instead. But the great object sought is to get railway communication at the least possible expense, and then to improve the line hereafter as the traffic improves.'

I have explained this divergence of opinion between the Government of India and the Bombay Government, for it illustrates their relations to each other. It is natural and right that the Supreme Government should look to the ultimate advantages to the Empire of any proposed scheme; it is also right that the Provincial Government, as was done in this case by Lord Reay, should primarily pay attention to local requirements, and should jealously safeguard the interests of the provincial finances.

Only second in importance to the development of railways running through British territory is the expansion of railways in Native States. The more enlightened native princes are fully alive to the advantages of railways in opening up their territories and increasing their prosperity. They have proved themselves ready to spend large sums on railway construction not so much as a commercial speculation, but as a duty which they owe to their people. Lord Reay steadily endeavoured to encourage this feeling. The Gáekwár of Baroda took the lead as a railway projector. But his desire to retain jurisdiction over local lines running through his territory causes a difficulty in the case of railways which pass partly through his dominions and partly through the British districts. The principal railways constructed up to the present time by the Gáekwár have therefore lain entirely in the State of Baroda.

They consist of two groups. The one to the south of Baroda comprises lines from Miyagaon and Vishvamitri on the Bombay, Baroda and Central India Railway, to Dabhoi, constructed in 1873 and 1881; and from Dabhoi to Bahádarpur and Chándod, constructed in 1879. The other, in the north of the State, which was completed in 1888, runs from Mehsana to Kherálu, and contemplates branches from Visnagar on this line to Vijápur and from Mehsana to Patán: the latter opened on the 20th July, 1891. On all these lines the Gáekwár exercises full jurisdiction, but as he has adopted the Indian Railway Acts, the law in this particular is uniform, although administered by Baroda courts. The jurisdiction question stands in the way of other schemes. The Baroda State is so intermixed with British territory that it is often impossible to get from one part of it to another without passing through our districts. There can be no doubt that divided responsibility is a great mistake. But where the lines are merely short branches serving isolated districts, there seems to be no vital reason for demanding the same absolute jurisdiction which must be exercised by the paramount power over the great trunk lines. It is hoped that a compromise may be arrived at, giving the Baroda State jurisdiction over branch lines passing mainly through its territories, while the British Government retains its authority over the trunk lines.

The two projects hindered by the jurisdiction question were, (1) a line from Anand, on the Bombay, Baroda and Central India Railway, westwards to Petlád and Sojitra, thence to Piploi and Nadiád, and so eventually to Cambay; and (2) a line from Surat eastwards to Songarh, and thence to Nandurbár in Khándesh. The latter project well illustrates the jurisdiction difficulty. On leaving Surat it would traverse 5½ miles of British territory, then 13 miles of Baroda, then 13½ miles of British, then 18½ miles of Baroda, after which it would pass into British territory and into minor tributary States which have no jurisdiction of their own. A compromise was however, arrived at with regard to the first of these schemes, and the line from Anand to Petlád was opened on May 5, 1890. The Gáekwár ordered the construction of a line from Mehsana to Viramgám[1], a direct result of the friendly relations between Lord Reay and His Highness. It will be of great benefit to the Káthiáwár system, as it connects it by a metre gauge line with the metre gauge main line, the Rájputána-Málwá. It only remains to add that, as in Sind, the cost of making and maintaining roads in many parts of Gujarát is extremely great, owing to the absence of metal, and that it is therefore eminently a province for the construction of railways.

The improvement of railway communications in Káthiáwár during Lord Reay's administration made more rapid progress than in Baroda. The division of the Káthiáwár peninsula into numerous Native States might have been expected to raise many difficulties but for the public spirit of the princes and chiefs. The Káthiáwár railway system was commenced under the rule of Sir Richard Temple by the opening of a line, in 1880, from Wadhwán to Bhaunagar, built at the expense of the Thákur Sáhib of the latter State, and of a second line, running through the State of Gondal from Dhoráji to Dhassa, and joining the Bhaunagar line at Dhola, in 1881. The advantages of these lines became so evident that it was resolved to expand them. Two railways were constructed, one from Jetalsar traversing the State of Junágarh to the port of Verávval, the other from Dhoráji through the State of Porbandar to the port of Porbandar. Lord Reay cut

[1] Opened on the 1st February, 1891.

the first sod of the latter line at Dhoráji on December 29, 1887, and took occasion to praise the public spirit of the Thákur Sáhib of Gondal, who had given up his first idea of making a railway to his capital, Gondal, in order to co-operate with the Administration of Porbandar in building a line to open up that port. At the same time his Excellency announced that Gondal was raised to a first-class State, and that the Thákur's salute was increased from nine to eleven guns. Lord Reay opened the line before he left India, the construction having been remarkably rapid.

An even more enthusiastic railway constructor is the Thákur Sáhib of Morvi. Not satisfied with building a line from Wadhwán to Morvi, he has gone outside the limits of his own State and extended it to Rájkot, whence it may possibly be prolonged through Nawánagar to the fine trading harbour of Saláya on the coast of Káthiáwár. This remarkable development of railways in the Peninsula of Káthiáwár reflects the greatest credit on everyone concerned; on the enlightened rulers of Bhaunagar, Gondal, Morvi, and Junágarh, and on the successive Governors of Bombay, Sir Richard Temple, Sir James Fergusson, and Lord Reay.

The only other railway in a Native State requiring notice is the Kolhápur State Railway. This line was commenced in February, 1888 (opened 1891). It was constructed by the Kolhápur Darbar, which provided all the money; but it is intended that, when complete, it shall be worked by the South Maráthá Railway Company as a branch of their system. The line runs from Kolhápur City to Miráj on the Southern Maráthá line, a distance of $28\frac{3}{4}$ miles, and was estimated to cost Rs. 22,72,520. This is a very large sum for construction alone, but the works were difficult and involve an expensive bridge over the Krishna River.

It is difficult in the case of the great trunk systems to show the local development during the five years under review. For long sections of those systems lie beyond the limits of the Bombay Presidency; and their extension or improvement is for the most part made quite independently of the Bombay Government. It must therefore be clearly understood that the following table is not, in regard to the three main systems, intended to claim for the Bombay Government the credit due for developments in which they had not a leading part. Its sole purpose is to present a bird's-eye view of the extension of railway communication in the Bombay Presidency, or directly connected with that presidency—of the lines, in short, which are popularly associated with Bombay; on which the prosperity of its British districts and Native States largely depends; and of which the direct control has been made over by the Supreme Government of India to the Bombay Government for the purposes of railway administration. In each system the working expenses have been deducted from the gross earnings. The Bhopal line is excluded, as it passed to the Indian Midland system before the close of the period under review.

RAILWAY SYSTEMS OF, OR CONNECTED WITH, THE BOMBAY PRESIDENCY, 1885 TO 1890.

	Miles Open.			Nett Earnings.		
	Jan. 1 1885.	Dec. 31 1889.	Increase.	1885.	1889.	Increase.
				Rs.	Rs.	Rs.
Bombay, Baroda and Central India (including Rájputána-Málwá and Cawnpur-Achnera Railways)	1,852½	2,106½	254*	1,53,37,863	1,84,14,472	30,76,609
Great Indian Peninsula (including Dhond-Manmád Railway, Khangaon and Amráoti Branches)	1,448	1,448	—	1,83,13,310	1,83,23,102	9,792
Southern Maráthá Railway (including Mysore State Railways)	354	1,275	921	1,40,338	11,83,649	10,43,311
Káthiáwár Railways	193	420½	227½	3,91,247	6,56,558	2,65,311
Baroda Railways	58¾	86½	27¾	55,623	73,530	17,907
Total . . .	3,906¼	5,336½		3,42,38,381	3,86,51,311	
Total Increase			1,430¼			44,12,930

Next in importance to railways as a means of communication come tramways. These convenient adjuncts to a comprehensive railway system have long received attention from the Bombay Government. During the period under review, the Indian Feeder Lines Company was started, in 1887, with the object of constructing tramways to the principal

[1] By lease of the Cawnpur-Achnera Railway from the Government of the N. W. Provinces.

places at short distances from the main lines of the railway systems. Lord Reay encouraged this useful project, and the Indian Tramways Act was extended to the whole of the Bombay Presidency except the cities of Bombay and Karáchi, where special Acts are in force and where tramway systems have for some years been in operation. The first undertaking of the new Company was to lay a horse-tramway from Násik City to the Násik Road Station on the Great Indian Peninsula Railway; the next project contemplated was a steam-tramway from the Barsi Road Station to Barsi. Of more importance is the scheme for constructing a tramway from Ahmadábád to the once famous but now decayed port of Dholera, a distance of seventy-seven miles. This is a large project, and the cost is estimated at not much under nineteen lakhs of rupees. But the wealth of Ahmadábád and the vitality of Dholera as a trading-centre seem to hold out promise of its success.

While the construction of railways and tramways, the modern means of communication which are transforming the face of India, forms an important part of the duties of the Bombay Railway Branch of Public Works Department and demands the careful attention of each successive Governor, roads, the primary means of communication, are not neglected. The policy of the British as the paramount power has been to cover India with a network of sound roads, which remain as a witness to the thoroughness of our engineers, as the Roman roads of Europe testify to the greatness of the conquering race of two thousand years ago. To enumerate the new roads commenced or completed, or the old roads improved or metalled during the five years under review, would tire out the most patient reader.

But to indicate the scale of the works undertaken, in spite of the general policy of retrenchment, it may be noted that in 1888-89 no less than Rs. 20,92,153 was spent upon communications, namely, roads, bridges, and ferries, in addition to Rs. 5,47,522 on establishment and tools. In that year, also, two important roads from Ghoda to Ambegáon and from Jamgáon to Kotul were commenced as 'parts of a scheme for opening up the hilly tracts of country in the north-west of the Poona, and the west of the Ahmadnagar Districts, inhabited by Kolis and Rámosis, whose condition will, it is hoped, be thereby improved [1].'

Bridges and ferries also come under the purview of the Public Works Department, as facilitating means of communication. It fell to Lord Reay's lot to open the great bridge across the Indus at Sukkur, over which the North-Western State Railway passes to the right bank of the river. This bridge, the finest example of the cantilever principle before the completion of the Forth Bridge, was, however, not built by the Bombay Railway Department, and was only inaugurated by Lord Reay in his capacity as Governor of the Presidency. Perhaps the most important undertaking of the kind by the Bombay Public Works Department during the five years was the reconstruc-

[1] *Administration Report of Civil Works of the Public Works Department, General Branch, Bombay Presidency, for the year* 1888-89, p. 11.

tion of the Ellis Bridge at Ahmadábád,—a work greatly needed both for the sake of the town itself and of the district across the river.

With regard to ferries, mention has already been made of the great ferry across the Indus from Kotri on the North-Western State Railway to Gidhu Bandar in connection with the proposed railway to Umarkot, of which it would form an important link. Many lesser ferries are maintained by the Bombay Government, and take the place of bridges where it is inexpedient to spend large sums on building.

In a province, like Bombay, with a long coast-line and numerous ports and harbours, it is hardly necessary to say that communication by sea is often cheaper and more convenient than by land. Many steamers ply between Bombay and other places on the coast. The mails from Bombay to Karáchi, the second city in the presidency, are, as I have mentioned, carried by steamers. The immigrants from Ratnágiri, who work in the Bombay mills, come to the great manufacturing city in steamers. An interesting point with regard to such steamship communication is that it rests in the hands of independent companies. Private enterprise supplies the need without the interference of Government, and to all appearance supplies it adequately.

Though steamship communication can be safely left to private enterprise, it is otherwise with regard to irrigation. The British Government in India is not only the great capitalist who has to provide for or guarantee undertakings requiring expenditure. It is also the great landlord, and in that capacity owes many duties to its tenants. Among such duties the construction and maintenance of irrigation works hold a leading place.

The importance of artificial irrigation in India, where the whole prosperity of the country depends upon the rainfall or other supply of water for agricultural purposes, is obvious, and the British Government has spent vast sums upon it. The general direction, as well as the financial control, of irrigation is retained by the Supreme Government of India, in the same way as it controls railway communication. But the Bombay Public Works Department has the administrative and executive management of irrigation works within the boundaries of the Presidency. It has also the power of sanctioning new works up to a limit of two lakhs of rupees, although the Government of India retains ultimate control by restricting the amount of the budget allotment to Bombay. In the exercise of these powers the Supreme Government has practically stopped all extension of the irrigation works in Gujarát and the Deccan, because they do not yield a direct return even approaching the interest on the capital expended upon them. The Bombay Government has not availed itself of the provision for undertaking such works provincially, that is to say, by making its provincial finances responsible for the interest on the outlay. Owing to the short term of five years for which the Provincial Contract runs, it would not have time to realise a substantial share in the profits of such works, while it would incur the risks of future contracts being so framed as to exclude the consideration of eventual revenue resulting from them. The Bombay Government therefore prefers to invest any portion of its balance or surplus revenue in the permanent improvement of the accommodation for public offices and of the means of communication. This expenditure involves no future obligations, and is, at the same time, of distinct advantage to the local administration.

An idea of the proportionate importance of irrigation among the works undertaken by the Bombay Government may be formed from the following figures[1]. Out of Rs. 72,57,620 actually expended by the Bombay Public Works Department, in 1889-90, on works and repairs, excluding the charges for establishment, Rs. 40,26,549 were spent on civil works, imperial, provincial, and local, including roads, buildings, &c.; Rs. 11,03,924 on military works; and Rs. 21,27,147 on irrigation.

In dealing with irrigation in the Bombay Presidency a wide distinction must be drawn between irrigation in the Province of Sind, where it is an absolute necessity, and irrigation in Gujarát and the Deccan, where it is of the nature of famine-insurance, and a convenience for improving agriculture.

Both systems are administered and reported upon to the Government of India by the Government of Bombay; but they are kept distinct, and the figures regarding them are shown separately.

[1] *Administration Report of Civil Works of the Public Works Department (General Branch), Bombay Presidency, for the year* 1889-90; Bombay, 1890, p. 3.

'The irrigation system of Sind,' says a Resolution of the Government of India, dated June 28, 1889, 'consists of a great network of canals, led off from the Indus, watering a country which is almost rainless and devoid of wells, and which but for these canals would produce hardly any crops except in basins flooded by the spill of the river. It also includes a system of embankments, whose object it is to shut in the flood-waters of the river and prevent its spill. But though these canals and embankments practically constitute one combined system, managed indiscriminately by the same engineering and collecting staff, they are distinguished for account purposes into four classes according to the nature of the funds employed in their construction. In the first class, major works, are four canals constructed from Loan Funds; in the second, minor works, for which Capital and Revenue Accounts are kept, are seven canals constructed from Revenue. The rest of the canals fall into the third class, minor works, for which only Revenue Accounts are kept, having for the most part been constructed from Revenue in earlier years, before a careful system of Capital Accounts was started. The fourth class, agricultural works, consists chiefly of the embankments in Upper Sind, which are less closely connected with irrigation than with the protection of the country and the retention of the river in its proper course. Few of these canals are entirely new, though all have been greatly improved under British rule.'

This paragraph gives some idea of the complicated system of accounts kept with regard to irrigation in Sind, and of the importance of such works to that province. The nature of the country and its peculiar climatic conditions render it entirely dependent upon the Indus for its agricultural prosperity. This has been recognised from the earliest times, and several of the Native dynasties laboured to maintain and improve a system of irrigation. But no previous Government ever attempted so much as the British have accomplished, and the methodical and persistent labours of a succession of great engineers are rendering no longer appropriate the sobriquet given to the province by Sir Richard Burton in one of his early books, entitled 'Scinde, or the Unhappy Valley.' Down to the end of the year 1888–89 Rs. 84,28,392 had been expended in Sind on the four major irrigation works. Of this sum Rs. 51,61,311 had been spent on the Eastern Nára Works, Rs. 16,73,079 on the Begári Canal, Rs. 12,54,874 on the Desert Canal, and Rs. 3,39,128 on the Unharwah. On the seven minor works, for which Capital and Revenue Accounts are kept, there had been expended up to the same date Rs. 32,73,637; of which the largest items were Rs. 13,88,713 on the Sukkur Canal, and Rs. 10,25,928 on the Fuleli Canals.

The irrigation works in Sind are divided into seven executive charges; the area of cultivation irrigated in each being shown in the following table. Much of this large area must, but for irrigation, remain absolutely barren; and even the localities which would obtain an overflow of the Indus greatly benefit from the regulation and storage of the supply. The figures are taken from the Sind Irrigation Revenue Report for 1888–89.

IRRIGATION AREA IN SIND, 1888–89.

	Government Land.	Jághir Land.	Total.
	Acres.	Acres.	Acres.
Begári Canals . .	279,236	82,434	361,670
Shikárpur Canals .	137,133	6,289	143,422
Ghár Canals . . .	428,552	16,822	445,374
Eastern Nára . .	213,700	4,000	217,700
Haidarábád Canals	334,370	48,427	382,797
Fuleli Canals. . .	252,494	54,921	307,415
Karáchi Canals . .	242,071	18,186	260,257
Total . .	1,887,556	231,079	2,118,635

To irrigate this area of 3310 square miles, 5916 miles of canals and 613 miles of *bunds*, or protective embankments, had to be maintained in the year 1888–89[1], and their totals steadily increase as fresh developments are initiated in the different districts. The annual outlay on this vast system of irrigation and protective works in Sind may be summarised thus:—Improvements, Rs. 1,69,009; maintenance and repairs, Rs. 11,81,720; cost of collecting the revenue, Rs. 3,91,630; total in 1888–89, Rs. 17,42,359[2].

Large as this amount is, it brought in a full return, not only in the increased prosperity of the province, but in actual revenue. It is extremely difficult to estimate the exact amount of this revenue, as it takes the shape of increased rent for irrigated land, rather than of a direct charge for the supply of water. It has been

[1] *Sind Irrigation Revenue Report*, 1888–89, p. 23. [2] *Ibid.*, p. 37.

customary in the Sind Irrigation Reports to calculate the estimated water-share of the consolidated revenue.

Mention has already been made of the complicated system of capital accounts, and of the existence of numerous minor works for which no capital account is kept, and it is therefore considered better to give the nett revenue of Sind irrigation works without attempting to introduce the question of how far this revenue ought to be reduced by a deduction of the interest on the capital sum expended on them. Subject to this proviso the following were the figures for 1888-89:—Canal Revenue, Rs. 44,69,436[1]; less expenses as shown in the last paragraph, Rs. 17,42,359; net revenue from Sind irrigation works, Rs. 27,27,077.

These figures are instructive. They show that the British Government is not only doing its duty to the people of Sind by constructing and maintaining irrigation works, but is doing so at a profit to the general revenue. 'It cannot be too constantly borne in mind,' says Mr. Arthur C. Trevor, the Acting Commissioner in Sind, on February 14, 1890, in reviewing the Report from which these statistics are taken, 'that practically the whole revenue in Sind depends upon its canal system, and on the facilities afforded for controlling, distributing, and utilizing the waters of the Indus, without which the province would be a desert. The marked development which has taken place of late years is due in a

[1] *Sind Irrigation Revenue Report*, 1888-89, p. 36; on p. 60 of the same Report, however, the figures of the actual receipts on account of canal revenue are given as Rs. 44,58,953, or Rs. 10,483 less than in the above table.

great measure to the influx of capital in connection with the Afghan war expenditure, to the outlet for surplus agricultural produce, afforded by the opening of the railway and the state of the European markets, and to the growth of intelligence and enterprise among the people. With these aids, the water poured into the country year by year has been much more completely utilized than previously[1].'

While irrigation is thus the life-blood of Sind, in the other provinces of Bombay, Gujarát and the Deccan, it is not so much a necessity in ordinary seasons as a means of famine insurance against years when the rainfall is abnormally low. In 1888–89 only 77,318 acres were irrigated (apart from the ordinary wells) in Gujarát and the Deccan—the same year in which 2,118,635 acres were irrigated in Sind. The following statement is instructive as showing the function of canal irrigation in Gujarát and the Deccan as a famine insurance, the irrigated area rising or diminishing according to the rainfall:—

IRRIGATION AND RAINFALL IN GUJARÁT AND THE DECCAN, 1883–89[2].

	Rainfall in Inches.	Acres Irrigated.
1883–84	31·42	32,864
1884–85	24·35	37,701
1885–86	22·80	57,567
1886–87	28·81	40,903
1887–88	26·35	44,303
1888–89	19·65	77,318

The value of irrigation works in the Presidency proper

[1] *Sind Irrigation Report*, 1888–89, p. 62.

[2] *Administration Report of the Public Works Department* (*Irrigation*), 1888–89, p. 1.

is therefore not to be under-rated. For the cultivators readily take advantage of them, when the rainfall is deficient.

From an engineering point of view, the works in the Deccan present features of interest unknown in Sind, as it is a more difficult task to retain and distribute water in a hilly country than on a flat plain watered by a great river. Especially is this true of the Níra Canal, originally conceived by Lieutenant-General J. G. Fife, R.E., and now being constructed. Lord Reay issued a special Minute in regard to the work on March 22, 1890. His Excellency pointed out that it was unfair to compare the financial results of irrigation works in Sind with those in the Deccan and Gujarát, and argued that irrigation schemes in the Presidency proper should be undertaken not only to afford relief in time of scarcity or famine, but with a view to the storage of the rainfall and its better distribution. In a speech delivered before the Bombay Chamber of Commerce on April 11, 1889, Lord Reay had already defined the position of the Government towards irrigation-works in Gujarát and the Deccan. 'In the meantime,' he said, after speaking of the amount of money expended[1], 'the anticipations, as regards the utility of works affording a supply during the monsoon months, had been fully tested, with the result that such works were of use in ordinary years only to a very limited extent, the people being very averse to the extended use of the means of artificial irrigation

[1] *Administration Report of Civil Works of the Public Works Department, Bombay Presidency (General Branch)*, 1888-89, pp. 1, 2.

for the ordinary crops grown at that season. This result is accounted for partly by the expense of manuring and preparing the fields for irrigation, and by the character and distribution of the rainfall, which, in ordinary seasons in most districts, renders artificial irrigation unnecessary, and, the people think, even injurious as respects the staple crop—jowári. In fact, the experience of the past twenty-five years may be said to be that a permanent supply of water, affording the means of irrigation all the year round, so as to admit of the more valuable rabi and perennial crops, such as wheat, gram, ground-nut, sugar-cane, and garden crops of all kinds, is essential to the success of the works. If the supply is not of this class, the works will not pay even their working expenses, and in ordinary seasons the supply, during the short period it is available, will in most cases run to waste, unutilised.

'It is further to be observed that the works themselves, though many of them anything but a financial success, are of great importance in seasons of drought, when the area of irrigation expands. The direct and indirect return may in such years be said to cover a large proportion of the loss in other years, when irrigation is not resorted to, though the same, or nearly the same, expenditure has to be incurred in keeping the works in order. Thus, in the past year, one of deficient rainfall, the works together irrigated 77,318[1] acres, as compared with 44,303 in 1887–88, and 40,903 in 1886–87, both years of good rainfall. These areas are small, as compared with those irrigated by canals in

[1] These are the corrected figures; the speech only gave the estimate.

Northern India; but there is a great difference in the configuration of the country and the sources of supply, and in the Deccan, with its steep confined valleys and rocky ground, with no large rivers affording a permanent supply of water, it is no small matter to have secured over 110 square miles of irrigated cultivation in a year, in which cultivation would, in the particular tracts concerned, have been impossible without the means of artificial irrigation.

'It has been suggested that some of the works, giving the worst financial results, should be abandoned; but as these are often of greatest assistance in years of drought, it is considered that this would be a mistake, as the benefit they confer directly on the ráyat and indirectly on the Government in increasing the food and fodder supply, is of almost incalculable local advantage. Experience goes to show that the future policy should be, when funds are available, to provide storage works to supplement the supply to those canals, which now only afford water for irrigation during the monsoon, and are only utilized to any considerable extent in seasons of drought. This will convert a machine ordinarily practically useless into one at all times affording means of a higher class of cultivation in considerable areas, and at the same time retain its efficiency as a means of mitigating the local effects of drought, by extending cultivation to those crops requiring water during the monsoon and early rabi season only, and which could not otherwise be raised.'

Public works specially designed for the benefit of the commercial community stand on a different basis from the provision of good means of communication and irrigation; they are destined for the advantage of a class well able to help itself, and which will find the capital necessary for any undertaking that promises good financial results as well as commercial advantages. The policy of Government is, therefore, to encourage, direct, and occasionally assist in the execution of works of commercial importance, but not itself to carry them out. Private enterprise may be trusted with the execution and maintenance of such works, and private enterprise, assisted by Government credit, has developed the two greatest commercial undertakings in the Bombay Presidency, the docks and harbour works at Bombay and Karáchi.

The Bombay docks, which are managed by the Bombay Port Trust, are among the finest in the world. The Prince's, which is the older dock, has an area of thirty acres, and contains sixteen quay-side berths. When necessary it can give accommodation for many more vessels by mooring them in a double row, and as many as twenty-four have been loaded and unloaded at one and the same time. The Victoria Dock is smaller, having only a water area of twenty-five acres, but owing to the method of its construction with projecting jetties, nineteen ships can be accommodated with quay-side berths at once. The quays in the Victoria Dock are 7425 feet in length, and in the Prince's Dock 6019 feet; a total of more than two miles and a half. Both are well provided with the modern means for loading and unloading ships. The quays are furnished with ninety-two portable hydraulic cranes, each capable of lifting a load of one and a half tons, in addition to five three-to-five-ton cranes, a twenty-ton crane, a thirty-ton crane, and a hundred-ton crane for lifting boilers and heavy machinery out of and into vessels. All the mechanical arrangements are highly efficient, and can load a steamship with 2491 tons of grain in bags in sixteen hours and a half.

The Bombay docks also contain transit sheds with an area of 651,741 square feet; warehouses with a floor area of 303,216 square feet, and a total accommodation of nearly twenty-two acres. Among these sheds is one at the north end of Prince's Dock specially adapted for the shipment of horses and troops, with a platform for the detrainment of artillery, from which the Indian troops were shipped for Egypt during the last Egyptian war. Through communication is maintained by three branches of lines, connected with the Great Indian Peninsula Railway. Cotton and grain, or other goods, can be brought straight from the district of production to the ship's side, and transferred into the vessel from the railway trucks by means of the hydraulic cranes. During Lord Reay's administration a new Graving Dock, twenty-six feet deep, was constructed at the north-west corner of the Prince's Dock; calculated for the largest steamers likely to pass through the Suez Canal for the next thirty years.

This vast and complete dock system is managed by an independent authority, the Bombay Port Trust, and is considered adequate at present for the commercial needs of the city. The Bombay Port Trust was constituted in June, 1873, and consisted originally of twelve trustees and a chairman, nominated by the Bombay Government. It received a grant of the former estate of the Elphinstone Land and Press Company, situated between the native town of Bombay and the harbour, and comprising about 250 acres of land and 5000 feet of harbour frontage, together with a large portion of the Government Reclamations and foreshore property. The value of these concessions was fixed at Rs. 2,11,70,754, on which sum the trustees were to pay 4 per cent interest for the first ten years and 4½ per cent afterwards.

The operations of the Bombay Port Trust were not at first financially successful, owing to the competition of the owners of adjoining private wharves, but in 1879–80 the Government purchased all the private foreshore-owners' rights, with one or two unimportant exceptions, for Rs. 71,45,000, and transferred them to the Trust. In the same year the constitution of the Trust was altered. The Bombay Chamber of Commerce was allowed to elect five of the trustees, the other seven and the chairman being, as before, nominated by the Government. The Prince's Dock, which had been four years under construction, was opened on January 1, 1880, having cost more than 80 lakhs of rupees, of which 76 lakhs were advanced by the Government at 4½ per cent. interest. The Prince's Dock proved too small for the demands upon it. The Victoria Dock, of nearly the same size and giving still greater facilities for shipping, was therefore undertaken, and on February 21, 1888, Lady Reay opened the first sluice of the new extension.

From 1880 to 1889 the management of Bombay Port Trust showed a steady surplus of revenue over expenditure, in spite of almost yearly reductions of dues, but in 1889–90 the general depression of trade exerted its natural influence on the trade of Bombay, and there was a deficit of Rs. 85,536, which was met from the reserve funds of Rs. 16,90,505 accumulated during the good years. Some idea of the magnitude of the interests involved may be formed from the statements that the capital expenditure of the Bombay Port Trust up to the end of the year 1889–90, deducting sales of land, &c., amounted to Rs. 5,08,56,602, that its revenue for 1889–90 was Rs. 41,97,746, and its expenditure, including interest on capital, Rs. 42,83,282, and that 645 vessels entered the two docks during that year.

The provision of adequate dock accommodation for commercial purposes, which could scarcely have been carried out without the assistance of Government, has proved a good investment of capital as well as a gain to the mercantile community. The question of constructing a dock for the ships of Her Majesty's Navy at Bombay stands on a different footing. That is a work of administrative expediency, which must be carried out by the Government itself, and which must justify its cost, not by interest on capital but in the increased capabilities of Bombay as a naval station. Hog Island, perhaps the future Birkenhead of Bombay, was purchased by the Government in 1864 as the fitting place for the purpose. A hydraulic lift was constructed, and successive naval authorities, since Captain Sherard Osborn (1867), have urged the formation of a dock on Hog Island, large enough to contain the largest ironclad, and the removal of the dockyard thither from Bombay.

A committee considered this project in 1883 and came to the conclusion that 'notwithstanding the many advantages Hog Island possesses as a site for a graving dock for the use of Her Majesty's ships, it would be premature to construct one there, unless Government are prepared to include in the scheme the provision of workshops and other conveniences in connection with the dock, so that the dock and the necessary establishments may be together; or are contemplating the removal to Hog Island of the whole of the buildings, machinery, and establishments of the Bombay Dockyard, a change of serious importance and involving a vast outlay of money.' Lord Reay felt the force of this argument, and, after consulting Rear-Admiral Sir F. W. Richards and Rear-Admiral the Hon. E. R. Fremantle, who successively commanded on the East India station during his administration, and Captain Hext, the Director of the Indian Marine, he adopted the view that the Government must rely on the Bombay Port Trust for accommodation until the finances were in a better condition; and that meanwhile no half measures should be taken in spending money on any scheme which after a time might prove inadequate.

The next most important port on the western side

of India to Bombay is Karáchi. Surat, Broach, Cambay, and other famous centres of ancient trade, have silted up and fallen into decay. But Karáchi, the creation of the British Government, has rapidly advanced in prosperity, and promises a still more vigorous growth in the future. The conversion of the Karáchi creek into a port for large sea-going vessels was first commenced upon a regular system in 1860, and the original works were directed to sheltering the bar by a breakwater and deepening the harbour. The next steps taken were the construction of the Napier Mole during the Commissionership in Sind of Sir Bartle Frere; and at a later date of the Merewether Pier, an iron-pile ship-pier at Kiámári at the head of the anchorage, called after Colonel Sir W. L. Merewether. The rapid expansion of trade caused by the construction of the North-Western State Railway, and the probability of Karáchi becoming the place of export for Punjab wheat, resulted in the formation of a Harbour Board in 1880, and the adoption of further plans for the development of the port.

The system of discharging cargo from the vessels in the anchorage into lighters, which carried it up the creek for a mile and a half to Karáchi, was seen to be both inconvenient and wasteful. In 1882, Sir Theodore Hope expressed a strong opinion that the right policy to adopt was to concentrate upon Kiámári, by providing direct railway communication along the Napier Mole and erecting ship wharfage with cranes and proper mechanical appliances. These ideas received prompt and vigorous effect. A loan of ten lakhs of rupees, of which 7¼ were advanced by the Bombay Government at 4½ per cent., was increased to 25½ lakhs; and the Government of India made a grant of 3½ lakhs for removing the 'Deep Water Point' and lengthening the East Groyne. A line was also extended to the wharves by the North-Western State Railway.

These works were executed with admirable rapidity. In February, 1883, the Merewether Pier was completed. In 1887 the first division of the ship wharf (named by Lord Reay on his visit to Karáchi after Mr. Erskine, late Commissioner in Sind) and the Napier Mole Boat Wharf were opened; and in 1888 the second division of the Erskine Wharf, with berths for three more ships, was finished. On April 1, 1887, the management of the port was transferred from the Harbour Board to a Karáchi Port Trust, constituted on the lines of the Bombay Port Trust.

The rapid advance of Karáchi in consequence of these improvements and of the opening of the Sukkur Bridge for traffic has been most remarkable. Whereas in the year 1882–83, in which Sir Theodore Hope paid his memorable visit, the revenue from port, pilotage and wharfage dues was only Rs. 3,01,374, it had sprung in 1889–90, the last year of Lord Reay's administration, to Rs. 7,21,778, and showed a profit over expenditure, excluding interest on capital, of Rs. 2,63,719. The importance of Karáchi is daily increasing owing to the wise encouragement given to the improvement of the port by the Government in advancing the necessary capital for engineering works, which would have been too costly or too risky for private enterprise in India.

The system of administration by Port Trusts has been found to be so efficient, that on April 1, 1889, the Aden Port Trust was formed for the management of that important Arab harbour. It is premature to speculate on what it may be able to effect. All other ports and harbours within the jurisdiction of the Bombay Government (apart from Bombay, Karáchi, and Aden) are directly under the Public Works Department. Indeed none of them are yet sufficiently important to justify the creation of a special local authority. Among works completed during Lord Reay's administration might be noted a new wharf at Dholera, a new pier at Dábhol, and the improvement of the port of Marmagáo by a Company. Marmagáo is now connected by the West of India Portuguese Railway with the Southern Maráthá system, but owing to the unsatisfactory state of the harbour and the insufficiency of sheds and sidings, the railway station is blocked in times of pressure. English capital might provide a remedy, but as the port is in Portuguese territory, further improvement may have to be preceded by international negotiations.

The Public Works Department also performs for Bombay the duties of the Trinity House in England. Its chief work in this capacity during Lord Reay's administration was the building of a new lighthouse at Vengurla, one of the pirate strongholds of the last century, at a cost of Rs. 18,137.

Another and very varied task of the Public Works Departments in India is the maintenance of what may be called the material fabric of government, that is of the buildings required for the use of the administrative departments. It is difficult to express in a few sentences the multiplicity of the needs which the Department has to satisfy in this respect. It has in Bombay to erect and maintain buildings for the service of imperial departments, such as the salt, opium, post office, and telegraph branches and the mint. Among many buildings of this class completed during the five years under review may be noted the custom-houses at Ratnágiri, Mahim, and Dábhol, and the Central Telegraph Office at Bombay.

Next come the requirements of the provincial administration, the District offices, including *kacheris* for the Mámlatdárs in the different *tálukás*, court-houses, jails and public distilleries. Among the prominent works of this class, commenced or completed during the period from 1885 to 1890, were the conversion of the magnificent relics of the Adil Sháhi dynasty at Bijápur into the head-quarter buildings of a British district at a cost of Rs. 3,63,450; the erection of the Yerrowda Juvenile Reformatory at Poona; with the Government Central Press, the new home of the Elphinstone College, and the Police Magistrates' Court at Bombay. There were also educational buildings, from the District school-house to the stately college, all of which are designed and constructed by the Public Works Department, besides hospitals, dispensaries, and lunatic asylums. The activity of Lord Reay's Government in regard to educational matters and to the relief of the sick, kept the Department very busy building during the five years.

The Wilson Free Church College at Bombay was completed, the Elphinstone College was moved to its present site, new buildings were added to the Victoria Jubilee Technical Institute, to the School of Art in Bombay, and to the Poona College of Science; the Sind Arts College and additions to the Muhammadan Madrasa at Karáchi were commenced. A new lunatic asylum was constructed at Ratnágiri; the Ripon Hospital at Ahmadnagar was completed; and various hospitals at Bombay, the gifts of generous citizens [1], which will extend both medical relief and medical education in the capital of the Presidency, were commenced.

In all these directions, the Bombay Public Works Department proceeded on former traditions, and in accordance with the policy pursued all over India. But in one respect the Bombay Government made a distinct departure during the five years. This was a complete scheme for housing the police throughout the Presidency. Up to 1882 the police force at the headquarters of each *tálukú* had, as a rule, to find their own quarters, accommodation being only provided for the guards on duty at the Treasuries. This proved prejudicial to efficiency, and in 1886 Lord Reay's Government initiated a scheme for providing quarters in the shape of Police Lines or Police Barracks throughout the Presidency. A regular type of building was adopted, and the work was pushed on vigorously and systematically on a regular plan. During the four years ending 1889-90 five and a half lakhs of rupees

[1] Some of these will be referred to in detail at the close of this chapter.

were expended on this necessary work. At the end of that period 2193 police had been housed under the new scheme; of whom 2112 are in specially erected lines and 81 in rooms added to existing lines. These quarters are all in the Districts. The question of housing the police in Bombay city stands on a different footing, owing to the great cost of any such project. But here also a commencement was made, and land has been reserved for Police Barracks near the Arthur Crawford Market, at Kolába and at Dádar.

Until a few years ago this summary would have exhausted the principal duties of the Public Works Department in Bombay. The State has long recognised its obligation to maintain and improve means of communication; many Eastern Governments encourage irrigation, if they wish for good returns in the shape of land-revenue; the best of them have done something to promote commerce; and every centralised administration, like that of India, has to look after its material fabric of court-houses and public buildings. But that it is the duty of the Government to endeavour to preserve the health of its subjects is a new doctrine. Sanitation is a new science; the laws of public health are imperfectly understood; and it is a matter of difficulty even in Europe to effect measures of sanitary reform. How much more difficult then must it be for a modern government, such as that of India, to introduce the Western ideas of sanitation into an Asiatic dominion, where the people oppose the traditions of centuries to attempts at reforming their daily habits? Under such circumstances innovations on established customs must be initiated very gradually, if the opposition is not to become active, instead of passive. Their forefathers never troubled themselves about pure water, drainage, or the removal of filth, the people argue; then why should the British Government disturb their peace and not let them live and die like their ancestors? Lord Reay realised the force of this argument. He preferred to encourage rather than to enforce sanitation, and an Act passed during his administration, the Bombay Village Sanitation Act of 1889, stimulated the promotion of sanitation by local authorities instead of making it a primary duty of the executive officers.

Sanitation, under its three main heads of providing a pure water-supply, efficient drainage, and the disposal of refuse, has for many years received the attention of the Bombay Public Works Department, and is likely to receive more, as public opinion is gradually formed. It stands on a very different footing in towns and villages; in the former the resources of modern engineering are severely taxed; in the latter but slightly.

The sanitary works undertaken by the Municipality of Bombay must be considered separately, as comprehensive schemes and sweeping measures are involved in dealing with the sanitary problems presented by one of the most populous cities in the world. Something may first be said of the sanitary works undertaken in the other cities of the Presidency during Lord Reay's administration. Foremost in this respect stands Ahmadábád, the ancient capital of the Muhammadan kings of Gujarát. Its enterprising municipality, after much consideration, adopted a scheme for supplying the city with water pumped from wells sunk in the bed of the Sabarmati River, at a cost of over six lakhs and a half of rupees. Hardly had these works been commenced, when it also undertook an elaborate drainage scheme, revised by Mr. Baldwin Latham, C. E., and inaugurated by Lord Reay in December, 1889. The Municipality of Poona, the capital of the Deccan, was not less interested in sanitary undertakings than the capital of Gujarát, as proved by the support given to all projects by the enlightened members of the Savarjanik Sabha. But zeal has not always been according to knowledge, and it is said that here the supply of pure water was poured into the city before a proper system of drainage had been provided for its exit. In some towns, as in Dhúliá, the municipalities and local boards are ready to spend money on sanitary works, and the engineers of the Public Works Department are kept busy in arranging schemes. The importance of scavenging and of surface-water drainage is also understood, and measures are generally taken to secure efficiency in these respects.

This progress is encouraging, but, as in Europe, the main difficulty is with the villages, and small country towns. What is needed for them is not the elaboration of schemes of drainage and water-supply, such as are wanted in large towns, but the creation of a healthy local opinion on the subject. How impracticable it seems to be to create such a local opinion is well shown in the replies to a circular sent out by the Bombay Government in 1884, which were printed under the title of 'Opinions of District Officers on the subject of Village Conservancy and Sanitation.'

There is a curious unanimity of opinion among these experienced officials that nothing can be done in a hurry. A passage from the opinion of Mr. T. D. Mackenzie, Collector of Broach, is worthy of quotation (p. 11). 'As regards Mr. Crawford's suggestion that it would "be very useful if Government were to offer prizes for the best essays on the practical conservancy of villages," I have only this comment to offer,—that in the month of November last I was in the municipal town of Bhiwandi in the Thána District, and on going to visit the principal school of the town, I found the classes—who are taught the Sanitary Primer—seated in blissful content over an open cesspool, into which poured water from ablution, water from cooking, filth of every sort and kind. I brought the matter to the notice of the Educational authorities, and I have no manner of doubt that when the Collector of Thána visits Bhiwandi next travelling season, he will find the state of affairs there precisely what I did. The in-born habits of hundreds of generations will not be eradicated by any number of essays on conservancy, however practical, or sanitary primers taught under such circumstances as I have described.'

Notwithstanding such discouraging opinions, the Bombay Government determined to make an effort, and after long consideration and many emendations passed the Bombay Village Conservancy Bill (Act I of 1889). It was a difficult bill to draft. There was the danger of discrediting sanitation by attempting too much. There was the risk that the villages would be encouraged to ask Government for assistance, which Government could not grant. Under this Act, villages which voluntarily undertake to keep themselves clean, to take care of their water-supply, and to prevent nuisances, are not to be affected. Villages, however, in which it is found to be necessary to take some steps to secure the observance of ordinary sanitary rules, may at the discretion of the Collector of the District be placed under a Sanitary Committee of three or more adult householders, with powers to make regulations, punish breaches of them, and raise money. In a third class of villages, those which are really small towns but not large enough to have municipalities, Sanitary Boards are to be formed, partly of residents and partly of officials, with a more extended authority.

'The intention,' says the Bombay Administration Report, 'is thus to constitute, wherever necessary, small local authorities, who, with the co-operation of the magistracy, will be entrusted with the important duty of attending to village sanitation. It is thought that without the aid of such local bodies, operating each within the sphere in which by its constitution it is most likely to possess influence, no attempt to introduce the minor measures of sanitary improvement, which everywhere beyond the limits of municipal districts are so urgently needed, will be successful; and it is believed that for a moderate measure of this nature the spread of enlightenment in the Bombay Presidency has prepared the people in all, except a few backward parts, and that the Bill will be generally acceptable as affording a simple means of remedying a condition of things which is admittedly the cause of wide-spread disease, and, to a very large extent, of the fatal epidemics with which the Presidency is so frequently visited.'

The Bombay Government also took the practical step of granting, from 1888–89, Rs. 10,000 annually to each of the Commissioners of the three Divisions, to be applied in aid of local funds and voluntary contributions, where such funds are appropriated to schemes of village water-supply.

The history of the growth of each great city has its individual features of interest. It is acknowledged all over the world that a capital, especially when it is not only the political but the commercial and intellectual capital, deserves and requires special attention from the State. Bombay city is more than the capital of the Bombay Presidency; it is also the great manufacturing town and the most important sea-port in India. Its material progress, both from the sanitary and the architectural point of view, demands, therefore, a particular mention in a chapter devoted to the consideration of Public Works.

The most important project undertaken by the Municipality of Bombay during the five years under review was the Tansa Waterworks scheme. The city was and is, for the present, supplied with water from the Vehar and Tulsi lakes. But the growth of the population has been so rapid that the supply from these sources, though comparatively recently provided, soon proved inadequate. The Municipality therefore decided on November 19, 1885, to adopt a magnificent project, that will provide the city with an inexhaustible water-supply. The main features of the scheme, which, when carried out, will afford another splendid proof of the public spirit of the citizens of Bombay and the skill of English engineers, have been officially summarised.

'A dam will be constructed across the Tansa River at a point behind the Mahuli hills, 53½ miles distant from the boundary of the island of Bombay. The height of the dam will be at first 109 and subsequently 133 feet above the bed of the river. The area of the proposed lake, when the dam is raised to its highest level, will be 8 square miles. The area from which the rainfall will be collected is 52 square miles. The available water-supply, after making deductions for evaporation, will be 100 million of gallons daily throughout the dry season. The water will be conveyed into Bombay by tunnels for 2½ miles, by conduits for 26¼ miles, and by iron pipes for the remaining 24⅜ miles. It will be carried over the Bassein creek on a bridge. The capacity of the conduits and tunnels will be sufficient to deliver a supply of 33 million gallons daily in Bombay. . . . . Its total cost will be 123 lakhs of rupees, which will be expended over a period of 7 years[1].' Lord Reay took the keenest interest in the progress of this stupendous engineering feat, and visited the works at Atgáon on January 24, 1890. By the close of the financial year 1889–90 considerable

[1] *Bombay Administration Report for* 1885–86, p. 70.

progress had been made, and $32\frac{3}{5}$ lakhs were already expended.

Drainage is as important in the economy of a great city as water-supply. The growth of the population and the low levels make this a serious question in Bombay. Mr. Baldwin Latham visited the city as a sanitary expert in January, 1890, and after making an exhaustive enquiry drew up a valuable report on the subject. The practical action to be taken on his report falls, however, beyond the period under review.

Next in importance to keeping people well by sound measures of sanitation and provisions for the public health, comes the need for curing, or at least relieving them, when they are ill. Lord Reay had this need much at heart, and hospital accommodation and administration received his earnest personal attention. He found the most liberal and generous help from wealthy citizens of Bombay in all endeavours to relieve the wants of their poorer fellow-citizens. The three chief native hospitals in the city of Bombay, in 1885, were the Jamsetjee Jejeebhoy Hospital, the Goculdas' Tejpal Hospital, and the Cama Hospital for Women and Children. The usefulness of these great institutions is now to be considerably increased. On March 9, 1889, Lord Reay laid the foundation of the Bai Motlibai Obstetric Hospital, so called from the benevolent lady who presented the valuable site, adjoining the Jamsetjee Jejeebhoy Hospital, as well as a lakh and a half of rupees for the expenses of its construction. A few months later he laid the foundation stone of the Petit Hospital for Women and Children in the same neighbourhood, for which Sir Dinshaw Manekji Petit presented a lakh and a quarter of rupees; and Lady Reay laid the foundation of the Avabai Bhownaggree Home for Nurses, founded by Mr. M. M. Bhownaggree. In connection with the Cama Hospital for Women and Children, presided over by Dr. Edith Pechey-Phipson, the trustees of the late Mr. Bomanji Edulji Allbless placed Rs. 66,000 at the disposal of Government for the erection of an Obstetric Hospital, and of suitable quarters for the resident lady-physicians at the Cama and Allbless Hospitals.

But a detailed enumeration of the princely benefactions for hospital purposes would fill many pages. I must therefore content myself with including them in the general list of donations by eminent citizens and inhabitants of the Presidency during the five years under review, at the close of this chapter. It is not too much to say that these munificent foundations have doubled the means for the relief of the native poor, and greatly extended the facilities for a sound medical education. It may be doubted if any city in the British Empire can boast of such a spontaneous and valuable addition to its charities within so short a period.

The Bombay Government was itself not behindhand in well-doing. The European Hospital for the use of poor Europeans resident in the city and of sailors from the ships in the port, and of railway officials and their families, had become insufficient. It was resolved by Government to erect a new European Hospital at a cost of Rs. 5,69,667 on the ruins of the old Fort George, to which Lord Reay, on laying the foundation stone in February, 1889, gave the name of St. George's Hospital. The late Mr. Sorabji Cowasji Powalla gave the money to build, on a site granted by Government, a Free Dispensary in the Fort. These and similar buildings have been designed by the Public Works Department.

Lord Reay felt that it was not enough for the Government to supervise the sanitary, charitable, and architectural institutions of Bombay for the time being. He believed that some general scheme should be arrived at with a view to direct the expansion of the city in the future. He accordingly appointed a strong representative committee, with Sir Frank Forbes Adam as chairman, to consider the whole question of the extension of the city of Bombay. The subjects placed before it included the preservation of open spaces, the removal of useless buildings or of noxious trades, the regulation of the Government terms for letting or leasing Government land, provision of new roads, reclamations, building regulations, sanitation, &c. The committee reported on October 31, 1887, and although many of its recommendations cannot yet be carried out, its report will remain as a valuable mine of information for guidance in the future. The most unanimous and earnest recommendation of the Committee, and of the principal witnesses before it, was that the native garrison of Bombay should be moved from the present Marine lines and lines at Bori Bandar to the cantonment at Kolába. The military authorities did not accept this view. They felt the importance of having troops at hand in case of a disturbance in the native town; and apart from this objection, the enormous expense of reclaiming sufficient land at Kolába must adjourn the question for some time. In one matter Lord Reay's Government was able to take effective action. This was in putting a stop to further alienation of Government sites, from a consideration of the rapid rise in value of all land in or near the city of Bombay.

An idea has now been given of the variety and multiplicity of duties performed by the Public Works Department in the Bombay Presidency,—a variety and multiplicity only equalled by the unavoidable intricacy of its accounts. Putting on one side the whole question of military works, which is discussed elsewhere, the Public Works Department carries out its labours under five separate heads, which produce five sets of accounts to be unravelled, in order to arrive at the financial results. Irrigation, railways, and certain civil buildings, such as those for the salt department, opium department, post and telegraph services, mint, currency office, and the Residency at Baroda, are Imperial charges, and are debited to the Government of India. Court houses, *kacheris*, police lines, jails, main roads serving more than one district, and the like, are Provincial charges.

The third category consists of local public works of all kinds, paid for out of the funds administered by the District Boards constituted under Bombay Act I of 1884, and which are entered in the accounts to Incorporated Local Funds. By this Act schemes for all new works or repairs estimated to cost more than Rs. 500, or in the case of roads more than Rs. 50 per mile, have to be prepared or approved by the Executive Engineer of the District, and all works costing more than Rs. 2500, and under certain circumstances even less than this amount, have to be carried out by the Executive Engineer. No charge is made to the District Boards for the services of the engineer, but for the use of the Government establishment under his orders, and for the official audit of the accounts a fixed charge of 12 per cent on the expenditure upon the local work is debited. This of course does not represent the amount of saving really effected for the local authority by employing the Government machinery, and is an aid given by the Government to maintain thoroughness in local public works and the efficiency of the establishment. Under the head, fourthly, of Excluded Local Funds is reckoned the expenditure undertaken for municipalities, port trusts, and native states on public works, which is charged for, as a general rule, at the same rate as for Incorporated Local Funds.

Fifthly comes the work undertaken on behalf of private individuals or bodies, who give sums of money for charitable institutions, such as hospitals and dispensaries, in which cases the services of the Public Works Department in designing, directing, and supervising are given free of charge. Works done under these circumstances, sometimes on a very large scale, are grouped under the heading of Contributions.

When this multiplicity of accounts is considered, with all the intricacies arising from the different heads of provincial public works and from the distinct but confusing specialities of Sind Irrigation, it is obvious that the management of the Bombay Public Works Department, apart from the technical engineering problems involved, must be a heavy burden for a thoroughly trained administrator. The Public Works Department, however, with the Military and Marine Departments, is in a special manner regarded as under the superintendence of the Governor.

'A very able Indian administrator wrote to me quite recently,' said Lord Reay in his speech before the Bombay Chamber of Commerce on April 11, 1889, 'that he himself had found the Public Works a subject on which it was hopeless to have a policy: this shows how extremely difficult the subject is. Our policy was to execute out of the funds at our disposal a maximum of works with a minimum of establishment[1].' As the amount allotted to public works was fixed independently of establishments annually, reductions in the expenses of headquarters establishments not involving the sacrifice of efficiency meant a further sum to be spent on works. The three main principles of policy which guided Lord Reay in such reductions were the simplification of direction, the consolidation of executive charges, and the separation of administration from direction. The easiest method of exhibiting the nature of his reforms is to compare the directing and higher executive staff of the Bombay Public Works Department as it stood on his arrival

[1] *Administration Report of Civil Works of the Public Works Department, Bombay Presidency* (*General Branch*), p. 1.

and after his reforms were effected. This presentment excludes the Railway Branch, which was entirely accountable to the Government of India and formed an independent secretariat.

Lord Reay found a headquarters staff of four officials, the Secretary to Government in the Public Works Department, the Chief Engineer for Irrigation and Joint Secretary to Government, and two Under-Secretaries; with four Superintending Engineers for the three divisions of the Presidency proper and for Sind. Lord Reay resolved, with the full concurrence of Sir Charles Elliott, to recur to the policy of Sir Bartle Frere, and abolished the office of Chief Engineer and Under-Secretary for Irrigation. He made the Secretary to Government a purely administrative officer, instead of a directing officer, and he made the four Superintending Engineers responsible and directing authorities in their several divisions over irrigation as well as over all technical matters within the scope of the Department.

In the Executive or Constructive staff Lord Reay found thirty-eight charges, of which fifteen were for irrigation. The seven irrigation charges in Sind he left undisturbed, but he abolished four of the eight irrigation charges in the Presidency proper and transferred the duties to the ordinary executive engineers in the districts in which the irrigation works were situated. This saved money, and it relieved the minor irrigation works from the expense of a separate establishment, thus giving them a better chance to show a good financial result. By amalgamations and redistributions the total number of Executive Engineers on the staff was reduced from thirty-eight to thirty-two, and was accompanied by a corresponding reduction of the subordinate, office, district accountant and temporary establishments.

In regard to the Public Work Accounts, the system previously in vogue was that of a Central Audit Office. This system, although perhaps the only one possible before the existence of railways and improved communications, had ceased to be suited to the times. It was necessarily slow; it irritated the executive engineers throughout the country by involving them in a mass of correspondence with the Central Office of Audit; it cost large sums not only in maintaining that Central Office, but in a staff of clerks at the headquarters of each Executive Engineer; it was unsatisfactory because, in Lord Reay's words to the Bombay Chamber of Commerce, 'accounts were compiled for purposes of audit.' Aided by Major Le Breton, the Examiner of Public Works Accounts, Lord Reay introduced a thorough change. He borrowed an idea from the Railway Companies, and established a system of travelling audit. The advantages of this reform need not be insisted on. It frees the Executive Engineer from much correspondence and book-keeping; it enables the travelling auditor to drop down at any time and examine the state of the books with the original vouchers; it settles disputed points on the spot. It is quick and efficient, economical, and easily worked.

It may be noted that these reductions of establishment were not attained by persuading officers to retire on large pensions or with large gratuities. A fortunate series of vacancies enabled them to be carried out without hardship to individuals or an increased burden of pensions to the Government. Thus, for instance, the retirement of Mr. J. H. E. Hart, the Chief Engineer and Joint Secretary for Irrigation, made it possible to leave his post unfilled without injury to anyone.

The financial result of these reforms in the Directing, Executive and Accounts branches of the Bombay Public Works Department has now to be seen. In his speech to the Bombay Chamber of Commerce on April 11, 1889, Lord Reay gave the following figures as his estimate of the yearly saving to be effected.

	Rs.
Engineering Establishment	48,000
Upper Subordinate Establishment	22,500
District Accountants	10,116
Office Establishments	28,128
Temporary Establishment	55,000
Account Establishment	43,464
	2,07,208

As a matter of fact they appear to have been greater than he anticipated. The cost of the establishment of the Bombay Public Works Department was Rs. 21,49,737 in 1885–86; it sank to Rs. 18,55,969 in 1889–90, and was estimated at Rs. 18,38,830 for 1890–91, a total saving of Rs. 2,93,768 or Rs. 3,10,909 according to the year adopted for comparison. Even more striking is the percentage of the cost of establishment to the cost of works and repairs at the two epochs. In 1885–86, with a total expenditure of 98⅛ lakhs and a revenue of 13¼ lakhs, the establishments cost 28·66 per cent; in the estimate for 1890–91, where the expenditure is estimated at 111½ lakhs and the revenue at 15 lakhs, the establishments amount to only 20·08 per cent.

The Government of India has once again introduced the dual system of administration with effect from 1889–90 by the creation of a Military Works Department. Formerly Royal Engineers had charge of civil and military works in some executive charges, while civil engineers looked after military works in other executive charges; and the Bombay Public Works Department received credit at the rate of 23 per cent on the total outlay on any work or repairs from the Imperial Funds. Now the Military Works Department will be more expensive, and the Bombay Department will lose this increment. A numerous staff of officers will be maintained for the military work, which is not enough in quantity to absorb a whole Branch; and they will no longer gain experience in civil works. But there are two sides to every question, and H.R.H. the Duke of Connaught recorded a Minute putting the case from an Imperial and Military point of view. 'In the Bombay Military Command,' he says, 'military works are administered by many agencies, i.e. Central Provinces, Central India, Rájputána and Bombay proper. References are consequently multiplied and unity of system lost. This, I believe, involves loss of economy and prevents money saved or not required in one direction from being transferred to another, where it is urgently required. I think Government cannot ignore the covenant made with Royal Engineer officers, that they should be suitably employed in military duties. I notice a great many reverting to the Imperial List owing to this cause.'

No department of Indian administration is more interesting than that of Public Works. The greatness of the difficulties to be surmounted, the engineering problems to be solved, have a fascination of their own. The variety of its undertakings seems bewildering, yet in that variety there is a charm. The routine of revenue or judicial administration, however absorbing it may be to the worker, is not easily made interesting to a casual observer or to a reader. But engineering is always attractive. It is one of the typical pursuits of the age. Great feats of constructive skill and of daring design dazzle the beholder, who sees, and the reader, who reflects. India is studded with such modern monuments. But it is right to remember that the Department, which supervises the irrigation of Sind, which built the Nira Canal, which designed the drainage and waterworks at Ahmadábád, and the architectural buildings that form so decorative a feature of Bombay City, can do efficiently its humbler although not less important duties: that it supplies hilly districts with their first roads, and policemen with their barracks.

In his Public Works' policy, Lord Reay's hands were strengthened alike by the high-minded loyalty of the officers of the Department, and by the generous benefactions made by Indian gentlemen for works of public utility. The foregoing pages have indicated, as far as an outsider can venture to indicate, the internal strain within the Department from the financial reforms and reduction of offices. However much that strain might be reduced by skilful readjustments and by fortuitous retirements, it must have taxed the loyalty of many of the officers concerned. The success of Lord Reay's Public Works' policy was mainly due to the noble spirit in which the Departmental officers accepted and carried out his reforms. He has himself acknowledged in eloquent terms, both while in India and in public speeches since his return to England, his sense of personal gratitude to the officers of that Department.

Lord Reay appreciated not less cordially the public spirit which induced many citizens of Bombay and residents throughout the Presidency to spontaneously come forward, and to ask the Government to undertake large works of general usefulness at their private cost. I have already referred to some of the princely benefactions of this class. The following paragraph summarises the principal ones which have come to my notice, and shows a total of Rs. 10,79,408 contributed by private benevolence to public works during the five years under review.

More than half of this large sum was contributed by one man, Sir Dinshaw Manekji Petit, who was most deservedly created a baronet in 1890. He is the second Bombay native gentleman who has received the distinction of an hereditary title, and in the liberality of his benefactions he deserves to rank with Sir Jamsetjee Jejeebhoy, who was created a baronet in 1857.

Both charitable and educational schemes in Bombay city benefited by Sir Dinshaw Petit's liberality. In January, 1888, he offered Rs. 1,25,000 for the erection of a Lying-in Hospital, which sum he afterwards allowed to be used for the construction of a Hospital for Women and Children, as an extension of the Jamsetjee Jejeebhoy Hospital. He also gave a lakh of rupees towards building a Home for Lepers near Bombay.

In promotion of education Sir Dinshaw presented the property known as the Hydraulic Press, valued at three lakhs of rupees, in exchange for the Elphinstone College buildings, which were converted into the Victoria Jubilee Technical Institute. He likewise gave Rs. 16,419 for the construction of a Patho-Bacteriological Laboratory in connection with the Veterinary College at Parell, and Rs. 6000 toward the erection of a Gymnastic Institution in Bombay. But he did not restrict his generosity to Bombay city. He also presented five and four-fifth acres of land at Poona for the site of the Pasteur Laboratory in connection with the Poona College of Science, and gave Rs. 11,500 and Rs. 10,000 for the foundation of charitable dispensaries at Bassein and Murbád in the Thána District. The total amount and value of the gifts of this great philanthropist for charitable and educational purposes during the period of Lord Reay's administration reached the sum of Rs. 5,68,919.

Coming to other benefactors, Bai Motlibai, widow of Mr. Nauroji Wadia, gave a lakh and a half of rupees and a valuable site of 20,954 square yards, adjoining the Jamsetjee Jejeebhoy Hospital, for the building of an Obstetric Hospital. Mr. Harkisondas Narottamdas gave a lakh of rupees for a Clinical Hospital for Women and Children; but the conditions made by Government were not acceptable to the donor, and the amount was therefore refunded. Mr. Framji Dinshaw Petit gave Rs. 75 000 for the erection of a Laboratory, fitted with the most modern appliances, in connection with the Grant Medical College at Bombay. The Allbless family, namely the trustees of the late Bomanji Edulji Allbless, the widow of Mr. Edulji Framji Allbless, and the sons of Mr. Dorabji Edulji Allbless, presented amongst them Rs. 72,000 for the establishment of an Obstetric Hospital on land adjoining the Cama Hospital, and of a mortuary for Parsis in connection with it, and also (with the assistance of Rs. 5000 from the Countess of Dufferin's Fund) for the building of quarters for the lady doctors of the Cama and Allbless Hospitals. Mr. Sorabji Cowasji Powalla gave Rs. 31,473 for a gratuitous charitable dispensary in the Fort, Bombay; Mr. M. M. Bhownaggree, C.I.E., Rs. 15,699 for a Home for Pupil Nurses in connection with the Jamsetjee Jejeebhoy Hospital; Mr. Pestonji Hormusji Cama Rs. 15,000 for nurses' quarters at the Cama Hospital; and Mr. Dwarkadas Lallubhai Rs. 10,000 for a Cholera Ward at the Jamsetjee Jejeebhoy Hospital, which was utilised instead for the establishment of an out-door Dispensary for Women and Children. Lastly, mention must be made of the gift of the Parsi Panchayat Fund of Rs. 2000 for the erection of a separate mortuary for Parsis in connection with the hospital, which bears the name of the best-known member of their body.

Turning from these munificent gifts made by citizens of Bombay for Bombay institutions, I regret that I have few details regarding the rest of the Presidency. But it may be that many smaller sums were given, which, though they do not equal the magnificent benefactions of the merchant princes of Bombay, yet represent as much charity, self-denial, and public spirit as the larger gifts. I have mentioned Sir Dinshaw Petit's establishment of two charitable dispensaries in the Thána District, and I have to add that the Ripon Memorial Committee founded the 'Ripon Hospital' at Ahmadnagar at a cost of Rs. 16,700 during the five years under review, and that Mr. Nusserwanji Manekji Petit gave Rs. 10,000 for a Charitable Dispensary at Wáda in the Thána District; Messrs. Dayabhai Tapidas and Domodardas Tapidas Rs. 5867 for a Laboratory, and a Lecture-Room for Science Classes at the Surat High School; and Mr. Dinshaw Pestonji Dalal Rs. 1750 for a Gymnasium in connection with the High School at Broach.

CHAPTER X.

FINANCE.

THE annual debate on the Indian Budget in the House of Commons affords an opportunity for Englishmen to get some idea of the difficulties and perplexities which beset Indian financiers. The problems caused by the depreciation of silver and the varying value of the rupee have long received the attention of Parliamentary economists who study the principles of currency and exchange. The questions of morality involved in the Government monopoly of opium, of expediency in regard to the salt tax, and of the adoption of Western ideas in imposing an income tax, are frequently brought before the English public. But it is the financial difficulties, expedients, and policy of the Government of India as a whole, that is of the Supreme Government, which are thus presented. Few Englishmen have any idea of the system pursued with regard to provincial finance, or in what manner the financial relations of the Supreme Government with the provincial administrations are regulated. These relations form the subject of the present chapter.

The policy of financial decentralisation, as inaugurated by Lord Mayo, established the system of Provincial Contracts. Those contracts are formulated after due enquiry every five years. The Government of India enters into an agreement with the eight Provincial Governments, and hands over to them the control of the administration and expenditure of nearly all departments, subject to limitations as to the creation of new appointments and other slight restrictions. To meet this expenditure the Provincial Government is granted the whole, or a specified proportion, of nearly all sources of revenue. A careful estimate is made of the probable revenue and expenditure under these heads, and specific sums are accepted as fixed amounts. Any expenditure in excess of those sums must be met out of the growth of the provincial allotted sources of revenue or by local taxation, and the Government of India can only be appealed to for financial assistance when the additional expenditure has clearly arisen out of circumstances which were not taken into consideration when the Contract was drawn up. On the other hand, certain departments of the administration, such as the Army, Military Works, the Post-office, Railways, Irrigation, Indian Marine, Telegraphs, the Mint, the raising of loans and the negotiation of the Exchange for home charges, are kept in the hands of the Supreme Government, which draws the whole of certain departments of revenue, and a specified proportion from others in each province, to defray its Imperial charges.

The history of these Provincial Contracts is extremely interesting, as they form a chief factor in the problems of Indian finance, and shows the steady growth of the system of fiscal decentralisation. The first Contract was made in 1872, and under it important spending departments, notably Education, Civil Buildings, Jails, and Police, were provincialised, but the chief revenue departments were not affected. Sir Richard Temple, in introducing the system, described it in his Financial Statement for 1871-72 in the following words:—'The Local Governments are to have a fixed annual allotment from the general exchequer for these particular services, and are to appropriate, as local income, all receipts connected therewith. They are to regulate (subject to certain general rules) all the expenditure on those services. If the existing income, namely, Imperial allotment *plus* departmental receipts, shall suffice for the requirements of that expenditure, then that is well. If it shall not suffice, then the Local Governments are not to apply to the Government of India for increased grants. They must raise what they need by local taxation, or by such like means (subject to our central control) if they fairly can. But if they find that they cannot fairly manage this, then they must necessarily do without the increased expenditure. However much the necessity for doing without the increase may be regretted, there is no help for it. This is the only way of following the good old rule of cutting coat according to cloth. However important progress and improvement may be, financial safety is more important still[1].'

The wisdom of the policy of decentralisation was justified by the results of the contracts of 1872. In making the second series of Provincial Contracts in

[1] *Report of the Finance Committee*, 1886: Calcutta, 1887; vol. i. p. 11.

1877, the principle was further developed, and the Government of India handed over to the provincial administrations some of the larger departments of revenue, such as Excise and Stamps, in the belief that financial decentralisation would render these departments more lucrative by more careful administration. Sir John Strachey, in his Financial Statement for 1877–78, thus stated his reasons for this belief. 'What we have to do,' he said, 'is not to give to the Local Governments fresh powers of taxation, but, on the contrary, to do all that we can to render fresh taxation unnecessary, and to give to those Governments direct inducements to improve those sources of existing revenue which depend for their productiveness on good administration. I have a strong conviction of the financial importance of this matter; and the importance is not merely financial, if I am right in believing that better administration would give us a large additional revenue of a thoroughly unobjectionable character, without the country feeling that any new burdens had been imposed upon it.

'How is this better administration to be obtained? The answer seems to me simple: it can be obtained in one way only,—not by any action which gentlemen of the Finance Department, or of any other Department of the Supreme Government, can take while sitting hundreds or thousands of miles away, in their offices in Calcutta or Simla,—not by examining figures and writing circulars,—but by giving to the Local Governments, which have in their hands the actual working of these great branches of the revenue, a direct, and, so to speak, a personal interest in efficient management. It may be very wrong, but it is true, and will continue to be true while human nature remains what it is, that the local authorities take little interest in looking after the financial affairs of that abstraction, the Supreme Government, compared with the interest which they take in matters which immediately affect the people whom they have to govern. When Local Governments feel that good administration of the Excise and Stamps, and other branches of Revenue, will give to them, and not only to the Government of India, increased income and increased means of carrying out the improvements which they have at heart, then, and not till then, we shall get the good administration which we desire; and with it, I am satisfied, we shall obtain a stronger and more real power of control on the part of the Central Government than we can now exercise[1].'

Sir John Strachey's forecast was justified. The sources of revenue wholly or partly provincialised produced larger sums, without unduly pressing upon the people. When therefore the Third Contract was made in 1882, the system was still further developed. The income from Forests and Assessed Taxes was equally divided between the Imperial and Provincial Governments, and even the Land Revenue, the most important source of income, was partly provincialised. Only such sources of revenue as were imperial in their incidence, were reserved in their entirety for the

[1] *Report of the Finance Committee*, 1886: Calcutta, 1887; vol. i. pp. 11, 12.

Imperial Treasury. These were Opium, Salt, Customs, the Mint and Tributes from Native States, with other local exceptions. A careful estimate of the assumed amounts to be collected and disbursed in each province was made, and the difference between provincial income and provincial expenditure was met by the assignment of a fixed percentage of the Land Revenue to each provincial administration.

This was the Contract which Lord Reay found in force when he assumed the government of the Bombay Presidency in 1885. The provincial expenditure sanctioned by it amounted to Rs. 342,45,900, from which must be deducted Rs. 69,04,000, entered under the head of Assignments and Compensations, which does not represent money spent, but Land Revenue excused in return for certain services and similar allowances, leaving an estimated real expenditure of Rs. 273,41,900. To meet this expenditure there was assigned to the Bombay Government an income of Rs. 349,29,900, or deducting the same sum of Rs. 69,04,000, which was purely a book entry, of Rs. 280,25,900. Provision was thus made for an estimated annual surplus of Rs. 6,84,000.

This income was derived from three sources First, the Provincial Government had the benefit of all receipts from the Administrative and Civil Departments such as Law and Justice, Police, and Education, which had been originally assigned to it by the First Contract in 1872. These sources were estimated in 1882 to produce Rs. 13,70,000. With these receipts must also be classed Rs. 6,31,000 from the Public

Works Department, and Rs. 3,76,500 from various Miscellaneous Receipts, making a total of Rs. 23,77,500. Second, the Bombay Government was allotted one-half of the revenue from Stamps, Excise, Forests, Registration, and Assessed Taxes, with two smaller sums of Rs. 60,000 and Rs. 79,000 from the Salt Tax and the Customs, making a second estimated total of Rs. 70,14,000. From these sources Rs. 93,91,500 were contributed towards the requisite income of Rs. 280,25,900. In the third place the balance, amounting to Rs. 186,34,400, was made up by the assignment of 59·8216, or practically three-fifths, of the estimated Land Revenue of the Presidency.

In 1885, at the beginning of the five years with which I deal, the estimates both for provincial revenue and provincial expenditure had been greatly exceeded. The actual receipts from the allotted sources of revenue for the year 1884–85 amounted to Rs. 304,64,957, or Rs. 24,39,057 in excess of the figure mentioned in the Contract of 1882. This increase was apparent in nearly every branch of the revenue. The most striking developments were in Excise—an advance of Rs. 8,92,780 on the Contract estimate; of Rs. 5,78,421 in Forests, of Rs. 2,68,576 in Land Revenue, of Rs. 2,38,427 in Police, of Rs. 1,86,044 in Public Works (Civil), and of Rs. 1,82,142 in Stamps; while the only remarkable decrease was Rs. 1,93,467 in Law and Justice. This improvement thoroughly justified Sir John Strachey's forecast in introducing the Provincial Contract of 1877. If it was in part due to the general prosperity of the province, it was also in part the result of vigorous administration. The Local Government felt that it had a real interest in getting as much as possible out of the sources of revenue, since it received a share for its own disposal.

But although the revenue had increased, the provincial expenditure had grown with still greater rapidity. From Rs. 273,41,900, which was the sum allotted by the Contract of 1882, it had advanced in 1884–85 to Rs. 304,04,895, an increase of Rs. 30,62,995. This was spread over nearly all the departments. The principal items of increase of expenditure over the original estimates were Rs. 12,59,241 in Public Works (Civil), Rs. 6,25,882 in Police, Rs. 2,92,729 in Forests, Rs. 2,51,558 in the collection of the Land Revenue, Rs. 2,29,713 in the Salt Department; while the only notable decrease was Rs. 2,31,719 in the collection of the Customs. Owing to this general increase in expenditure, the actual surplus of revenue over expenditure in the year 1884–85 was only Rs. 60,062 as against the estimated surplus of Rs. 6,84,000.

Yet in spite of the narrow margin the Bombay Government was not imperilling the financial safety of the presidency. For by the terms of the Provincial Contracts the administration was bound to keep a minimum balance of 20 lakhs of rupees to meet any sudden demand, or supply any great need, such as might be caused by famine or pestilence. For this reason an ample balance was allowed to the Bombay Government when the Provincial Contract was settled in 1882. The balance carried over from the Contract of 1877 amounted to Rs. 21,04,872, to which was added a special grant of Rs. 8,00,000 to be spent on productive public works, making a total of Rs. 29,04,872. Certain other special grants amounting to Rs. 27,63,000, and included in the opening balance, need not at present be taken into consideration. Not satisfied with maintaining the prescribed minimum, the Financial Department of Bombay largely increased it. Indeed, in the original estimates for the year 1886–87, the last year of the Third Contract, the balance was estimated at 55½ lakhs. But at this time the Government of India was itself in too great need to allow the provinces to hold such large sums to their credit, and appropriated 20 lakhs of the Bombay balance. After this deduction the closing balance of the Third Contract stood at 35½ lakhs, or a surplus of more than 6 lakhs over the opening balance.

The financial straits of the Government of India caused by the Penjdeh incident and consequent military preparations on the North-West frontier, by the occupation of Upper Burma, and still more by the loss on Exchange caused by the depreciation of the rupee, rendered the utmost economy imperative in every province and in every department. It was evident that not only the provincial balances must be borrowed or taken by the Supreme Government, but that terms more favourable to the Supreme Government must be made when the next Provincial Contract was fixed. The settlement of the fourth Provincial Contract in 1887 was the most important financial event during Lord Reay's tenure of office in Bombay. The necessity for retrenchment was clearly perceived by the Bombay Government, and it loyally co-operated with the Supreme Government in the disagreeable duty. Bombay's prosperity, as shown by her accumulated balances, the rapid increase of her revenue and ten years' freedom from famine, made it certain that she would have to contribute more largely than in 1882 to the needs of the Government of India. The Supreme Government did what it could to meet its deficit by imposing an Income-tax in 1886, but its expectation was that by taking a larger share of the provincial revenues it would avoid the necessity of further taxation.

In February, 1886, during the last year of the Provincial Contract of 1882, the Government of India took its first step in this direction by appointing a Finance Committee 'for the purpose of examining expenditure, whether Imperial or Provincial, and reporting to the Government what economies are therein practicable'; and of 'turning their immediate attention to the revision of the arrangements now in force between the Imperial and the Provincial Governments.' The Committee was so constituted as to represent the various departments of the Government and the European and Native communities both in Northern and Southern India. It consisted of Mr., now Sir, C. A. Elliott, as President, Mr. Justice, now Sir, H. S. Cunningham, of the Calcutta High Court, Ráo Bahádur Mahadeo Govind Ranade, of the Bombay Presidency, Mr. J. Westland, Comptroller of Finance, Lt.-Col. A. J. Filgate, Accountant-General Public Works Department, Mr. H. W. Bliss, of the Madras Civil Service, Mr. Robert Hardie, Secretary and Treasurer of the Bank of Bengal, and myself. Circulars were sent out to all the Provincial Governments and many public bodies and associations, and sub-committees were appointed; of which the most important was the Travelling Sub-Committee, consisting of Mr. Elliott, Sir H. S. Cunningham, Mr. Westland, Colonel Filgate, and Mr. Bliss.

This Sub-Committee went from province to province, and was assisted in its enquiries by local members added to it by each Provincial Government[1]. Its examination into provincial expenditure was thorough and minute, and it collected a valuable body of statistical information. The Finance Committee was not able to complete the whole of its programme before its dissolution in December, 1886; but it drew up and presented a full and valuable report on the Provincial Contracts, on which the Fourth Provincial Contract of 1887 was based. According to this report Bombay could well afford to increase its contribution to the Imperial Treasury. The Finance Committee proposed, therefore, that Bombay should surrender an additional Rs. 27,06,000 a year to the Government of India, while Madras was to give up Rs. 14,07,000, the North-Western Provinces Rs. 12,65,000, Bengal Rs. 11,52,000, Assam Rs. 1,86,000, and the Central Provinces Rs. 1,85,000. In the Punjab revenue and expenditure only just balanced, and no alteration could be made in the terms of the Contract. The condition of Burma

[1] In Bombay Mr. W. Lee-Warner (now Political Secretary to the Government, 1891), and Sir Forbes Adam, then Chairman of the Bombay Chamber of Commerce, were added as members.

was so disturbed that the recommendation was that the former Contract should be provisionally renewed for a short period.

So enormous an addition as 27 lakhs of rupees to Bombay's contribution to the Government of India could not be obtained without general and sweeping retrenchments in all branches of the provincial expenditure. This was what the Finance Committee recommended, and they pointed out how the reductions might best be made. To take the most conspicuous examples, they recommended that the expenditure on Education, which stood according to the Budget Estimate for 1886–87 at Rs. 16,57,000, should be fixed under the new Contract at Rs. 13,90,000; while the expenditure on Public Works (Civil), then estimated at Rs. 46,99,000, should be reduced to Rs. 27,00,000. These proposals roused strenuous opposition. The Bombay Government had embarked on important educational schemes, including the promotion of Technical Education, under the sanction of the Supreme Government. It now found them threatened with shipwreck. It had also pledged itself to important buildings for aided schools and colleges, and to feeder roads for the railways. It now found the allotment for Public Works cut down to a figure only sufficient to carry out annual repairs and to leave barely a lakh of rupees for Original Works. The Bombay Government, therefore, protested vigorously, and with a measure of success. For when the new Contract was settled finally, it obtained Rs. 15,22,000 for Education, and Rs. 29,30,000 for Public Works (Civil); as against the

Finance Committee's proposals of Rs. 13,90,000 and Rs. 27,00,000.

The new Contract was finally concluded by a Resolution of the Government of India, dated March 11, 1887. Besides fixing different sums for the various heads of revenue and expenditure, based on the results of the past five years and the enquiries of the Finance Committee, it contained important changes in the method of allotment. All the receipts of the Provincial, Civil, and Administrative Departments, together with Public Works (Civil) and certain Miscellaneous Heads, were left to the Provincial Government. On the other hand, Opium, Mint, Tributes from Native States, Military and Public Works (Military) were treated as Imperial Revenue, together with Salt, Customs, Post Office, Telegraphs, and Irrigation, subject to trifling exceptions. This partition was on the same lines as the previous Contract. Similarly the receipts from Forests and Registration were again equally divided between the contracting parties. Under the other main revenue heads, important alterations were made in the manner of distribution. Excise, the most lucrative source of income next to Land Revenue, had shown an extraordinary power of expansion. It was now no longer equally divided, but three-fourths of its yield were assumed by the Imperial Government, while one-fourth was left to the Bombay administration. In some degree to compensate for this deprivation, three-fourths of the revenue from Stamps were assigned to the Provincial Government instead of one-half; together with one-half of the

Assessed Taxes, less a small deduction for the surplus profits of Railways [1].

But the most sweeping alteration was in regard to the Land Revenue. Instead of the Provincial Government's receiving a proportion practically equivalent to three-fifths of this the largest source of revenue, after the deduction of the book-heading of assigned land revenue, it was only to take one-fourth. But as, on these terms, it would be unable to meet its expenses, it was to receive under the head of Land Revenue a fixed lump sum of Rs. 81,87,000.

Nothing proves more clearly alike the continued prosperity of the Bombay Presidency during the period from 1882 to 1887, and the success of its administrators, than a comparison between the figures adopted for the Contracts at these two dates. Land Revenue, excluding Assignments, was estimated at 328 lakhs in 1887 as against 311 in 1882; Excise at 91 lakhs instead of 64; Assessed Taxes at 29 lakhs instead of 13; Forests at 31 lakhs instead of 16; Stamps at nearly 46 lakhs instead of 41; Registration at Rs. 3,93,000 instead of Rs. 2,80,000. Under one of these heads, Assessed Taxes, the increase was due to improved legislation, but in the other cases it was the result of good administration and continued prosperity.

Under the chief Civil Heads the estimate was only Rs. 15,17,000 as against Rs. 13,70,000. It would have been greater had there not been a falling off in the income from Law and Justice, which was estimated only to produce Rs. 5,20,000 annually be-

[1] Government of India Resolution, 11 March, 1887, p. 2.

tween 1887 and 1892 instead of Rs. 7,59,000, which had formerly been expected. Lastly, Miscellaneous Heads were estimated at Rs. 2,66,000 from 1887 instead of Rs. 2,92,500, and the receipts from Public Works (Civil) at Rs. 7,53,000 instead of Rs. 6,31,000. In short, the revenue assigned to the Bombay Treasury was estimated at Rs. 360,73,000 in 1887 as against Rs. 349,29,900 in 1882; or deducting the calculations for assignments, at Rs. 279,64,000 *nett* in 1887 instead of Rs. 280,25,900 in 1882.

While the natural tendency of the Finance Committee and of the Government of India was to take the figures of the estimated revenue as high as possible, the opposite tendency appeared with regard to the allowances to be made for provincial expenditure, which were estimated as low as possible. Nevertheless the steady growth of expenditure, fostered by the large surpluses and balances of the past five years, had grown to a height which it was very difficult to check, and the new Contract had to admit a general increase. The cost of the collection of revenue, which formed the largest item in the provincial expenditure, was almost certain to rise with the revenue, and it was felt to be bad policy to interfere with the efficiency of the machinery which filled the treasury. The estimate on these accounts was fixed for 1887 at Rs. 162,17,000 as against Rs. 161,92,700 in 1882. But the increase was really far greater than that. Although the cost of collecting the Land Revenue, for instance, had slightly fallen, Assignments had risen from Rs. 69,04,000 to Rs. 80,09,000. To balance this the charges for the collection of the Imperial Salt Revenue, estimated in 1882 at Rs. 7,72,000, and of the Customs, estimated at the same date at Rs. 5,50,000, were wholly removed to the Imperial Account.

Even larger and yet equally necessary was the increase of expenditure granted in the Civil and Administrative Departments. These charges, which by the Contract of 1882 stood at Rs. 128,17,000, had, notwithstanding the efforts of the Finance Committee, to be fixed at Rs. 141,80,000 in 1887. The most serious additions were of Rs. 7,62,000 to Police and of Rs. 4,67,000 to Education, but all showed some advance except Law and Justice, and Marine, in which were effected trifling reductions of Rs. 41,000 and Rs. 17,000 respectively. In Miscellaneous also there was an increase from Rs. 17,55,000 fixed in 1882 to Rs. 20,61,000 estimated in 1887, and in Provincial Postal and Telegraph Charges from Rs. 89,000 to Rs. 1,18,000. Lastly come Public Works (Civil), estimated in 1882 at Rs. 29,40,200 and in 1887 at Rs. 29,30,000. This trifling reduction does not however truly represent the check caused to Public Works in Bombay by the financial necessities of the Government of India. For in the interval between the two contracts the expenditure had risen to over 45 lakhs, now reduced in 1887 to 29 lakhs.

Finally, the Provincial Expenditure was fixed in 1887 at the same sum as the Provincial Revenue, and the example set in 1882 of allowing an annual estimated surplus of Rs. 6,84,000 was not followed.

The history of the fourth Provincial Contract between the Government of India and the Government of Bombay, made in 1887, and its terms, have been described at length not only because its arrangement formed the most important event in the financial history of the five years under review, but also because of the light it throws on Provincial as opposed to Imperial Finance and on the principle of financial decentralisation. When it had been finally concluded, the Bombay Government loyally made the best of the situation. It was entirely successful. The revenue continued to expand in a remarkable manner to the benefit of both the Imperial and the Provincial Exchequer. It may be admitted that the Bombay system of fixing and collecting the revenue is an expensive one. But it is justified by results, and is held by its advocates to be more economical in the long run than a less exact and cheaper system. Besides encouraging the growth of the revenue, the Bombay Government kept a close eye on expenditure. Lord Reay's reforms in the Public Works Department, by means of which he reduced the expenses of establishment without destroying efficiency, and was enabled to use the savings for actual works, have been described. They are typical of the retrenchment policy pursued by the Bombay Government during the period under review. Under such prudent management, Bombay successfully responded to the pressure brought to bear on it by the Finance Committee of 1886.

Under these circumstances, with a large balance and

a flourishing revenue, in spite of the heavy demands made upon Local resources under the new Contract, Bombay was again called on, in the second year after the settlement of the Contract, to give aid to the Government of India. The loss on Exchange and the military expenses kept the Supreme Government in a state of deficit. It could only meet the heavy demands for the defence of the North-Western frontier and Burma, together with the low rate of the rupee, by further contributions from the provinces. Lord Reay personally sympathised with the difficulties of the Government of India. He loyally recognised that it was the duty of the provinces to assist it. But at the same time he felt keenly disappointed that Bombay should be mulcted of its hard-gained savings, as he had intended to use them for the promotion of the moral and material wellbeing of the people.

The question of this further aid to the Government of India was discussed in a Conference, consisting of one representative from each province, held at Calcutta, under the presidency of Mr. J. Westland, in December, 1888. The Bombay representative was Mr., now Sir, J. B. Richey, who argued the case for his Presidency with much tenacity. He maintained that Bombay was more closely taxed than any other province, and that its large balance was due to its strict efficiency of administration. He held that the true remedy was to establish an equally efficient revenue system all over India. Bengal, where the Permanent Settlement prevents any enhancement of the Land Revenue, he pointed out as an instance of a lightly-taxed province.

I am not concerned to oppose or defend Mr. Richey's views about Bengal, and shall briefly remark that I do not agree with them. But his attitude illustrates a useful result of financial decentralisation, in that it not only spurs the financiers of each province to make the best of their own resources, but makes them critical of other systems throughout India. Mr. H. E. Stokes, the Madras representative at the Conference, took the same view as Mr. Richey, and also urged that the mere possession of a large balance, without reference to the circumstances under which it had accrued, should not be a ground for a new demand by the Supreme Government. However, after stating his case, Mr. Richey consented to a surrender of $17\frac{1}{8}$ lakhs from the Bombay balance to the Government of India.

This important Conference was not summoned solely to assess a further requisition upon the provinces. 'The problem of which the Government of India seeks the solution,' said Mr. Westland, 'is this. At present, when the Government of India desires to revise the contracts, each province is taken separately, and the revision of each is made entirely without regard to the circumstances affecting the rest. This system necessitates laborious investigation, and is, moreover, in the opinion of the Government of India, attended with other disadvantages. Is it possible, then, to lay down a rule or standard by which, when the necessity for revision arises (say, by reason of the increase of the demands falling on the Imperial share of the Revenues), an assessment can be made which shall be, at least in a general way, fair as between the several provinces concerned?'

The fact of this idea having been mooted shows that the Government of India was not entirely satisfied with the working of the Provincial Contracts. Indeed, various other systems were mentioned if not officially proposed. One of these might be called the 'minimum' theory. By it, budgets would be framed for each province, in which the minimum estimate of expenditure would be fixed, and all surplus revenue over that amount would go to the Government of India. Provincial balances, reply the advocates of the Provincial Governments, would thus become a thing of the past, and the Provincial Governments would become merely collecting and executive bodies. The existing financial federation of the provinces and consequent decentralisation would be *de facto* superseded by financial centralisation.

Another suggested system was the 'tribute' theory. According to this plan the whole scheme of Provincial Contracts would be abolished. Each province would be informed how much would be wanted from it, for a term of years, and left to raise its 'tribute' and the revenue for its ordinary expenditure as it liked: subject of course to Imperial supervision and control. This plan seems simple, but grave dangers lurk in it. It would be a matter of considerable and recurring difficulty to fix the tributes equitably, and the most heavily burdened would be sure to murmur. Moreover, so thorough a measure of decentralisation would tend to disintegrate India and might lead to fiscal hostilities between different provinces.

Another view was to classify the chief taxes, allocating some entirely to the Government of India, and the others to the Provincial Governments. This obviously could not be approved by the Government of India. One of the main reasons for decentralising certain sources of revenue, as clearly put by Sir John Strachey in introducing the Second Provincial Contract in 1877, was that the Supreme Government should profit by the greater keenness of the Provincial Governments in looking after the income, of which a part was allotted to themselves.

Meanwhile the Government of India made efforts by retrenchments, and by fresh taxation, such as the Income-tax and the increase of the Salt-tax, to meet the extraordinary and heavy expenses forced upon it by the North-Western defences, the occupation of Burma, and the fall in the value of the rupee. But its greatest source of supply is of course from the Provincial Governments.

A striking feature in the history of provincial finance in India is the testimony afforded to the value of decentralisation. In other departments decentralisation may have political advantages and disadvantages, more or less immediate or remote. But in financial matters it brings a sure reward in the shape of improved revenue and economical expenditure. In no province has this truth been more fully proved than in Bombay. The extraordinary elasticity of the revenue during the period from 1885 to 1890 may have been partly due to natural causes, such as the absence of famine, internal free trade, and better communications. But it was also directly due to the combined efforts of all concerned in the Bombay administration, who strove earnestly to improve the revenue, in order that the appliances for the moral, intellectual, and material progress of the people might be augmented by the additional income thus secured.

CHAPTER XI.

EXCISE AND GENERAL TAXATION.

THE Land Revenue is not only the largest, but also the most important source of revenue in India. It is in the direct collection of rent, and in the fulfilment of the recognised duties of a great landlord, that the administration of an Indian Province differs from that of a European State. But although the collection of the land-tax and the performance of the work of estate-agents form the chief functions of the revenue officers of the British Government in India, they are not the only ones. Revenue is raised in many other ways; both by direct and indirect taxation. The collection of these taxes does not involve the same minute examination into the details of rural economy, or exert the same influence on the prosperity of the people as a whole. It is nevertheless of great importance.

Taxation may be direct or indirect, but in both cases the same canons for its regulation are laid down: that it should be levied equitably, that it should be collected economically, that it should not encourage vice, that it should trench as lightly as possible on the necessities of existence, and interfere as little as possible with industry. The British Government in India carries out these principles by its endeavours to enhance the revenue from intoxicating drugs and to mitigate the incidence of the taxation on salt, by the abolition of internal transit duties, and by a reduction, almost amounting to an abolition, of the import duties on sea-borne trade.

In considering taxation in the Bombay Presidency, I purpose to treat at some length the questions arising out of the excise policy. During the five years under review (1885–90) that policy was keenly debated and criticised. I shall then more briefly deal with the revenue from salt, opium, customs, assessed taxes, stamps, and registration.

Of all revenue, that which is raised by the taxation of intoxicating liquors and drugs is perhaps the most defensible, both on grounds of political economy and morality. The discouragement of intemperance is a duty of every Government, and the accepted method consists in enhancing the cost of intoxicants by imposing taxes on their manufacture and sale. The system by which the Government of Bombay tries to attain this end, in other words, its excise administration, needs careful explanation, as it has been asserted by advocates of temperance in England that the Government of India has inverted the natural order of the excise question. It has been stated that instead of looking upon the taxation of intoxicants as a means of promoting temperance, the Government of India considers the revenue derived from this taxation of such paramount importance that it has fostered the taste for stimulants and given undue facilities for their sale. Without entering on the general controversy, I shall endeavour to faithfully present the facts in the single presidency with which this volume deals.

In Bombay, as in other provinces of India, it is the poorest and most wretched class of the inhabitants which indulges most freely in intoxicating liquors. On the one hand, the Bráhmans and high castes as a rule abstain altogether from strong drinks, or are strictly temperate in the use of them. On the other hand, the aboriginal tribes, such as the Bhils and Kolis, are hard drinkers. Some of them, like the Vágris and Kátkaris, are reported to almost starve themselves in food, or to eat rats, rather than give up their liquor[1]. Like many uncivilised tribes, these aborigines are incapable of self-restraint, and, when they drink, they drink to excess. Next to them come the depressed and backward classes, including many of the low-caste Hindus, who spend a large proportion of their earnings on drink. The trading classes hardly indulge at all, and scarcely ever to excess. In Sind the mass of the population is Muhammadan, and the followers of the Prophet are forbidden the use of liquor.

Geographical as well as racial differences are also to be observed. The cultivator in the Konkan, who has to work in a damp and rainy atmosphere, finds liquor an absolute necessity. The nearer he lives to the sea,

[1] *Report on the Economic Condition of the Masses of the Bombay Presidency* (1888), p. 8.

the more he drinks, and it was pointed out in 1888 that of 220 shops in the District of Ratnágiri at that time for the sale of liquor, no fewer than 170 were situated within fifteen miles of the coast[1]. I should remark, however, that the population is thickest and has most spare cash for luxuries in the coast tracts. In the Karnátik, also, the large numbers of Jains and Lingáyats, who never touch stimulants[2], lower the average of consumption per head, just as the large proportion of Bhils and aboriginal tribes in Khándesh and parts of Gujarát tend to raise it in those districts.

Taking into consideration these two factors, racial tendency to over-indulgence and geographical or climatic inducements to drink, and with a warning as to the inaccuracy of excise figures for certain districts, it is interesting to notice the incidence per head of excise taxation in the different parts of the Bombay Presidency proper, excluding Sind. The average was officially returned during the period under review at 7 anas 6 pies[3], say sevenpence halfpenny. A rupee may be taken as equal to about one shilling and fourpence; an *ana* is one-sixteenth of a rupee, or say equal to one penny; a *pie* is one-twelfth of an ana, or six pies equal one halfpenny. This average of 7 anas 6 pies ($7\frac{1}{2}d.$) per head for the whole Presidency proper was exceeded in Bombay City

[1] *Report on the Economic Condition of the Masses of the Bombay Presidency* (1888), p. 90.

[2] *Ibid.*, p. 81.

[3] *Ibid.*, Appendix IX, Abkári Details.

and Island, where the incidence per head amounted to 2 rupees, 11 anas, and 3 pies; in Surat District, where it reached 1 rupee, 5 anas, and 1 pie; in Thána and Kolába, where it was 15 anas and 2 pies, and 11 anas and 7 pies respectively; and in Broach, where it was returned at 7 anas and 10 pies. The average was closely approached in Poona and North Kánara, where the incidence of excise taxation per head came to 7 anas and 5 pies, and 7 anas and 4 pies respectively.

These figures are instructive. They justify the special inquiry and subsequent special excise legislation which took place during the five years under review in Bombay City, Surat, Thána, and Kolába. They also illustrate what I have said about racial and geographical influences. It is noticeable, however, that neither Khándesh nor the Panch Mahál̇s are ranked among the worst drinking districts, in spite of their large aboriginal population. But this is due rather to the difficulty of checking illicit distillation in their sparsely populated or jungly parts than to the non-consumption of liquor. Poona, however, holds an exceptional position, and it is stated: 'In Poona toddy drinking is getting more frequent near the city'[1], and 'town labourers of the lower castes spend part of their earnings in drink[2].'

After noticing the hardest drinking districts, it is only fair to particularise the most temperate: namely

[1] *Report on the Economic Condition of the Masses of the Bombay Presidency*, p. 27.
[2] *Ibid.*, p. 75.

Kaira in Gujarát, where the incidence of excise taxation is returned at only 5 pies per head, or less than a halfpenny, and Sátára and Ahmadnagar in the Deccan, where it is returned as 1 ana and 1 pie, and 1 ana and 6 pies, or say one penny and one penny halfpenny, respectively. While the average incidence of excise taxation per head for the Konkan division of the Presidency is 8 anas and 9 pies, and for the Gujarát division 6 anas and 8 pies; for the Karnátik division it is only 4 anas and 5 pies; and for the Deccan only 4 anas. All these figures compare favourably with the high rate of 2 rupees, 11 anas, and 3 pies for Bombay City and Island. But it must be remembered that Bombay is a capital, with a large European element and a floating population of sailors and factory hands; and that illicit distillation can be more easily checked in a city than in a country district.

There is an idea in England that the drinking of intoxicating liquors was forbidden by all religions in India, and that it has been reserved for the British administration to introduce the prevalent vice of England into her dominions in the East. It is only too well known that the contact of the civilised races of Europe with African, American, and Polynesian savages has often resulted in the deterioration, if not destruction, of the latter from the use of cheap intoxicants. It is argued that something similar has occurred in India. The aboriginal tribes have always been, and always will be, heavy drinkers, but it is supposed that the British excise policy has introduced the use of liquor among the higher castes, in spite of their religion. Sir Richard Temple, a former Governor of Bombay, in his speech in the House of Commons on April 30, 1889, exposed this fallacy at some length. It is, however, a fallacy so currently accepted in this country that his remarks deserve quotation in full.

'I have fortified myself,' said Sir Richard Temple, 'with what I conceive to be the very best native opinion to be obtained on that matter. I refer to Rájendra Lála Mitra, who is, I believe, one of the most learned and accomplished Hindus of this generation. He is profoundly versed in all the ancient religious beliefs of his country, and is a master not only of the Indian classics, but also of our Western tongue. In his elaborate work on the Indo-Aryans he has a chapter on "The Spirituous Drinks of Ancient India"; and he writes without bias either way—without any theory to sustain or to overthrow—and merely with the intent to portray Hindu manners by citations from authoritative writings. After some discussion, he goes on to say: "Elders, anchorites, sages, and learned men, forming the bulk of the priestly class, doubtless abstained from them (spirituous drinks), as they do now; so did a good number of thousand respectable householders; but they constituted only a fraction of the sum total of the community. And Sanskrit literature, both ancient and mediæval, leaves no room for doubt as to wine having been very extensively used in this country at all times and by all classes."

'A quotation from classical poetry runs thus: "How will you, dear one, of wine-reddened eye, who have quaffed delightful liquor, drink the mist-befouled water which I offer with my tears?" In one of the Sacred Books a goddess, girding herself to prepare for combat with a demon, says: "Roar, roar, ye fool, for a moment only till I finish my drinking." After adverting to the authority of the Tantra Books in modern Hinduism, our author cites several passages, from which I select one: thus Siva, the god, says: "Oh sweet-speaking goddess, the salvation of Bráhmans depends on drinking wine. I impart to you a truth, oh mountain-born, when I say that the Bráhman, who attends to drinking, forthwith becomes a god. True knowledge can never be acquired, goddess dear, without drinking wine. Therefore should Bráhmans always drink." And again: "Whoever, after being initiated in the salvation-giving spell, fails to drink wine, is a fallen man in this iron age." Lastly our author, after describing the supposed effects of Soma beer upon the Celestials, adds: "The effect of this liquor upon the gods could only have been assumed from the knowledge of what it was upon the worshippers."'

I am not concerned to advocate the excise system of the Government of Bombay, but to explain it. And I should frankly state that I think Sir Richard Temple presses the practical significance of the above quotations too far. For while the use of liquors can thus be proved in ancient India, there can be no question that the caste-restraints of Hinduism at the present day put a stringent check on drinking among the higher and more respectable classes of the community.

Moreover, although the Temperance party in England are wrong in asserting that the excise policy of the British has introduced into India the practice of taking stimulants in spite of the religion of the people, it must be admitted that drinking has increased throughout India, and especially in the Presidency of Bombay, of late years. This, however, is not to be attributed to the effect of the policy of the Government, but to general causes over which the Government can exercise little or no control. The spread of railways and mills, of European practices and European ideas, tends to destroy the old prejudice against liquor. The creation of large industrial capitals, such as Bombay, better wages, and a monthly surplus stimulate the drinking habit among the factory operatives, as in similar industrial communities in other countries. The general increase in prosperity of the agricultural and industrial classes has given them more money to spend on articles not of prime necessity, among which intoxicants must be included. These and similar economic causes have led to increased consumption of intoxicants. But it must be remembered that increased consumption, proceeding from such causes, does not necessarily mean increased intemperance.

It may be interesting here to mention the principal stimulants used in the Bombay Presidency and the localities where they are consumed. Imported alcoholic drinks, such as European beer, wine, brandy, whisky, and gin, or Aska and Sháhjahánpur rum, are too expensive for the mass of the population, and are consumed chiefly by the European residents and soldiery, or by natives who imitate European customs and have the means to gratify their inclination. The bulk of the inhabitants of the Presidency are quite contented with what is called 'country liquor.' This may be divided into toddy and distilled spirits.

Toddy, which is consumed to a greater or less extent in every district of Bombay, is the sap of the cocoa-nut or date-palm, and forms, when it is fresh drawn, a wholesome and innocuous beverage. It is otherwise with the country-made spirit. Almost all the spirit made in the districts of Gujarát and the Deccan is distilled from the dried flowers of the Mahuá or Mowra tree. This tree grows abundantly in several of the northern districts of the Presidency, where its flowers are collected in the forests by the Bhils and other wild tribes. Mahuá flowers are also imported in large quantities from the Central Provinces. In the city and island of Bombay, and in the districts of Thána and Kolába, both mahuá spirit and the spirit distilled from palm toddy are sold. In Ratnágiri and on the coast of the North Kánara District toddy spirit alone is used. In the inland or above *ghát* division of Kánara, and in the Karnátik districts of Belgáum, Dhárwár, and Bijápur, the spirit consumed is for the most part jágri, which is distilled from molasses[1]. In Sind distilled liquor is only drunk by a few Hindus, and the mass of the population, being good Muhammadans, prefer bháng, a narcotic which

[1] *Bombay Administration Report for* 1882–83, p. 245.

is usually prepared by bruising hemp heads into pulp, straining the pulp with water through a piece of cloth, and sweetening the decoction with sugar [1].

One of the aims alike of the Supreme and the Bombay Government has been to level up the taxation on country-made liquor to that on imported liquor. It is a truism that excessive customs duties promote smuggling, and that too highly-pitched excise duties lead to illicit distillation. In the Bombay Presidency it is found, to borrow a term from the language of the political economists, that the 'margin of smuggling' is much higher than the 'margin of illicit distillation.' That is to say, it is possible to collect a higher rate of customs duties without encouraging smuggling, than of excise without encouraging illicit distillation. This is inevitable. It might be possible to maintain as efficient supervision for excise purposes in the city of Bombay, as on the coasts for customs protection, but it would be impossible in sparsely populated country districts without an enormously expensive preventive establishment. It is improbable, therefore, that the excise on country-made liquor can ever be made exactly equivalent to the customs duty on imported liquor, although it may be possible to make them approximate more closely than they do at present.

The above considerations apply to customs duties levied on liquors imported by sea. With regard to importation by land from neighbouring Native States, the difficulty has been met in another manner. It is

[1] *Report on the Economic Condition of the Masses of the Bombay Presidency* (1888), pp. 47, 98.

impossible to maintain adequate preventive establishments along such an extended and interlaced land frontier as the Bombay Presidency possesses, especially where the territory of the British and of Native rulers overlaps and intersects. The British Government has, therefore, found it more economical to lease the excise administration of the smaller Native States. That is to say, it pays the rulers of these States fixed sums of money per annum, and in return receives a monopoly of the rights of manufacturing and selling liquor in their dominions. This monopoly the Government lets out to liquor farmers, generally to the lessee of the farm in the neighbouring British sub-divisions. Identity of taxation and administration is thus secured with regard to the smaller Native States within the limits of the Presidency. Such a sweeping measure for protection of the excise is not feasible with the larger bordering States of the Gáekwár of Baroda and the Nizam. With the Nizam a special convention has been made, by which no liquor shops are to be allowed within three miles of the British frontier. With the Gáekwár, whose territories not only adjoin but are interlaced with the British districts, a more elaborate treaty was negotiated during the period under review.

The customs on sea-borne imported alcoholic drinks, or 'potable liquors,' as they are termed in the returns, may first be considered. So large a proportion of the total customs revenue is derived from this source, that it was stated in 1882–83 that 'the Customs Department must now be regarded as maintained for the protection of the excise revenue and the registration of trade[1].' In 1884–85 no less than Rs. 15,11,330, out of the nett total of Rs. 15,75,325 collected as import duties in all the ports of Bombay and Sind, was levied on potable liquors[2]; and in 1889–90 (after the addition of Rs. 4,27,761 from the petroleum duty) the proportion stood at Rs. 21,37,017 out of Rs. 26,80,458[3]. It should be noted that the liquor imported at the Bombay ports is not all consumed in the Presidency, but also goes in part to other provinces.

In examining the detailed figures which make up these totals, it appears that the revenue from the customs duties on ale, beer, and porter rose from Rs. 18,684 to Rs. 46,059 during the five years under review (1885–90); the revenue from wines and liqueurs fell from Rs. 2,11,726 to Rs. 2,04,830; while the revenue produced by the duties on imported spirits increased from Rs. 12,80,808 to Rs. 18,86,038. The duty derived from the importation of spirits is therefore far in excess of that from all other alcoholic liquors.

A noteworthy point with regard to imported spirits is the increase in the proportion of whisky to brandy. The whisky comes from the United Kingdom, the brandy mainly from France. The only other imported spirit requiring notice is rum. A considerable quantity of rum is imported from the Mauritius. But it does not represent all the rum consumed in the Bombay Presidency, for a good deal comes overland

[1] *Bombay Administration Report for* 1882–83, p. xxx.
[2] *Ibid.*, 1885–86, Appendix IV. D (3).
[3] *Ibid.*, 1889–90, Appendix IV. D (3).

from the distilleries at Aska in the Madras Presidency and Sháhjahánpur in the North-Western Provinces. Of the brandy of the cheaper and coarser sorts, a large quantity is imported in the wood, to be used for mixing with and fortifying the alcoholic strength of country liquor, or to be watered down, bottled, and sent up country for consumption.

During the period under review the general Indian Tariff Act of 1887 came into force in the Bombay Presidency, January 1887. It introduced two useful modifications. First, the duty on spirit of the strength of 'London proof' was raised from four to five rupees, to be increased or reduced in proportion as the strength of the spirit exceeded or was less than 'London proof.' This regulation seems to have had the desired effect, for it is stated that, in consequence of the new tariff, there was in 1889–90 'a decrease in the importations of over-proof potable spirits, together with an increase in those of under-proof spirits[1].' The second change was not so important. By the former tariff, all perfumed spirits, such as Eau de Cologne, were admitted duty-free, if in bottles not exceeding four ounces in capacity. This remission was largely taken advantage of for the importation of perfumed spirit, which was drunk as a stimulant instead of being used for toilet purposes. By the new Tariff Act the remission was abolished, and 'the effect of the change was to enhance the revenue, and at the same time to check almost entirely the importation of bastard Eau de Cologne.'

[1] *Bombay Administration Report for* 1889–90, p. 142.

Turning from the import duties on liquors to the excise, or as it is called from an old Persian word the *abkári* administration, it may first be observed that imported liquors contribute to the excise as well as to the customs revenue. Special licenses have to be purchased from the Excise Department for the retail sale of foreign liquor. The income from these licenses only amounts, however, to 3 per cent of the excise revenue, but their existence has to be noticed, as one of the complaints which led to the appointment of the Bombay City Abkári Commission by Lord Reay arose out of them. Foreign and country liquor licenses, that is to say licenses to retail foreign and country liquor, had been separated in 1884 on the following grounds urged by the Commissioner of Abkári. 'It seems to me,' he wrote, 'undesirable that foreign liquor should be allowed sale in the same shops as liquor of Indian manufacture. The rates of duty levied on foreign liquor are largely in excess of those levied on the liquor ordinarily manufactured in Bombay and other parts of India, and the practice followed in Bombay gives the proprietors and retail liquor shops special opportunities of foisting off on unsuspecting or half-intoxicated customers, as highly taxed liquors imported from Europe, spurious liquor concocted from cheap Indian materials. The revenue suffers in consequence and consumers do not get fair value for their money.'

Against the separation of foreign liquor and country liquor licenses, which was adopted on this recommendation, the Bombay retailers strongly protested, and their grounds for complaint were examined by the

Bombay City Abkári Commission in 1885. But the complainants tried to prove too much, and the Commissioners supported the policy of the Government in these words. 'The chief objection of the country-liquor sellers to the separation of the licenses is that it reduces the consumption of country liquor and increases that of foreign spirits; but as the foreign spirit sellers contend that it increases the consumption of country liquor at the expense of foreign spirits, it is probable that neither class has been prejudiced to any material extent; and since the separation of licenses certainly helps to prevent adulteration, it is not desirable, in our opinion, to revert to the former system of allowing the sale of both foreign and country spirits in the same shop[1].'

Proceeding to the excise on country-made spirits, the Bombay Government seeks to raise the highest rate from them, compatible with the prevention of illicit distillation. This rate must vary in different countries according to the strength of the preventive establishment and the possibility of efficient supervision. Just as illicit stills were common in the Highlands and Islands of Scotland, and in the West of Ireland, and are even now occasionally found there, so in the wild sparsely-inhabited parts of Khándesh and the Panch Mahéls, and in the mountains and forests of the Konkan, illicit distillation proves very difficult of control. The aim of the Bombay Excise Department is, there-

[1] *Report of the Commission appointed to consider the working of the Abkári Act in the town and island of Bombay:* Bombay, 1885, p. 3.

fore, to levy the highest rate of taxation on liquor manufactured in the province, which shall not encourage illicit distillation, on the same principle that the Bombay Customs Department imposes the highest rate of customs duty which shall not encourage smuggling. The Bombay Government has framed its excise policy in order to attain this end, and has enormously increased its excise revenue.

The increase in the amount of the excise revenue between 1884–85 and 1889–90, however, is not proportionately so great as the increase in the Customs revenue from potable liquors. The gross revenue from excise in the Bombay Presidency in 1884–85 was Rs. 81,137,83, and the nett revenue, deducting refunds, drawbacks, and the cost of collection, Rs. 77,38,384. In the year 1889–90, the gross revenue had risen to Rs. 99,10,524 and the nett revenue to Rs. 93,43,677, showing an increase of Rs. 16,96,741 gross and Rs. 16,05,293 nett. The present system and the increased efficiency of the excise administration which accompanied its introduction date from 1878; and the praise or dispraise for its results has by common consent been assigned to Mr. Pritchard, now Sir Charles Bradley Pritchard, K.C.I.E., for many years Commissioner of Abkári, to whose ability as an administrator all parties render justice. In order to understand Mr. Pritchard's reforms, it is necessary to show the nature of the previous excise system.

The old system was one of monopolies with local modifications. The monopoly of manufacturing and retailing intoxicants in certain groups of villages, sometimes in whole tálukás, was sold by auction to farmers of the excise. This system possessed the obvious advantage of bringing in a revenue in lump sums without entailing expensive establishments. But its disadvantages were those inherent in all financial schemes for farming monopolies. From the revenue point of view it was unprofitable, for only capitalists could afford to purchase these farms, and their tendency was to combine to keep down the prices offered. From the moral point of view it was impolitic, because the farmers naturally tried to push their sales, and neither endeavoured nor desired to put a check on consumption. From the consumers' point of view it was objectionable, as the farmers, having the monopoly of manufacture as well as of sale, made their liquor as cheaply as possible, since they had no inducement to turn out a good and therefore an expensive article. The only persons to whom the system was satisfactory were the farmers themselves, who made large fortunes.

The new system was introduced in order to check these evils. It was intended to enhance the revenue, regulate consumption, and secure a good quality of liquor. It was hoped to effect these objects by extending the use of public and central distilleries, erected by Government, in which the farmers had to make their liquor and pay a fixed duty per gallon upon it. The right of retailing, and in the majority of districts of manufacture, was still sold to farmers, but they were obliged to sell sound liquor which had been tested and passed by Government officials. The Government was enabled to check drunkenness by raising the rate of duty per gallon.

Practically there are two systems, known as the central and the public distillery system. According to the central system, the farmer for the district has to produce his liquor in a central distillery which is a Government building, under strict Government control. No one else can manufacture liquor in the district. Inspectors note the quantity and quality of liquor which leaves the distillery, and trace it to the retail shops, which are limited by the Collector to the wants of the district. According to the public distillery system, there is not one farmer for the whole district, but a number of subdivisional farmers of excise for each part thereof. These men must all obtain their liquor from a public distillery, but in that distillery there are several manufacturers, each with a license to manufacture liquor, and each manufacturing to supply his own retail trade or to sell to other dealers. Lord Reay was personally in favour of separating, so far as practicable, the manufacture and the retail trade.

The chief difficulty to be met was the difficulty of restraining illicit distillation and smuggling. Under the central distillery system constituting a monopoly of manufacture, the liquor farmers have an interest in restraining illicit distillation, and they are said to have even employed *fakirs* as a detective agency. But under the public distillery system, the farmer who retails and does not distil may be willing to run the risk of retailing liquor which has paid no duty, for the extra profit[1].

A further disadvantage of the new system lay in the retention of the farmer monopolists. It is true that the farmers were shorn of their power of selling bad liquor by being obliged to manufacture in the Government distillery or to purchase their liquor from it. Nor did they merely pay, as formerly, a lump sum for the privilege of retailing liquor, which had enabled them to make large fortunes by getting their farms at too low a price, and had induced them to vigorously push their sales. They were obliged instead to pay a still-head duty per gallon on a guaranteed minimum consumption. This came to the knowledge of the English temperance advocates in the House of Commons, and they not unnaturally argued that it constituted a direct incentive to drunkenness. They urged that a liquor farmer might guarantee, for instance, a sale of 100,000 gallons and pay duty on that amount; but that finding he could only sell 80,000 gallons at a profit, he would part with the remainder at so cheap a rate as to encourage drunkenness.

It might be supposed that self-interest would prevent the farmers from doing a ruinous business of this sort; but the economic hypothesis is gainsayed by the facts. Hence Lord Reay thought it right to try the experiment in Thána and Kolába of raising the duty by competitive tenders for payment per gallon of actual consumption instead of on a guaranteed mini-

[1] *Bombay Administration Report for* 1885-86, p. 153.

mum consumption: assimilating it gradually to the English system which probably will in the end be adopted. Under both systems the Government had recourse to competition, and in both systems competition led to bad results. Under the former system it sometimes tempted a guarantee of a larger consumption than was warrantable; under the second system a guarantee of a higher duty than could be recouped from the consumer. The latter system led to illicit distillation and to illicit retail traffic; the former was said to promote the sale of drink.

It therefore seemed necessary to restrict unlimited competition, and to estimate what Government had a right to assume as a minimum consumption: not allowing a wide departure in the tenders above or below the amount thus assumed.

One thing was clear, that the central and public distillery systems, by which the manufacture of liquor is supervised, are preferable to the former out-still system, by which the monopolist manufactured practically without control. But for some time it proved difficult to introduce the better system into districts where sparseness of population or other special causes made illicit distillation easy. During the five years of Lord Reay's administration, it was introduced into Sind, into three tálukás of the Panch Maháls, and from January 1, 1888 even into Khándesh, where the quantity of mahuá trees presents an element of peculiar difficulty. Practically speaking the out-still system had almost completely disappeared by 1890. Sir Richard Temple felt himself justified in saying, during the debate in the House of Commons on April 30, 1889, 'that the out-still system existed only in very remote parts of the province, and it is being done away with.'

The reforms introduced by Mr. Pritchard before Lord Reay's arrival, and the increased efficiency of the preventive establishment, which resulted, roused a strong opposition from every branch of the liquor trade in Bombay city. Fortunes were no longer to be made by the larger capitalists who used to take liquor farms, and the small retailers suffered also. Equally disgusted were the liquor consumers, who found the prices enhanced and a greater stringency in the prevention of illicit distillation. The opposition was skilfully managed. The liquor trade presented petitions to the Bombay Government, while at the same time it made common cause with the real temperance advocates, especially with the temperance party in the House of Commons, and pretended that its opposition to the new Government system arose from its zeal for the sobriety of the people. The chief centres of this movement were the city of Bombay and the districts of Thána and Kolába on the coast, to the north and south of the capital. Thána especially is a great drinking district, and the people resented a rise in the price of intoxicants. They therefore, under the guidance of the liquor-sellers, refused to buy liquor made at the public distillery, and their agitation was for a time confounded with another and quite genuine movement which was concurrently taking place among disinterested advocates of temperance in India. In the city of Bombay, the liquor-sellers were a powerful and wealthy body, and they made their complaints loudly known through the Press.

There were therefore two elements of opposition. Earnest advocates of temperance were then, as, to the honour of the leaders of Indian public opinion be it said, they are always, urging the repression and discouragement of drinking habits among the people. The liquor-makers and liquor-dealers were resisting the new regulations, which compelled them to give better liquor at a reasonable price.

The cry was raised, and by some of the real temperance party in perfect good faith, that the Government, in its zeal to increase the revenue unduly, was increasing the tax on fresh toddy as severely as on distilled spirit. It was asserted that toddy was a mild and innocuous drink, slightly stimulating, but not intoxicating. It was called 'the poor man's beer.' The opposition urged that the poor man, unable to obtain his favourite drink, was taking to spirits. There was enough truth in these statements to lay the foundation for a bitter attack on the Abkári Administration, and to induce the Bombay Government to revise the excise demand on freshly-drawn or raw toddy.

It is true that raw toddy, when just drawn from the tree, is a wholesome and non-intoxicating beverage. But it appears from the report of Surgeon-Major Lyon, Chemical Analyst to the Bombay Government[1], that 'in toddy collected in pots, which have

[1] Dated March 3, 1883; reprinted as an appendix to Lord Reay's *Minute on Abkári*, published in Nov. 1889.

been previously used for the same purpose, fermentation appears to commence before the pots are removed from the trees,' and that 'the process of fermentation appears as a rule to be complete, and the toddy appears to attain its maximum of alcoholic strength within about 24 hours after the removal of the pot from the tree.' Without going into the elaborate figures of this report, it may be said that cocoa-nut, date, and brab toddy respectively attain an average alcoholic strength of 7·15, 5·8, and 3·9 per cent of proof spirit three hours after being drawn, and of 10·0, 8·0, and 4·7 per cent eight hours after being drawn. In order to explain what this means, the Government Analyst proceeds to state that the alcoholic strength of London small beer is equivalent to 2·2, of London porter to 7·3, and of ale to 12·0 per cent of proof spirit. It appears then that the raw toddy, which its advocates liken to lemonade or ginger-beer, very speedily becomes a strong drink which deserves to be subjected to proportionate taxation.

Further, it must be noted that it is extremely easy to distil strong spirit from the toddy when fermented. I cannot do better than quote, almost verbatim, Mr. Pritchard's description of the process. He says: 'A pot of fermented toddy can be converted into a ready-charged still, and distillation can be set going anywhere in less than five minutes. All the apparatus necessary, besides the pot of toddy, is an earthen saucer (and a little wet earth) with which to close tightly the mouth of the pot; also a small bowl to be placed floating on the surface of the toddy in the pot. If a pot of fermented toddy thus made up is set to boil, and the saucer which closes its mouth is kept cool by pouring water on it, the spirit given off from the toddy in the shape of steam is condensed on the under side of the saucer, and drips from the saucer into the bowl floating on the toddy ready to receive it. Two or three bottles of strong spirit can be made by this simple process in a couple of hours from an ordinary-sized pot of toddy. The distillation can be carried on anywhere, in the houses, or in the fields, or in the jungles; wood and water are plentiful in all the coast tálukás. It was the common custom of the country to make toddy spirit in this primitive fashion before the reforms of 1877-78. A similar practice prevailed in Bombay. Toddy distillation in the same fashion was carried on in the houses and cocoa-nut gardens all over the island. Toddy spirit,' concludes Mr. Pritchard, 'is made to this day in the same fashion in the public distilleries in Dádar and Chaupáti in Bombay, the only difference being that the stills used are large copper pots, with metal lids to close their mouths,—the pot-stills in which whisky used to be made in Scotland and Ireland.'

Under these circumstances, the rapid fermentation of toddy and the ease with which strong spirit can be distilled from it, the Bombay Abkári Department had believed itself justified in treating raw toddy as inchoate toddy spirit, and imposed taxes on it accordingly. This roused the opposition in Thána and Kolába, as has been already said, and in the island of Bombay. The cry against the Excise Department was warmly taken up; the Fazandárs or owners of cocoa-nut, date and brab trees loudly protested; and in 1885, the year in which Lord Reay took up his office, the Bhandáris, who form a class of hereditary tree-tappers and toddy-drawers, struck work.

The Bhandáris formed an interesting class, and had, as they believed, an hereditary claim on the indulgence of the Government. A curious petition from them presented in 1735, is extant. It is too long to quote in full, but the Resolution passed by the Government of that date upon the petition may be inserted here. 'Bombay Castle, Saturday, November 1, 1735. At a consultation present: The Hon'ble John Horne Esq., President and Governor, George Taylor, Esq., John Braddyl, Esq., George Percival, John Lambton; W. Draper, indisposed. Read and approved our last consultation. The President lays before the Board a petition, which had been presented to him by the heads of the Bhandáris, as entered after this consultation, setting forth the difficulties they labor under thro' the excessive high rent paid for the arrack farm, as the drawing and distilling arrack are the only means they have to depend upon for their support and sustenance, and offering to take the said farm among themselves and to pay the sum certain of ten thousand rupees per annum, which it is never to exceed or go under.

'The President also acquaints the Board that on discoursing with the heads of the said Bhandáris he had with some difficulty prevailed on them to give twelve thousand rupees per annum for the sole liberty of selling toddy and arrack, and had thereupon sent for the present farmer to know if he was inclined to relinquish his contract, who, though he confessed that he had hitherto suffered by it, was in hopes to retrieve his loss during the time remaining of his contract, and therefore was unwilling to give it up.

'The Bhandáris being a very useful set of people, and of all our inhabitants the most to be depended on in any exigency, they being of a military caste, and having on several occasions behaved with courage, we should be very glad to preserve those already upon the island, as well as to encourage others to come and settle among us; the increase of their number would tend to the better security of the place, which, during the time that our vessels are out, we are sorry to say is but ill-provided for, and the method now proposed will, we hope, not only prove effectual for that end, but in our opinions it is adventageous to our Hon'ble Masters.

'It is therefore unanimously agreed humbly to recommend the same to them for their concurrence, and by the time we receive their answer the present contract will be expired.'

Lord Reay, like his predecessor of a century and a half before, received a petition from the Bhandáris. In it they represented that in 1690 a tax at the rate of one rupee, eight anaṣ a year was levied on each toddy-yielding tree; that this rate was increased to three rupees a year by 1833; to six rupees in 1859; to seven rupees in 1874; and to nine rupees in 1876. By the Abkári Act of 1878 many restrictions were placed on their trade, and the rate per tree was steadily increased to 18 rupees per tree. In 1884 a change was made, and the tree-tax was replaced by a tax of one rupee, ten anas, per imperial gallon of Rási, and of two rupees, six anas, on Fenni. This final arrangement had, the Bhandáris declared, ruined their trade, and reduced the 10,000 persons hereditarily engaged in it in Bombay to starvation.

Lord Reay resolved to deal with the whole Abkári administration in Bombay city by means of a Commission, and on July 22, 1885, he appointed Sir Frank Souter, Mr. J. H. Grant, C.S., and Mr. Sorabjee Bengali, for that purpose. They were ordered to enquire into not only the grievances of the Bhandáris and Fazandárs, but also into those of the wholesale and retail liquor-sellers in the city and island of Bombay. They presented their report on October 29, 1885. I have already noticed their recommendation on one of the two principal complaints of the liquor-sellers with regard to the separation of the sale of imported and country liquor. On the other, of which the gist was a complaint of spiteful opposition and of knock-out tactics in the auction sales of licenses, they recommended that instead of unlimited competition for such licenses a preference should be given to former holders.

On the raw-toddy question, the Commissioners reported in favour of reducing taxation upon it, and in March 1886 a Government Resolution was passed, fixing a tax of five rupees on each date, and of ten rupees on each cocoa-nut and brab tree tapped for raw toddy. In the following year it was further ordered, with the idea of maintaining a cheap supply of the raw toddy, that each tree-foot booth-keeper in the city and island of Bombay should be obliged to sell pure and undiluted raw toddy at a price not exceeding nine pies for eight drams. In Bombay city where the preventive regulations are more easily enforced these reforms worked satisfactorily, and the Revenue drawn from raw toddy which the strike had stopped represented a considerable item.

This change having been made in Bombay, a similar change was granted to the petitioning coast tálukás of Thána and Kolába. Tree-foot booth licenses were ordered to be issued at ten rupees each.

Lord Reay, with the whole experience and knowledge which very full discussions with his colleagues could yield, thus sums up the results of the facilities given in favour of unfermented cheap raw toddy in Thána and Kolába. 'It is sometimes urged,' runs his Minute on Abkári, dated November 1889, 'that illicit distillation is an imaginary peril in districts where toddy trees grow, as long as a sufficient amount of raw toddy is placed at the disposal of the people. With regard to this assertion it will be as well to bear in mind, that, under the system which prevailed in Thána in 1888 and which was specially designed to favour the sale of raw toddy, 175,000 gallons 25° O.P. of illicit spirit are believed to have been passed into consumption according to one estimate and 400,000 gallons 25° O.P. according to another. The increase in quantity of raw toddy made available in Thána in 1888–89 as compared with 1886–87 was estimated at 641,539 gallons and in Kolába at 154,029 gallons. The

[1] P. 8.

increase in the Salsette and Bassein tálukás alone amounted on that estimate to 484,684 gallons, while in Panvel and the Alibág Bágáyat of Kolába the increase was estimated to amount to 157,939 gallons, while in the rest of the Kolába District there was a falling off.

'It is certain that this toddy was not consumed in the raw state, and the contemporaneous fall in the revenue from licit mowra and toddy spirit is only too significant. In 1886–87 in Thána the revenue from licit consumption amounted to Rs. 6,94,540; the estimate for 1888–89 is Rs. 4,94,670; in Kolába the figures are Rs. 3,05,151 and Rs. 2,77,306. Other arguments point to the same result. The price of raw toddy used to be 6 pies per bottle at the tree foot and 8 pies per bottle in the shops. In Umbargáon and Dáhánu the prices were 4 pies and 6 pies per bottle. The ordinary price in 1888–89 rose to 9 pies per bottle everywhere. The explanation of this cannot be that with a large increase of the supply of raw toddy, the demand for raw toddy increased to such an extent as to justify this increase of price. There is only one conclusion which can be drawn from these facts: that illicit distillation must have prevailed. It was partly due no doubt to the increase of the rates charged for licit country spirit resulting from enhanced competition for the contracts. But the facts also show the very great difficulties under which the Preventive Establishment labours to put down illicit manufacture of spirit, and the absolute necessity for the careful regulation of the sale of raw toddy.'

The increasing consumption of intoxicating drink in the Bombay Presidency seems greater in figures than it is in fact. Under the old farming system it was impossible to know what amount of liquor was actually consumed. The new and more exact system has only been introduced gradually. Nearly every year has seen a fresh District or part of a District brought under the central distillery system. It is therefore impossible to effectively compare the figures of one year with those of another. The increased excise revenue does not necessarily mean increased consumption, but, to some extent, better regulated and more vigilantly taxed consumption. As the preventive establishment improves in efficiency, the figures will continue to show an apparent increase in consumption by the increase of the revenue. But this increase is partly due to the growing prosperity of the people, partly to a more vigilant system of excise, and partly to a larger consumption of liquor.

The revenue from the excise on country-made liquor forms, as has been said, more than 90 per cent of the total revenue collected by the Bombay Abkári Department. The rest is contributed by licenses for the sale of imported liquor; for the sale of intoxicating drugs, other than opium, and from miscellaneous sources. Intoxicating drugs, other than opium, practically mean hemp (gánja) and the preparations made from it, such as bháng and charas. The greater part of the revenue derived from the sale of these drugs is collected in Sind, where the Muhammadan population, being debarred by their religion from liquor, use narcotic drugs instead. Of the total contributed under this head in 1889-90 more than one-half came from Sind[1].

The revenue from opium is an imperial head of taxation, and does not come within the purview of a volume on a provincial administration. The large opium revenue collected in Bombay is collected for the Supreme Government of India. The cultivation of the poppy is forbidden throughout the Presidency, and by special treaties and conventions in all the smaller Native States. The Bombay opium revenue, amounting in 1889-90 to over 189 lakhs of rupees, is derived from pass fees at the rate of Rs. 650 per chest on Baroda and Málwá opium brought into Bombay for export to China and other countries. For actual consumption in the Presidency a certain quantity is bought by the Bombay Government in the market, and issued from Government depôts to licensed retail vendors.

Salt became a permanent source of the Bombay excise revenue in 1838, when an excise duty of eight anas per maund took the place of town and transit duties[2] in the Bombay Presidency. In 1869 it amounted to one rupee 13 anas per maund, levied either as an excise or an import duty. It was raised to two rupees eight anas per maund in 1877 and reduced to two rupees in 1882. The Bombay Salt Department was reorganised in 1872, and by the Salt Act of 1873 the manufacture, storage, and sale of salt was brought

[1] *Bombay Administration Report for* 1889-90, Appendix V. C(3).

[2] *Ibid.*, 1882-83, p. 242.

under complete Government control. The policy of Mr. Pritchard, as head of the Salt Department, was to close small private works (whose turn-out was less than 5000 maunds of salt a year) owing to the disproportionate expense of their supervision, and to concentrate the manufacture in large works.

The Bombay salt-works are of two kinds. The most important from brine-wells are at Khárághoda and Udu on the Rann of Cutch, where there are respectively 235 and 250 salt-pans, which can turn out over 76 million maunds of salt a year. The other class are sea-salt works—chiefly in Kolába and Thána Districts on the coast. The sea-salt varies much in colour, weight, size, and compactness of grain, while the Cutch salt, which is made in brine-wells, is more uniform. There are also large salt-works at Maurypur-Moach in Sind for the supply of that province. With a view to preventing smuggling, the British Government has bought up the sources of salt in Jodhpur and other Native States.

It was of even more importance for the Bombay salt revenue to get control of the manufacture of salt in the Portuguese sea-coast territories of Goa, Daman and Diu. This was secured by the Portuguese Treaty of 1878, which came into operation on January 15, 1880. By its provisions the manufacture of salt in Portuguese India was handed over to the British Government in return for an annual payment of four lakhs of rupees, and an allowance of fourteen pounds of salt per head yearly, at a low rate of purchase, for every Portuguese subject within Portuguese boundaries.

During the five years under review (1885–1890), the most important measure affecting the Salt Department was the increase of the duty from 2 rupees to 2 rupees 8 anas a pound, which came into force in January, 1888. This increase was much to be regretted, but the financial exigencies of the Government of India necessitated the step. The revenue from salt is imperial, and rose from 146 lakhs in 1884–85 to nearly 207 lakhs in 1889–90. The careful overhauling of the working staff of every branch of the Provincial administration, rendered necessary by the requirements of the Supreme Government, effected a saving in the expenses of the Bombay Salt Department of Rs. 31,848 a year. The Bombay Salt Act of 1890 contains stringent provisions against illicit manufacture of salt—provisions carefully elaborated by the Bombay Government during the period under review. In addition to excise, opium, and salt, two other smaller sources of revenue require notice—the Customs and the Assessed Taxes.

The Customs duties have, in accordance with the fiscal policy of England, been so greatly reduced and simplified that the function of the Customs establishment is now mainly to protect the excise and to register trade. The Bombay revenue from this source did, however, increase from 19 lakhs of rupees to 31 lakhs during the five years under review, of which increase 4 lakhs was due to fresh taxation. This revenue was almost entirely derived from duties on imports, and chiefly on imported liquors. In 1889–90, out of 31 lakhs raised by customs duties, more than 28 lakhs was derived from imports. Of the 28 lakhs more than 24 was levied on imported liquors (as against about 15 lakhs in 1884–85), and Rs. 61,462 on arms, ammunition, &c. A new import duty imposed during Lord Reay's administration was levied on petroleum and mineral oils. It came into force in February, 1888, and in 1889–90 produced more than 4 lakhs of rupees. The only export duty is on rice, which brought in Rs. 3,25,087 in 1889–90.

Under the heading of Assessed Taxes a considerable increase from 12½ lakhs of rupees in 1884–85 to more than 33' lakhs in 1889–90 is to be observed. The increase was caused by the supersession of the former License Tax by the new Income Tax in 1886. This measure, it had been expected, would meet with much opposition, like the former Income Tax, but as a matter of fact it was introduced into the Bombay Presidency without any difficulty. Though not a proportionate income tax in the modern sense, it was roughly graduated. Incomes under Rs. 500 were exempt; incomes over Rs. 500 and under Rs. 2000 paid 4 pies in the rupee, and those over Rs. 2000 paid 5 pies in the rupee. Salaries, both official and non-official, earnings of professions, companies and securities were alike subjected to taxation. The tax on official salaries and on Government securities is deducted before payment.

As might have been expected, more than half the total amount realised was collected in the city of Bombay, where the wealth of the Presidency is largely accumulated. In the Administration Report for 1886-87, the year after the first collection of the tax, some very interesting details as to its incidence and distribution outside Bombay are given[1]. In the Mofussil or rural districts it appeared that the average amount levied from each income assessed was 23 rupees, 1 ana, and that only one person was assessed in every 310 of the population. The incidence of the tax on the population at large was 1 ana, 2·27 pies. Looking at the tax-payers alone, the incidence (outside Bombay city) was highest in Aden and Karáchi, and next in commercial districts like Khándesh, Broach, Sholápur, Poona, and Ahmadábád: and lowest in Thar and Párkar, the Panch Maháls, and Ratnágiri. The smallest number of incomes assessed was in Ratnágiri, and next in order in Thána, Kárwár and Sátára, while the largest number was in Ahmadábád and next in Surat. The number of incomes between Rs. 500 and Rs. 750 amounted to a little over 50 per cent of the entire number brought on the roll. The assessments on money-lenders formed nearly 33 per cent of the Mofussil assessments, and the only other occupations largely represented were 'general' merchants, piece-goods and grain merchants and village shopkeepers. Outside Bombay city the salaries taxed were found chiefly in Dhárwár, on account of the railway offices there, in Karáchi, Poona, Aden and Ahmadábád. Under the head 'Companies,' there were few Mofussil assessments except in Karáchi, Ahmadábád and Broach.

[1] P. 174.

In 1889–90 the incidence of the Income Tax on the persons assessed was returned at Rs. 75 in Bombay city, Rs. 47 in Aden, Rs. 26 in the Central Division, Rs. 25 in the Northern Division, Rs. 22 in Sind, and Rs. 21 in the Southern Division. The only falling off from the collection made in 1888–89 is in the Northern Division, and it is said to be caused by the loss experienced by the people of Surat owing to the great fire in that city in April, 1889.

Two other sources of revenue must receive a short mention here. One of these, Stamps, is important to the Treasury, because it returns a larger income than either Customs or Income Tax, while it is cheaply and easily levied. It is also regarded as an index to commercial prosperity, as it gives evidence of the amount of business done. The other, Registration, is of the greatest economic importance, and its contribution to the revenue is merely incidental to its general usefulness.

The Bombay revenue from Stamps rose considerably during the years under review, from 44 lakhs of rupees in 1885–86 to 52 lakhs in 1889–90. Commercial and general stamps, which afford evidence of commercial activity, including inland revenue stamps, foreign bill stamps, share transfer stamps and bills of exchange, afforded a revenue of nearly 24 lakhs of rupees in 1889–90 as against 13 lakhs in 1884–85; while court-fee stamps, including probate, showed a decline from 31 lakhs in 1884–85 to 28 lakhs in 1889–90.

The revenue derived from Registration is of secondary importance, and it is difficult to know in what chapter to mention it. Yet I should be reluctant to pass over in silence a system which many a European State might envy. By the Bombay Regulation IX of 1827 a register of deeds was established in every district of the Presidency in order to preserve copies not only of title-deeds to property, but also of other important documents. By this Act fees were levied varying from 2 to 5 rupees for the registration of deeds, according to their length, and these fees were the perquisite of the Superintendent of Registers, who was generally the assistant judge. On January 1, 1865, however, a change was made, and a regular Registration Department was formed under the control of a Registrar-General, a title altered to Inspector-General of Registration in 1871. This step was followed by the establishment of an 'ad valorem' fee for registration in addition to the copying fee. Many classes of deeds may be registered under this admirable system, wills, certificates of sale, adoptions, certificates of value, legal documents, translations, &c. The work is carried out by about 26 Head-Registry and 219 Sub-Registry offices, under the supervision of an Inspector-General, a Branch Inspector-General for Sind and five Inspectors. There is also an additional Registrar of Joint-Stock Companies.

Although the collection of revenue is quite a secondary object of the Bombay Registration Department, it is not the less satisfactory to note that owing to the great and rapid increase of work done and consequent fees, and to economical management, it now returns a handsome surplus. Like the stamp revenue, the increase of registration is a sure sign of commercial prosperity.

During the year 1884–85, the number of deeds registered in the Bombay Presidency amounted to 106,976, the largest number up till then recorded; in 1889–90 the number had risen to 154,326, an increase of nearly 50 per cent. The augmentation of income is still more striking: for whereas the Bombay Registration Department only showed a profit of Rs. 76,620 in 1884–85, rather more than 2 lakhs of rupees were divided between the Imperial and Provincial Treasury as the profits of Registration in 1889–90. This was not entirely due to the increase of work done, as Lord Reay made various reductions in the establishment in 1887, of which the most notable were the amalgamation of the Inspectorship-General of Registration and Stamps with the Inspectorship-General of Prisons, and the abolition of one of the Inspectorships. The increase in the number of Joint-Stock Companies also deserves to be mentioned. In 1885–86 there were 188 companies with a nominal capital of Rs. 11,30,36,430 of which Rs. 8,79,53,222 was paid up, on the Registrar of Joint-Stock Companies' books. In 1889–90 there were 219 companies with a nominal capital of Rs. 13,59,89,930, of which Rs. 10,19,64,356 was paid up.

In this chapter I have endeavoured to give a view of the general taxation of an Indian province (apart from the land-revenue and municipal imposts), and of how it was affected during the period under review from 1885 to 1890. To sum up the most important fiscal changes carried out during Lord Reay's administration. He was responsible for none of the three great alterations made by the Government of India, the raising of the Salt Tax, the imposition of the Income Tax, or the passing of the Import Duty on Petroleum. I have therefore touched but lightly on these points. But the Abkári policy was a purely provincial question, in which the Supreme Government did not interfere. Lord Reay's Excise policy, like his Forest reforms, was keenly canvassed, and brought his name prominently before the English public. It caused him deep anxiety, but he had the satisfaction of knowing that he had not shrunk from attacking one of the most difficult and delicate problems with which an Indian Governor can be called upon to deal. He found a violent agitation going on against the excise system. He quieted that agitation, keeping steadily in view the guiding principles of raising the maximum of revenue from the minimum of consumption, the discouragement of undue competition, and the limitation of the number of retail liquor shops to the actual needs of the population.

CHAPTER XII.

Protection of Person and Property: Justice, Police, Jails.

THE administration of justice throughout the Regulation Districts of the Bombay Presidency is, under the Letters Patent of 1865, entrusted to the Bombay High Court of Judicature, sitting at Bombay. All the districts of the Presidency proper, excluding Sind, are now Regulation Districts, the last Scheduled or Non-regulation District, the Panch Mahâls, having been made Regulation in 1885[1], the first of the five years under review. Sind is still a Non-regulation Province, although the law is practically administered in the same way as in the Presidency proper, and the Court of the Judicial Commissioner in Sind takes the place of the High Court at Bombay.

The Bombay High Court of Judicature consists of a Chief Justice and six Puisne Judges. The Chief Justice is appointed in England, and is an English lawyer of repute; the six puisne judges are selected partly from the Covenanted Bombay Civil Service and partly from practising barristers of a certain standing. The Chief Justice throughout Lord Reay's tenure

[1] *Bombay Administration Report for* 1885–86, p. 56.

of office was Sir Charles Sargent, a highly experienced judge, who had been the last Chief Justice of the Ionian Islands during the English occupation, and who, after serving on the Bombay bench for many years, succeeded Sir Michael Westropp as Chief Justice in 1882. One of the noteworthy appointments made to the puisne judgeships during Lord Reay's tenure of office was that of Mr. Kashinath Trimbak Telang, C.I.E., a Hindu advocate of approved learning in jurisprudence and eminent in the practice of the law. Lord Reay had throughout the five years the aid of an accomplished lawyer as a Member of his Council, as both Sir Maxwell Melvill and Sir Raymond West were former judges of the Bombay High Court.

The Bombay High Court has both ordinary and extraordinary civil and criminal jurisdiction, and exercises original and appellate functions[1]. It also supervises the administration of justice by the different Civil and Criminal Courts of the Regulation Districts. Ordinary original jurisdiction is exercised in matters, both civil and criminal, which arise within the limits of the town and island of Bombay. In virtue of its extraordinary jurisdiction the High Court may in civil cases remove and itself try any suit brought in any Court under its superintendence, and may in criminal cases exercise jurisdiction over all persons residing within the jurisdiction of any Court subject to the superintendence of the High Court. The most important functions of the Bombay High Court are,

[1] The following paragraphs are condensed from the *Bombay Administration Report for* 1882–83, p. 21 et seq.

however, those which it exercises as a Court of Appeal. In civil matters it entertains appeals (1) from the judgment of one Judge of the High Court, or from the judgment of any Division Bench of the High Court, the members of which are equally divided in opinion and do not amount in number to a majority of the High Court, and (2) from the decisions, except in cases where no appeal lies, of all Civil Courts under its superintendence.

In criminal matters it is, subject to the limitation just mentioned, a Court of Appeal from the decisions of all Sessions Courts. It is also a Court of Reference and Revision in criminal cases, and all capital sentences passed within the limits of its appellate jurisdiction have to come before it for confirmation. It further exercises the functions of an Insolvent Court, and possesses the civil and criminal jurisdiction of an Admiralty and Vice-Admiralty Court in prize causes and other maritime questions arising within its jurisdiction. It has also been invested with testamentary jurisdiction, and has matrimonial jurisdiction over Christians. One of its judges officiates as Judge of the Pársi Matrimonial Court. Matrimonial decrees by District Courts require confirmation by the High Court. In the province of Sind, the Court of the Judicial Commissioner, called the Sind Sadar Court, occupies, in matters of appeal and revision, the position of the High Court; but his decrees in matrimonial cases require confirmation by the High Court of Bombay. The District Judges in Sind have no matrimonial jurisdiction.

Under the superintendence of the Bombay High Court and the Sind Sadar Court, the administration of justice is carried out by the rural or local judges. In civil matters these officers are divided into four grades, District and Assistant-District Judges, and First Class and Second Class Subordinate Judges. A Second Class Subordinate Judge has original jurisdiction in suits of less than Rs. 5000 in amount or value, and a First Class Subordinate Judge in all civil cases, except suits in which Government, or any officer of Government in his official capacity, is defendant. An Assistant District Judge may try such original suits of less than Rs. 10,000 in amount or value as the District Judge refers to him. The officer who presides over the principal Court of original civil jurisdiction in each district is the District Judge. He exercises a general control over all Courts within his charge, and refers to the Assistant Judge such suits as he deems proper. He also arranges for the guardianship of the persons and the management of the property of minors and lunatics, and hears and decides a variety of petitions regarding certificates of heirship, certificates to collect debts due to deceased persons, suits for winding up partnership under the Indian Contract Act, and applications of many kinds. The District Judges of Poona and Surat are in addition Judges of the Pársi Matrimonial Courts in those towns, and the former, as Agent for Sardárs in the Deccan, decides under a Regulation of 1827 cases in which members of the local nobility are interested. In some districts there is employed also an Assistant Judge 'with full powers,' who has all the jurisdiction of a District Judge in civil judicial matters and nearly all the administrative powers.

The power of appeal in civil causes is carefully regulated. In cases not exceeding Rs. 5000 in value or amount, an appeal lies on both matter of fact and of law to the District Judge from the decrees of a Subordinate or Assistant Judge. From the decision of a District Judge in appeal, a special appeal on points of law only lies to the High Court. An appeal from the decrees of a Subordinate or Assistant Judge in cases exceeding Rs. 5000 in value, and of a District Judge in all original suits, lies to the High Court. From the decisions of the High Court a further appeal lies to Her Majesty in Council, when property in dispute is of the amount or value of Rs. 10,000 or upwards, and such an appeal may also be allowed in other cases of special importance or involving grave questions of law.

Turning to criminal jurisdiction, the highest district tribunals are known as Courts of Session. These are presided over by three grades of officers, the Sessions Judge who is the District Judge in civil matters, the Joint Sessions Judge who is an Assistant Judge 'with full powers,' and the Assistant Sessions Judge who is an ordinary Assistant Judge. The Sessions Judge is empowered to try any offence, and to pass upon any offender any sentence authorized by law, subject in the case of a capital sentence to confirmation by the High Court. The Joint Sessions Judge can only try cases which by general orders of Government he is empowered to try, or which are made over to him by the Sessions Judge, but he has equal powers on the bench with the latter. The Assistant Sessions Judge can only try such cases as are referred to him by the Sessions Judge; sentences of imprisonment for more than three years passed by him require confirmation by the Sessions Judge, and in no case can he pass sentences of imprisonment or transportation for more than seven years.

The High Court and the Courts of Session are the superior criminal courts, but ordinary criminal work is disposed of chiefly by the executive district officers, who, in addition to their revenue duties, are invested with magisterial powers. They are divided for this purpose into three grades. Magistrates of the Third Class can inflict imprisonment not exceeding one month and fines not exceeding fifty rupees; Magistrates of the Second Class can inflict imprisonment not exceeding six months and fines not exceeding two hundred rupees; and Magistrates of the First Class can inflict imprisonment not exceeding two years and fines not exceeding one thousand rupees. Magistrates of the First and Second Class may also pass sentences of whipping. In each district the Collector or chief revenue officer, under the title of the Magistrate of the District, has special powers of controlling magistrates of all classes within the limits of his executive charge, and an appeal lies to him from the sentences of any Magistrate of the Second or Third Class within his district. First and Second Class Magistrates may, under the title of Sub-Divisional Magistrates, exercise, when so empowered, many of the functions of the Magistrate of the District within the sub-division placed under their charge.

As compared with the administration of justice in some other parts of India, a characteristic feature of the Bombay system is its more complete separation of the persons by whom the executive and the higher judicial functions are exercised. After a preliminary training in revenue and executive work, covenanted civilians elect to remain in the revenue or to enter the judicial branch of the service, and they do not afterwards pass from the one to the other. The grade of Assistant Judge provides a training for the office of District and Sessions Judge[1]. This is giving rise to a curious anomaly. The ablest members of the Covenanted Civil Service usually prefer the executive branch, and a difficulty is occasionally found in manning the judicial branch, while the most able and accomplished natives, who delight in legal subtleties, apply themselves to that line. There is therefore a possible danger of appeals lying from learned subordinate judges to comparatively inexperienced covenanted civilians superior to them in the judicial hierarchy.

In addition to these ordinary courts, Small Cause Courts, invested with summary powers for the recovery of small debts and demands, have been established in the city of Bombay and in the six large towns of Ahmadábád, Broach, Karáchi, Nadiád, Poona, and Surat. The Judges of the six Mofussil Small Cause

[1] *Bombay Administration Report for* 1882–83, p. 23.—Standing information.

Courts have jurisdiction in money suits, within these towns, up to Rs. 500 in value, and their decisions are final, save in so far as they are subject in reference to points of law to the High Court, or to the supervision of the High Court in its extraordinary jurisdiction. The Presidency Small Cause Court has cognisance in suits not exceeding Rs. 2000 in value, arising within the island of Bombay. Mention must also be made of the Cantonment Magistrates, exercising jurisdiction in civil matters up to Rs. 200 within their cantonments.

The Bombay Judicial Service, whose grades and functions I have just described, forms a very numerous body. In the City of Bombay, there are the High Court, with its original jurisdiction, the Small Cause Courts and three Presidency Magistrates. In the Regulation Provinces, or the Presidency proper, there are thirteen District Judges, one Joint Judge, and two Assistant Judges 'with full powers.' In their capacity as criminal judges these form the sixteen Sessions and Joint Sessions Judges, and there are also three ordinary Assistant Judges who are Assistant Sessions Judges. For original criminal work there are 18 District Magistrates, 122 Magistrates of the First Class, 192 of the Second Class, and 221 of the Third Class. For the lesser civil work there are the Small Cause Courts, three Cantonment Magistrates with powers of a Small Cause Court Judge, 14 First Class Subordinate Judges, and 86 Second Class Subordinate Judges.

In Sind there are, besides the Sadar Court, four District Judges, including the Deputy Commissioner of Thar and Párkar, who in their criminal capacity form three Sessions Judges and one Assistant Sessions Judge. For original criminal work there are in Sind five District Magistrates, 24 Magistrates of the First Class, 59 of the Second Class, and 57 of the Third Class. For civil work in Sind there are one Small Cause Court, one Cantonment Magistrate, and 13 Subordinate Judges with seven Mukhtiyárkars, seven Head Munshis, and one Deputy Collector in Thar and Párkar possessing powers to try civil suits.

These judges and magistrates were all stipendiary. There were also during the year 1889–90 in the Presidency proper 84 Special or Honorary Magistrates, but none in Sind, and of these 84 Honorary Magistrates, 48 formed eight Benches of Magistrates. In that year six of the members of High Court were Europeans, and one was a Hindu, Mr. Kashinath Trimbak Telang. Of the Sessions, Joint Sessions, and Assistant Sessions Judges only five were natives. Of the 122 Magistrates of the First Class 79 were Europeans: while of the 413 Second and Third Class Magistrates, all were natives except seven and five Europeans respectively[1].

The law administered by these numerous judicial authorities is that of the Indian codes. Of 180,962 persons brought under trial in 1889–90, 72,566 were convicted. Many of the cases, however, were merely breaches of the Forest Act, the Abkári Act, the Municipal Acts, and other petty offences. For real crime it is necessary to consult the analysis of offences returned as true. These numbered 112,018 in 1889–90,

[1] *Bombay Administration Report for* 1889–90, pp. 49, 50–55.

of which the largest classes were 24,015 of hurt and 11,249 of theft. The offences affecting human life returned as true amounted to 420, and 273 cases of murder were brought to trial during the year. The number of capital sentences affirmed by the High Court of Bombay and the Sadar Court of Sind for the five years ending 1889–90 averaged 28 per annum.

It is interesting to note the geographical distribution of crime, and elaborate returns are issued every year on this subject. Taking the six districts in which the proportion of reported offences to population is lightest, for each of the five years under consideration (1885–1889 inclusive) it is found that the following four are always among them, Ratnágiri, Dhárwár, Bijápur, and Kánara, and it may be mentioned that Sátára, Belgáum, and Sholápur are not far behind. This speaks well for the morality and peaceable character of the inhabitants of the Karnátik, Southern Konkan, and Southern Deccan. In the four best districts the average for the five years is one offence for every 481 of the population in Ratnágiri, for every 437 in Dhárwár, for every 375 in Bijápur, and for every 325 in Kánara. The remarkable immunity from crime of Ratnágiri has given rise to comment, and it is recorded that 'the inhabitants of Ratnágiri, though they have the reputation of not shrinking from litigation and of being zealous in the prosecution of their claims in the Civil Courts, are certainly a most peaceable and law-abiding people.'

Coming to the other end of the scale, it is observed

that among the six districts in which most crime is reported, the same four are always to be found. The average for the five years 1885–89 of offences reported to the number of population is one for every 99 in Poona, for every 105 in Karáchi, for every 118 in Thána, and for every 152 in Haidarábád. It is noteworthy that two of these districts are in Sind. To what Poona owes its unenviable pre-eminence it is difficult to say; but it is remarkable that Thána, which both in Forest and Abkári matters made itself particularly noticeable by its attitude of opposition, should rank among the most criminal districts. Thána has steadily progressed in its ratio of criminality, whereas all the other districts have fluctuated from year to year. Thus Thána stood fourth in 1885 and 1886 with a proportion of one reported offence to every 148 and 146 of its population respectively, third in 1887 with one to every 111, second in 1888 with one to every 101, and at the head of the list of criminal districts in 1889 with one offence to every 84 of the population.

It is not necessary to particularise the details of the work of the Civil Courts in so minute a manner, but the reports show that whereas only 147,875 suits were disposed of in the various Civil Courts in 1884–85, the number had risen to 197,452 in 1889–90. This great increase may fairly be attributed to increased prosperity and commercial activity rather than to increased litigiousness.

The expenditure on the establishments maintained for the administration of civil and criminal justice is necessarily very large, but, as will be seen, the law-courts pay more than half their expenses from stamps and fees. Thus in 1884–85 the total expenditure of the Civil, Revenue, and Criminal Courts amounted to Rs. 42,19,995, and the receipts to Rs. 22,24,750, while in 1889–90 the expenditure had risen to Rs. 43,28,555 and the receipts to Rs. 29,47,095.

Turning to the judicial history of the period under review, there are only two cases which need special mention. The first was the riot of the Talávias at Broach in 1885. The Talávias are a wandering low-caste, dwelling mainly in the territory of the Gáekwár of Baroda. Several efforts have been made to induce them to settle down, but in vain, and a colony which had been formed for them had to be abandoned. In 1885 a number of these people encamped near Broach, where for some months they behaved in an eccentric though on the whole inoffensive manner.

But on November 22, 1885, about seventy-five of the Talávias, whose fancied grievances against the Government had been stimulated by their priests, entered Broach in search of the Collector of the District. Not finding him they fell upon Mr. Bruce Prescott, the Superintendent of the Bombay, Baroda, and Central India Railway Police, whom they met driving along the road in his dog-cart. They attacked him with sticks and bill-hooks and wounded him so severely that he died in three hours. After threatening the Bank of Bombay at Broach, the Talávias passed on through the town. Outside they met a small body of police, with whom they had a short fight. At the first volley fired by the police, five of the Talávias were killed and five wounded, and after the second they fled, pursued by the police, who captured many of them. During the fight, three of the policemen were wounded, one so severely that he died from his injuries.

The leader of the Talávias, Lakha Bhagat, was tried with others at the Broach Court of Sessions, when he and two other ringleaders were sentenced to death and fifty-one of the rioters to penal servitude for life. Seventeen of the latter sentences were cancelled by the High Court, but the more serious penalty was confirmed, and the three ringleaders were hanged[1].

The second case deserves notice because out of it arose important questions of judicial procedure which gave rise to much controversy. Mr. Arthur Travers Crawford, C.M.G., of the Bombay Civil Service, Commissioner of the Central Division, having been charged with corruption, and with borrowing money from natives and from his official subordinates, was tried by a special Commission, consisting of Mr. Justice Arthur Wilson, of the Calcutta High Court, Mr. J. W. Quinton, at that time a Member of the Board of Revenue of the North-Western Provinces and since murdered at Manipur, and Mr. R. J. Crosthwaite, then Judicial Commissioner of the Central Provinces. This Commission opened the inquiry at Poona in October, 1888, and held sixty-seven public sittings. In its report it found Mr. Crawford not guilty of the graver charges of

[1] *Bombay Administration Report for* 1885–86, p. 51.

corruption or of borrowing from official subordinates. He had himself pleaded guilty to borrowing money from natives within the Division of which he had administrative charge.

The Bombay Government was bound by the Act[1] under which Mr. Crawford was tried, not merely to review the Report of the Commission, but to pass its own decision on the facts brought to light by that Report. Its unfavourable decision together with the Report of the Commission were submitted to the Secretary of State. Finally, the Secretary of State in his Despatch of March 29, 1889, declared 'that the character and consequences of the pecuniary embarrassment to which Mr. Crawford had brought himself disclose a condition of things altogether lamentable and inconsistent with the possibility of the proper administration of the Division, at the head of which he was placed, or indeed of the due performance of his public duties anywhere.' He therefore ordered the removal of Mr. Crawford's name from the list of the Bombay Civil Servants.

Such cases are fortunately very rare in India, so

[1] Act XXXVII of 1850. Sir Raymond West's Minute on the case begins thus: 'The Commissioners appointed to investigate the charges preferred against Mr. A. T. Crawford, having now presented their Report, the duty devolves on Government under Act XXXVII of 1850, of pronouncing on the proof or failure of proof of malversation. In discharging this duty, Government must obtain all the assistance from the report and the proceedings of the Commissioners which those records can afford, but it is bound, using these valuable aids, to form its own judgment on the innocence or culpability, and the degree of culpability of the accused officer.' The view taken by the Government of Bombay, upon a consideration of the whole statements before it, was more unfavourable to Mr. Crawford than the conclusions arrived at by the Commission in their Report to Government.

rare that the Crawford case stirred public opinion to the depths. In accordance with Indian precedents, and with a view to preventing evidence being kept back through fear, the Bombay Government authorised the offer of a complete indemnity to witnesses who might have given gratifications or money to Mr. Crawford or his supposed agents. Under this indemnity many persons came forward to give evidence. The Bombay Government prepared to fulfil its pledge, while marking its displeasure on those who had offered bribes. But the Secretary of State issued instructions to the Bombay Government that 'the general rule must be that those who have given bribes must be deprived of magisterial and other functions.' The statute of George III under which this decision was arrived at had not previously been applied, as regards this provision, in India. When Her Majesty's Government determined to apply it in this case, a serious dilemma arose. On the one hand, it was impossible that the solemn pledge of indemnity given by the Bombay Government should be disregarded. On the other hand, it was impossible that officers who had obtained their places by corruption should continue to hold their appointments unless they had yielded to undue pressure, which, as shown in Sir Raymond West's minute, had concussed them to make these payments. Apart from the new statutory question thus imported into the case, it was generally recognised that unless a complete guarantee had been given to the witnesses, the enquiry would have been a mere farce. It is absurd to suppose that the victims of an alleged system of extortion in India would come forward to give evidence, unless they were assured that the fact of their having been coerced into submission to the alleged system of extortion would not be used to their further detriment. It was also recognised that, unless the British Government were to be regarded as willing to wink at an alleged system of corruption on a large scale by a highly placed British officer, an enquiry was absolutely demanded. Under these circumstances, with the English statute on the one side and the actual and acknowledged facts and necessities of such a trial in India on the other, the Governor-General in Council determined to intervene, and to pass a modified Act of Indemnity.

When the Bill was introduced into the Supreme Legislative Council of India on September 19, 1889, Mr. Hutchins, now Sir P. P. Hutchins, K.C.S.I., said: 'This Bill indemnifies all of them [i.e. the incriminated native officials or "Mámlatdárs"] against suits and prosecutions, but will not relieve any who have made corrupt payments without any extreme pressure from the other penalties, which have been incurred under Statute 49 of George III. It was not considered right that the guarantee against official departmental punishment or loss should be maintained. In all cases the rights and liberties of Her Majesty's subjects must not be left at the mercy of judges and magistrates, who have corruptly purchased their offices and powers. The dismissed men, however, should be given a pecuniary compensation for this partial non-fulfilment of the guarantee. Eight officials have been dismissed and others will shortly be disposed of, who clearly do not fall under the category of persons who have paid money under great pressure. It cannot be imputed to the Bombay Government in removing these men that they are breaking their own guarantee, for their promise has to this extent been over-ruled by the Secretary of State and the Government of India. The whole question has been reduced to a single issue of facts, whether payment can or cannot be regarded as having been extorted. When this issue has been decided, the dismissal follows necessarily in consequence, not by the act of the Government of Bombay, but of the appellate authorities, which enjoined that such a course of action should be pursued.'

The Viceroy on the same occasion spoke with equal clearness: 'Nothing could be more unfortunate than to allow an impression to prevail that such engagements were liable to be lightly set aside, but the desire to support the presidential Government did not constitute a ground for legislating with the express purpose of retaining in office, and in the discharge of judicial and administrative functions requiring the highest integrity, persons who had not only become legally incapable of serving the State, but who had shown themselves guilty of deliberate and voluntary corruption. Government believed that having to choose between a partial cancellation of guarantee and the retention in office of men self-convicted as unworthy of public confidence, the partial cancellation of guarantee was the lesser evil. The indemnity given by the Bombay Government had promised: first, exemption from punishment for an indictable offence; secondly, protection from private suits or prosecutions; thirdly, retention of office in spite of statutory incapacity in cases even of the most serious offenders. The guarantee would hold good except in regard to the retention of office, and compensation will be given for the loss of this.' The difference of opinion between the Supreme and the Local Government was of a somewhat technical character turning on the definition of undue pressure and 'extreme pressure.' The Bombay Government did not consider that the guilt of deliberate and voluntary corruption had been legally established against the Mámlatdárs.

In the House of Lords, the Secretary of State for India, Lord Cross, explained at some length that the non-confirmation of the complete guarantee did not imply a censure on the Bombay Government. 'I wish to take this opportunity,' he said, 'of publicly stating that Lord Reay deserves much credit for the manner in which he has endeavoured, I hope successfully, to put a stop to bribery and corruption in his province.' And again: 'In conclusion, I must take this opportunity of stating that Lord Reay has certainly done his utmost to give full effect to the pledges which he gave, and has acted all through with the highest sense of honour, and although he was, in my judgment, ill-advised in the particular course which he took, and which I have not been able to sanction, I have every confidence in his administration, and can bear testimony to his continuous and successful efforts to promote the moral, social, and material prosperity of the people committed to his charge.'

After a consideration of the whole case, however, Lord Reay deemed it his duty to place his resignation in the Viceroy's hands. The Viceroy urged that not only was there no sufficient ground for this step, but that the resignation of the Governor of Bombay would be detrimental, under the circumstances, to the public interests and liable to be misunderstood. The Secretary of State took the same view, and Lord Reay refrained from pressing the matter further.

During the five years under review, no serious change was made in the judicial administration. It was otherwise with the police. The Police Bill, passed by the Bombay Legislative Council in April, 1890, was one of the important measures of the five years. Equally important questions arose as to the housing, drilling, and organising of the district police.

There are two distinct bodies of police in the Bombay Presidency, the stipendiary police and the village police. The former comprise three separate branches: the District Police, the Bombay City Police, and the Railway Police. Of these the District Police, numbering over 18,000 officers and men, form a semi-military corps, partly armed and drilled, who are enlisted not merely for the preservation of the peace, but also as an organised force in case of disturbances. The village police, on the other hand, are the hereditary servants of the village communities and guardians of the local peace, and are paid by perquisites or by rent-free lands.

The District Police are managed or commanded by a Superintendent of Police in each district, who has complete executive control over his force, under the general direction of the Magistrate of the District. Each Superintendent has one or more Assistant-Superintendents, and probationers under him. Both Superintendents and Assistant-Superintendents are invested with magisterial powers to conduct proceedings preliminary to trial. The police sub-division of a district is identical with the táluká, but the Faujdár, or chief constable of a sub-division, holds a position inferior to that of the Mámlatdár, who is in revenue charge of the táluká. The Faujdár is, however, independent of the Mámlatdár in his executive control of the police under him, and is only answerable to the Superintendent or Assistant-Superintendent. The regular police in each sub-division are divided into outposts under the charge of head constables, for the patrol of the sub-division [1].

The system of District Police has its merits, and in past days was the only one possible. But with the improvement of communications it became necessary to make some attempt to secure uniformity of control and supervision, without infringing on the executive authority of the district officers. For this purpose a Commissioner of Police had been appointed as early as 1855; but the office did not answer expectations and was abolished in 1860. The need for a central controlling authority, however, made itself more and more

[1] *Bombay Administration Report for* 1882–83, pp. 23, 24.—Standing information.

apparent. In the districts there was a general want of uniformity in drill and in procedure; at headquarters the Government felt the need of a trained adviser in police questions. Sir James Fergusson, the predecessor of Lord Reay, pressed this point, but his views met with a steady opposition from the district officers and the Commissioners of Divisions, who were entrusted with the general supervision of the Police, and who argued that such a measure of centralisation would diminish the authority of the district officers. Sir James Fergusson thus stated the question in a Minute dated February 11, 1884: 'Why should not the police require special supervision as well as jails, schools, and hospitals? We rightly require the district officers to visit these and to report upon them through the Commissioners; but we do not dispense with special and skilled visitors. Yet there is quite as much need for skilled supervision of the police in point of discipline, conduct, and practice as of jail officials and prisoners . . . . . The plan I would propose is this: not to revive the Police Commissioner, but to create an Inspector-General, who shall visit every district annually and report to Government once a year, but in special cases as often as may be necessary, upon the efficiency, discipline, composition, and management of the police. . . . . . I would in no way alter the present powers and relations to the police of the District Magistrate. The relative functions of the Magistrate and the Inspector-General are as distinct here as they are in England or in Bengal.' Sir James Fergusson's views prevailed, and Colonel Wise was appointed Inspector-

General of Police in the Bombay Presidency on January 6, 1885, a few weeks before Lord Reay's arrival in India.

The appointment proved a complete success. There was a general levelling-up of the district police force. Uniformity of drill, clothing, and arms was secured; police lines were constructed by the Public Works Department on a regular system; and the force became at the same time better disciplined and better organised. Equally satisfactory was the effect on the performance of the true duties of a police force, the prevention of crime. A police manual was compiled, codifying the orders and instructions on which the police were to act. Crime was more carefully registered, and a consolidated report on the whole work of the force took the place of the four separate reports of the four Commissioners. Fuller statistics were secured, especially with regard to the supervision of released convicts and suspected characters, and a special branch was formed under the Personal Assistant to the Inspector-General of Police for the purpose of collecting intelligence on the social and political condition of the people. This branch also undertakes the compilation of a weekly Police Gazette, giving the names and descriptions of those 'wanted.'

The advantages experienced from the creation of a central controlling authority over the District Police led the Bombay Government to pass a Police Bill, in order 'to give legislative definition to the Inspector-General's authority and functions, and, in settling these, to review and re-define the relations to the Police system of the Commissioners and District Magistrates.' By this

Bill, which was introduced by Sir Raymond West into the Bombay Legislative Council on December 12, 1889, and read a third time and passed on April 9, 1890, full control over the mechanism and discipline of the police force was given to the Inspector-General of Police, while the authority of the Magistrate of the District, as the officer in whom centre both magisterial and executive powers, is maintained and emphasised. At the same time advantage was taken to re-arrange the provisions of the police law, to revise them, and to introduce some new enactments suggested by the deficiencies of the previous law. Whenever extended authority has been given to the magistracy or to the police for the purpose of preserving order and maintaining the general welfare of the public, precautions have been taken to prevent abuse of the powers thus conferred. Sections have also been introduced with the intent of securing gentleness and humanity on the part of the police in the discharge of their duties. But the main aim of the Bill is to define the respective authority of the Inspector-General and the local and district authorities. This has been done by reserving questions of internal economy to the former, and of discipline and direction to the latter.

In addition to the District Police there are two other special bodies of stipendiary police employed in the Presidency. Of these the most important is the Bombay City Police. As is the case in other capitals and great seaports, the work of this force is more arduous than that of the force in country districts, and the Bombay City Police is a picked body of men. During Lord Reay's administration it had the misfortune of losing its chief, Sir Frank Souter, C.S.I., C.I.E., who died on June 5, 1888. He had been Commissioner of Police in Bombay for twenty-four years, and was knighted on the occasion of the Prince of Wales's journey through India, in recognition of his long and valuable services.

The other special force is the Railway Police—divided into three branches employed on the (1) Bombay, Baroda and Central India, (2) the Great India Peninsula, and (3) the Southern Maráthá Railways. Its special duty is to protect these lines, and most of its work is directed towards preventing thefts. It also registers the amount and value of property stolen while in transit, and endeavours to recover it.

The numbers of the stipendiary police, in all the three forces, increased slightly during the five years under review. The largest increase was in the Railway Police—from 1051 to 1338 officers and men, mainly due to the formation of the Southern Maráthá Railway Police. The total increase in the three forces was from 21,384 officers and men in 1884 to 21,890 in 1889. The Bombay Police thus form an important reserve force of armed men, if any crisis should denude the Presidency of its regular military troops. The larger portion of the police are Muhammadans and Maráthás. In 1889–90 it is stated that 66 per cent of the subordinate officers and 30 per cent of the men in the District Police had sufficient education to write an intelligent crime report[1].

[1] *Bombay Administration Report for* 1889–90, p. 44.

With regard to distribution wide divergencies appear. Thus there is one policeman to every 1286 of the population in Ratnágiri, one to every 1218 in Belgáum, and one to every 1173 in Kaira. At the other end of the scale one policeman is kept for every 326 of the population in the Panch Mahals, one for every 336 in Karáchi, and one for every 367 in Thar and Párkar. On the other hand, calculated on the area, there is only one policeman for every twenty-three square miles in Thar and Párkar as against one for every five square miles in Ratnágiri. The total cost of the police administration in every branch rose from Rs. 47,88,353 in 1884–85 to Rs. 50,45,441 in 1889–90. Of this expenditure about 38 lakhs of rupees were spent in the salaries and pay of the various police forces.

Very different in character to this regular semi-military police, which in some respects resembles the Royal Irish Constabulary, is the Bombay Village Police. The village watchmen are the servants of the village community, and are under the charge of the Police Pátel,—who generally but not always conducts also the duties of Revenue Pátel. The special duties of the village policemen are to prevent crime and public nuisances, and to detect and arrest offenders, within village limits. The Police Pátel has to furnish the Magistrate of the District with any information demanded, to keep him informed as to the state of crime, and as to the health and general condition of the community in his village. 'The actual importance of the village police,' it is recorded in

1882[1], 'cannot for one moment be overlooked. Without the aid of the village police not a single offence could be traced out. They are the real backbone of the detective police. They know all that is going on, and know every one in the villages.'

Having described the various police forces, whose duty it is to prevent crime and arrest offenders, and the judicial system which tries arrested prisoners, it remains to briefly advert to the jails in which convicted prisoners are confined. There are twenty-six district jails, and fifty-six sub-jails in the Presidency, with one great central jail at Yerrowda, near Poona, all under the supervision of the Inspector-General of Prisons. Land was purchased during the period under review for a new jail in Bombay City. Some of the convicts are employed in extra-mural gangs, and have been engaged in fitting Bijápur to become the headquarters of the former district of Kaládgi, and on canal works at Mhaswad, Gokák, and the Nára. The average daily convict population for all jails was 6,959 in 1889-90, and in that year the total number of convicts admitted into the jails of the Presidency was 17,111. The gross cost of the maintenance of prisoners in 1889–90 was Rs. 5,42,423, or 70 rupees, 7 anas, and 4 pies per prisoner. But the actual cost of rations per prisoner was only 29 rupees, 8 anas, and 10 pies; or £2 each *per annum*, at the exchange rate of 1*s*. 4*d*. *per rupee*.

I have now very briefly explained the principal arrangements for the protection of person and pro-

[1] *Bombay Administration Report for* 1882–83, p. 23.—Standing Information.

perty in the Bombay Presidency. Such protection constitutes the first duty of government, and the expenditure on law and justice, including jails and police, is by far the largest item of provincial expenditure. Taken together, they cost in 1889–90 nearly 100 lakhs of rupees: as, against, for example, 15 lakhs allotted by the Provincial Contract of 1887 to education.

CHAPTER XIII.

LOCAL GOVERNMENT: MUNICIPALITIES AND DISTRICT BOARDS.

THE extension of local self-government to India is a question that can be looked at from many points of view. The educated natives and their European friends advocate the establishment of municipalities and local boards both as affording training grounds for learning the duties and responsibilities of administration, and as the necessary sequel of the English political axiom 'no taxation without representation.' The taxpayer looks upon such schemes as a fresh method for raising money from him. The trained English administrator is apt to disparage the practical results—results which he could have accomplished more speedily and more thoroughly on his own authority. The Government of India bears all these considerations in mind. It has insisted on the creation of municipalities and local boards, but it protects the taxpayer by limiting the amount of local taxation, and it checks extravagant or perverse administration by close supervision, and when needful by interference.

The question of local administration is bound up

with that of local taxation. In India there are three sorts of taxation and expenditure—imperial, provincial, and local. Of the relation between imperial and provincial finance I have already spoken, relations which have rapidly developed under Lord Mayo's decentralising policy. Local financial administration by local bodies of local income for local purposes is a yet further development of the same principle of decentralisation.

The comparison between local taxation in India and rates in England cannot be carried far, for many matters which are locally administered in England are in India directly managed by the provincial governments. Thus in India, police, hospitals, the greater parts of public works, and until recently education, were paid for out of the provincial revenue. Primary education, sanitation, and purely local roads and improvements are now left to local administration in the Bombay Presidency. But very little more can be handed over in the rural districts, because the Government of India feels that when a cultivator has paid his land-tax, great caution should be exercised in laying further burdens upon him.

The success of any thoroughgoing scheme of local self-government depends upon the possibility of finding local men able and willing to conduct it. Has India got a sufficient supply of such men? And how are they to be found? At the first hopeful start of the experiment, it was asserted that the most intelligent natives would strive for a share in the local government, and that the vast majority of the people would hail its concession as a boon. But it was soon discovered that local self-government meant local taxation, and that the promotion of education, sanitation, and public works intended for the general good of the community, might seem to the average taxpayer dearly purchased, if increased burdens were laid upon his individual shoulders.

To the Government, he argued, local self-government might be a convenient method for raising funds without increasing the incidence of general taxation; but to the urban taxpayer it was practically a new device for getting more money out of him under a different name. In rural districts the one-ana cess calculated on the land-revenue is a fixed quantity.

When, therefore, it was found that local self-government in towns implied increased taxation for local purposes, and not the administration of a part of the general funds, its popularity waned. Lord Reay met with a curious instance of this. He received a deputation of the inhabitants of a small town, which was to be turned into a municipality. They represented to his Excellency that they were too poor and inexperienced to receive such a boon, and begged to be excused from the honour and expense of a system of local self-government. Lord Reay discussed the question with them, and finally remarked that he had heard that the policy was approved by the people. To this the deputation demurred, declaring that local self-government was not intended for such poor people as those of their town.

In the larger cities, where competent men can be

found to fill local offices and perform local duties, the question arises as to what is the best method to select them. The natural bias of the English administrators of India (as of any other highly capable bureaucracy) was in favour of nomination. On the other hand, the principle of representation has a special charm to the educated natives of India, who naturally hope that the time will come when a proportion of seats in the Provincial Legislative Councils, if not in the Legislative Council of the Government of India, may be filled by election. The result has been to work out the experiment of municipal government on a joint system of nominated and elected candidates. In some municipalities and local boards, sufficient interest is taken to bring forward good and suitable candidates, but it cannot be denied that in others the principle of nomination has proved so far the most suitable.

In 1884 a new impulse had been given to local self-government in Bombay by the Local Boards Act (Act I of 1884) and the Bombay District Municipal Act Amendment Act (Act II of 1884). The task of the Government during the next five years, the period dealt with in this volume, was mainly to watch the working of the new system. An interesting experiment was introduced by the establishment of an educational franchise at Poona. This important municipality was reconstituted by a Government Resolution, dated June 26, 1885. The governing body was formed of 20 elected and 10 nominated Commissioners. Of the 20 elected members, 16 were to be elected by persons paying municipal taxes to the amount of not less than Rs. 3 per annum, and the remaining four by a special body of electors. 'Having regard,' says the Resolution of the Bombay Government, 'to the existence in Poona of a very large and intelligent class of educated native gentlemen, who have already shown great interest in municipal administration and in the promotion of education, the Governor in Council is willing to give a greater extension to the elective element in Poona than has been thought desirable in other municipalities.' The special body of electors then formed consisted of Fellows and Graduates of any University, Barristers-at-Law and Advocates of the High Court, Pleaders holding a sanad from the High Court, Jurors, Honorary Magistrates, Licentiates of Medicine, Surgery, or Civil Engineering, and masters of departmental and registered schools, together with Sardárs, persons on whom the British Government has conferred the titles of Ráo Bahádur, Khán Bahádur, Ráo Sáheb, or Khán Sáheb, servants of Government, or of any public body, corporation, or company, registered under the Indian Companies Act, whose salary is not less than Rs. 30 a month, or former servants, whose pensions are not less than Rs. 15. Together with the new franchise, the Poona Municipality received the right to elect its President.

More wide-reaching were the new provisions for Bombay city. Bombay is at once a great capital, a great port, and a great manufacturing centre. It has a population of over three-quarters of a million within municipal limits, and is therefore larger than Manchester or Liverpool, Birmingham or Glasgow. In such a city the question of self-government is of the utmost importance. Every advance of sanitary science makes large demands upon its resources, and the problems suggested by its rapid growth in wealth and population are extremely complicated. It has a powerful body of wealthy and philanthropic citizens; but of citizens belonging to various races, and imbued with very different conceptions as to what municipal administration should attempt, and as to the methods by which it should work. The administration of Bombay City was one of the difficult questions to be solved by Lord Reay's Government, and among his most far-reaching pieces of legislative work was the passing of the Bombay City Municipal Act [1].

Municipal government had been established on its modern basis in Bombay, as in the other Presidency towns, in 1856. Many subsequent measures had modified or developed it, notably in 1865, 1872, and 1878, and when Lord Reay's Government undertook to legislate, the constitutional law of Bombay City was embodied in eleven separate enactments. The first purpose of the new Bill was to consolidate the law, but in doing so important alterations were introduced. Its provisions, drafted by Mr. J. R. Naylor, aided by Mr. Ollivant, the Municipal Commissioner, were divided into twenty-one chapters. At first received with strenuous opposition, it was carefully revised by a Select Committee of the Legislative Council, with whose members Lord Reay discussed the alterations. It

[1] Act IV of 1888; received the assent of the Viceroy on 8th Sept., 1888. This Act is analysed in the *Bombay Administration Report for* 1887–88, pp. 61–65, and has attracted notice on the Continent of Europe.

eventually passed with general approval. One of the chief modifications introduced during its passage was the regulation for handing over the primary schools to the Municipal Corporation.

By this Act of 1888 the government of Bombay was vested in a Municipal Corporation and a Town Council. The Municipal Corporation consists of 72 members, of whom 56 are elected and 16 nominated by Government. Of the 56 elected members, 36 are elected by municipal taxpayers, or as we should call them the ratepayers, and resident graduates of any University in the United Kingdom or India, in ward elections; 16 are chosen by Her Majesty's Justices of the Peace; two by the Senate of the University of Bombay; and two by the Bombay Chamber of Commerce. The Town Council consists of twelve members of the Corporation, four nominated by Government and the remainder elected by the Corporation. The Municipal Commissioner appointed by Government is present, with a right to speak, at meetings of the Corporation and of the Town Council. The Town Council is intended to be the Standing Committee of the Corporation to work out the details of such schemes as the Corporation determine to adopt. It is also to exercise control over the municipal finances. Both the Corporation and the Town Council elect their President and Chairman. The Municipal Commissioner is the executive officer of the Corporation.

The powers of the Corporation of Bombay under the new Act include the following, among others too numerous to specify in detail: sanitation in all its branches, street cleansing, drainage and water-supply, the registration of vital statistics, the regulation of building, primary education, the maintenance of the fire-brigade, and the care of hospitals for contagious diseases. The most important matters of which it has no control are the charges arising in connection with the administration of justice, police, stipendiary magistrates, and jails. It exercises full control over the city finance, except that it can raise no new loan without the consent of the Governor in Council. The Government also reserves the right of nominating auditors for the municipal accounts.

The municipal revenue of Bombay City rose from Rs. 43,83,973 in 1885–86 to Rs. 53,42,170 in 1889–90. The chief items are the Consolidated Rate at 8 per cent, which rose from Rs. 14,61,304 to Rs. 16,61,697; water rates from Rs. 6,65,370 to Rs. 11,23,006; liquor and tobacco licenses from Rs. 3,22,927 to Rs. 3,34,672; and the Halalkor or sweeper cess from Rs. 3,16,786 to Rs. 4,73,919; while town duties fell from Rs. 6,79,292 to Rs. 6,67,065; and wheel tax, cabs, and tolls fell from Rs. 3,37,010 to Rs. 3,25,616. During the same period, from 1885–86 to 1889–90, the expenditure of Bombay City increased from Rs. 40,76,940 to Rs. 50,42,405. The principal items were interest on the Municipal Debt, which rose from Rs. 7,87,527 to Rs. 14,85,711; Public Works from Rs. 9,64,842 to Rs. 13,03,528; and Public Health from Rs. 9,99,322 to Rs 11,96,577. As might be expected from these last figures the Municipal Debt largely increased during the period under review from Rs. 1,10,43,843 to Rs. 2,68,52,640.

Apart from the passing of the Bombay City Municipal Act, the most important events in the administration of Bombay City during the five years under review were the increase of hospital accommodation; the initiation of technical education; the Tansa Water Supply Scheme for bringing a practically unlimited supply from the Tansa Lake; the report of the Bombay Extension Committee; and the completion of the defences of Bombay Harbour.

These have, however, been described in other chapters. But special mention should be made of the hearty expressions of loyalty evoked in the City by the Jubilee of the Queen-Empress in 1887. The Corporation spent Rs. 24,052 on illuminations, and presented an address to Her Majesty by the hands of the late Captain Morland, the Chairman of the Town Council, who received the honour of knighthood upon the occasion. Among the grants for public purposes made by the Corporation the most liberal was one of Rs. 80,000 to the Victoria Jubilee Technical Institute.

A curious episode was the strike of the scavengers in the Health Department in July, 1889, which caused very serious inconvenience.

The importance of Bombay City and the large interests with which it deals tend to dwarf the other municipalities in the Bombay Presidency. The latter considerably increased during the period under review, and numbered 161 in 1889–90 of varying size and population. Some of these municipalities are flourishing. Ahmadábád, for instance, is particularly well administered, and has undertaken two expensive schemes for drainage and water-supply. But good local administration is not universal. Broach was a conspicuous instance of bad administration, and one or two of the smaller municipalities, such as Parántij and Mehmedábád, had to be superseded.

The smaller municipalities derive the greater part of their income from octroi duties. The Bombay Government fully realises the objections to this mode of levying taxation, and takes special care that the octroi duties shall not become transit duties on through trade. But the municipalities have a rooted objection to direct taxation, and cannot see the reason of the Government's dislike of octroi duties. It was because Parántij repeatedly refused to abolish octroi taxation that it was superseded[1]. Mr. G. F. M. Grant, the Acting Commissioner for the Southern Division, writes in his report for 1888–89[2]: 'Neither the people nor their representatives (as a rule) approve of direct taxation, which cannot, if properly levied, be evaded, and which openly attacks their pockets. The dislike on the part of Municipal Commissioners is perhaps based partly on the fear of incurring unpopularity, but I believe that all but the most intelligent are averse to the system.'

The octroi is, therefore, in Bombay the important feature of District municipal finance. Out of Rs. 23,51,272 raised by the District municipalities in

[1] *Bombay Administration Report for* 1889–90, p. 67.

[2] *Report on Municipal Taxation and Expenditure in the Bombay Presidency for* 1888–89, p. 71.

1889–90, no less than Rs. 13,32,464 was collected by the octroi. The income thus collected is, however, supplemented to a greater or less degree by various means of direct taxation according to the circumstances of particular localities. In Sind, for instance, Rs. 4,34,691 out of a total municipal revenue of Rs. 5,17,610 are raised by the octroi, and in certain municipalities it forms the sole source of local income. On the other hand, the three municipalities in the Panch Maháls, with certain others, such as Kurla and Bándra which are practically suburbs of Bombay, levy no octroi duties whatever. The following statistics are of course exclusive of the great municipality of Bombay City.

The direct taxation levied for local purposes in the district municipalities amounted in 1889–90 to Rs. 10,18,808. It is divided into many different heads. The most lucrative is the tax on houses and land which brought in Rs. 3,68,908, of which only Rs. 37,998 were raised in Sind. Next come the Conservancy cess, Rs. 1,96,764; and tolls, Rs. 1,67,776. The other direct taxes for local purposes produce not more than a lakh of rupees.

Some of these other local taxes are pretty general, such as the tax on vehicles, which is raised nearly everywhere. Others are purely local, such as the pilgrim tax in Kaira; a tax on fishing-boats and shops in Kolába; on mills, kilns, &c. in Thána; on trade registration and musicians in Poona; on looms in Ahmadnagar; on snuff and stones in Sátára; booth fees in Dhárwár; camping fees on carts in Kánara;

and a trifling dog tax in Ahmadnagar, Násik, Sholápur, Belgáum, and Kánara[1].

In addition to the local revenue raised by taxation, direct or indirect, the district municipalities derived Rs. 9,96,322 in 1889–90 from other sources. The largest items in this amount were Rs. 2,13,322 from grants-in-aid from provincial or local funds; Rs. 3,09,160 from the rent of municipal lands, receipts from public gardens, &c., of which the largest share, Rs. 1,38,044, was received in Karáchi; and Rs. 1,42,825 from markets. It is noteworthy, considering that the transfer of schools to the municipalities took place during the period under review, that only Rs. 78,771 was derived from school fees in 1889–90.

The local revenues of Bombay municipalities, excluding Bombay City, amounted from taxation and miscellaneous receipts to Rs. 33,47,594 in 1889–90. But to complete the amount at their disposal during the year in question must be added the further sum of Rs. 6,78,530 derived from loans, deposits, and advances. Of this total the two largest items were two loans, each of over two lakhs of rupees, raised for public works by the municipalities of Surat and Ahmadábád[2].

The heads of the expenditure of this large municipal revenue, which in 1889–90, excluding interest on local loans, amounted to Rs. 35,31,809, may be classed

[1] *Bombay Administration Report for* 1889–90, Appendix V. G. (1).

[2] The account stands thus: Municipal taxation, Rs. 23,51,272; miscellaneous receipts, Rs. 9,96,322; loans, deposits, advances, Rs. 6,78,530. Total at disposal of Bombay Municipalities, excluding Bombay City, 1889–90, Rs. 40,26,124.

under the items of office establishment, collection of municipal rates and taxes, public safety, public health, public instruction, public convenience, and miscellaneous. On the first, second, and last of these heads, which absorbed Rs. 1,84,699, Rs. 1,88,636, and Rs. 1,25,183 respectively, nothing need be said, but the other four merit a more detailed examination. They represent the true work of municipalities, work which is, as in Europe, often regarded with dislike by the townspeople, but which is nevertheless necessary for the welfare of every urban community.

Public health, including sanitation in its widest sense, forms the largest branch of district municipal expenditure, and accounted in 1889–90 for Rs. 15,12,863. Mention has already been made of some of the most extensive engineering works undertaken by the Bombay Public Works Department at the expense of the municipalities. Thus the ancient city of Ahmadábád, the second most populous city in the Presidency, with a population of 124,767 according to the census of 1881, raised large loans and expended large sums on sanitary works. The town is honeycombed with cesspools which have been used for generations; the walls of the houses to the height of several feet bear traces of being impregnated with sewage; and the water-supply from wells is foul. Two extensive schemes have been undertaken for drainage and waterworks, and Lord Reay did all in his power to encourage the Ahmadábád municipality in well-doing on his visits to Gujarát.

Surat, the third most populous municipality in the

Presidency, with a population of 107,154 inhabitants in 1881, has to encounter the same difficulties as Ahmadábád in adapting the methods of modern sanitary engineering to an ancient and crowded community. It was also during the period under review ravaged by fire and threatened by flood, and had to undertake extensive works against the latter danger. Poona, the fourth largest municipality, discussed new schemes for drainage and completed its water-supply; but its task is complicated by the neighbourhood of two adjoining local authorities, the Poona Suburban Municipality and the Poona Cantonment.

Medical relief, including the maintenance of dispensaries, absorbed Rs. 1,42,334 of the Bombay municipal expenditure (exclusive of Bombay City) in 1889–90, and vaccination Rs. 17,162; while Rs. 85,888 were spent in that year on watering the streets.

Next to public health, the public convenience makes the largest demands on the municipal revenues, and in 1889–90 no less than Rs. 7,75,758 was expended on different undertakings coming under this head. Much of the work is done by the Bombay Public Works Department, and it includes markets, streets, and bridges. Among such work taken in hand during the period under review may be noted the Empress Market at Karáchi; the widening of the streets at Surat in the rebuilding of the portion of that city devastated by the great fire in 1888[1]; and the opening of the Reay market in Poona.

In the chapter on Education, I have mentioned the

[1] *Bombay Administration Report for* 1889–90, p. 67.

transference of the primary schools to the local authorities (which in the provincial towns are the municipalities) under the system of grants-in-aid and Government inspection. This measure is important in its influence on the progress of education, by stirring up a more lively interest on the part of the citizens, and also marks an advance in the application of the system of local self-government. Public instruction has become a serious item of municipal expenditure, amounting in 1889–90 (not including Bombay), to Rs. 5,19,682. Against this must be set the receipt of Rs. 78,771 in school fees.

Lastly comes the head of public safety, under which the sum of Rs. 2,25,038 was expended in 1889–90. Of this the greater proportion, Rs. 1,74,677, was spent on lighting the streets; and Rs. 46,932 (a very inadequate sum) on protection from fire. In certain districts, Dhárwár, Bijápur, and Thar and Párkar, the municipalities spend nothing whatever on fire-protection: in others containing important towns, namely, Kánara, Haidarábád, Belgáum, and Násik, the yearly expenditure does not exceed Rs. 200. But it may be expected that such disasters as the great fire at Surat will arouse other municipalities to a sense of the absolute necessity of establishing efficient means for the extinction and prevention of fires.

The 161 District municipal bodies in the Presidency were composed in 1889–90 of 2272 members, of whom 1380 were nominated and 892 elected. But this does not fairly represent the progress of the elective principle, for the backward province of Sind possesses an excessive proportion of nominated to elected members. Deducting the 26 municipalities in Sind, the 135 municipalities of the Bombay Presidency proper were composed of 1912 members, of whom 1091 were nominated and 821 elected. Taking individual districts, the proportion was highest in Poona, where in 12 municipalities there were 90 nominated and 90 elected members; and in Ratnágiri, where in 5 municipalities there were 40 nominated and 40 elected members. The ratio was lowest in the Panch Mahâls, where all the members of the 3 municipalities were nominated; and in Kaira, where in 11 municipalities there were 103 nominated to 23 elected members. From another point of view the 1912 members of the municipalities in the Presidency proper consisted of 516 official and 1396 non-official members, and of 1765 natives to 147 Europeans[1]. The nominated non-official members are carefully selected to secure due representation for classes, trades, professions, or castes, which do not obtain their fair share of municipal honours and responsibilities at the polls.

Turning from municipal to rural self-government, District Local Boards or Local Funds Committees were constituted by the Bombay Act IV of 1869. Under that Act they were to be presided over by the Collector of the District, and to consist of certain district officials and of one inámdar and six local landholders nominated by Government. They had to administer the local cess of one ana in the rupee of land tax for local purposes. The Táluká (or sub-divisional)

[1] *Bombay Administration Report for* 1889-90, Appendix III, H.

Local Funds Committee was to be presided over by the Deputy or Assistant Collector, and to bring the wants of the Táluká or sub-division before the District Committee. Act I of 1884 made many changes in this arrangement, and introduced the elective principle. It enacted that the president of any local board might be nominated or elected, but if nominated, a vice-president was to be elected by the board. It gave executive authority to the Táluká Boards, who receive an assignment of money, calculated in the proportion of the one-ana cess to be spent for purely local purposes. During the five years under review (1885–90) this Act was being practically worked out. Additions were made to the responsibilities of the Local Boards, and an increased share in local administration, especially with regard to primary education.

It was also during this period that the elective scheme for rural self-government came into force. For many reasons, not the least of which is the practical difficulty of distance, it is hardly to be expected that rural local boards should be as well attended as urban municipalities by the elected members, and it will take a longer time to awaken the rustic mind to the importance of local self-government than among the quicker-witted townspeople. It has not been found possible to introduce the elective principle into the more backward Tálukás. In the Panch Mahál̇s no members are yet elected to the Local Boards, in Thar and Párkar only two out of 38, in the Upper Sind Frontier only four out of 34, and in North Kánara only 24 out of 105.

There are in the Bombay Presidency, including Sind, 23 District Local Boards and 198 Táluká Local Boards. These are composed of 3430 members, of whom 40 are ex-officio, 1847 are nominated, and 1543 elected. The only district in which the elected outnumber the nominated members is Shikárpur in Sind. In 1889-90, allowing for two vacancies, there were 791 officials and 2637 non-officials serving on these boards, or looking at it from another point of view, 217 Europeans to 3211 natives[1].

The income received by these 221 Local Boards, District and Táluká, in 1889–90, amounted to Rs. 46,38,320. Towards this Rs. 3,05,558 came from the Sind Village Officers Cess Fund, Rs. 1,43,633 from the Government Central Book Depôt, and Rs. 36,079 from the Steam Boilers Inspection Fund, which sources have been added to the Local Funds since the passing of Act I of 1884. The Local Funds under that Act brought in Rs. 41,53,048 during the year 1889–90. By far the largest part of this sum came from the local rate or cess of one ana in the rupee of land-revenue, namely, Rs. 24,27,994. The other main heads were Rs. 2,31,588 from tolls on ferries, Rs. 1,38,014 collected under the Cattle Trespass Act, Rs. 1,29,474 from school fees, Rs. 1,21,499 tolls on roads and bridges only collected in the Central Division, Rs. 1,00,007 from fishery fees in Sind, Rs. 82,773 from sand and quarry fees, and Rs. 49,843 from tolls on roads alone, collected in the Southern Division[2].

[1] *Bombay Administration Report for* 1889–90, Appendix III, G. (1).
[2] *Ibid.*, Appendix V, F. (4).

The distribution of this local revenue shows the comparative rural wealth of the different districts, and varies from Rs. 42,006 in Thar and Párkar, Rs. 58,484 in the Upper Sind Frontier, Rs. 64,020 in the Panch Mahals, and Rs. 1,11,404 in Kolába, to Rs. 2,53,317 in Shikárpur, Rs. 2,59,198 in Thána, Rs. 2,74,099 in Dhárwár, and Rs. 3,71,748 in Khándesh. It is still more interesting to note the incidence per head of population of the local taxation in the different districts, which varied in 1889-90 from 11 pies in Ratnágiri, 1 ana 1 pie in Násik, and 1 ana 3 pies in Sholápur, to 4 anas 3 pies in Surat, 5 anas 5 pies in Shikárpur, and 8 anas 4 pies in Broach.

The expenditure of these Local Boards in 1889-90 for local purposes amounted to Rs. 40,02,036[1]. More than one-half, namely, Rs. 20,40,796, was spent on public works, including original works and repairs, executed either by civil officers or the Bombay Public Works Department. The greater part of the sum was spent on communications, chiefly district and purely local roads, which absorbed no less than Rs. 12,90,618. The only other notable item under this head is Rs. 2,88,310 for water-supply and waterworks; and it is interesting to observe that Rs. 12,531 were spent in the Southern Division on the planting of roadside trees. Next to public works in the rural budget comes education or public instruction. The primary schools were transferred to the Local Boards during the term of Lord Reay's administration under the grant-in-aid system, and in 1889-90 Rs. 12,90,679

[1] *Bombay Administration Report for* 1889-90, Appendix V, F. (1).

were spent upon them, or nearly one-third of the total rural expenditure. Other items worthy of record are Rs. 77,792 on hospitals and dispensaries, and Rs. 89,589 on vaccination.

The foregoing summary of the work undertaken by the district municipalities and district and Táluká local boards gives a fair idea of what is being done by local self-government in the Bombay Presidency. It will be observed that, with the important exception of the management of the police, it corresponds with the work undertaken by the local authorities in England. But the problems of local taxation and expenditure are only one side of the great issues raised in Bombay by the establishment of local self-government. The creation of municipalities, and the extension of the elective principle for urban communities, were the characteristic features in this respect of Lord Reay's administration. The Bombay Municipal Act, perhaps the greatest legislative achievement of his government, must be recognised as a sagacious and timely effort to deal with the most complicated question of local government in the Presidency—namely, the government of its capital.

CHAPTER XIV.

MILITARY AND MARINE.

THE Bombay army is commanded by a Lieutenant-General, with the title of Commander-in-Chief in Bombay. He has a seat in the Bombay Council, and is assisted by a complete staff, headed by an Adjutant-General and a Quartermaster-General, but is himself subordinate to the Commander-in-Chief in India. Most military questions affecting the Bombay army pass through the hands of the Military Secretary to the Bombay Government, who also acts as secretary in the Marine and Ecclesiastical Departments. The successive Commanders-in-Chief of the Bombay army during the five years under review were, as I have already mentioned, Lieutenant-General the Honourable Sir Arthur Hardinge, K.C.B., younger son of the first Viscount Hardinge Governor-General of India from 1844 to 1848; Lieutenant-General Sir Charles George Arbuthnot, K.C.B.; and Lieutenant-General H.R.H. the Duke of Connaught.

The Bombay army has a brilliant record of its own. But it is beyond the scope of this book to even enumerate the series of wars by which South-western India was won from the Muhammadan and Maráthá princes, who had divided between them the heritage of the 'Great Mogul.' One or two regimental episodes must suffice. The 1st Bombay Native Infantry (Grenadiers) co-operated with the 42nd Highlanders in the famous defence of Mangalore by Lieutenant-Colonel John Campbell in the third Mysore War. The siege lasted from May, 1783, to January, 1784, and when the city surrendered, Tipú Sultán allowed the remnant of the garrison to retire with the honours of war to Bombay. The 3rd, 5th, and 7th Bombay Native Infantry took a conspicuous part in the pitched battle of Seedaseer, when Tipú Sultán endeavoured to check the column from the Malabar Coast, on its march to join in the siege of Seringapatam. The 2nd and 13th Bombay Native Infantry formed part of the force under Sir David Baird, which sailed from India in 1801 across the Indian Ocean and up the Red Sea to Cosseir, whence it marched across the desert to the Nile. It descended the Nile in boats, and joined the English army sent to Egypt to expel the French. Its perilous journey has been most fully described by a French writer, the Comte de Noë. It was the 2nd Bombay Native Infantry also, under the command of Captain Staunton, which, unsupported by any British soldiers, fought the Maráthá army at Korygáon in 1818. Bombay regiments served in the first Afghan war, and in the conquest of Sind by Sir Charles Napier.

During the Mutiny, only two regiments, the 21st and 27th Bombay Native Infantry, followed the example of the Bengal Sepoys, and rose in open revolt. Unfortunately the honours of the Bombay army suffered eclipse for a moment during the second Afghan War by the disaster at Maiwand : due not to want of bravery in the troops, but to unskilful tactics. Only for a moment, however. The 28th Bombay Native Infantry served with marked distinction in the Soudan campaign of 1885; and the Bombay contingent despatched to take part in the conquest and occupation of Upper Burma in 1885–86 did its duty right well.

During the five years from 1885 to 1890 important questions arose as to the abolition of the Commandership-in-Chief in Bombay, and as to bringing the Presidency army into more direct relations with the Supreme Government under the Commander-in-Chief in India. The Army Commission, whose report was laid before Parliament in 1884, had recommended the abolition of the three Presidential armies, and the substitution of four army corps. On these questions I, as a civilian, do not here offer an opinion of my own, but confine myself to indicating the main line of argument on both sides.

One of the principal issues raised was whether the change proposed would produce over-centralisation. The Army Commission gave expression to the view that there is something anomalous in the existence of three separate Presidency armies with three distinct systems of administration, in the same country, all serving the same Central Government. 'The majority of the Commission,' says the Report, 'are much impressed by the evils of the present Presidential system, the defects of a war administration worked by separate and dispersed agencies, and by the three sets of separate Staff and Army Departments. We cannot close our eyes to the grave embarrassments to military affairs caused by the numerous and circuitous channels through which the smallest detail has to filter. The anomaly is not merely useless, but hurtful to the efficiency of the army.'

To remedy these evils the Commission recommended the formation of four army corps, two of which would be identical with the present Madras and Bombay armies, while the other two would be constituted from the eastern and western portions of the Bengal army. There would be one Headquarters Staff at Simla, instead of the three independent Presidential staffs. The lieutenant-generals commanding the army corps would be more distinctly subordinate to the Commander-in-Chief in India than are the Commanders-in-Chief of Bombay and Madras at present. The military secretariats of the Madras and Bombay Presidencies, and the connection of these Presidency Governments with military affairs, would be curtailed or abolished.

On the other hand, it was represented that the financial saving from such reconstruction would not be very great. The Headquarters Staff at Simla would have to be strengthened to make up for the reduction of the Presidential staffs. There would be four lieutenant-generals commanding army corps and one full general commanding the army in India in chief, in place of two lieutenant-generals commanding the Madras and Bombay armies and one full general commanding in chief, as at present. An advantage would be that the Commander-in-Chief in India would be freed from his special duties as Commander-in-Chief of the Bengal army. He would, with his Headquarters Staff, be thus enabled to devote himself to the supervision of the army in India, considered as an organic whole, in the same way as the Government of India in its civil administration controls the provincial governments. The danger was the possibility of over-centralisation, and the consequent impairing of local responsibility and local energy.

Lord Reay looked at the question without being biassed by his position as a provincial governor. He pointed out that the establishment of an independent Commander-in-Chief with a Central Staff need not lead to over-centralisation. He argued that the four army corps of Bengal, Madras, Bombay, and the Punjab might retain all their local characteristics and be treated as four units or 'four watertight compartments,' each with its own Medical Staff, Commissariat, Transport, and Accounts department. In these departments he considered too much centralisation had already been introduced, although fully recognising the need for uniformity. He recognised that the lieutenants-general commanding them might be made as immediately responsible for their efficiency and economy as are the Presidential Commanders-in-Chief at present. If this principle was strictly observed he held that the change from presidential armies to army corps might be worked so as really to lead to decentralisation, and that the Headquarters Staff might more effectively devote itself to the interests of the Indian army as a whole; its connection with the executive details of the Bengal army being severed. The Commander-in-Chief in India would naturally retain his seat on the Viceroy's Council, and there could be no objection to the lieutenants-general commanding the army corps in Madras and Bombay being members of the Councils of the governors of those provinces, as the Commanders-in-Chief of the Madras and Bombay armies have heretofore been.

Turning from this general question to the actual history of the Bombay army during the five years under review (1885–1890), the first important event was the transfer of the Belgáum District command from the Bombay to the Madras army in November, 1885. In return the Nágpur District was transferred from the Madras to the Bombay army, on October 1, 1888. This exchange, which the Bombay Government regretted, shows that the distribution of troops is not necessarily affected by the limits of the different Presidencies. Belgáum is a Bombay District; Nágpur is in the Central Provinces; while, as a further example, the Quetta District command, which is upon the Sind frontier, was transferred from the Bombay to the Bengal army.

On the same day as the transfer of the Nágpur command was effected, October 1, 1888, a general reorganisation of the commands and staff was introduced. The terms Divisions and Brigades were abolished, and the senior commands, previously styled Divisions, and First and Second Class Brigades, were divided into two classes only, and called First and

Second Class Districts. One Major-General's command, the old Northern District, was suppressed. Some of the stations within its limits were transferred to the Bombay District, and the rest were formed into Second Class Districts. The Second Class Brigade at Nasirábád was also reduced to a station, commanded by a Colonel on the staff. The Divisional and Brigade Staffs in the Adjutant-General's and Quartermaster-General's Departments were amalgamated; and the officers holding appointments in these departments were designated District Staff Officers, First Class, and District Staff Officers, Second Class, in lieu of their former cumbrous titles of Assistant and Deputy-Assistant-Adjutant-General, and Assistant and Deputy-Assistant-Quartermaster-General. Three Brigade-Majors were abolished, and Station Staff Officers were allowed at certain stations instead. The Station Staff Officers were divided into four classes instead of three, and the staff salaries of the first, second, and third classes were increased.

This important reform in the Adjutant-General's and Quartermaster-General's Departments consequent on the reorganisation of the district commands, was accompanied by not less important changes in other branches of the departmental organisation. On February 1, 1887, the Commissariat Supply and Transport Departments of the Bombay army were amalgamated. In July, 1887, their staff was reorganised; and on September 21, 1889, orders were issued that from October 1 in that year their presidential staffs should be formed into one central department for all India under the orders of the Commissary-General-in-Chief and under the administrative control of the Government of India.

The Commissary-General in Bombay selected by Lord Reay was Colonel Wilhelm Luckhardt, C.B. and Aide-de-Camp to the Queen, an extremely able officer. He reorganised the important spending departments under his control, introduced drastic reforms and put down many abuses. The result was a saving of three lakhs of rupees. He paid special attention to the vital question of transport, and largely substituted mules for the comparatively useless elephants and camels.

Even more interesting was Colonel Luckhardt's attempt to make the transport followers of military value, instead of incumbrances to the progress of an army. He obtained leave in July, 1887, to teach these followers the work of carpenters, blacksmiths, masons, &c. in the transport workshops, and to pay them half the rates allowed to departmental workmen, while they were employed as artificers. The scheme was tried as an experiment for one year. It proved a success and resulted in a financial saving, and the Government of India in July, 1889, sanctioned its continuance. Another point of Colonel Luckhardt's administration was his advocacy of the substitution of the draught for the pack system, and his endeavours to find a style of cart suitable for rough ground and strong enough not to break down when heavily laden.

While speaking of reforms in the army departments, mention should also be made of the abolition of the

Bombay Clothing Agency on October 1, 1889, in consequence of the recommendation of the Finance Committee. The separate presidential Judge-Advocate-General's departments were amalgamated on April 1, 1888 into one, under a Judge-Advocate-General for India. A considerable saving was effected by the substitution of one Deputy-Judge-Advocate-General and one Assistant-Judge-Advocate-General for the Bombay army in the place of the former establishment of a Judge-Advocate-General and two Deputy-Judge-Advocates-General.

These important measures of reform and consolidation in the higher grades and in the staff of the Bombay army were introduced partly as a result of the recommendations of the Finance Committee, and partly as steps towards the scheme of reconstruction propounded by the Army Commission. Whether or not that scheme be ever adopted in its entirety, the measures just described have tended alike to efficiency and economy.

With reference to the British regiments stationed in Bombay during the five years from 1885 to 1890, it may be briefly noted that in 1885 the strength of each battalion of infantry was augmented by the addition of one hundred privates. Measures were also taken, under a scheme formulated by the Government of India in 1887, to replace the old canteens by regimental institutes containing both refreshment and recreation departments.

In the Bombay Native Regiments more important changes were made. A distinguishing characteristic of the Bombay, as of the Madras, army has been the maintenance of the 'dilution' system. By this system regiments composed of members of a single caste or a single race are avoided, in contradistinction to the practice which formerly prevailed in the Bengal army. The argument in favour of 'dilution' was strengthened by the experience of the Mutiny in 1857. The only two Bombay regiments which mutinied were the 21st Native Infantry, which was composed solely of Púrbiahs, and the 27th Native Infantry, composed solely of Maráthás[1]. Generally speaking, Maráthás and Rájputs, Sikhs and Patháns, may be seen serving together in the ranks of the regular Bombay regiments.

The Maráthás are alike the most numerous and the most warlike inhabitants of the Bombay Presidency proper. Of their military aptitude in the past there can be no doubt: for it was the Maráthás who broke the power of the Mughal Empire. But the development of the mill industry and the improvement in the condition of agriculture tends yearly to diminish the number of Maráthá recruits. The hardy inhabitants of the District of Ratnágiri who formerly enlisted in large numbers, now prefer to earn the livelihood which their barren soil denies, in the factories of Bombay rather than in the ranks of the army. 'At the present day,' it is said[2], 'the Bombay army is greatly dependent for its supply of recruits on the Native States of Central India.' To this general statement the three Balúch regiments form a marked exception. These regiments

[1] *Memorandum on Army Corps* versus *Presidential Armies* (Bombay, 1888), p. 7.

[2] *The Calcutta Review* for October, 1889, p. 244.

are not 'diluted,' nor is the supply of recruits for them likely to be diminished for many years to come. Indeed, in 1887 the Government of India, recognising the high military qualities of the Balúchis, proposed that three more regiments of the Bombay Native Infantry should be localised in Sind and Balúchistán, and recruited from the frontier tribes. This scheme was not carried out, owing to representations by the Bombay Government.

I now turn for a moment to the different sections of the Bombay Native Army. In the artillery, the two Bombay Mountain Batteries (Native) were increased from four to six guns each in 1885, and the field of recruitment for them was extended to the Punjab in 1889. The Bombay Native Cavalry was increased by one regiment and by the addition of a fresh squadron to each regiment, in 1885. In the same year the 1st and 2nd Bombay Lancers were equipped throughout with lance, sword, and carbine. In 1887 the Aden troop also was armed with the lance instead of the sabre. In the Bombay Native Infantry far-reaching changes were made. Under the system introduced into the whole native army of India in 1886, the Bombay Native Infantry regiments of the old organisation were linked together into regiments consisting of three battalions each; the new battalions being identical with the old regiments. Of these new regiments, one, consisting of the 4th Rifles, the 23rd Light Infantry, and the 25th Light Infantry was on the proposal of H.R.H. the Duke of Connaught formed into a Rifle Corps in 1888. The 4th Rifles were armed with long Sniders in 1887, and in 1888 the Government of India sanctioned the issue of Martini-Henri rifles to certain Native Infantry regiments.

Another point worthy of notice was the assimilation of the system of enlistment for the Bombay Native Army to that prevailing in the Bengal Native Army, in 1887. Under it, a soldier can claim his discharge after three years' service if his regiment is within 10 per cent of its establishment in time of peace. The formation of a Reserve for the Native Infantry, sanctioned by the Secretary of State in 1885, and established in connection with the Bombay army in 1887, is of the nature of an experimental measure.

The British troops in the Bombay Presidency, in 1889–90, numbered 12,604 officers and men, and the Native army 26,902 officers and men; total, 39,506. The English force comprised 21 batteries and troops of artillery with 84 guns (excluding the heavy ordnance at Bombay, Aden, and Karáchi), one regiment of cavalry, nine regiments of infantry, and 34 engineers. The Native army consisted of two Mountain Batteries of artillery with 12 guns, one regiment of engineers, nine regiments of cavalry, numbering 4516 officers and men, and 28 regiments of infantry numbering 21,353 officers and men. The English army contained 391 commissioned officers, 1262 non-commissioned officers, and 10,951 men. The Native army was composed of 326 English commissioned officers, 548 Native commissioned officers, 2811 non-commissioned officers and 23,217 men[1].

[1] *Bombay Administration Report for* 1889-90, Appendix III, I (1).

The total cost of the Bombay army under the various Budget grants for 1889–90 amounted to Rs. 265,33,687. Of this sum Rs. 62,23,872 was allotted to the English army, and Rs. 74,64,636 to the Native army[1]. What are termed Effective Services, including the staff, the commissariat, ordnance, medical, barrack, clothing, and remount establishments, and the administration of martial law, absorbed no less than Rs. 113,06,028. Some of the items under this head deserve further details. The commissariat, for instance, including establishments, supplies, and services, cost Rs. 54,35,212; a sum which gives an idea of the magnitude of the department with which Colonel Luckhardt had to deal; ordnance, Rs. 14,08,219; medical establishments, services, and supplies, Rs. 11,43,982. Non-effective Services, namely pensions and rewards, came to Rs. 15,39,151.

Among the items under Effective Services is a sum of Rs. 3,15,654 for Volunteer Corps. The number of volunteers in the Bombay Presidency amounted to 4394 officers and men. Of these, 2735 belonged to the three Railway Volunteer Corps, composed of the men employed on the three great trunk lines running from Bombay—the Bombay, Baroda, and Central India; the Great India Peninsula; and the Southern Maráthá. The Bombay Volunteers include artillery, rifles, and light horse; and the Sind Volunteers comprise the Karáchi Naval Volunteer Corps formed in June, 1889. The formation of a similar corps of Naval Volunteers

[1] *Bombay Administration Report for* 1889–90, Appendix III, I (2).

at Aden was sanctioned by the Bombay Government in January, 1890.

In addition to the cost of the Bombay Army must be reckoned the expenditure on military works, which may be divided into Defence and Ordinary Works. I have already referred to the separation of the Military Works from the Bombay Public Works Department, in the last year of Lord Reay's administration. The Government of Bombay recognised the distinction between original defence works, needing supervision by Royal Engineers and ordinary military works, such as barracks and store-houses. Lord Reay fully acknowledged the expediency of a special supervision, and indeed of a special department, for the former. Indeed, shortly after his arrival he successfully urged acceleration of harbour defence works. But he protested against the concentration of ordinary military works under a central department of military works at the distant headquarters of the Government of India. The Bombay Public Works Department had shown itself thoroughly competent to carry out the building and repair of barracks and stores. Lord Reay maintained that, by its knowledge of local prices and requirements, it could do such work more economically and quite as efficiently as the new branch of Military Works directly dependent on the Simla Department.

Defence works stand on a different footing. It was part of the policy of Lord Dufferin to fortify the great seaports of the Indian Empire against attack by sea. Recent naval manœuvres show with what ease a modern ship of war can capture or destroy even the largest city, unless protected by effective heavy ordnance. Foremost among the seaports of the Indian Empire are Bombay, Aden, and Karáchi. Elaborate defence works (of which it would be improper for me to enter into the details) were undertaken during the five years under review for the protection of these cities. The preparation of the designs and the execution of the works have been carried out by a special staff of Royal Engineer officers at each station under the direction, since 1887, of the Inspector-General of Military Works. Coast batteries have been erected, heavy modern ordnance has been supplied, and a network of submarine mines has been arranged in connection with each of these three harbours. Three torpedo boats of the latest pattern arrived for Bombay and two for Karáchi in 1889. Schemes for defence in case of an attack have been drawn up, and rehearsals of them were carried out in the presence of H.R.H. the Duke of Connaught at Aden in November, 1889; at Karáchi in January, 1890; and at Bombay in March, 1890[1]. During the five years from 1885 to 1890, Rs. 64,54,284 were spent on the special coast defences of Bombay, Aden, and Karáchi, of which Rs. 6,51,099 have been refunded by the Home Government as a moiety of the expenditure at Aden.

The Secretary in the Military Department is also the Secretary in the Marine Department to the Government of Bombay, and the headquarters of the Indian Marine are at Bombay. The old Indian Navy,

[1] *Bombay Administration Report for* 1889–90, p. 68.

maintained by the East India Company, and with a glorious record of service on the coasts of India and in the Persian Gulf, was abolished on April 30, 1863. It was believed that the work which it performed could be more economically done in another fashion, and six ships of the Royal Navy were subsidised for the purpose at a yearly cost of £70,000. This expectation was not altogether realised. The transport of troops to Aden and from one Indian port to another, the inspection of lighthouses and the guarding of the convict settlement on the Andaman Islands, were scarcely duties for the Royal Navy. In 1877 a separate Indian Marine was accordingly organised. It constructed a regular service out of the local establishment which had gradually grown up for these special duties, and took over the dockyards at Bombay and at Kidderpur near Calcutta. In 1882 Captain H. W. Brent, R.N., was appointed the first Director of the Indian Marine, and had the arduous task of despatching the Indian contingent to Egypt. He was succeeded in 1883 by Captain John Hext, R.N., who filled the office of Director of the Indian Marine throughout the five years under review.

The Indian Marine mans five troopships, the 'Canning,' 'Clive,' 'Dalhousie,' 'Mayo,' and 'Tenasserim,' besides the two turret-ships 'Abyssinia' and 'Magdala,' six torpedo boats, and several smaller vessels. The Government of India also owns the five great troopships which carry the reliefs between England and India, the 'Serapis,' 'Euphrates,' 'Crocodile,' 'Jumna,' and 'Malabar,' but which are officered and manned by the Royal Navy. The ordinary work of the Indian Marine is the transport of the reliefs between one Indian port and another. But in case of a military expedition, a much greater strain is placed on its resources. Thus in 1885, just before Lord Reay's arrival, it carried to the Soudan in its own vessels and in hired transports, between February 22 and April 16, 3366 officers and men of the Indian Army, with 11,521 followers, 835 horses, 2279 mules and ponies, 4155 camels and other animals.

On a still larger scale was the work of the Indian Marine in transporting troops for the conquest of Burma in 1885–86. It embarked in its own and in hired ships 14,629 officers and men, with 6565 followers, 494 horses and other animals; and in 1886 18,389 officers and men, with 7371 followers, 3054 horses and other animals. Its officers did good service on the Irrawadi in the Burma campaign; two of them earned the Distinguished Service Order and several have been mentioned in despatches. During the five years under review the Indian Marine received steady encouragement from the Government of India. Its officers have been graded in the Indian precedence list, but just complaints are made that it has not yet received a fair share of recognition from the Lords of the Admiralty.

CHAPTER XV.

SIND, ADEN, AND THE PORTUGUESE POSSESSIONS.

HITHERTO I have treated the Bombay Presidency as a whole. But before ending this volume, I must explain at some length an important question which arose afresh during the five years under review in regard to the outlying province of Sind. I shall then very briefly refer to certain transactions in the more distant settlement of Aden, and in the Portuguese Settlements on the Bombay coast.

The province of Sind, as already stated, is cut off from the Presidency Proper by Native States, and presents administrative problems distinctively its own. Its Muhammadan population, its entire dependence on irrigation for agricultural prosperity, its comparatively recent conquest, and its sparsely inhabited tracts, contrast with the conditions prevailing in Gujarát and the Deccan. It accordingly forms, to a certain extent, a separate administrative unit. The Commissioner in Sind exercises larger powers than the Commissioners of the Northern, Central, and Southern Divisions of the Presidency. The Judicial Commissioner of Sind possesses nearly all the powers of the Bombay High Court. The Districts of Sind are still Non-Regulation, and many enactments of the Bombay Legislative Council are not extended to them. The administrative system on the whole resembles that of the Central Provinces, except that the Commissioner in Sind is subordinate to the Government of Bombay, while the Chief Commissioner of the Central Provinces is directly under the Government of India.

The connection of Sind with the Bombay Government has not, however, been always regarded as essential, and in 1888 the Government of India decided to recommend the transference of Sind to the Lieutenant-Governorship of the Punjab. Lord Reay, on being consulted by the Governor-General in Council, objected, and after a full consideration of his arguments, the transfer was not carried into effect. The question seriously affected the Bombay Government, and the decision to maintain the *status quo* was not arrived at without much discussion. The proposal is, however, of old standing and has an instructive history. The following summary shows the long-protracted deliberation which is given to such a question of territorial jurisdiction by the Indian Government, and briefly indicates the arguments from time to time put forward on both sides. They may be divided into historical, geographical, administrative, military, and commercial.

Sir Charles Napier conquered the Amírs of Sind in 1843, and was appointed Governor of the province on its annexation by Lord Ellenborough. He held the office until 1847, doing arduous work in settling a country disturbed by long licence and misgovernment. On Napier's resignation, the administration of Sind was placed under the control of the Bombay Government. In February 1856 the Government of India proposed to establish a Lieutenant-Governorship on the north-west frontier of the empire, to include both the Punjab and Sind. The project was, however, negatived by the Court of Directors on financial and other grounds. In November, 1858, after the abolition of the East India Company, the Secretary of State for India ordered the formation of the Lieutenant-Governorship of the Punjab. The composition of the new province was left to the Government of India. It decided, in a large measure owing to the admirable administration of Sind by Sir Bartle Frere, then Commissioner, and to the difficulty of communications with the North, that Sind should remain attached to the Bombay Presidency. Twelve years later, Lord Mayo had again to consider the question of re-arranging the jurisdictions of the Local Governments, and among them the transfer of Sind. No step was immediately taken, but in 1876 the Secretary of State sanctioned the transfer of Sind to the Punjab, and on August 15, 1879, the Government of India applied for sanction to bring the new arrangements into force from January 1, 1880. The events at Kábul, however, and the continuance of the Afghán war, caused the proposal to be postponed. From this narrative it will be seen that one school could fairly argue that the subordination of Sind to the Bombay Government was accidental, and that there had long been a consensus of opinion in favour of eventually separating it.

On the other side, the history of actual facts may be opposed to the history of opinion. It may be true, urge the advocates for retaining the *status quo*, that the subordination of Sind to Bombay had been regarded as a temporary measure. Nevertheless the arrangement has now lasted for nearly fifty years; and when a temporary arrangement lasts for nearly half a century in India, it must be treated as practically permanent. They argue that the very facts which weighed with the Government of India against actual separation in 1858 and 1879, namely the admirable administration of Sir Bartle Frere and the Afghan war, show that the unanimity of opinion was, upon the two occasions when the matter was most maturely considered, overpowered by practical considerations in favour of the existing system. To this answer it is rejoined that these considerations against the transfer were of a temporary character.

The geographical arguments for and against the transfer of Sind are apparent from a glance at the map. On the one hand, Sind is separated from the boundaries of the Bombay Presidency by the Native States of Rájputána and Cutch, while it marches on its northern frontier with the Lieutenant-Governorship of the Punjab, and on its western frontier with the recently ceded districts of Balúchistán. Its most important physical feature, and the one on which its agricultural prosperity depends, the Indus river, is formed by the five streams which give the Punjab its name. It would seem natural, therefore, that the whole course of the mighty river and its affluents should be under one government. The difficulty of communication with the Punjab, which formed an objection to the inclusion of Sind within that Lieutenant-Governorship in 1858, has been removed by the completion of the North-Western State Railway. Lahore can now be more easily reached by train than Bombay by steamer. To these geographical arguments may also be added ethnological and religious considerations. The people of Sind are less alien in habits and religion to those of the Punjab and Balúchistán than to those of Bombay. The prevailing religion of Sind is that of Islám, which has comparatively few followers in the Bombay Presidency.

On the other hand it is urged that the geographical argument of Sind being watered by the great river of the Punjab is not conclusive, for it might be alleged on behalf of the amalgamation of part of Madras with Bombay, and against the separation of Assam from Bengal. The close connection between Sind and the Punjab resulting from the completion of the North-Western State Railway may some day be balanced by the construction of a Bombay line across the Rann of Cutch from Karáchi to Káthiáwár. It is true that the Sind population is chiefly of the Muhammadan religion, but these Muhammadans are the descendants of the original Hindu inhabitants, who were converted to the faith of Islám during the reign of the Ummayide dynasty of Khalifas, and are ethnically related to the people of Gujarát. This is proved by the Sindi language, which differs more from Punjabi than it does from Gujaráti, and has much in common with the latter vernacular. The class from which Native officials in Sind are chiefly drawn is that of the Hindu Amils. The Bombay Presidency proper contains Maráthi-speaking, Gujaráti-speaking, and Kánarese-speaking races, and has to deal with the Hindu, Pársi, and Lingáyat religions. The addition of another language and another dominant religion in Sind does not complicate its government.

The administrative arguments are more weighty. The Province of Sind is and, under British rule, always has been an administrative entity. It is administered by a Commissioner, whose powers resemble those of the Chief Commissioners of Assam and the Central Provinces. Its districts are Non-Regulation like those in the latter governments. Its judicial machinery is complete in itself. It can therefore be separated with a minimum of friction or inconvenience. It has its own interests, which are independent of those existing in the Bombay Presidency. Its agricultural system, dependent on irrigation works and canals, differs from that of the Deccan, the Konkan or Gujarát. Its physical configuration, with its one great river, its sandy soil and frequent deserts, its absence of mountains and of forests, presents peculiar conditions. Its commercial prosperity depends on the trade of the north-west of India, mainly upon wheat, while that of the Bombay Presidency proper depends on the trade of the western and central districts of the Peninsula, mainly on cotton.

In reply to these considerations, the opposing school justly urges the success which has been attained by the existing system. For nearly half a century, Sind has been administered, as a separate organisation it is true, but by Bombay officers and upon Bombay principles. Bombay administrators, like Sir Bartle Frere and Colonel Sir W. L. Merewether, have built up a most efficient government. A special revenue system, based on the condition of the province, under the name of irrigational settlements, has been introduced by the instrumentality of Mr. H. N. B. Erskine, C.S.I., who was Commissioner in Sind during the early part of Lord Reay's administration. Education has been put on a sound footing by a special Inspector of Schools, Mr. H. P. Jacob. The Bombay Public Works Department has paid particular attention to the requirements of Sind, and has successfully laboured, with the aid of its slowly acquired special knowledge, to maintain and extend the network of irrigation canals. Sind has certainly not suffered by its connection with Bombay in the past.

Nor would the separation be unattended with difficulties. The Sind public records are inextricably mixed up with those of the rest of the Bombay Government, and it would be a very expensive and prolonged task to separate them. Bombay, moreover, is the principal maritime province of India. The Bombay Government is peculiarly suited to deal with the special questions connected with the management of ports and harbours. Sind has a considerable seaboard, and its wealthiest and most progressive city is the important port of Karáchi. The Punjab has no ports and no maritime administration. It would have to create a fresh machinery for the single harbour of Karáchi, and there would be a danger of disagreement between the neighbouring maritime jurisdictions of Sind (if a part of the Punjab) and Bombay.

The fourth series of considerations are military. It was owing to the inconvenience of a division of political responsibility upon the North-Western frontier that the Government of India resuscitated the idea of the separation of Sind from Bombay in 1876. The unity of frontier policy was impaired by a portion of the frontier being subject to the Government of the Punjab and a portion to that of Bombay. It was felt that since the completion of the North-Western State Railway the whole frontier ought to be treated strategically as a whole. In the event of a war the existence of two military authorities on the frontier might prove a source of weakness.

To these considerations the opposed school of administrators rejoin that, since 1876, circumstances have undergone a change. That Sind is no longer strategically a frontier province. That by the Treaty of Gandamak the former Afghán districts of Pishin and Sibi were assigned to the British Government, and Quetta is held on a perpetual lease from the Khán of Khelát. These accessions have been formed into a separate government of British Balúchistán, under the rule of the Agent to the Governor-General at Khelát as Chief Commissioner.

The military district command at Quetta now

pertains to the Bengal Army, like the other military commands on the Punjab frontier. It is true that the ultimate base of operations, the North-Western State Railway, runs through both the Punjab and Sind. But the southern line of primary operations has been pushed out from Sind into Balúchistán by the construction of the railway from Sukkur to Sibi, with a loop line through the Bolan to Quetta, and from Sibi up the Nari gorge and the Harnai valley to Pishin, and onwards towards the Khojak pass. A military road has been made through the Bori valley connecting Pishin with the Punjab, and a cantonment has been established at Loralai.

On more general military grounds, it is argued that if the Bombay Army were deprived of its three Balúch battalions and the Sind Horse, its prestige and usefulness would be impaired; that it is necessary for its efficiency that it should have to garrison an outlying province like Sind, sufficiently close to the frontier to maintain the spirit of alertness for actual warfare.

From the commercial point of view, the most important city in Sind is Karáchi, and Karáchi is the port of export for the produce not only of Sind but of the Punjab. It would be for the advantage of the trade of the Punjab that its outlet should be under the control of its own administration. This argument would certainly be conclusive if Bombay and the Punjab were independent states, for it is natural that every state should strive for a maritime outlet of its own for its commerce. But the Bombay Presidency and the Punjab are not rival states. They form part of one empire. The Government of India would, in case of a conflict of interests, take care that the Bombay Government should not prejudice the interests of the Punjab. Meanwhile the experience gained by the Bombay Government in the management of Bombay itself, the greatest port of India and one of the greatest in the world, has proved of inestimable advantage to the interests of Karáchi. The development of that harbour during Lord Reay's administration, the extensive works undertaken for its improvement by the Bombay Public Works Department, and the formation of the Karáchi Port Trust on the model of the Port Trust which has done so much for the prosperity of Bombay, have been already mentioned. The consideration that the Bombay Presidency is the maritime province of India has weight both from the commercial and the administrative point of view. It is an advantage to have the two most important centres of coast defence (the ports of Karáchi and Bombay) under the same Local Government. As a matter of fact, the great commercial houses, which control the export wheat trade of Karáchi, are more closely connected with Bombay than with Lahore or Delhi, and have generally their headquarters at Bombay.

If Sind is separated from Bombay, what is to be done with it? Two projects have been brought forward. According to one of them, Sind, with the recently ceded districts in Balúchistán, would be formed into a Chief Commissionership similar to those of Assam and the Central Provinces. But in these days of easy communication by railway and telegraph, the tendency is to diminish rather than to increase the number of administrative units. Economy can thus be secured without prejudice to efficiency, and it is likely that in any rearrangement of Provinces a reduction in the number of local governments will be made.

The other project is to unite Sind with the Lieutenant-Governorship of the Punjab. This was the scheme favoured by Lord Lytton's Government in 1876, and adopted by Lord Dufferin's Government in 1888.

Of the people of Sind, those who pay attention to the manner in which their province is governed disliked the idea of separation. On May 18, 1888, the Sind Sabha of Karáchi, describing itself as 'a body established for the representation and advancement of the public interests of the people of Sind,' drew up a 'humble memorial' on the subject to the Viceroy in Council. The Memorial ably set forth the leading arguments mentioned in the foregoing paragraphs in favour of retaining Sind under the Government of Bombay. Although this document may seem rather to furnish evidence of contentment with the existing state of things than to appreciate the reasons—political, commercial, and military—which now point to a change, it deservedly carried some weight. Upon a full consideration of the objections urged by the Bombay Government, and of the expression of opinion in Sind, the Government of India refrained from further action in the matter for the time being.

During the discussions as to separating Sind from Bombay arose a question of amalgamating the Central Provinces with that Presidency. This proposal was regarded with approval by Lord Salisbury in 1876, when the transfer of Sind was under consideration, as affording compensation for the loss which the Bombay Presidency would experience. It was again carefully discussed during the five years under review, 1885–1890; and it will probably be revived when the question of territorial redistribution comes up for final decision. The Central Provinces were acquired by the British from the Maráthás, and many experienced administrators have thought that the time is at hand for reuniting those Provinces with the main portion of the Maráthá country under the Government of Bombay. If the double project is ever carried out, Sind would be amalgamated with the Punjab into a strong frontier Province stretching down the whole valley of the Indus from the Himálayas to the sea; while the Bombay Presidency would embrace all the British provinces of Western and Central India commanded by the railway system which has its sea-outlet at the port of Bombay. Meanwhile the general question of transfer of territory to or from Bombay remains in abeyance. But as this question fundamentally affects the future of the Bombay Presidency, I have thought it well to present it in a clear light.

With regard to Aden, I propose merely to summarise the more important administrative events during the five years under review, 1885–1890. Aden may be considered as a fortress, a settlement, and a port. As a fortress, commanding the entrance to the Red Sea, and as a coaling station, the defence of Aden is a matter of supreme importance to the whole British Empire. The English Government recognise this fact, and the English War Office furnished designs for a series of defensive works to render Aden impregnable. The Home and the Indian Governments divide the expense, but the works have been carried out partly by the Bombay Government, partly by the Western India Imperial Defences Branch, and the garrison is supplied by the Bombay Army. The defensive works were completed during the period under review, and both the Governor and the Commander-in-Chief of Bombay had reason to believe that all that was then possible has been done to secure the safety of the great stronghold which commands the road to India.

As a settlement, Aden is administered by a Resident, who is also the Brigadier-General commanding the troops stationed in the fortress. The Resident has full magisterial authority, together with jurisdiction as a judge of the Vice-Admiralty Court and in matters connected with the suppression of the slave trade. The Resident has six assistants under him, one of whom is the Cantonment Magistrate. It being found inexpedient to keep a large population within the limits of the fortress, the village of Shaikh Othman was purchased in 1880 in order to lay out a suitable settlement for the civil part of the inhabitants. It is situated about five miles from Aden, and has been so rapidly taken into favour that it now contains about 10,000 inhabitants. An Aden Municipality has been formed, including Aden proper and Little Aden on the two peninsulas, which form the limits of the fortress, and Shaikh Othman. Like all the other Bombay Municipalities, it pays its chief attention to sanitation. This Municipality raised a local revenue of Rs. 1,52,178 in 1889-90, and one of Lord Reay's last acts was to make arrangements for the establishment of a good civil hospital in connection with it.

As a port and coaling station, Aden is the centre of a large and increasing trade. In 1889-90 no fewer than 1615 vessels visited Aden, of which 1461 were merchant steamers with an aggregate tonnage of 2,427,760 tons[1]. Of these only 970 were British steamers, and their number showed a decrease, owing to the fact that passing ships prefer to take in their coal at Perim, where there are no port dues. The value of the seaborne and inland trade, exclusive of Government stores and treasure and cargo manifested for transhipment on importation, amounted in 1889-90 to Rs. 671,79,699, a large increase over the average for the five years under review[2]. Considering the magnitude of this trade, Lord Reay's Government determined to extend to Aden the system which had proved so beneficial at Bombay, and by Act V of 1888 created an Aden Port Trust. This new body, of which the First Assistant Resident is chairman and all the members are nominated by Government, at once obtained

[1] *Bombay Administration Report for* 1889-90, pp. 71 and 116.
[2] *Ibid.*, p. 113.

a dredger of 1000 tons capacity and prepared to deepen the harbour at an expense of Rs. 9,30,967, to be spread over five years. The receipts of the Port Trust during the year 1889–90 amounted to Rs. 1,97,723, of which Rs. 1,17,298 were derived from port dues. The expenditure on dredging alone amounted to Rs. 1,40,433 [1].

The functions of the Resident at Aden are not however confined to the settlement. For Aden has many dependencies. The most important of these is the little island of Perim, situated in an important strategic position at the entrance of the Red Sea. It is defended by a small garrison, and largely used as a coaling station. During 1889–90 588 steamers, of which 528 were British, called at the island, four-fifths of them to take in or discharge coal [2]. Besides Perim, the Resident at Aden has control over the Massah Islands and Eibat Island, purchased by the British Government in 1840, and the Kooriah Mooriah Islands ceded by the Imám of Mascat in 1854; islands which are however chiefly valuable for their guano deposits. The coast tribes from Perim to Ras Sair are also under British protection, and in 1886 the Bombay Government established a protectorate over the large island of Socotra, 150 miles E.N.E. of Cape Guardafui. By this arrangement the native ruler engaged to protect shipwrecked vessels of whatever nationality, and to enter into no agreement with any nation but the English.

[1] *Bombay Administration Report for* 1889–90, p. 74.

[2] *Ibid.*, p. 71.

A British protectorate is also maintained from Aden over the Somáli coast, along the African seaboard of the Gulf of Aden. It is important for the prosperity and safety of Aden that this district should not be controlled by any foreign power; for its safety, because it enables England to effectually close the Gulf of Aden; for its prosperity, because it supplies Aden with live stock, and Somális are the labourers of the settlement. The Somáli Coast protectorate extends from Ras Jibuti to Bandar Ziyada, that is from 48° 15′ to 49° E. long., and is divided for political purposes into the two sub-residencies of Bulhar-Berbera and Zaila. It contains three ports, Bulhar, Berbera, and Zaila, and there is every prospect that under British protection a flourishing trade will spring up in connection with them. One function of the Resident at Aden is, under the orders of the Bombay Government, to maintain the Somáli coast line. That line is held, not as a base for expansion inland, but to increase the security of Aden. Towards the close of Lord Reay's administration, however, it became necessary to penetrate the interior. In August, 1889, the Mamasan Esa tribe treacherously attacked Bulhar and killed 67 of the inhabitants. A punitive expedition was therefore despatched in January, 1890, under the command of Captain Domvile, consisting of 60 cavalry, 30 sappers 170 native infantry, and 10 men of the Royal Navy, with two Gardner guns, which defeated the Esa tribe, who came in voluntarily and made their submission after the return of the force[1].

[1] *Bombay Administration Report for* 1889–90, pp. 29 and 70.

It seems a long stride from so recent an acquisition as Somáli-land to the relations of the oldest European power in Asia with the Government of Bombay. Yet it is with the Government of Bombay, which has grown out of an item in the dowry of a Portuguese princess, Catherine of Braganza, when she wedded the English king Charles II, that the successors of Vasco da Gama and Affonso de Albuquerque, Francisco de Almeida, and João de Castro have to deal. All the Portuguese possessions now remaining in India, Goa, Damán, and Diu, lie within the limits of the Bombay Presidency, and involve frequent communications between the Governor of Bombay and the Governor-General of Portuguese India.

The fact that the Portuguese settlements are imbedded in British territory rendered a clear understanding necessary, if they were not to become nests for smugglers and caves of Adullam for broken men of various sorts. During the five years under review, the Portuguese Treaty of 1878 remained in force; by which Portugal surrendered her right to manufacture salt and other rights, in return for certain allowances and a subsidy of Rs. 4,00,000 a year. I have mentioned that this subsidy was hypothecated for the construction of a railway from the Portuguese port of Marmagáo to join the Southern Maráthá Railway. That line will make Marmagáo the outlet for the cotton of Bellary, and greatly promote the prosperity of the Portuguese territory of Goa. It was completed during the period under review (1885–1890), and its opening was celebrated by an international ceremonial, at which the Governor-General of Portuguese India and Lord Reay were both present.

Great as may be the importance of this event on the prosperity of Portuguese India, it did not excite so much interest as the closing of the ancient schism in the Roman Catholic Church in India by the Concordat between the Pope and the King of Portugal, signed on June 23, 1886. In the days when Portugal was the Christian nation which kept the road to Asia round the Cape of Good Hope, Roman Catholic hierarchies were established in India, China, and Japan, and the King of Portugal, though not yet 'Fidelissimus,' received the right to nominate to those bishoprics. But the power of Portugal in the East dwindled as rapidly as it had grown. Four centuries rolled by, and when Roman Catholic missionaries built up new congregations of converts in districts within the limits of the tolerant sway of England, the new Roman Catholic Churches felt it unjust that they should be subject to bishops appointed by the Portuguese sovereign of an insignificant portion of India, or by his nominee, the Archbishop of Goa. The result of this feeling was a strife between the Vicars-Apostolic of the Pope, at the head of various missions in British or Feudatory India, and the bishops of the Portuguese Church in India. I have explained the character of this *Schisma Lusitanum* in my 'Indian Empire.' It suffices here to remark that the Pope naturally desired to preserve his direct supremacy over such of his flock in India as were not resident within Portuguese limits; that it was also natural for the Portuguese nation to resent any subtraction from the shadow of their former greatness in the East, even though the substance of it had long departed. The agreement arrived at was to the effect that from September 1, 1886, the Roman Catholic Church in India should be divided into the eight ecclesiastical provinces of Agra, Bombay, Calcutta, Colombo, Goa, Madras, Pondicherry, and Verapoli, each presided over by its own archbishop. Seven of these provinces were to be directly ruled by the Pope, but the eighth, the province of Goa, was left to the King of Portugal. The Archbishopric of Bombay holds in certain respects an intermediate position. The province of Goa was to consist of the dioceses of Goa, Damán, Cochin, and Mailapur, and to these sees the King of Portugal retains the right to nominate. The Archbishop of Goa keeps his title of Primate of the East and Patriarch of the East Indies, and has the right to preside at all the Plenary Councils of the Indies which are to be held at Goa.

Incidentally it may be noted that this arrangement will somewhat complicate matters with regard to the Roman Catholic Church in the Bombay Presidency. The province of Bombay consists of the archdiocese of Bombay and the diocese of Poona. The former of these sees extends over Bombay, Gujarát north of the Narbáda, Cutch, Rájputána, Sind, and Balúchistán; and the latter over the Southern Konkan, Khándesh, and the Deccan up to the limits of Haidarábád, Mysore, and North Kánara. But on the other hand, the Bishop of Damán, one of the suffragans of the

Archbishop of Goa, will have jurisdiction over Damán, Diu, Gujarát south of the Narbáda, the Northern Konkan, Bassein, and the islands of Salsette and Trombay. At the same time nine churches in the archdiocese of Bombay with their schools fall under the jurisdiction of the Bishop of Damán, and ten churches and institutions in the diocese of Damán under that of the Archbishop of Bombay. It is a compromise which, to be successful, must be worked in a conciliatory spirit.

INDEX.

Abkári: *see* Excise.

Aboriginal tribes, efforts for their education, 182, 183; their forest life, 196, 197; their wasteful cultivation in forests stopped, 217; right to collect forest produce, 218; drinking habits, 364.

Abyssinians in the Konkan, 30.

Accidents, considered in 'classing,' 241.

Achárya, Ráo Sáheb Rámchandra Trimbak, member Forest Commission, 203.

Adam, Sir F. F., President Bombay Chamber of Commerce, 73; Chairman Jubilee Technical Institute, 173; Bombay Extension Committee, 327; additional member Finance Committee, 350.

Aden, Port Trust formed, 315, 479; incidence of income-tax, 397; Volunteers raised, 461, 462; defence works, 463; history, 1885–1890, as a fortress, 478; as a settlement, 478–479; municipality, 479; as port, 479–480; trade, 479; dependencies, 480.

Administration of Bombay, affected by the land system, 10, 11; its excellence, 77

Adoption in Native States, 88.

Advances to cultivators, 269, 270.

Agriculture; question of agricultural education, 158, 159, 166–168; chair of, founded at Baroda, 168; services of the Survey to, 264; appointment of Director of, 265.

Ahmadábád, district in Gujarát, 27; subsoil-water assessment in, 253; tálukdári tenure, 256; incidence of income-tax, 397.

Ahmadábád city, the Gujarát College, 152, 153; medical school at, 155; Jubilee Celebration at, 271; railway communication with Bombay, 281; proposed tramway to Dholera, 295; the Ellis Bridge rebuilt, 297; water-works and drainage, 319, 320, 441; has a Small Cause Court, 409; excellence of its municipality, 438.

Ahmadnagar, district in the Deccan, 31; its first settlement, 236; very little drinking in, 367; local taxes, 439, 440.

Ahmadnagar city, High School transferred to local authorities, 140; Ripon Hospital at, 317, 339.

Ajrá, Jubilee Bridge at, 125.

Akalkot, Native State in the Deccan, 31.

Akbar, Emperor, incorporated Sind in Mughal Empire, 23.

Ale, beer, and porter, import duty on, 374.

Alexandra Native Girls' School, Bombay, 185.

Alienation Settlements, 265–268.

Allbless family, their charitable gifts to Bombay, 326, 338.

American Missionary Society opened school at Bombay (1814), 129.

Anand, railway to Godhrá from, continued to Ratlám, 282; railway to Petlád, 291.

Animal hospital at Surat, 15.

Anjuman-i-Islam, the, at Bombay, 179.

Appeals, course of, 406.

Apte, Mr., Principal of Fergusson College, Poona, 150.

Arbuthnot, Lt.-Gen. Sir C. G., Commander-in-Chief, Bombay, 60, 61, 449.

Army, the Bombay; history, 449–451; question of its abolition, 451–454; reorganisation of commands, 454, 455; departmental reforms, 455–457; British troops, 457; Native troops,

457-460; numbers, 460; cost, 461; the Volunteers, 461, 462.
Army Commission (1884), its recommendations, 451, 452
Art, schools of, at Bhúj, 153; the Jamsetjee Jejeebhoy at Bombay, 169, 170.
Asoka, eighth edict in Thána, 30; efforts to convert the Deccan, 31; the Karnátik, 45.
Assessed taxes, 396.
Assessment, method of, under Bombay Survey system, 242; subsoil water assessment, 251-254.
Auckland, Lord, settled education controversy (1839), 130.
Aundh, Native State in the Deccan, 31; left to the Collector of Sátára on breaking up of Sátára Jághírs, 119, 120.
Aurungzeb, his attempts to conquer the Deccan, 33-36.

Bahadurji, Dr., appointed professor at Grant College, 156.
Báhmaní dynasty in the Konkan, 30; the Deccan, 32.
Baillie, A F., quoted, on roads in Sind, 285, 286.
Baird, Sir D, expedition to Egypt (1801), Bombay troops in, 450
Bálásinor, Jubilee Municipal Hall, 125.
Balúchís, numerous in Sind, 25; the Balúch regiments, 458, 459.
Bándra, Convent School at, 185; no octroi levied at, 439.
Bánsdá, Native State in Gujarát, 27; Jubilee Dharmsálá, 125.
Bária, Native State in Rewá Kántha, refused to abolish transit duties, 123.
Baroda, Native State in Gujarát, 27; under Supreme, not Bombay Government, 80; railway extensions in, 289-291.
Baroda, Gáekwár of, character, 94; political attitude, 95, 96; founded chair at Grant College, Bombay, 156; and chair of Agriculture at Baroda, 168; his College at Baroda, 176; attitude on railway jurisdiction question, 290, 291; excise convention with Bombay Government, 373.
Barsi, tramway to, 295.
Bassein, Dispensary founded at, by Sir D. Petit, 337.
Belgáum, district in the Karnátik, 44; large advances to cultivators in, 269; freedom from crime, 411; proportion of police to population, 426; dog-tax in, 440; military command of, transferred to Madras (1885), 454.
Bengali, Sorabjee, member Bombay City Abkári Commission, 389.
Berbera, Port in Somáli Coast Protectorate, 481.
Bhágdári tenure, 259.
Bhandáris or toddy drawers strike of, in Bombay Island, 387; petition in 1735, 387, 388; settlement of their grievances, 388, 389.
Bháng, decoction of hemp, drunk in Sind, 371, 372; excise on, 392, 393
Bhaunagar, Native State in Káthiáwár, change in framework of government, 98; administrative history (1870-1890), 105-115; Jubilee Waterworks, 124; railway to Wadhwán, 291.
Bhaunagar, Mahárájá of, education, 107, 108; marriage, 108; popularity in his State, 115; endowed the Lady Reay Nurse Fund, 156.
Bhils aboriginal race, riots in Mewár and Pol, 120; supported dacoits in Mahi Kántha, 122; religious movement among, 124; efforts to educate, 183; a forest tribe, 197; advances to, in Khándesh, 269; heavy drinkers, 364.
Bhor, Native State in the Deccan, 31; placed under charge of Collector of Poona, 119; refused to abolish transit duties 123.
Bhor Ghát, trains allowed over at night in monsoon, 278.
Bhownaggree, M. M., founded Nurses' Home at Bombay, 156, 326, 338.
Bhúj, School of Art at, 123; Jubilee Waterworks, 124.
Bijápur, district in the Karnátik, 44; first survey settlement of, 236; freedom from crime, 411.
Bijápur city converted into head-quarters' station of a British district, 316; by a convict gang, 427.
Bisset, Major W. S., quoted on pressure on B. B. and C. I. Railway, 281, 282.
Blanford, W. T., quoted on geology of Gujarát and Sind, 18.
Bliss, H. W., member of the Finance Commission (1886), 349, 350.
Bombay, Baroda and Central India Railway, 281, 282.
Bombay Chamber of Commerce frequently consulted by Lord Reay,

73; elects deputies to the Port Trust 310; to the Municipality, 435.
Bombay City, a great port, 13; government transferred to (1687), 49; railway routes from 278–281; new terminus, 279; the docks, 308, 309; the Port Trust, 309-311; the dockyard, 311–312; new buildings, 316; the Tansa Waterworks scheme, 323-325; drainage, 325; hospitals, 325–327; the Extension Committee, 327, 328; excessive drinking in, 366; protests against the excise policy, 383, 384; the Bombay Abkári Commission, 389; heavy incidence of income tax, 396; its Small Cause Court, 409; the Bombay City Police, 424, 425; Municipality, 433-437; the Municipal Act of 1888, 434-436; its budget, 436, 437; Jubilee celebration, 437; Volunteers, 461; defensive works, 463.
Bombay City Abkári Commission, its appointment, 389; its recommendations on licenses, 377; on raw toddy, 389.
Bombay City Municipal Act (1888), 434-436.
Bombay City Extension Committee, 327, 328.
Bombay Education Society, 129, 130.
Bombay Island ceded to Charles II (1661), 31.
Bombay Presidency, its geology, 17, 18; geographical divisions, 19; mountains, 19; rivers, 19–21; *see* Excise, Land-system, &c.
Bombay Roman Catholic diocese, 484, 485.
Brab, strength of toddy from, 385.
Braddyl, John, member of Bombay Government (1735), 387.
Bráhmans, Maráthá, chief administrative caste in the Bombay Presidency, 12; their share in the Maráthá Confederacy, 39; founded the Fergusson College at Poona, 150; their keenness for education, 176.
Bráhmans, Nágar, their old monopoly of government in Bhaunagar, superseded, 98; their able rule in Bhaunagar, 107.
Brandis, Sir D., first Inspector-General of Forests in India, 192.
Brandy, importation of, 374, 375.
Brent, Capt. H. W., R.N., first Director of the Indian Marine, 464.
Bridges, maintenance of, 296, 297; Jubilee at Ajrá, 125; railway at Sukkur, 296; Ellis at Ahmadábád, 297.
Broach, district in Gujarát, 27; tálukdári tenure in, 256; bhágdári tenure in, 259; heavy incidence of excise taxation, 366; of income-tax per head, 397; of rural local taxation, 447.
Broach City, gymnasium founded at, by Mr Dalal, 339; has a Small Cause Court, 409; riot of Talávias at (1885), 413, 414; bad municipality, 438.
Buck, Sir E. C., sanctioned agricultural chemist and Pasteur Laboratory, 159.
Buddhist remains in the Konkan, 30; in the Deccan, 32; at Upárkot in Junágarh, 117.
Bulhar, port in the Somáli Coast Protectorate, attacked by the Esa tribe, 481.
Burma, expedition to (1885), Bombay troops in, 451; their despatch from Bombay, 465.

Caldwell, Bishop, quoted on Maráthá language, 43.
Cama Hospital for Women and Children at Bombay, 325, 326.
Cama, Pestonji Hormusji, benefactions to Bombay City, 338.
Campbell, Sir George, quoted on Madras land system, 245; on Bombay system, 260.
Campbell, James, his Bombay Gazetteers, 15.
Campbell, Lt.-Col. John, his defence of Mangalore (1783), 450.
Cantonment Magistrates, 409.
Capital sentences have to be confirmed by the High Court, 404; number of (1885-1890), 411.
Carter, Dr. Vandyke, founded Reay Lectureship at Grant College, 156.
Castle Rock, ceremony of opening Portuguese Railway at, 280.
Cattle-breeding encouraged in the Panch Maháls, 211.
Central Provinces, question of uniting with Bombay, 477.
Chalukya dynasty in the Deccan, 32.
Chiplunkar, S. H., represented complainants before the Forest Commission, 209.
Church Missionary Society established schools in the Konkan, Deccan, and Sind, 129.
Clarence, Duke of, his lion hunt in Junágarh, 118.

Classing in Bombay Survey System, 240-242.
Clock-tower, Jubilee, at Sádra, 124.
Colleges in the Bombay Presidency, 145.
Commandership-in-Chief in Bombay, question of abolishing, 451-454.
Commanders-in-Chief in Bombay; *see* Arbuthnot, Connaught, Hardinge.
Commercial activity in the Bombay Presidency, 14; evidenced by the revenue from stamps, 398.
Companies, Joint Stock, increase in number of, 400.
Competition, evils of, in excise administration, 312.
Concordat of 1886, ending the Portuguese schism, 482-484.
Connaught, Duke of, Commander-in-Chief in Bombay, 61, 449; favoured an Indian Sandhurst for Indian nobles, 92, 93, 184; quoted on Military Works Department, 334, 335; formed a Rifle Corps, 459; present at defence rehearsals, 463.
Contracts, Provincial, History of, 341; the first, 342; the second, 342-344; the third, 344; the fourth, 348-356.
Cooke, Dr. T., Principal of the Poona College of Science, 158; advocated a degree and course in agriculture, 159; efforts for practical agricultural education, 167; member of the Forest Reorganisation Committee, 220.
Council, the Bombay, 50; its share in the Government, 70-73.
Crawford, A. T., trial of, by a Special Commission, 414, 415.
Crawford Commission, question of indemnity arising from, 415-417; debate on the Indemnity Act, 417-419.
Crime, statistics and distribution of, 411, 412.
Cross, Lord, Secretary of State for India, dismisses Mr. A. T. Crawford, 415; speech in the House of Lords on Lord Reay's policy, 419, 420.
Crosthwaite, R. J., member of the Crawford Commission, 415.
Cultivated area, increase in, 264, 273.
Cunningham, Sir H. S., member of the Finance Committee (1886), 349, 350.
Customs, Internal, between Native States, endeavours to abolish, 85; maintained by Ráo of Cutch, 101.
Customs, sea-borne, on potable liquors, 373-375; affected by the Tariff Act, 375; revenue from, 395, 396.
Custom-houses, new, 316.
Cutch, Native State in Gujarát, 27; Political Agent only gives advice, 82; question of a railway through, 284.
Cutch, Ráo of, character of, 104; fosters the School of Art, 123; gives money for the relief of his subjects in Bombay, 124.
Cutch, Rann of, no difficulty in making railway over, 284; the salt-works on, 394.

Dábhol, new pier at, 315; custom-house, 316.
Dacoity put down in Junágarh, 118; prevalence and suppression in Káthiáwár, 120-122; among the Kolis in Poona District, 219.
Dakshina, grant by the Peshwás for education, 129, 146.
Dalal, Dinshaw Pestonji, founded gymnasium at Broach, 339.
Damán, Catholic diocese of, 484, 485.
Dángs, The, Native States in the Deccan, 31; thinly populated, 81.
Daphlápur, Native State, political charge removed to the Collector of Bijápur, 119.
Datubhai, Ibrahim, founded a hospital at Mándvi, 124.
Davison, Captain, signed Joint Report of 1847, 236.
Deccan, area and population, 31; history, 31-38; problems of administration, 41.
Deccan Agriculturists' Relief Act (1879), 244, 273.
Deccan College, name given to Poona College (1864), 149; would not merge with Fergusson College, 151, 152; its Law Class, 157.
Deccan Education Society founded Fergusson College, 150.
Decentralisation, Provincial, favoured by Lord Reay, 69; progress of financial, 340.
Deers Leap, waterfall on the Tápti, 20.
Defence Works at Bombay, Karáchi, and Aden, 462, 463.
Departments of the Bombay Government, 50, 70.
Dharampur, Native State in Gujarát, 27; Jubilee Dispensary at, 125.
Dharmsála, Jubilee, founded at Bánsdá, 125.
Dhárwár, district in the Karnátik, 44; survey settlement of, 236; freedom

from crime, 411; local taxes, 439; its rural taxation, 447.
Dhárwár, town, Rájá of Kolhápur educated at, 90; Lingáyat Association, 181; railway centre, so paid much income-tax, 397.
Dholera, proposed tramway to Ahmadábád, 225; new wharf, 315.
Dhoráji, railway centre in Káthiáwár, 291.
Dhrángadrá, Native State in Káthiáwár, reduced transit duties, 123.
Dhúliá, sanitary works at, 320.
Dispensaries: Jubilee, at Dharampur, 125; founded by Mr. Powalla at Bombay, 327, 338; at Bassein and Murbád by Sir D. M. Petit, 337; at Wáda by Mr. N. M. Petit, 339.
Distillation, Illicit, difficulty of checking, 372, 377, 380; on its increase from toddy, 391.
Distilleries, Central and Public, different systems, 380.
Diu, Portuguese port, dispute with Junágarh settled, 118.
Dnyánoba, Maráthá poet, 43.
Docks, the Bombay, 308-311.
Dockyard at Bombay, question of removal to Hog Island, 312.
Dogs, local taxes on, 440.
Domvile, Capt., R.N., his expedition against the Esas, 481.
'Downward filtration' theory of education, 131, 134.
Draper, William, member of Bombay Government (1735), 387.
Drawing, increase of classes in, 170, 171.
Drinking intoxicants, increase of, in India and Bombay, 370, 392.
Drugs, narcotic, excise on, 392, 393.
Dufferin, Lord, opposes needless interference with Provincial Governments, 69; laid foundation stone of Sind College at Karáchi, 153; efforts to fortify Indian ports, 462.
Dufferin Fund, Lady, for trained nurses, supported by Bombay Native Princes, 124.

East, Mr., designed water-supply for Bhaunagar, 110.
Eau-de-Cologne, importation for drinking purposes stopped, 375.
Edar, Native State, jail outbreak in, 122.
Education; of Native Princes, 89-94, 183, 184; encouraged in Baroda, 95; Gondal, 100; Bhaunagar, 114; Native States generally, 123; its history in Bombay, 128-134; primary, 134-138; secondary, 138-143; bifurcation of studies, 143-145; higher education:—general, 145-153; the colleges, 145; Deccan College, 147-150; Fergusson, 151; Gujarát, 152; Sind, 153; professional, 154-159; Grant Medical College, 154-156; Law School, 156, 157; Poona College of Science, 157-159; Bombay University, 159-161; aided for directly managed schools, 161-163; payment by results abandoned, 163, 164; technical education, 164-176; in agriculture, 166-168; Veterinary College, Bombay, 168, 169; Bombay School of Art, 169, 170; the teaching of drawing, 170, 171; Victoria Jubilee Technical Institute, 171-173; technical education at Poona, 173, 174; in Sind, 175, 176; education in the Deccan and Gujarát, 176, 177; in Sind, 177; education of Muhammadans, 177-180; Lingáyats, 180, 181; depressed castes, 181, 182; aboriginal races, 182, 183; female education, 184, 185; general effect of, 186, 187; summary of advance in (1885-1890), 188.
Education, Bombay Board of (1840-55), 130, 131,
Education Commission, Indian (1882), 133, 134; recommendations on primary education, 137; quoted, on Bombay secondary education, 139, 140, 141; on aided education, 161, 162; condemned payment by results, 163; quoted, on education of Muhammadans, 178; of low castes, 182.
Education Despatch of East India Directors (1854), 131, 132.
Educational Franchise, established at Poona, 433.
Egypt, Baird's expedition to (1801), Bombay troops in, 450.
Eibat Island, dependency of Aden, 480.
Election of representatives, question of, 432; proportion of elected members in district municipalities, 443, 444; Local Boards, 445, 446.
Elliott, Sir C. A., approved changes in Public Works Department, 331; Chairman Finance Committee (1886), 349, 350.
Elphinstone, Mountstuart, services to education in Bombay, 129: views on

Hindu education, 146, 147; founds Poona Sanskrit College, 147; Minute on Education, 148; quoted on forests of the Konkan, 197; attempts at a land settlement, 231, 232.
Elphinstone College, founded at Bombay (1827), 130; moved to a suitable site, 152, 317; Professor of Persian appointed at, 179.
Engineering education, provision for, 157, 158.
Erskine, C., first Director of Public Instruction, his policy, 132, 135.
Erskine, H. N. B., Commissioner in Sind, advocated railway to Umarkot; 286; wharf at Karáchi called after, 314; author of irrigational settlements, 472.
Esa tribe, expedition against (1890), 481.
Excise or Abkári administration, attacks on, 363, 364; its aims, 372; purchased in Native States, 372, 373; revenue produced by, 378; monopoly system, 378, 379; central and public distillery systems, 380; duty on minimum or guaranteed consumption, 381; out-still system, 382, 383; raw toddy question, 384, 391; general results, 392; excise on drugs, 393.
Exhibition, Industrial, at Poona, 174.

Fagel, Baron, maternal grandfather of Lord Reay, 57.
Fazandárs, opposition of, to taxation of toddy, 316.
Fergusson, Sir James, Governor of Bombay, encouraged railways in Káthiáwár, 292; quoted on appointment of Inspector-General of Police, 426.
Fergusson College, Poona, founded without consulting Supreme Government, 68; its history and growth, 150, 151; refused to merge with Deccan College, 151, 152.
Fernandez, T. R., surveyed Bhaunagar State (1872–79), 113.
Ferries, 297.
Ferry across the Indus at Kotri, 284, 297.
Field, definition of a, under Survey Settlement, 238-240.
Fife, Lt.-Gen. J. G., designed Níra Canal, 305.
Filgate, Lt.-Col. A. J., member Finance Committee (1886), 349, 350.
Finance Committee (1886), 349–351.
Financial Conference at Calcutta (1888), 357, 358.
Financial relations of Supreme and Provincial Governments; *see* Contracts, Provincial.
Fire, Protection from, in Bombay City, 436; in District Municipalities, 443.
Fire at Surat, 398, 443.
Forest Act Amendment Law (1890), 214.
Forest Commission (1885), 202–209.
Forest Establishment Reorganisation Committee (1889), 220-222.
Forestry, class in, at Poona College of Science, 158, 159, 221.
Forests, their extent in India, 189, 190; influence on climate, 191; scientific forestry in India, 191, 192; early conservancy in Bombay, 192, 193; the Forest Department, 193; locality of Bombay forests, 194; Forest Settlements, 195, 196; aboriginal tribes, 196, 197; forest villages, 197, 198; forests in Thána and Kolába, 198, 199; rapid destruction, 199; agitation in Thána, 199–202; appointment of Forest Commission, 202-204; Lord Reay's speech, 204–208; report, 208–209; grazing in forests, 209-212; woodcutting, 212–214; *ráb* cultivation, 214, 216; *dalhi* cultivation, 217; care of wild tribes, 218, 219; importance of demarcation, 219, 220; working plans, 220; Forest Establishment Reorganisation Committee, 220-222; Forest Officers made subordinate to Collectors, 221, 222; revenue from forests, 223.
Fraser, Mr., appointed tutor to Rájá of Kolhápur, 90.
Fremantle, Rear-Adm., Hon. E. R., consulted on removal of Bombay dockyard, 312.
Frere, Sir Bartle, perceived the merit of Sir M. Melvill, 65; laid foundation stone of Deccan College (1864), 149; employed in the settlement of Indápur, 233–235; efforts to improve Karáchi harbour, 313; recurrence to his Public Works Departmental arrangement, 331; his government of Sind, 468, 472.

Gáekwár, the; *see* Baroda.
Gánja (hemp), excise on, 392.
Gaurishankar Udeshankar, Diwán of Bhaunagar, 105, 106.

Geology of the Bombay Presidency, 17, 18.
Gháts, Western, 19-21; forests of, 194.
Gibson, Dr., first Conservator of Bombay forests, 192; quoted on the agitation in Thána (1851), 199, 200.
Gidhu Bandar to the Eastern Nara, railway proposed from, 284-288.
Goa, Roman Catholic Archbishop of, position under Concordat (1886), 484.
Goculdass Tejpal Hospital at Bombay, 325.
Godhrá-Ratlám railway, 284, 287.
Goldsmid, H. E., settled Indápur táluká, 233-235; signed Joint Report (1847), 236.
Gondal, Native State in Káthiáwár, excellent administration, 100, 101; dacoity, 121; jail outbreak, 122; railways through, 291, 292.
Gondal, Thákur of, character, 99, 100.
Goudsmit, Prof., Lord Reay's tutor at Leiden, 57.
Government of Bombay, form of, 50-53; Lord Reay's attitude towards, 74-77.
Government of India, its relations with the Provincial Governments, 67, 68; did not approve of an Indian Sandhurst, 92; passed Forest Act Amendment Law (1890) at request of Bombay Government, 214; controls railways and irrigation, 275, 276, 298; difference as to proposed railway in Sind, 287-289; granted money for Karáchi harbour works, 314; financial relations with the provinces, 341-345; with Bombay, 345-354, 357-360; passed Act of Indemnity for witnesses at Crawford Commission, 417-419; difference of opinion, 419; recommended severance of Sind, 467.
Grant, Sir Alex., Director of Public Instruction, introduced grants in aid to schools, 161, 163; friendship with pupils, 187.
Grant, G. F. M., quoted on dislike of municipalities to direct taxation, 438.
Grant, J. H., member Bombay City Abkári Commission, 389.
Grant, Sir Robert, Governor of Bombay (1835-38), interest in medical education, 154.
Grant Medical College, Bombay, history, 154, 155; the Petit Laboratory, 155; new professorship added, 156.
Gray, Brig.-Surgeon W., quoted on Grant College, 155.
Grazing in forests, question of, 209-212.
Great India Peninsula Railway, 277-279.
Greaves, Lt.-Gen. Sir G. R., opposed idea of Indian Sandhurst, 184.
Greeks, the, their dealings with the Konkan, 30.
Griffiths, Mr., Principal School of Art, Bombay, 169.
Gujarát, Province of, boundaries and population, 27; history, 28, 29; problems of government, 29; Lord Reay's visits to, 176, 441; difficulty of making roads, 291.
Gujarát College, Ahmadábád, transferred to a Local Board, 152, 153.

Haidarábád, District in Sind, 23; bad roads, 285, 286; excessive criminality, 412.
Haidarábád City, 26; medical school at, 155; railway designed from, 284.
Harbours in the Bombay Presidency, 13; improvements in Karáchi harbour, 313, 314; smaller harbours, 315.
Hardie, Robert, member Finance Committee (1886), 349.
Hardinge, Lt.-Gen. Hon. Sir Arthur, Commander-in-Chief in Bombay, 60, 449; used selection not seniority in filling commands, 75.
Haug, Martin, head of Sanskrit Department, Poona College, 148, 149.
Hemp (gánja), excise on, 392.
Hext, Capt. John, Director of the Indian Marine, consulted on removal of Bombay Dockyard, 312; at head of the Indian Marine (1885-90), 464.
Hog Island, question of removing the Dockyard to, 311, 312.
Hope, Sir T. C., recommendations on Karáchi harbour, 313, 314.
Horne, John, Governor of Bombay (1735) on Bhandári's petition, 387.
Horse-breeding encouraged in Bhaunagar, 109, 110.
Hospitals: in Gondal State, 100; in Native States, 124; services to medical education in Bombay, 154, 155; new in Bombay, 325-327.

Howard, Mr., Director of Public Instruction, 161.
Humfrey, Major, reorganised Junágarh police, 118; put down dacoity in Káthiáwár, 121.
Hurford, Miss, Principal of the Poona High School for Girls and Female Training College, 185.
Hutchins, Sir P. P., speech on Mámlatdárs Indemnity Act, quoted, 417, 418.

Immigration into sparsely populated districts, 273.
Improvements, tenant's right to profit by his, 243, 247, 248.
Inám Commission, 266.
Income-tax re-imposed (1886), 396; proceeds and incidence, 397, 398.
Indápur táluká, result of first survey settlement of, 234-236.
Indian Feeder Lines Company, 294.
Indian Midland Railway, 278.
Indus River, 19, 20; bridge over, at Sukkur, 296; ferry over, Gidhu Bandar to Kotri, 284, 297; importance as irrigating Sind, 300.
Industrial Association of Western India, 174.
Industrial Museum, the Reay, at Poona, 174.
Institutes, Jubilee, at Palánpur and Radhánpur, 124; regimental, 457.
Irish Presbyterian Missionary Society, established schools in Káthiáwár, 129.
Irrigation, a duty of the Indian Government, 297, 298; under Supreme Government, 298, 299; amount spent on, 299; in Sind, 300-304; in the Deccan, 304, 305; Lord Reay's remarks on irrigation works in the Deccan, 305-307.
Irrigation Settlements in Sind, 255, 256.

Jacob, H. P., quoted on technical schools in Sind, 175, 176; services to education in Sind, 177, 472; to Muhammadan education, 180; recommends monitor system, 187.
Jágri, spirit from, drunk in the Karnátik, 371.
Jails in the Bombay Presidency, 427.
Jail outbreaks at Bhaunagar, 111; at Edar and Gondal, 122.
Jains, numerous in the Karnátik, never drink intoxicants, 365.
Jaipur, Mahárájá of, Lord Reay's opinion of, 97, 98.
Jamábandi of a village, 268.
Jamkhandi, Native State in the Karnátik, 44.
Jamsetjee Jejeebhoy, Sir, gave lakh of rupees for the Deccan College (1863), 149; founded hospital at Bombay (1843), 154.
Jamsetjee Jejeebhoy Hospital at Bombay, works in harmony with Grant Medical School, 154; extended by foundation of Petit and Motlibai Hospitals, 155, 325.
Jamsetjee Jejeebhoy Mechanical Engineering School, part of the Victoria Jubilee Technical Institute, 172.
Jamsetjee Jejeebhoy School of Art at Bombay, 169, 170.
Janjira, Native State in the Konkan, 30.
Jasdán, Chief of, character and administration, 102, 103.
Jath, Native State in the Deccan, 31; political charge removed to Collector of Bijápur, 119.
Jawhár, Native State in the Konkan, 30.
Jodhpur, proposed railway through, 284; salt works purchased, 394.
Jodhpur, Mahárájá of, Lord Reay's opinion of, 97.
'Joint Report (1847),' defined Bombay Survey Settlement, 236.
Jubilee, the Queen's (1887), memorials of, in Native States, 124, 125; the Victoria Jubilee Technical Institute at Bombay, 171-173; fund raised by Lingáyats to commemorate, 181; celebration by Tálukdárs at Ahmadábád, 271; general rejoicings at Bombay, 437.
Judges, Local, powers in civil matters, 405, 406; criminal matters, 406, 407; number of, in Bombay proper, 409; in Sind, 410; proportion of natives, 410.
Judicature, Bombay, High Court of, constitution, 402, 403; powers, 403, 404.
Judicial Department, 70, 71.
Judicial system in Gondal State, 100; in Bhaunagar, 114.
Junágarh, Native State in Káthiáwár, description, 117, 118; suppression of dacoity, 118; settlement with the Portuguese, 118; railways in, 119, 291; transit duties abolished, 123.
Justice, Administration of, in Bombay

Presidency; the High Court, 403-405; civil courts, 405, 406; appeals, 406; criminal courts, 406, 407; magistrates, 407, 408; Small Cause Courts, 408, 409; expense of, 412, 413.

Kadarbux, Káthiáwár dacoit, executed (1886), 122.
Kádirdád Khán, Khán Bahádur, his technical schools, 175, 176; services to education in Sind, 177.
Kaira, District in Gujarát, 27; narvádári tenure in, 259; small amount of drinking in, 367; proportion of police to population, 426; pilgrim tax levied, 439.
Kamal, Maráthá land settlement, 229, 230.
Kánara, North, District, 44; need of labour in, 273, 274; average consumption of intoxicants in, 366; free from serious crime, 411; local taxes on carts, 439; dogs, 440
Kánarese-speaking districts; *see* Karnátik.
Karáchi, District in Sind, 23; excessive criminality in, 412; proportion of police to population, 426.
Karáchi City, great port of the future, 13; growth and trade, 25, 26, 474, 475; the Sind College at, 153; Madrasa, 180; need of railway facilities, 282, 283; history of port and harbour, 313, 314; Port Trust, 314; incidence of income-tax, 397; has Small Cause Court, 409; the Empress Market, 442; volunteer corps, 461; defence works, 463; protests against severance from Bombay, 476.
Karnátik, the Bombay, 44; its population, 44; history, 44, 45; not given to drinking intoxicants, 365; chiefly jágri, 371; freedom from crime, 411.
Kárwár, important port, 13
Káthiáwár, Peninsula in Gujarát, 27; the number of Native Chiefs, 96; their diversity, 98; Bhaunagar, 98, 99, 105-115; Gondal, 99-102; Jasdán, 102, 103; Lakhtar, 103; not all good, 104; Junágarh, 117-119; Agency Police formed, 120; which suppressed dacoity, 121; railways in, 291, 292.
Kátkaris, forest aboriginal tribe, 197; heavy drinkers, 364.
Kelkar, Ráo Bahádur Yeshvant Moreshwar, Secretary to Forest Commission (1885), 204.
Khairpur, Native State in Sind, 23; sparsely populated, 81; administration of, 115-117.
Khándesh, District in the Deccan, 31; immigration into, 273; introduction of central distillery system, 382; incidence of income-tax in, 397; amount of rural local taxation, 447.
Khárághoda salt-works, 394.
Khoti tenure in the Konkan, 258.
Kolába, District in the Konkan, 30; amount of forest in, 197, 198; shared Thána's complaints against Forest laws, 198; represented before Forest Commission (1885), 209; *ráb* cultivation, 214, 215; spare land in, 273; large amount of drinking, 366; temperance movement in, 383; increase of drinking, on lowering tax on toddy, 390, 391; sea-salt works in, 394; local taxes on fishing boats, 439; amount of rural taxation, 447.
Kolába Cantonment, question of removing native garrison of Bombay to, 327, 328.
Kolába Forest Sabha represented complainants before Forest Commission (1885), 209.
Kolhápur, Native State in the Karnátik, 44; thickly populated, 81; recent dynastic history, 89; abolition of import and export duties, 122; construction of railways in, 292, 293.
Kolhápur City, foundation of Technical School, 123.
Kolhápur, Rájá of, education of, 89, 90.
Kolis, forest aboriginal tribe, 197; enquiry into their condition, 219; excessive drunkenness, 364.
Konkan, its population, 30; history, 30, 31; forests, 194, 198, 199; khoti tenure in, 258; climate causes inhabitants to drink, 364, 365.
Kooriah Mooriah Islands, dependency of Aden, 481.
Korygáum, Battle of (1818), 450.
Kurla, municipality levies no octroi, 439.
Kurundwád, Native State in the Karnátik, 44.
Kwájas, Muhammadan commercial class, numerous in Sind, 25.

Laboratories: the Petit in connection with Grant College, Bombay, 155, 328; Pasteur at Poona College of Science, 159, 337; Bacteriological at Veterinary College, Bombay, 168,

337; Physical at the Jubilee Technical Institute, 173.
'Ladder theory' in education, 137, 140.
Lakha Bhagat, leader in Talávia riot at Broach (1885); hanged, 414.
Lakhtar, Thákur of, character, 103.
Lallubhai, Dwarkadas, founded dispensary at Bombay, 338.
Lambton, John, present at resolution on Bhandáris (1735), 387.
Land administration, interest of, in Bombay, 9, 10; British system introduced into Bhaunagar, 113; its basis in India, 224-226; different in each province, 227, 228; early land settlements in Bombay, 229; the Maráthá, 229, 230; Elphinstone's views, 231, 232; Pringle's settlement, 232, 233; Williamson's settlement, 233, 234; settlement of Indápur, 234-236; the Joint Report (1847), 236; the survey system, 237, 238; definition of a field or number, 238, 240; classing, 240; accidents, 240, 241; irrigation value, 241; assessment, 242; the survey tenure, 243, 244; its advantages, 245, 246; revision of settlements, 246, 247; tenant's right to improvements, 247, 248; position class, 249, 250; subdivision of 'numbers,' 250, 251; subsoil water assessment, 251-254; work of Survey and Settlement Department, 254, 255: irrigation settlements in Sind, 255, 256; unpopularity of revised settlements, 261; alienation settlements, 265 268.
Land Records and Agriculture, Department of, 263, 264.
Land Revenue, collection of, in Bombay, 268, 269; its amount and division between Supreme and Bombay Governments, 345, 346, 353; cost of collecting, 354, 355.
Language, the Sindí, 24, 471; the Maráthí, 42, 43.
Lansdowne, Lord, Viceroy of India, opposed unnecessary interference with Provincial Governments, 69; speech on Mámlatdárs Indemnity Bill, 418, 429.
Latham, Baldwin, revised the drainage scheme at Ahmadábád, 320; consulted on drainage of Bombay, 325.
Law School at Bombay, 156, 157.
Le Breton, Maj, Examiner Public Works Accounts, his reforms, 332.
Lee-Warner, W., quoted on the workshops, Poona College of Science, 174; on Bombay education (1885-90), 188; additional member of Finance Committee (1886), 350.
Legislative Council, the Bombay, 50; debate on the land system in, 261, 262; on Bombay City Municipal Act, 434, 435.
Licenses, separation of foreign and country liquor, in Bombay, 376, 377.
Lighthouses under Bombay Public Works Department, 315.
Lingáyats, zeal for education, 180; their Jubilee fund, 181; petition on Bráhman monopoly of office, 181; total abstainers, 365.
Lions still found in Junágarh, 117.
Literature, Sindí, 25; Maráthí, 43, 44.
Local Boards in rural districts, 444-448; introduction of election, 445, 446; their number, 446; income, 446; expenditure, 447.
Local Government, approved by Lord Reay, 78, 79; expediency of, in India, 429-432; elected *versus* nominated members, 432; municipalities, 432-444; local boards, 444-448.
London Missionary Society founded schools in Gujarát, 129.
Luckhardt, Col. W., Commissary-General in Bombay, reorganised his departments, 456.
Lunatic Asylum built at Ratnágiri, 317.
Luseria, School for Bhils established at, 183.
Lyon, Surgeon-Maj., Analysis of and report on toddy, 384, 385.

McAfee, Mrs., Principal Ahmadábád High School for Girls, 185.
Macaulay, Lord, won victory for Anglicists against Orientalists in Indian education, 130.
Mackay, Donald James, Lord Reay; *see* Reay.
Mackay family, history of, 54-57.
Mackenzie, T. D., quoted, on village sanitation, 321.
Mackichan, Dr., appointed Vice-Chancellor, Bombay University, 160, 161.
Macnaghten, Principal of Rájkot College of Native Princes, 107.
Magistrates, powers of, 407, 408; numbers, 409, 410; honorary, 410.
Mahi Kántha, group of Native States in Gujarát, 27; Bhil riots in, 120;

Agency Police formed, 120; transit duties abolished, 123.
Mahi river, 20.
Mahim, new custom-house built at, 316.
Mahuá spirit, 371.
Maiwand, Battle of, 451.
Málik Ambar, land settlement of, 229.
Mámlatdárs, revenue duties of, 268; the Mámlatdárs Indemnity Bill, 416-420.
Mándvi, hospital founded at, 124.
Mangalore, Bombay troops in the defence of (1783), 450.
Maráthá country divided into Konkan and Deccan, 30.
Maráthás, a conquering race, 11; India conquered by the British from, 12, 37, 38; conquest of Gujarát, 28; struggle with Aurungzeb, 35, 36; extension of their power, 36, 37; system of organised pillage, 37; character of the Maráthá Confederacy, 39, 40; collapse of their financial system, 42, 230; character of the people, 42; language, 42, 43; literature, 43, 44; land settlement, 229, 230; join the army less, 458.
Marine, Indian, headquarters at Bombay, 463; organised (1877), 464; size, 464, 465; services in transporting troops, 465.
Marmagáo, port in Portuguese territory, 13; railway completed from, 280, 482; harbour improvements needed, 315.
Massah Islands, dependency of Aden, 480.
Matrimonial cases, jurisdiction in, 403, 404.
Maurypur-Moach, salt-works at, for Sind, 394.
Mayo, Lord, Viceroy of India, his decentralisation policy, 67, 68; views on education of Native Princes, 91; decentralised finance, 340; considered separation of Sind from Bombay, 468.
Mayúr Pandit, Maráthá poet, 43, 44.
Medical education in Bombay, 154-156.
Mehmadábád, municipality superseded, 438.
Mekránis, their dacoities in Káthiáwár, 121, 122.
Melvill, Sir Maxwell, his career, 64, 65; character, 65-67.
Merewether, Col. Sir W. L., his administration of Sind, 472.
Merewether Pier, Karáchi, 313, 314.
Military Commissions for younger sons of Native Princes, 92, 93, 184.
Military officers, question of appointing to civil posts, 75, 76.
Military Works Department formed, 334, 462.
Mill, John Stuart, drafted Educational Despatch (1854), 131.
'Minimum theory' of relation of Imperial and Provincial finance, 359.
Miráj, Native State in the Karnátik, 44.
Missionaries, services to education in Bombay, 128, 129; their Colleges in Bombay, 145.
Mitra, Rájendra Lála, quoted, on use of intoxicants in ancient India, 368, 369.
Monsoon, course of the, in the Bombay Presidency, 17.
Morland, Sir H., Chairman of Bombay Town Council, knighted on occasion of the Jubilee, 437.
Morvi, Native State in Káthiáwár, 102; railways in, 292.
Morvi, Chief of, character, 101, 102; a railway builder, 292.
Motlibai, Bai, founded hospital in Bombay, 155, 325, 337.
Movar Sadháni, dacoit leader in Káthiáwár, 121, 122.
Mudhol, Native State in the Karnátik, 44; abolished transit duties, 123.
Mughal Empire incorporated Sind, 23; conquered Gujarát, 28; endeavoured to subdue the Deccan, 33-36.
Muhammadans, the majority in Sind, 23; their educational backwardness, 178, 179; efforts to improve, 178, 179; their land settlement in the Deccan, 229; do not drink liquor, 371, 392.
Municipal Hall, Jubilee, at Bálásinor, 125.
Municipalities; in Gondal State, 101; Poona, 432, 433, 442; Bombay, 433-437; the Bombay City Municipal Act, 434-436; the district municipalities, 437-444; number, 438; local taxation: octroi, 438, 439; direct, 439, 440; expenditure: on public health, 441, 442; convenience, 442; instruction, 442, 443; safety, 443; proportion of elected members, 443, 444; Ahmadábád, 441, 442; Surat, 442; Aden, 479.
Munro, Sir Thomas, settled the Karnátik, 45.

Murbád, dispensary founded at, by Sir D. M. Petit, 337.
Mutiny of 1857, Bombay army only slightly affected, 450, 458.
Mysore Railways, worked by Southern Maráthá Company, 279.

Nadiád, Agricultural Society's experimental farm, 168; has Small Cause Court, 409.
Nágpur, District command transferred to Bombay army (1888), 454.
Nágpur-Bengal Railway, 278, 279.
Nám Deva, Maráthá poet, 43.
Napier, Gen. Sir C. J., conquered Sind, 23; first Governor of Sind, 467, 468.
Nára Canal, Eastern, railway proposed to, 284, 287.
Narbadá river, 20.
Narottamdas, Harkisondas, munificent offer of a Hospital, 338.
Nárukot, Native State, its small population, 81.
Narvádári tenure, 259, 260.
Nash, Lieut., helped to settle Indápur táluká, 235.
Násik, District in the Deccan, 31; first survey settlement, 236; local dog-tax, 440; incidence of rural local taxation, 447.
Násik town, tramway to Násik Road Station, 295.
Native Chiefs in Bombay, their varying character, 83; instances of bad chiefs, 86-88; right of adoption, 88; education of minors and younger sons, 89-93; characters of rulers of Baroda, 94-96; Bhaunagar, 98, 99; Gondal, 99-101; Morvi, 101, 102; Jasdán, 102, 103; Lakhtar, 103; Cutch, 104; Khairpur, 115-117; advantages of the maintenance of a Native Chief, 115.
Native States, numerous in Bombay, 12, 13; area and population, 80; variety, 81, 82; duties of British Political Agents, 82, 83; policy pursued towards, 84, 85; question of railway jurisdiction, 85, 86; interference occasionally justified, 86 88; Baroda, 94-96; Káthiáwár, 96-115; Gondal, 100, 101; Bhaunagar, 105-115; Khairpur. 115-117; Junágarh, 117-119; break up of the Sátára Jághírs, 119; Bhil riots, 120; dacoity, 120-122; abolition of transit duties, 122, 123; education, public works and hospitals, 123, 124; celebration and memorials of the Jubilee, 124, 125; railways in, 289 293; right of excise purchased by the British Government, 372, 373; of opium growing, 393; of salt making, 394.
Nawánagar, Native State in Káthiáwár, Dacoity in, 121; transit duties abolished, 123.
Naylor, J. R., Acting Member of the Bombay Council, 64; drafted the Bombay City Municipal Act, 434.
Níra Canal in the Deccan, 305.
Nizam, Excise Convention with, 373.
North-Western State Railway, 282, 283.
Nulkar, Ráo Bahádur Krishnáji Lakshman, member of Forest Commission (1885), 204.
'Number' or field, definition of, 238-240.
Nurse Fund, Lady Dufferin's, supported by Native Princes, 124.
Nurse Fund, Lady Reay's, endowed by Mahárájá of Bhaunagar, 156.
Nurses, Home for, founded by M. M. Bhownaggree, 156, 328, 338.
Nutt, Capt. H. L., tutor to Mahárájá of of Bhaunagar, 108.

Octroi duties, levied by municipalities, 438, 439.
Ollivant, J. E., Municipal Commissioner, helped to draw up Bombay City Municipal Act, 434.
Opium revenue in Bombay, 393.
Osborn, Capt. Sherard, recommended removal of Bombay Dockyard, 312
Out-still system, abolished in Bombay, 382, 383.
Ozanne, E. C., Director of Land Records and Agriculture, member of the Forest Commission (1885), 203; his experiments on *ráb*, 215; services to agriculture, 265.

Pálanpur, Native State in Gujarát, 27; Agency Police formed, 120; transit duties abolished, 123; Jubilee Institute built, 124.
Panch Mahâls, District in Gujarát, 27; encouragement of cattle breeding 211; advances made for rebuilding houses, 270; immigration into, 273; central distillery system introduced, 382; light amount of income-tax, 397; made a Regulation District (1885), 402; proportion of police, 426; small receipts of local rural taxation, 447.

Parántij, Municipality superseded 438.
Parsi school for girls at Bombay, 185; gift by Panchayat Fund for a mortuary, 338.
Pasteur Laboratory founded at Poona College of Science, 159; on site given by Sir D M. Petit, 337.
Pechey-Phipson, Mrs. Edith, head of Cama Hospital, Bombay, 326.
Peile, Sir J. B., member of Council, career and character, 61, 62; efforts for Muhammadan education. 279.
Percival, E. H., Joint Administrator of Bhaunagar, his administration, 105-115; quoted on advantage of maintaining Native Princes, 115.
Percival, G., present at Resolution about Bhandáris (1735), 387.
Perim, Island near Aden, growing importance as a coaling station, 479, 480.
Perry, Sir T. Erskine, President Bombay Board of Education, his policy, 131, 139; professorship of jurisprudence founded to commemorate, 156, 157.
Petit, Sir D. M., arranged removal of Elphinstone College to another site to make room for Jubilee Technical Institute, 152, 171, 172, 337; founded hospital for Women and Children at Bombay, 155, 325, 337; and Bacteriological Laboratory at Bombay Veterinary College, 169, 337; created a baronet (1890), 336; other benefactions, 337.
Petit, F. D., founded Laboratory at Grant Medical College, 155, 338.
Petit, N. M., founded dispensary at Wáda, 339.
Petroleum, duty on, imposed (1888), 396.
Peyton, Lt.-Col., member of Forest Commission (1885), 203.
Phaltán, Native State in the Deccan, 31; left under political charge of the Collector of Sátára, 119, 120.
Phythian, Mr., First Principal of the Jubilee Technical Institute, 172.
Police Administration, in Gondal State, 100, 101; in Bhaunagar, 111; Agency Police formed to suppress dacoity, 120; the appointment of an Inspector-General of Bombay Police, 421-423; his reforms, 423, 424.
Police Bill (1890), 423, 424.
Police, the Bombay; the District Police, 421, 422; Bombay City Police, 424, 425; Railway Police, 425; numbers and constitution, 425; distribution and cost, 426; Village Police, 426, 427.
Police lines built, 317, 318.
Political agents, their duties in Native States, 82.
Political Department, 80, 82.
Poona, District in the Deccan, 31; schools for aboriginal tribes opened in, 183; Koli discontent, 219; settlement of Indápur and rest of district, 234-236; discontent at revised settlements, 261; roads made to open up hilly tracts, 296; average incidence of excise, 366; heavy income-tax paid, 397; excessive criminality, 412.
Poona City, its colleges, 146-152; medical school, 155; industrial exhibition, 174; educational advantages, 176; terminus of South Maráthá Railway, 279; sanitary works, 320; drinking increasing, 366; has a Small Cause Court, 409; new Municipal Act, 432, 433; local taxes, 439; municipal works, 442; the Reay Market, 442.
Poona College, its history (1852-64); 148, 149; created Deccan College, 149.
Poona College of Science, its history, 157; engineering, agriculture and forestry taught, 158, 159; Pasteur laboratory added, 159; its workshops, 173, 174; new buildings, 317.
Poona Sanskrit College, founded by Elphinstone, 147; defended by him, 148; English Department founded (1842), and became Poona College (1852), 148.
Porbandar, railways in, 291, 292.
Port Trusts: Bombay, 309-311; Karáchi, 314; Aden, 315, 479, 480.
Portuguese, the, a conquering power in the Konkan, 30: dispute between Diu and Junágarh settled, 118; always accompanied by friars and priests, 129; completion of West of India Portuguese Railway, 280, 281, 482; ceded excise rights by treaty (1878), 394, 395. 482; relations with Bombay Presidency (1885-90), 482, 483; end of the schism, 483-485.
Position class introduced into survey settlement, 249.
Pot numbers, or subdivisions of fields, 239, 250, 251.
Powalla, S. C., founded Dispensary at Bombay, 327, 338.

Prescott, Bruce, murdered by Talávias at Broach, 413.
Pringle, R. K., his land settlement, 232, 233.
Pritchard, Sir C. B., Acting Member of Council, 63; as Commissioner advocated railways in Sind, 286; his excise administration, 378; opposition to his reforms, 383; quoted, on the manufacture of toddy spirit, 385, 386; his Salt Policy, 394.
Public Instruction, Department of, founded (1855), 132; *see* Education.
Public Works, in Baroda, 95, 96; Bhaunagar, 110, 111; in Native States, 124; importance and variety in India, 274, 275; railways, 275-294; tramways, 294, 295; roads, 295, 296; bridges, 296; ferries and steamships, 297; irrigation, 297-307; the Bombay Docks, 308-312; Karáchi harbour works, 312-314; lighthouses, 315; material fabric of government, 315-318; buildings, 316, 317; police lines, 317, 318.
Public Works Department, only administers railways, 277; and irrigation, 298; intricacy of accounts, 328; reforms in the staff, 330-332; in Public Works Accounts Branch, 332; saving effected, 333, 334; formation of Military Works Department, 334.

Quetta District command transferred to Bengal, 454.
Quinton, J. W., member of Crawford Commission, 414.

Ráb Cultivation, 215, 216.
Rádhanpur, Native State in Gujarát, 27; joint Hindu and Muhammadan ministers, 120; Jubilee Institute, 124.
Railway Jurisdiction in Native States, question of, 85, 86, 96.
Railway Police, 425.
Railways, strategic value of, 47, 48; encouraged by Native Chiefs; Gondal, 100: Morvi, 102; Bhaunagar, 111; Junágarh, 119; Great India Peninsula Railway, 277-279; Southern Maráthá, 279-281; West of India Portuguese, 280. 281; Bombay, Baroda and Central India, 281. 282; Godhrá-Ratlám, 281; North-Western, 282-283; question of in Sind, 282-288; in Baroda, 289-291; Káthiáwár, 291, 292; Kolhápur, 292, 293; table of progress (1885-90), 294.
Rájkot, railway to, 292.
Rájkot, College for Native Princes at, difficulties inherent in, 91, 92; religious education advised by Thákur of Lakhkar, 103; decline in popularity, 183, 184.
Rájpipla, Native State in Gujarát, 27; school for Bhils at, 183.
Rájputána, Lord Reay's opinion of its chief princes, 97, 98.
Rámdrúg, Native State in the Karnátik, 44.
Ranade, Ráo Bahádur Mahadeo Govind, member of the Finance Committee (1886), 349.
Ratlám, Railway to Godhrá, 281, 282
Ratnágiri, District in the Konkan, 30; very closely occupied, 273: proportion of liquor-shops near the coast, 365; toddy drunk, 371; incidence of income-tax very light, 397; singularly free from crime, 441; proportion of police to population, 426; rural local taxation very light, 447; people prefer working in Bombay mills to enlisting in the army, 458.
Ratnágiri Town, Industrial School, 175; custom house, 316; lunatic asylum, 317.
Reay, Lady, Nurse Fund, endowed by Mahárájá of Bhaunagar, 156.
Reay, Lord, ancestors, 54-57; education and career, 57-59; appointed Governor of Bombay (1885), 59; attitude towards the Council, 69-71; the Secretariat, 71-73: views on patronage, 74; tours, 76: preferred individual discussion to meetings of Council, 76, 77; attitude towards Native Chiefs, 84, 86, 88-94, 97, 98, 103, 104; cut first sod and opened railway to Veráwal, 119; views on primary education, 137, 138; on secondary education, 142-144; efforts to merge the Poona Colleges, 150-152; on medical and legal education, 156, 157; agricultural education, 159, 168; expectations from 'aided' schools, 163, 164; definition of technical education, 165, 166; opened Jubilee Technical Institute, 172; encouragement of Gujarát, 176; and of Sind education, 177; reply to the Lingáyats, 181; on female education, 185; speech to the Forest Com-

mission, 204–208; defended Survey and Settlement Department, 248; views on sub-soil water assessment, 253; opened West of India Portuguese Railway, 280, 483; obtained the Godhrá-Ratlám railway, 282; and Mehsana-Viramgám railway, 291; cut first sod Dhoráji-Porbandar railway, 292; opened Sukkur Bridge, 296; speech on irrigation works in the Deccan, 305–307; inaugurated Ahmadábád drainage works, 320; interest in Bombay hospitals, 325–327; speech on Public Works policy, 330; reforms in Public Works Department, 331–334; quoted, on raw toddy question, 390, 391; aims of his excise policy, 401; praised by Lord Cross, 419; resignation refused, 420; interview with a deputation declining municipal government, 431; opinion on army corps *versus* presidential armies, 453, 454; against the severance of Sind, 467.
Reay Industrial Museum at Poona, 174.
Reay Lectureship at Grant College, 156.
Reay Market at Poona, 442.
Reay Workshops at Bombay School of Art, 170.
Regimental Institutes, 457.
Registration Department, 398–400; revenue from, 400.
Rewá Kántha, Native States in Gujarát, 27; transit duties abolished in all but Bária, 123.
Rice, export duty on, 396.
Richards, Rear-Adm., Sir F. W., consulted on transference of Bombay Dockyard, 312.
Richey, Sir J. B., member of Council, 62, 63; representative of Bombay at the Financial Conference (1888), 357, 358.
Ripon Hospital at Ahmadnagar, 317, 339.
Ripon Textile School in Victoria Jubilee Technical Institute, 172.
Roads, made in Bhaunagar, 111; badness in Sind, 285, 286; difficulties of making in Gujarát, 291; in the Bombay Presidency, 295, 296.
Roberts, Gen. Sir F., opposed idea of an Indian Sandhurst, 184.
Roman Catholics, early educational efforts of, 128, 129; college at Bombay, 145; convent school at Bándra, 185; ending of Portuguese schism, and new arrangement of dioceses, 483–485.
Rum, import of, 374, 375.

Sabarmati River, 20.
Sachín, Native State in Gujarát, 27.
Sádra, Jubilee Clock Tower at, 124; Bhils educated at, 183.
Saint George's Hospital at Bombay, 327.
Salisbury, Lord, Secretary of State of India, approved cession of Central Provinces to Bombay, 477.
Salmon, Captain, captured dacoit leader (1885), 121.
Salt Act (1890), 395.
Salt; history of salt-tax in Bombay, 393, 394; salt works in, 394; cession of salt rights in Native States, 394; in Khairpur, 117; in Portuguese territories, 394, 395; the tax increased (1888), 395.
'Sandhurst, an Indian,' favoured by Lord Reay and the Duke of Connaught, 92, 93; opposed by Sir F. Roberts and Sir G. Greaves, 184.
Sángli, Native State in the Karnátik, 44.
Sanitation, 318, 319; sanitary works at Ahmadábád, 319, 320; at Poona, 320; sanitation in villages, 320, 321; Bombay Village Sanitation Bill, 321–323.
Sargent, Sir Charles, Chief Justice of Bombay, 403.
Sátára, District in the Deccan, 31; slight use of intoxicants, 367; freedom from crime, 411; local taxes, 439.
Sátára Jághírs, historical group of Native States, broken up (1887), 119; transit duties abolished, except in Bhor, 123.
Savanúr, Native State in the Karnátik, 44; its small size, 81.
Sáwantwádi, Native State in the Konkan, 30.
School, description of indigenous, in Bombay, 136, 137; *see* Education, Schools of Art, Technical Schools.
Scots Brigade in Holland, 54–56.
Scottish Missionary Society, its educational work in Bombay and the Konkan, 129; the Wilson College, Bombay, 145.
Secretariat, the Bombay, 52; Lord Reay's attitude towards, 71–73; and opinion of, 77, 78.

Seedaseer, Battle of, Bombay troops in, 450.
Sethna, Mr., appointed a Law Professor by Lord Reay, 157.
Settlements, Land; *see* Land Administration.
Sháhbudin, Kázi, founded scholarships for Muhammadans, 179, 180.
Shikárpur, District in Sind, 23; amount and incidence of local rural taxation, 447.
Shikárpur Town, 26.
Shilotri tenure in the Konkan, 259.
Sholápur, District in the Deccan, 31; first survey settlement, 236; heavy incidence of income-tax, 397; freedom from crime, 411; local taxes, 440; incidence of local rural taxation, 447.
Sims, Proctor, carried out public works at Bhaunagar, 110, 111.
Sind, history, 23; population and religions, 24, 25; trade and commerce, 25, 26; towns, 26; problems of British rule, 26, 27; technical schools, 175, 176; education, 177; babúl reserves, 194; irrigation settlements, 255, 256; advances to cultivators, 269; Managership Sind Encumbered Estates abolished, 270, 271; question of railways, 282, 288; badness of roads, 285, 286; irrigation, 300-304; *bháng* drunk, 371, 372; excise on bháng, 392, 393; central distillery system introduced, 382; salt-works, 394; non-regulation, 402; Judicial Commissioners Court, 401, 405; number of judges and magistrates, 410; municipalities depend on octroi duties, 439; question of severance from Bombay, 467-477;—historical arguments, 467-469; geographical, 469-471; administrative, 471-473; military, 473, 474; commercial, 474, 475; what would be the result, 478; local memorial against, 476.
Sind College at Karáchi, 153.
Sindí language, 25, 471.
Sivají, pillaged Surat, 28; crowned at Ráigarh, 31; his reign, 35; dynasty, 39.
Small Cause Courts, 408, 409.
Socotra Island, protectorate established over (1886), 480.
Somáli Coast Protectorate, 481.
Soudan, expedition to the, Bombay troops engaged in, 451; the transport of, from Bombay, 465.
Souter, Sir F. H., Commissioner of the Bombay City Police, member Bombay City Abkári Commission, 389; death, 425.
South Maráthá Railway, its extension, 279, 280.
Sridhar, Maráthá poet, 43.
Stamps, revenue from, 398.
Staunton, Major, won battle of Korygáum (1818), 450.
Steamship companies serving Bombay, local traffic, 297.
Steel, Vet.-Surg., first Principal of Bombay Veterinary College, 168.
Stokes, H. E., Madras member of Calcutta Financial Conference (1888), 358.
Strachey, Sir John, quoted on Provincial Contracts, 343, 344.
Sukkur, gaining importance from the railway, 26; bridge over the Indus at, opened by Lord Reay, 296.
Summary Settlement Act, 267.
Surat, District in Gujarát, 27; heavy incidence of excise on drink, 366; incidence of rural local taxation, 447.
Surat City, animal hospital at, 14; pillaged by Sivají, 28; headquarters of the Bombay Government to 1687, 49; the Arabic College, 179; the Tapidas Laboratory, 339; income-tax from, affected by the great fire, 398; has a Small Cause Court, 409; its municipal undertakings, 441, 442.
Surgána, Native State in the Deccan, 31.
Survey and Settlement Department; for its work, *see* Land Administration; its work almost at an end, 262, 263.
Survey Tenure, 243, 244, 247.

Talávias, riot of, at Broach (Nov. 1885), 413, 414.
Tálikot, Battle of (1565), 32, 40.
Talpur Mirs, dynasty in Sind, 23.
Táluká Boards, 445.
Tálukdári tenure in Gujarát, 256, 257.
Tálukdárs of Gujarát, schools for, 184; their indebtedness and special legislation to relieve them, 257, 258, 271, 272; celebration of the Jubilee, 271.
Tánkha settlement, 229.
Tansa Water-works, scheme to supply Bombay, 323-325.
Tapidas, Dayabhai and Domodardas, founded Laboratory at Surat, 339.

Tápti River, 20.
Tariff Act (1887), 375.
Taxation, *see* Assessed Taxes, Excise, Stamps, &c.
Taylor, George, present at resolution on Bhandáris (1735), 387.
Teak trees, Government rights to, reserved in Bombay, 192, 193; granted to occupants, 214.
Technical education, Lord Reay's encouragement of, 164, 165; definition of, 165, 166; in agriculture, 166–169; art, 169–171; mechanics, 171–176.
Technical Institute, Victoria Jubilee, at Bombay, 171-173.
Technical Schools, at Kolhápur, 123; Poona, 173, 174; in Sind, 175, 176.
Telang, Kashinath Trimbak, appointed a Law Professor, 157; a Judge of the High Court, 403.
Temperance movement in Thána and Kolába, 383, 384.
Temple, Sir Richard, Governor of Bombay, encouraged forestry, 193, 195; promoted railways in Káthiáwár, 291, 292; quoted, on the first Provincial Contract, 342; on consumption of intoxicants in ancient India, 368, 369; on abolition of the out-still system, 382, 383.
Tenures in Bombay: the survey, 243; tálukdári, 256, 257; khoti, 258; shilotri, 259; bhágdári and nárvadári, 259, 260; of alienated holdings, 265, 266,
Thákurs, a forest tribe, 197.
Thána, District in the Konkan, 30; forests in, 197, 198; agitation against forest laws, 199 202; orders issued on grazing in forests, 211; on *ráb*, 216; much cultivable waste, 273; heavy incidence of excise per head in, 366; temperance movement, 383; toddy licenses, 390; led to illicit distillation, 391, sea-salt-works, 394; excessive criminality, 412; local municipal taxes, 439; large amoumt of local rural revenue, 447.
Thána Forest Association, presented case for agitators against forest laws, 209.
Thar and Párkar, District in Sind, 23; prosperity and need of a railway, 285; incidence of income-tax light, 397; proportion of police to population, 426; small amount of local rural revenue, 447.
Thompson, Mr., of Khedwára Mission, attempts to educate Bhils, 183.
Toddy, 371; its strength, 384, 385; easy to make spirit from, 385, 386; taxation of, 388, 389; reduced (1886), 389, 390; Lord Reay's minute on, 390, 391.
Torpedo boats supplied for defence of Bombay, and Karáchi harbour, 463.
Tramways, 294, 295.
Transit duties in Native States, progress of the abolition of, 122, 123.
Transport, military, efforts to improve, 456.
Trees planted in Bhaunagar, 114; forest trees of Bombay, 194; planted on road-sides by Local Boards, 447.
Trevor, Mr. A. C., quoted on the importance of irrigation to the revenue of Sind, 303, 304.
'Tribute theory' of relations of Imperial and Provincial finance, 359, 360.
Tulsi Lake supplies Bombay with water, 323
Turkarám, Maráthá poet, 43.

Udaipur, Maháráná of, Lord Reay's opinion of, 97.
Udu, salt-works at, 394.
Umarkot, railway designed from Gidhu Bandar to, 284.
University of Bombay, founded (1857), 133; refused to grant degree in agriculture, 158, 159; its importance to Bombay education, 159, 160; bill for its reorganisation suspended, 160; Dr. Mackichan appointed Vice-Chancellor, 160, 161.
University Schools Final Examination, 143.
Upárkot in Junágarh, Buddhist caves at, 117.
Upper Sind Frontier, District in Sind, 23; small amount of local rural taxation, 447.

Vaccination, progress in Gondal State, 100.
Vágris, aboriginal tribe, heavy drinkers, 364.
Várlis, forest tribe, protected against forest rules (1851), 200.
Vehar Lake supplies Bombay with water, 323.
Vengurla, new lighthouse constructed at, 315.
Veráwal, port in Junágarh State, railway made to, 119, 291.
Veterinary College, Bombay, founded

(1886), 168; given a laboratory by Sir D. M. Petit, 169.
Vidal, G. W., Chairman Forest Commission (1885), 203; member Forest Establishment Reorganisation Committee, 220.
Village communities, coparcenary, traces of, in Gujarát, 259, 260.
Village Conservancy Bill, 321, 323.
Village Police, 426, 427.
Volunteer Corps, 461, 462.

Wáda, dispensary founded at, by N. M. Petit, 339.
Waddington, Mr., Principal of Gujarát College, 153.
Wadhwán, Girasia School at, 184; railway to, from Bhaunagar, 291; Morvi, 292.
Wadia, Nauroji N., first honorary secretary Victoria Jubilee Technical Institute, 173.
Wards Estates, 270.
Water supply, Bhúj and Bhaunagar, 124; Ahmadábád, 319, 320; Poona, 320; Bombay, the Tansa scheme, 323-325.
West, Sir Raymond, member of Council, his character, 63, 64; evidence on secondary schools, 141, 142; his University Reorganisation Bill, 160; quoted, on the finding of the Crawford Commission, 415, 416; introduced Police Bill, 424.
West of India Portuguese Railway, completed, 280, 281, 482.
Westland, J., member Finance Committee (1886), 349, 350; Chairman Financial Conference (1888), 357-359.
Whisky, increase in importation of, 374.
Williamson, Thomas, his views on land settlement, 233.
Wilson, Mr. Justice Arthur, Chairman Crawford Commission, 414.
Wilson College, Bombay, 145, 317.
Wines, import duties on, 374.
Wingate, Sir George, helped to settle Indápur táluká, 235; signed Joint Report (1847), 236; reduced 'classing' to a system, 240
Wise, Col., appointed first Inspector-General of Police, 426; his reforms and administration, 427.
Wodehouse, Sir Philip, Governor of Bombay, appointed the Joint Administrators of Bhaunagar, 105.
Women, allowed to study at Grant Medical College (1884), 155; female education in Bombay, 184, 185.
Wordsworth, Dr., Principal of Deccan College, 149; influence on his pupils, 187.
Wroughton, R. C, member of Forest Commission (1885), 203.

Yadava dynasty in the Deccan, 32.
Yerrowda, Juvenile Reformatory at, 316; Central Jail, 427.

Zaila, port in Somâli Coast Protectorate, 481.

THE END.